Minor League Mom

*A Mother's Journey Through
the Red Sox Farm Teams*

Pamela Carey

MINOR LEAGUE MOM
A Mother's Journey through the Red Sox Farm Teams

BARKING CAT BOOKS is an imprint of New River Press

Barking Cat Books website is: www.barkingcatbooks.com
New River Press website is: www.newriverpress.com

Cover by Francisco Rivera

FIRST EDITION

Library of Congress Control Number: 2009924083

ISBN: 978-1-891724-176

DEDICATION

To Charley, my husband of forty-three years,
Who loves his family above all else,
Who taught me to be a Red Sox fan on our first date,
Who nurtured, advised and supported us so that Tim and Todd could
follow their dream,
As could I.

To Tim, Todd, Alison and Trish,
Who allowed me to open their lives to public scrutiny, and
Who are the role models their children will someday want to emulate.

To the classy heroes of Fenway Park, past and present,
Who demonstrated honesty, loyalty and team above all else,
Without whom my sons would not have dreamed their dream.

To the knowledgeable fans of Red Sox Nation,
Who made me a believer and
Who taught me the virtue of patience.

1

How It Began

June 1, 1992. I was home alone, inside on a perfect early summer day in New England; pacing, eating, washing dishes, making beds, anything to keep me occupied while I waited for the phone call that never seemed to come. I was nervous. I had good reason. It was the day of the amateur baseball draft.

Tim and Todd were two of the hundreds of players major league teams were considering to play pro ball. All day, friends and relatives had been calling to find out any news. My husband Charley was at a meeting. Todd was working at Brown. Tim was taking finals at Dartmouth. So it was just me and the phone. If any team was serious about Todd, then he'd have a difficult choice: Leave Brown before his senior year or give up a shot at major league ball.

Of course, I'm being overdramatic. Todd could wait until he graduated to try pro ball, but the bonuses went down each year a player waited. It was still a difficult choice. If he were chosen, he'd have to promise us he'd finish Brown in the off-seasons.

And Tim deserved a shot at pro ball, too, yet he had already committed to teach English in Taiwan. Would he want to give that up? Would either of them have an opportunity to make the choice? We just didn't know.

The only people who had an idea, whose suggestions, advice, and reports counted, were the baseball scouts; the experts upon whom the fate of many baseball careers depend.

Who are these guys who have so much power? Pat Jordan in A False Spring gave me insight into the lives of baseball scouts. Most of them had undistinguished yet solid minor league careers. They were rewarded with managerial positions in the backwaters of organized ball. Then, as they aged and developed an accurate and trusted eye for talent, they were further rewarded with full-time jobs scouring a section of the country in search of sure-fire phenoms. They had to be stingy with the $100,000 bonuses they were authorized to offer, yet they could not let the athletes go to the competition, who'd be sniffing around the same hot prospects. Such was the life of the scout: constant travel, daily attendance at games and sticking their necks out for untried athletes.[1] Charley and I first noticed the scouts at American Legion games. James "Mac" Wright was the Cumberland (R.I.) Legion Coach, and Tim was one of his favorites because he reminded Mac of his own son.

When Tim turned sixteen, he impressed college coaches and professional scouts as the starting catcher for our Legion team. That year they had a good run into the regional playoffs and in attendance was Charley's college coach and the boys' mentor, John Winkin. One or two scouts would show up for these games and they'd follow the same rituals: sit behind home plate in their lawn chairs, eat sandwiches they picked up at Subway, drink coffee from thermoses, and chatter away to each other.

Every once in a while they'd scribble something on their clipboards or time a kid's pitch with a stopwatch, but it all seemed very informal to us.

Charley and I steered away from them.

They all came to the same Dartmouth or Brown games in the same freezing weather we did, and after a while I began to hope our boys would always play superior games when these men were around. I never dreamed the scouts were there to see Tim or Todd. Those college games were some of the best times of our lives, when we planned vacations around spring baseball trips to Florida, Louisiana, Arizona, or Maryland and once even to Honolulu, when both Brown and Dartmouth were invited to the same tournament.

Were we parents carrying our baseball support to the point of addiction? I think not. Charley and I went to the Hawaiian beaches between games – the ultimate baseball mom's reward. My mom and dad accompanied us, and my dad became a minor TV celebrity, as all games were broadcast live on the islands. At those Brown-Dartmouth games, the camera focused on him sitting behind home plate. He was juggling his Styrofoam cup of coffee, his score card, and two hats, alternating between his Brown hat and Dartmouth hat each half inning.

When the regular season began, Charley and I and my parents (who lived three hours from us) followed the boys throughout New England, New York, and Pennsylvania. We often set up assembly lines to make peanut butter and jelly sandwiches for the teams between games of a double- header.

We invited both teams to our house for lasagna when Brown hosted Dartmouth, loving every minute that the boys, their friends, and coaches were there. I happily served plates of food in the din of the dining room, while young men stood around gulping down the meal, or sprawled on the family room floor to watch hockey playoffs on TV. I could not help but wonder how my two sons, how all these young players, seemed to have grown into young men in the blink of a fastball.

In 1991, Tim, a junior at Dartmouth, was named All-Ivy-League catcher. Todd was named the same year as a sophomore shortstop at Brown. With these honors I learned for the first time about the politics of baseball.

The New England College All-Star Game was to be played in Fenway Park, Boston's major league field. Lou Merloni, the shortstop for Providence College, had his name on the ballot, while Todd's was left off, despite an equally remarkable record. It was no coincidence that the Providence College Coach would also be the All-Star Coach. Other New England coaches saw the injustice and submitted Todd's name on the ballot. He indeed played – half the game, *in left field*!

I began to realize then how the network of college coaches worked.

They talked constantly, even outside their own leagues. That network could have a great impact on the opportunities for kids who wanted to play in prestigious summer leagues to get into pro ball. And then there was the shadowy presence of professional scouts who checked on the players through their contacts with the coaches. Charley's father, who played three years in the Cardinals organization before he got hurt, maintained that a draftee rose in an organization according to the influence of the scout who signed him.

Here's one scouting report on Tim and Todd. This report is from someone who observed them for years - actually their whole lives. It's written by their mother. Me.

Personalities

<u>Tim</u>: *Outspoken, take-charge leader, unwavering in his commitment to any chosen activity. Mature, focused, disciplined about fitness as well as intellectual pursuits. All-Star ice hockey defenseman, known as "The Enforcer." Protector of younger brother, will fight through difficulties with calm determination. Closes the gap between skill and success with hard work.*

<u>Todd</u>: *Naturally gifted athlete, learned early and quickly how to measure up to older brother. Outstanding talents as a forward in ice hockey and infielder in baseball. Sense of humor, but content to be alone or with a small group of friends. Academically gifted if pushed, self-disciplined in anything that interests him. Has the ability to go to the major leagues if he believes in himself.*

Physical Attributes

<u>Tim</u>: *6'3," 220lbs., throws right, bats left, solid catcher's body, enhanced by a six-day-a-week workout schedule. Resilient response to injuries, including broken fingers, thumb, and nose; concussions; sprained knees and ankles; bone bruises.*

<u>Todd</u>: *6'2," 180 lbs., throws right, bats left, quick instincts, fast on his feet, easy*

grace, tremendous velocity on his arm.
Few injuries, including stitches, rib bruises, concussion, break near the thumb-
pad on his hand.

Statistics
<u>*Tim*</u>*: Batted .347 junior year of college, .310 senior year. Outstanding defensive*
catcher; strong, accurate arm; captain. "The best leader a coach could ask for
and a joy to have around," said Dartmouth Coach Bob Whalen.

<u>*Todd*</u>*: Batted .329 junior year of college, led team in runs scored and hits (a*
University record). Fluid fielder, outstanding arm, distinguishing him from all
other shortstops in the Ivy League.

As I said, these are unbiased, objective reports I could have submitted to major league teams, if they'd only asked!

Around six o'clock on June 1, the phone finally rang. It was Bill Enos, the New England scout for the Boston Red Sox. He called to inform Todd that he'd been drafted in the ninth round by the Red Sox. Since the Sox had no first-round pick that year, they had actually picked Todd eighth from all the players around the world.

I wanted to shout, cry, scream. Something! But I was home alone and everyone in the family was busy. These were the days before cell phones.

I had to wait until Charley and Todd came home together from Providence.

I sat down and had a glass of wine. The news began to sink in. Despite his limited number of games (only twenty a season plus other non-league games), and the low-key non-scholarship program in the Ivy League, Todd's play had attracted a major league team!

I was so happy for Todd that I'd forgotten to ask about Tim. Enos had said nothing about him. He did say he wanted to set up a meeting with Todd. Todd wanted Charley to negotiate for him, a formality because major league teams offered standard amounts for each level of the draft. Todd was offered cash to pay for his last year at Brown and an equal amount as an additional bonus. His salary would be $850 a month for the four-month season.

Bill Enos, the rambling, cigar-chomping 71-year-old scout, soon to retire after fifty-five years in baseball, came to our house five days later with his wife Grace. Bill had a contract in his hand. Grace welcomed all of us to the Red Sox family with a gift of napkin rings for me and Bill went on and on with his baseball stories, scoffing at Todd's concern about giving up his senior year. "What's two semesters to an Ivy Leaguer? You'll finish them in the off-seasons. No problem." Todd signed the contract, wearing his new Red Sox hat.

I served cheese and crackers and kept the conversation light, but I wondered about the two semesters. Would he indeed go back? When the Enoses left, Todd asked us if we thought he was doing the right thing.

"You've worked too hard not to go after your dream," we told him, and asked him to reassure us that he would complete his degree as soon as he could. A few days later, his plane ticket for the Sox rookie camp in Winter Haven, Fla., arrived. Inside the package was a note that Tim should contact Bill Enos as soon as he graduated.

Before Todd boarded the plane a few days later, he muttered to Charley and me, "Thanks for everything you have done for me," and gave us big hugs. That one moment made all those hectic years worthwhile.

The day after Tim graduated, Bill and Grace Enos were back again, this time with a contract for Tim. The Sox were offering him a free agent's contract, with a bonus of $1000 and the same $850/month salary as Todd's. Bill asked him, "Do you want to play professional baseball badly enough that you will give up everything else?" Tim did not hesitate, signed immediately, and had to make profuse apologies to the YMCA in Taiwan, where he was supposed to teach. At the airport as he was leaving for rookie camp three days after college graduation, he was interviewed by a Providence TV station. Asked for his reaction to signing with the Red Sox just days after his brother, Tim replied, "It's just like a dream." He would miss Todd in Winter Haven by five days. Todd had already been assigned to the next level.

Bill's question to Tim, "Do you want to play professional baseball badly enough that you will give up everything else?" grew loud in my mind as I walked around our now empty summer house, played tennis, or worked in the garden. Of course, Tim did, and Todd, too. What young ball player would answer differently? Were they merely caught up in the romance of a chance to play a boy's game and make big money? I stopped this useless line of thinking by reminding myself that they both had Ivy League educations behind them. In that case, what were they doing on a ball field?

A scout had plucked the two of them from thousands of New England kids, dangled some money, and said, "Now go see what you can do!" He didn't mention that the odds are literally one hundred to one against either of them ever wearing the Red Sox uniform in Fenway Park. He didn't tell them about all the late night bus rides and the fast food and the loneliness and the roller coaster of streaks and slumps, of playing and sitting on the bench, of questioning your own sanity and the press questioning your abilities, all for $850 a month, which must cover food, apartment, transportation, and fun! He never mentioned the worst part – the not knowing, for months at a time, whether management thought you had a future in baseball or not. Could Tim and Todd handle all that? Could I handle all that?

2

A Mom's Record

I guess to everyone except Charley and me it seemed almost a miracle that our two sons had signed contracts with the Boston Red Sox within ten days of each other in June of 1992. To us at the time, it was a natural extension of their abilities, an attainment of the next level they'd worked so long to achieve. Of course, we watched on television some of the 338 legendary brother combinations who had played in the major leagues: the Ripkens, Cansecos, Gwynns, Alous, Niekros, Alomars, Martinezes, DiMaggios, etc. But it was only after the mayhem of negotiations, signing, college graduation for Tim, packing, and departures that we had time to reflect on what had occurred: two brothers, sixteen months apart in age, who had attended opposing Ivy League schools, had become minor league players for the same professional organization. Soon after they'd left for the rookie league in Winter Haven, Charley and I collapsed on the beach.

"What your boys have accomplished is truly remarkable," said a long- time friend, sitting in a beach chair. "It's an infinitesimal percentage of high school and college players in the country that are offered pro contracts. No one can convince me that it would have happened without the support and guidance from both of you."

Coming from John Cipollini, a self-taught guru of baseball, confidant of college coaches and scouts, as well as the coach of an American Legion ball team, this compliment startled us. But in retrospect, he probably was right. As parents, Charley and I had spent great chunks of our lives at baseball fields, watching hundreds of games. It was impossible to describe each of us individually without a partial description of the love for the game.

Certainly, I had watched ballgames in solitude in front of a black and white screen after school during my youth, when the Yankees participated in the World Series during the '50s. I'd watched at old Yankee Stadium, as part of a peer group on whose male members I was eager to make an impression.

I had also played field hockey and softball after school, but that was secondary to the hours, months, and years right through college I spent prancing in front of crowds of spectators as a cheerleader. I was a product of the '50s and early '60s, when access to organized sports for women was limited to cheering on the men, and little else. We were encouraged to excel in academics, drama, student government, writing, dance, art. I was accustomed to speaking before the entire student body of 1,200 as an officer of the high school student government. But interscholastic sports participation? Not for us ladies.

As I observed more and more of Tim and Todd's baseball careers, I began to understand what Roger Khan said in Good Enough to Dream: "the nature of the game is so complex that players reach their peaks relatively slowly...Baseball is a damn hard game to master."

I began to realize that Kahn's description of the complexity of the game was correct. A good player has to be able to reason and react quickly, and he has to know what to do with the ball before it is hit, based on the thousands of times he has been in that situation before: the same ball-strike count, the same number of outs, the same number of runners on base. Even something as deceptively simple as running the bases can become a humiliation, and no mother wants to sit through that!

I knew Tim and Todd had the intelligence the game required, but they needed the skills. What I didn't know was that Khan's words would define my sons' young lives, and as a result, mine, at least for a time. As they tried to master the game, to reach its highest levels, I would be with them every step of the way, recording their attempts through the one professional organization to which our family had devoted its whole fan support: the Boston Red Sox.

It was after I'd met Charley at Colby College (he was an All-New England player and son of a St. Louis Cardinals minor leaguer), married him, and moved back to New England following our four years in the Air Force that I became a Red Sox fan. The realization came slowly as to what a tremendous burden this is. Cleveland Amory described it best in Fenway by Peter Golenbock. He said that the frustrating, tantalizing "almost" that happens through the years is what makes it so painful.

We develop built-in defense mechanisms to allow ourselves never to get too excited or too hopeful. We know in our lifetimes we may only win the World Series once (2004) or twice (2007), and our children may never witness it again. Yet we don't really want to get over this addiction to a team that has let us down so frequently over the past eighty-six years. After all, we're New Englanders, and pain, inner tragedy, and suffering, as part of our Puritan heritage, make us better able to cope with whatever is coming next. What are we to do with our newfound success when we're so used to reliving and combating the pain – expect another championship, only to be let down again? We will, after all, be rewarded, if there is a heaven.[2]

By 1992, I already knew the joys and frustrations of being the ultimate baseball mom, the mom who drove her sons, sometimes to two different games at the same time, sat in the stands, washed their uniforms, soothed their losses, and followed them as they played in Rhode Island, Massachusetts, Connecticut, New Hampshire, Maine, Florida, Louisiana, Arizona, Virginia, the Carolinas, Maryland, Hawaii, Ohio, New Jersey, and New York, right into the professional leagues.

3

The Real Beginnings

It began at the beach. Charley would play "rundown" with the boys between two bases in the sand. This went on endlessly, often with many aspiring athletes taking turns as the base runners. Charley was always one of the fielders positioned on a base, until finally he would give up from exhaustion. Then it moved to our backyard with the neighborhood kids, including sisters, using hardballs from the beginning. When they outgrew the backyard, they moved to the street. Charley pitched to one and all after work, on baseball fields, any field, and especially during family vacations.

There were trips to Boston's Fenway Park, beginning when Tim and Todd were almost four and five; then organized Little League and Babe Ruth, ages nine through fifteen. Through it all, Charley coached, the boys learned to play, and I drove, sat, and watched. Not only baseball, but All-Star ice hockey too. Leagues melted into each other's seasons, four seasons a year, practices, and games, denying us school vacations because of tournaments in inaccessible or tundra-like places like Peoria, Ill., or Sault Ste. Marie, in the Upper Peninsula of Michigan.

So began our baseball/hockey life. I say "ours" because it was a shared effort; the whole family involved every step of the way. Why? Because Charley and I believed then, and still do, that sports can have a deep influence on a child's development physically, mentally, and emotionally.

Take Tim, for example. Charley's Little League catcher had been hit in the face by a pitch, and although the boy had on a mask, he had had enough of catching and quit right in the middle of a game. Tim was just nine, but he was on the team and Coach Charley had no other options: Tim became the catcher. Mike and Luke Ryan point out in It's Where You Play the Game that becoming a catcher changes a kid's life. First he improves, say the Ryans, merely by playing the position, catching 2,000 pitches a season, losing weight, becoming mobile, faster, more confident. The catcher becomes a team leader, develops perseverance, and will always be hardworking and successful, no matter what he does in life. I think that defines Tim to this day.

Success breeds success in kids. It doesn't have to be in sports, but it might as well be. Team settings develop leadership qualities, common goals, the ability to handle praise and criticism, wins and losses. So Charley and I drove all over New England investing our time in baseball and hockey games, investing in what we considered to be important aspects of our sons' lives.

We missed "normal" activities like weddings; our social life centered around the hockey team parents. The laundry piled up, the grass sometimes grew long, and the boys' late-night homework made rising early a challenge. But our commitment became a way of life, habitual, accepted, and in many ways, exciting. The boys knew we loved them and we praised them for their accomplishments. By age thirteen they had to have summer jobs, washing pots and pans in a restaurant or weeding at a nursery. We allowed no sense of entitlement.

Nor did we let up on our academic expectations. I worked the English/Social Studies beat, while Charley patrolled the Math/Science. As a former English teacher, I went after every dangling modifier and misspelling. We expected Tim and Todd to put as much time into developing their writing, math, and science skills as their skating or fielding. They knew there would be consequences if their grades dropped: the extracurricular activities would go.

The most grueling schedule occurred when the boys were involved in Babe Ruth baseball (pre-driving ages thirteen through fifteen). Charley was still their coach. We all lived in Westport, Mass., for the summer, an hour's drive from our home in Rhode Island. Charley would go directly from work in Providence to our house in Rhode Island to change before the games. I'd make sure Tim had a couple of hours of sleep after working for a landscaper. He and I would leave the beach to pick up Todd at the bus station, where he returned from his commute to a summer writing course.

The three of us would proceed to the ball field every night. After the game, we'd forge ahead in two cars to a fast-food restaurant, then head back to the beach. Some nights, after extra innings, it would be midnight before we got to bed. When that summer was over, Charley and I agreed that for our health and our marriage, he should step down as coach.

During most days of the year, I had knots in my stomach because of the schedule. I had a master's degree in English, but after teaching junior high and high school for four years, I stayed home when the boys arrived.

When Tim turned nine, I tried to get back into high school teaching. There was a glut of teachers then, so I decided to pursue interior design. That meant another degree and more training: three more years at Rhode Island School of Design at night, with an apprenticeship during the day.

Tim and Todd Carey, Little League days.

During those years, when he wasn't traveling on business, Charley took over all the homework duties, while I often worked on projects till sunrise. When I opened my own business, I was either meeting clients or traveling to the Design Center in Boston, always back at the school in time for carpool.

Charley and I held the boys accountable for their actions, and we had to be accountable ourselves. It was all about respect for us as parents, respect for authority. There was never any question whose decisions we supported in a school matter: it was always the educator. When Tim was hanging from a neighbor's tree, it accidentally split in half. He saved his allowances and bought the neighbor a smaller version of the same tree.

When they were old enough to drive, we allowed the boys to stay in the Rhode Island house alone one summer, while Charley and I stayed at the beach in Massachusetts. Any signs of partying or not showing up for their camp counseling jobs would have ended that privilege. We trusted them, and they repaid that trust by adhering to our rules, by learning to cook, do laundry, and clean up. Whatever happened in that house that summer bore no evidence afterward! Of course, I ran my interior design business out of the Rhode Island house, delivered casseroles, and picked up our mail there before joining the rest of the family at the evening games. I also threw loads of dirty uniforms into the washing machine.

We held Tim and Todd accountable for any commitment they agreed to, and we tolerated no quitting of sports activities, despite the inconvenience of conflicting practice/game times, work schedules or fatigue. The commitment was as much Charley's and mine as it was the boys'. Sometimes we would head out in different directions with a boy in each car and, frequently, a change of clothes for each of us.

We never pushed them into any sport or activity; never felt we had to live vicariously through them. Charley was vice-chairman of a $15 billion corporation, and I had my own business after a career in teaching.

We encouraged them simply because they loved to play. They were also excellent students, piano, trumpet, or sax players, Cub Scouts, Big Brothers, karate students and boyfriends. One could say that those frantic, early years laid the foundation for the dream of professional baseball, however unconsciously. As a family, we had already worked together to make difficult things happen – the boys through their self-discipline, talents, and commitments to goals, and we as parents by giving them the opportunities and encouragement to become strong, independent young men.

By Todd's junior and Tim's senior high school year, both boys had distinguished themselves in two varsity sports and in a variety of academic ways, earning them the attention of many colleges through coaches' letters of interest and visitations to games. So the Careys began a new phase of life so familiar to so many: the college decision.

The author with son Todd in his Brown University days.

4

Academia
and Athletics

The elaborate ritual about getting into college was really about fear; fear that they weren't good enough to get accepted for higher education, to get accepted by their peers, to get accepted for life's higher challenges. Life became an entrance exam, even for the kids not planning on college.

During their junior year of high school, both boys' personalities became irascible. By the end of that year, however, they began to realize that doors to higher education would crack open if they could excel in academics, and in not only one, but two sports. By their senior years, their personalities had returned to normal. We attributed the sudden welcome change to letters of interest that were being received from baseball and hockey coaches throughout the country.

In between those letters of interest from college coaches and the final acceptance letters was a lengthy, fun, sometimes tense, and certainly exhausting process for all of us. Tim received over 100 of these letters from baseball and hockey coaches, and Charley and I helped weed through them for school location, size, academic standards, and type of athletic program. We began making visits to campuses during his junior year and the summer immediately thereafter. On each campus, we had a pre-arranged meeting with the baseball or hockey coach. There was an almost instant like or dislike once the boys stepped onto a campus. In one case, as we walked with a guide through the venerable, cathedral-like buildings, both boys asked us to please get them out of there. The coaches' personalities were also a strong factor in their selections. We learned to distinguish between those coaches that were making false promises and those who were sincere.

To this day we owe a huge debt of gratitude to Brandeis Baseball Coach Pete Varney. We visited him first because the campus was closest to our Rhode Island home. He advised us that we were missing an opportunity by not applying to the Ivy League, because of the boys' credentials. He had been courting Tim, so his advice meant possibly losing him for his own team.

In the Ivy League, academic indexes were computed for each athlete's application. This was based on rank in high school class, SAT scores, and grade point average. The athletes had to fall within one standard deviation of the overall student body academic index. If the student was slightly below, but an outstanding athlete, the coach that wanted him on his varsity team had to appeal to the Admissions Office. There are no offers of monetary scholarships for athletes in the Ivy League, and our boys were ineligible for financial aid everywhere. In no cases was spending money offered, nor rented apartments, nor loaned cars, nor female escorts. Coach Frank Castelli at Brown came to our house during Todd's junior year of high school and promised only one thing: "If you decide to come to Brown, you will be my starting shortstop as a freshman." He was true to his word.

The application process demands a little fancy footwork on the part of the athlete, as each coach exerts constant pressure in the high school junior and senior years when he can make contact, as specified by NCAA rules. In addition to the NCAA rules, there is a restrictive set of Ivy League conference guidelines that limits everything from out-of-season practices to the number of calendar dates (it was 20) a team is allowed to play games in the spring. This contrasts sharply with the number of games some schools in the Sun Belt play – as many as 70. The Ivy League has other obstacles in recruiting players. As I mentioned earlier, there are no athletic scholarships; the conference has a low baseball profile among pro scouts; there are high academic demands; and the League does not offer the lavish, minor-league-quality complexes that attract many recruits to the big programs.

Eventually in the application process, a college coach will demand that the recruit commit to apply for early admission to that school, thereby enhancing with another prospect the coach's "preferred" list he would submit to the Admissions Department during normal admission months.

This demand always occurs after the athlete has been treated to an all- expense-paid trip to the school and every conceivable treat by his prospective teammates (sometimes illegally). The applicant is allowed five such visits by NCAA rules, and they are an absolute imperative to gain familiarity with the campus, coaches, and teammates. If the prospect truly feels a connection to one school, and believes in the coach's integrity (that the applicant would, indeed, be admitted during early acceptance procedures), then this process works smoothly. But if the applicant commits prematurely to early admission and is then denied admission, he is out in the cold for his other choices, since coaches at other schools remove the applicant's name from their preferred lists as soon as they learn of his early commitment. So, the prospect has to learn to be honest with the coaches, without fully committing himself. At one point, a college coach actually began screaming at Tim over the phone because Tim refused to apply for early admission. Charley interceded.

The process can become so tense that the prospective applicant may actually withdraw and let his parents or a sibling take over, especially if the parents have certain favorite choices. Bill Reynolds, in <u>Fall River Dreams</u>, chronicled the recruiting of our nephew, Chris Herren. At the time, the Boston Amateur Basketball Club coach, Leo Papile, called Chris "the best high school player in the country." During the extremely intense recruiting process, Reynolds reported these comments by Christopher:

"I'm sick of it. I don't even open the mail anymore. I just pick it up to see who it's from, and put it down. And I don't like it when the coaches come to Fall River. I don't mind playing in front of them at national tournaments, but when they come here, it's not the same. I don't know. I guess it's good for the city, for the younger kids to see the coaches around. But I don't like it."

The recruiting process had taken on a life of its own, hovering over everything, invading nearly all discussions. In Fall River it had become the topic of conversation, outweighing the upcoming mayoral elections, the teacher negotiations, and the strong rumors that river boat gambling was going to come to Fall River. Where was Chris Herren going to go to college?

It all seemed to be wearing on him, the endless questions, the speculation about where he was going. He couldn't walk down a corridor in school without someone asking him that question. He was afraid to answer the phone, for fear it would be another coach. A couple of times when he did answer it and it was a coach, he quickly said he was Michael (his brother), that Chris wasn't home. He got a beeper so his friends would have a way to reach him. He seemed more guarded, more irritable. In school he was distracted, falling behind in a couple of his subjects, which were outward signs of increasing inner turmoil.[3]

Although Tim and Todd were never harassed by the press, and the family was never plagued by incessant phone calls, we were nevertheless extremely relieved when each son could tell us where he truly felt most comfortable. Because of their strong academic backgrounds, as well as their talents on the ball field and hockey rink, letters of acceptance arrived during their senior years from Harvard, Dartmouth, Brown, West Point, Amherst, and Colby. I was extremely relieved when Tim accepted Dartmouth instead of West Point, since Charley had served in the Vietnam War during the first year we were married, and I didn't want a son of mine in combat. In the back of my mind was the possibility that their sports careers might continue post-college, with the exception of West Point.

Todd accepted Brown University, only twenty minutes from our house, with the promise that he would not be coming home on weekends. In fact, after he settled in, we actually had to give him two weeks notice to visit if we were ever going to see him! Providence and Boston provided ample social life.

Both boys' choices were perfect for their personalities and interests. Tim's focus on the Far East began in high school as a karate student, and continued as an instructor. He was intent on seeing Charley's slides of his days in Vietnam. He never wavered in his interest in the Orient, and from the first day on campus at Dartmouth College, he was committed to majoring in Asian Studies. He loved the natural surroundings of Hanover, New Hampshire, and took advantage of them. When his baseball career finally ended, he lived in Japan, learned to speak fluent Japanese, then entered graduate school, again in Asian Studies/International Relations.

Tim was unwavering in his dedication to any chosen activity, and his earnestness was genuine. He completed academic assignments because he was interested in the subject matter; Todd did so because he had to.

Tim's focus was always clear; his world existed in black and white. He tolerated no lapses in concentration or effort from himself or his teammates. When he broke his thumb playing baseball and had a cast made to fit his glove, he never missed a game. When a skate gouged his forearm in the National All-Star hockey championship in Peoria and he had two layers of stitches down to the bone to stop the spurting blood, he returned later to the tournament.

After partying one night at his Dartmouth fraternity, he was sprawled out near the toilet bowl the next morning. Around three that afternoon, his frat brothers checked on him and found him in the same position. Mike Phy, a diminutive premed student with emergency room experience, decided Tim's affliction was more than a simple hangover. He dragged the 6'3" Tim to the hospital emergency room down the street, where Tim's appendix was removed in an emergency procedure. I headed up to Dartmouth's Hancock Medical Center. Tim was kept for additional rest that night and released the following morning. Instead of heading directly home for a forced vacation, he insisted on climbing three flights of stairs to take a test in his CPR course. At the time we didn't realize how important that course would be.

Six months later, Tim was called upon to perform CPR on a fellow teammate, Peter Kiernan, who'd collapsed in the Dartmouth field house.

After Tim administered CPR for over ten minutes, the Rescue Squad arrived.

Tim accompanied Peter, son of the governor of Maine, in the ambulance, stayed in his room until the family arrived, and visited constantly during the days before Peter succumbed. The governor attempted to run his state from the hospital room. Tim became a focus for the media, despite the governor's attempts to envelop him in the family's privacy. Television newsmen demanded that Tim reproduce the event on the floor of the field house. As a result, Tim went underground, living at a friend's apartment off-campus while being tutored. The governor's family helped Tim accept Peter's death by explaining that he had succumbed because of an electrical malfunction in the brain. Tim had given them the days they needed to say good-bye. He developed instant maturity. At age twenty, he had looked death in the face, and had seen the best and worst aspects of fellow humans. His experience with the media made him a polished spokesman for the Red Sox while playing "A" ball in Lynchburg, Virginia.

Self-discipline, single-mindedness, perseverance, ambition – all these qualities Tim possessed, but they did not assure his success in professional baseball. Just as having talent and being a winner were not necessarily synonymous, likewise, possession of the above virtues without superior talent did not guarantee success. In addition, bonus money that the organization distributed to its top prospects, salary, internal politics, and personality clashes had to be factored in. Tim had weathered a broken thumb, broken fingers and nose, concussions, sprained knees and ankles, bone bruises on his shoulder, hips, and coccyx, not to mention the gash down to the bone in his forearm from a hockey blade. But he only weathered two years in pro ball.

Todd's personality, distinct from Tim's, had displayed itself even in infancy. Tim would generously drop his stuffed animals one by one into Todd's bassinet, but Todd learned to articulate his wants and exert his rights early. Sixteen months younger, he would not let Tim take advantage of him. When a new toy dangled in front of his jumper seat, he'd begin bouncing in excitement so high that we thought he'd fling himself onto the floor. He played for hours alone, building empty shoeboxes into rooms full of furniture he made from scraps. Tim was the gregarious one, always surrounded by friends, the leader of the pack. Todd had several young sidekicks in elementary school who proceeded to move away to other states. After that Todd grew wary and contented himself with one close buddy.

Through high school, he was the younger brother who tagged along, who played all the games with his big brother's friends and had to measure up. After all, Tim was always there to help or stick up for him. Rather than becoming a wimp, Todd developed "cojones." During a Halloween party, the kids had to bob for apples. After Tim and all his buddies had grabbed the apples with their teeth, it was Todd's turn. At first, he was unable to secure the fruit with his bite, so he pursued it until his head was completely immersed under the surface and he could immobilize it against the bottom.

But little brother could play protector, too. In the National Pee Wee All-Star hockey championship in Peoria, Tim's forearm was unintentionally slashed to the bone by an opponent's blade in the first game. Charley immediately left with Tim for the emergency room. After receiving two layers of stitches, Tim returned to the locker room to gather his equipment. Suddenly the door banged open and Todd blew in. "What are you doing here?" Charley asked in amazement.

"I knocked out the SOB who got Tim," he replied, "but I'm out of the tournament!"

It was amazing to Charley and me that they had bonded so closely. Todd displayed clowning qualities in childhood that became a subtle wit in adulthood. Tim would throw his head back and dissolve in laughter at some of Todd's antics.

Charley and I saw no outward jealousy or resentment, until one night at dinner. Todd was a junior in high school and Tim was a senior. Todd screamed, "I'm sick of trying to get good grades like Tim! I don't care if I go to college!"

"What do you think you'll do the rest of your life, Todd?" Charley asked.

"I really don't care. I'd be happy working in a gas station so I don't have to put up with this crap to get into college."

Charley quickly dispelled any such notion by telling Todd that working in a gas station would not be an option open for him, given his abilities. When he was interviewed in the papers and on local television after being awarded Most Valuable Player in the state high school hockey championships (an award Tim had received the previous year), his verbal skill and poise surprised us. It was only when Mike Szostak published an article in The Providence Journal on June 3, 1991 about their playing as opponents for the first time (in the Ivy League) that we, as parents, learned how much rivalry existed between them:

...We grew up together playing in the same league (said Todd). In high school we were always on the same team, competing for points in hockey or batting average in baseball. Now we're on different teams. It's hard to be as fiercely competitive against each other. When we (Brown) play Dartmouth, I want to beat Dartmouth, but I want Tim to do well.

The same was also true on opposing fields in the Great Lakes League in Ohio during one college summer. During the ten days at the end of their first pro season in 1992, they ended up together on the Elmira Red Sox.

Their teammates claimed they distanced themselves, and during the following spring training, teammates had no idea the two were brothers.

The life lessons learned in high school – self-preservation through distancing from a competitor – allowed each to maintain his self-esteem and also the brother relationship. The stakes were raised in the pros, because careers were on the line. Finally, when Tim was released from the Red Sox in 1994, the first and only person he wanted to talk to was Todd. "He's the only one who knows what I've been through," was Tim's comment. Later, the first person to visit Tim while he was teaching in Japan was his brother.

During Todd's junior year of college (after which he was drafted into the pros), he stole nineteen bases, including home with no runners on, and was caught only three times. But playing two sports meant there would be injuries. Like his brother, he ended up with stitches, rib bruises, a concussion, as well as a break near the thumb-pad. The latter, if it had been in the actual thumb-pad, would have meant no future growth to that digit. During one week, I took our twelve-year-old Todd into a walk-in clinic three times. Some of the injuries occurred while he played knee-ball in the house with his brother. But

Tim and Todd, the high school years.

by law, the medical personnel had to make a follow-up call to our home to see if Todd were a battered child.

In general, his older brother, the defenseman and catcher, was usually there to protect Todd. Tim would retaliate against anyone who went after his younger brother by flinging the opponent into the boards in ice hockey, or knocking him down when the opportunity arose, and pouncing all over him. I used to hide my face in embarrassment. Tim became known as "The Enforcer" on the ice, and together they gained the reputation of the Hanson brothers in the movie, *Slap Shot*.

During his junior year of college, when the scouts became more numerous at each baseball game, Todd developed back pain. The Brown team physician determined from x-rays that Todd's ailment was muscular, although his pelvis was tilted at an irregular angle. Years of scooping up balls in the infield had taken their toll. After three months of chiropractic treatment, Todd and his Brown coach set up an appointment with the Patriots' former orthopedic surgeon. Todd was referred back to an orthopedic in Providence, who gave him exercises to relieve the pain. To this day, he uses those exercises. Baseball season began two months later, and the scouts were none the wiser.

Todd's natural ability was always a source of frustration to his brother. The Puritan ethic, that hard work would be rewarded, seemed to have escaped him entirely. Todd didn't jog during pre-season until college, and never lifted weights on a regular basis until well into his pro career. Tim, on the other hand, had health club memberships in two states and would only take one day off per week from his routine. Later, in the rookie league with the Red Sox, Tim would learn that hard work didn't always mean guaranteed play. Free agents just didn't get the playing time that drafted players got. But by then, Tim's workouts had become a way of life.

Todd would take the field and scoop up grounders with the long fingers of his right hand as if they contained the suction of a vacuum cleaner. In one smooth motion, his 6'2" frame would uncork from the crouch, and his right arm would flail from behind, unleashing in a fluid, continuous arc a ball that grew in velocity as it neared its destination. Said Brown Coach Frank Castelli in a <u>Providence Journal</u> interview:

...His throw picks up speed as it nears first base. That's what separates him from 20,000 other guys. And he's got good power with the bat, too....

As a freshman, he took the field every day and he learned a lot of things. I knew he was good but this is a different level and there's no success right away, but Todd stuck with it and got better. A lot of freshmen get discouraged and get worse...Todd learned from those things. He developed the desire to go out there and take ground balls 'til he got it right. He's willing to stand out there and take it and he has the mental discipline to play 160 games in a pro season....[4]

In his junior year at Brown, Todd batted .329, leading the team with 34 runs and almost 50 hits. The latter tied a record at Brown that would later be broken by his good friend and teammate Dave Murphy. Todd began to swing with an uppercut so that he could pull the balls over the right field fence, thereby impressing the scouts. Charley had taught both boys to bat lefty from the beginning. We could always tell when Todd's swing was meant to hit a homer, but instead produced a pop-up or fly ball to the right.

His efforts to beat out bunts for singles, something at which he had excelled, became non-existent so that he would impress as a long-ball hitter.

Tim's batting average his junior year of college was .370, due not to home runs, but to singles and doubles. A couple of scouts watching sophomore pitcher Bob Bennett at Dartmouth began to watch Tim, as well.

But his senior year, on a losing team with no offense, Tim was looked upon to provide all the offense and his usual reliable defense. As a Captain, he was pressing hard for the team, as well as for his professional chances, since he hadn't been drafted after his junior year. His average dropped to .310, and the season ended early without fanfare, due to inclement weather.

Nevertheless, as he watched Bennett, then his brother, get drafted on June 1, 1992, Tim never stopped his daily workout routine. His "drill sergeant" attitude that had earned him that nickname was deeply ingrained, and finally, after he graduated from Dartmouth in early June, he got a break. Red Sox scout Bill Enos knew that for $43,500 he had a bargain: two smart, hard-working brothers in the Sox organization for the price of one junior-year draftee (Todd). Baseball is an incestuous business and it didn't hurt that Enos was the Dartmouth coach's godfather. Nevertheless, the professionals distrusted Ivy League players. Ivy Leaguers had so much going for them that they were tough to negotiate with, and generally were not committed to a professional career as a ballplayer.

5

Lower League Labyrinth

Perhaps a brief history is appropriate here, most of which is documented in Bruce Chadwick's Baseball's Hometown Teams. Entering the twentieth century, the minor leagues had become the largest and most successful sports organization in America. In 1908, there were 30 minor leagues operating coast-to-coast, with 214 teams. Within a few years, scouting systems enabled the major league teams to draw from semipro and minor leagues across the country. Sometimes hopeful players acted as their own agents. In 1916, one major league team, the Chicago Cubs, had been in business for forty years.

Branch Rickey instituted the farm system in 1916, when he became manager of the St. Louis Cardinals. He inherited a team with an inferior scouting system and little cash. With no other prospect for improving a weak major league team, he acquisitioned little-known players solely to develop them into his own major leaguers.

By 1917, however, the forty-two minor leagues had shrunk to twenty, and then nearly all went out of business with the advent of World War I, the Black Sox scandal, and the Pacific Coast scandal. But during the era of the roaring twenties and thirties, with folks anxious to find an escape mechanism, the eight remaining minor leagues had again swelled to twenty-five. In addition, the Negro Leagues provided traveling teams in small towns where there weren't always minor leagues, as well as in those where they were established. The Depression and unemployment reduced the leagues back down to sixteen.

In 1919, a clause in the agreement among minor league owners had been inserted stating they could bid whatever the market would bear for top players, thereby eliminating the outright possession of minor leaguers by each local owner. The local owners sought to draw back the crowds in the early 30's by installing permanent lighting systems, thus allowing night games for those who were employed during the day. By 1949, a record fifty-nine leagues operated with 10,000 players. Attendance hit a record 41.8 million at minor league parks.

With the advent of the televised major league "game of the day," attendance at minor league parks plummeted again in 1956 to 17 million. Air-conditioning at home made it far more comfortable to be seated in the living room than out at the local park, trying to catch a faint breeze. Little Leagues had been organized in the '50s; seashore and lakeside developments had sprung up with summer recreation; the late fifties and sixties saw the advent of pro football, basketball, golf, tennis, and bowling.

Major league teams began buying franchises in cities where successful minor league teams operated.

By the spring of 1956, owners of major league teams realized that the demise of the minor leagues would mean the end of their funded player pool. The owners got together to provide $500,000 stabilization fund to save the minors in the fifties, and by the end of the decade, additional hundreds of thousands were funneled to a player development fund by major league owners.

In 1962, their efforts at reclassification created Class AAA, AA (merging the former second and third tiers of minor leaguers), and various levels of Class A (formerly Class C and D), as well as the rookie leagues. In addition, they agreed that players' salaries and most of their playing expenses would be assumed by the major league teams, and that no fee would be levied when a player was promoted from the minors to the majors. The farm development system would be assured by minor league owners' profits from the sale of tickets, souvenirs, food, and beverages. All promotions, management of the minor league teams, and everyday expenses would be borne by the minor league owners from those profits.

Baseball's Hometown Teams mentions the first institution of a draft:

"...The new agreements also included a well-structured draft system in which the major league team drafted each player, signed him to a major league contract, and assigned him to one of their minor league teams."

The first amateur draft was held in 1964. In the '70s and '80s, minor league baseball fever again began sweeping the country. Cable TV stations and super stations broadcast the major leagues, creating interest. There was accessibility to minor league fields and free parking. Three wildly successful baseball movies were released (*The Natural, Bull Durham,* and *Field of Dreams*). A new breed of owner, schooled in streamlined marketing techniques and promotions and in running small businesses (souvenir shops), provided inexpensive entertainment for families. Finally, nostalgia for simpler times drove people back to the park for oldies music, goofy kids' contests between innings, and family picnics.

Today, with major league players holding out for multi-millions that the average fan cannot conceptualize in his wildest dreams, two hundred minor league teams operate more or less independently of major league teams (that is not to say that the managers are not told by phone from the organization's head office which players to put on the field the following day). Minor league owners must operate the ballpark, pay park personnel, some travel expenses (rundown buses!), and provide heavy-duty marketing. Minor leaguers' salaries are paid by the major league club. Baseball is a business.[5]

6

Early Innings

So the saga began. Todd arrived in Tampa with a newly-signed catcher from Vanderbilt, Jeff Martin, and boarded a van for a three-day stay at the Holiday Inn in Winter Haven.

The music and parties went on till 3 a.m. among the recruits from Venezuela and the Dominican Republic, who, though unable to speak English, had found "The New World."

After three successful days hitting and fielding with Frank White (the manager of the rookie team in Winter Haven), Todd was told that although Frank would like to keep him so he could develop his talent, he had orders to send Todd on to the Sox Elmira team in the New York-Penn League (one level above the rookie team). Todd flew out with a couple of pitchers. At that point, I trusted all management decisions.

Under Dave Holt in Elmira, Todd once again stepped into a starting position as the only shortstop on the team. Within a week, a third-team All-American, Bill Selby from the University of Southern Mississippi, arrived.

Bill and Bob Juday from Michigan State would switch off at second and third. Todd, eager to impress, began a month of self-imposed pressure and tremendous adjustment, hitting between .175 and .200. He and a catcher from Ohio, Marc Senkowitz, had left the Elmira Holiday Inn because the Sox only paid for their first few days after arrival. They had rented a room in a small house on a residential street in Elmira and purchased forty-dollar bikes for grocery shopping and transportation to the ballpark. Shortly thereafter, Todd's brakes let go. We later drove his car to Elmira, as well as our own, on our visit in late July. My mother kept him supplied with brownies, Pop Tarts, and cartons of juice via care packages.

The Red Sox minor league teams were six in number and were positioned in this order from the bottom up: Rookie team (Winter Haven); "A" teams (Elmira, N.Y.,

Winter Haven, Fla., and Lynchburg, Va.); "AA" team (New Britain, Conn.); "AAA" team (Pawtucket, R.I.).

From the Holiday Inn in Winter Haven, Tim moved with draftee Joe Hamilton, also an Enos choice from Massachusetts, to a new condo directly behind center field. After a week it became obvious that players who were getting the most playing time were those who were high-round draftees with big bonuses. After all, Enos had told Tim when he signed the contract, "They always need catchers." Tim was one of three behind the plate, rotating every third day and DH'ing. After a while, Frank White started playing the guys who were working the hardest. But at first, Jeff Martin, drafted in the thirteenth round, started most of the time behind the plate. The Rookie team played its games at noon, so catchers usually lost eight to ten pounds per day in the 95-104-degree heat. In the seventh inning of a game with the field temperature at 104 degrees, Frank White made substitutions.

"How are you doing, Tim?" he asked.

From his catching crouch, Tim replied, "I'm feeling good, Coach." He began to rise as the coach's voice filtered through.

"Hit the showers, Tim."

He spent off hours sleeping in the air-conditioned condo and lifting weights with the team one mile away. A bike became a necessity for Tim, also.

Charley and I planned our first trip to see Todd in Elmira. We asked him if there was anything we could bring him, and he requested long-sleeve blue undershirts to wear under his uniform for night games. I had to search Massachusetts and Rhode Island to find them. We proceeded resolutely to Dunn Field on our anniversary, in time to watch batting practice around 6 p.m. All games began at 7 p.m., with the exception of Sundays, a distinction from the Rookie League, whose games were at noon. Todd had left tickets in our name at the "Will Call" booth, but we were unaware of them and paid.

All baseball fans can recollect the rush of adrenaline and anticipation as they enter a baseball stadium from the concession ramps. I am always thrilled and astounded by this. The dark tunnel-like passageway opens at the end to a Technicolor green so wide that I have to turn my head to take it all in. Bleachers filled with kaleidoscope color and hawkers enticing with the aromas of hot dogs and promises of "Peanuts!" and "Cold Coke!" bombard my senses all at once. In the minor league parks, billboards in red, orange, black, and blue promote local businesses across the outfield fence. Wooden planks groan from the weight of fans of all ages in shorts, jeans, and obligatory baseball caps rushing to the restroom or to the ground-level concessions. And on the field are the bright white, red, blue, or gold uniforms of the players.

As I entered Dunn Field in Elmira that day, I saw our son on the infield dressed in the navy blue major league uniform of the Red Sox. Nothing in later years ever reproduced my thrill of pride at seeing him that first time. He was standing at the dugout fence signing autographs on balls, bats, gloves, and programs handed to him by kids lined up and down the aisles. He had been expecting us, and looked up every so often to see if we had arrived. When he caught sight of us, he gave a wave. We became instant celebrities proceeding down the aisle toward him; a path cleared, and whispers repeated, "Those are his parents." My focus was to get to him to deliver a hug, but in deference to his surroundings, all I could do was wave back and deliver a huge smile. My pride was printed on my face.

Todd got a hit in the bottom of the ninth to tie the game before 6,000 fans. The Elmira team lost in fourteen innings, to put their record at 5-7. Charley and I had our romantic anniversary dinner at an all-night Perkins Restaurant with Todd around midnight – par for the course for a baseball mom. The second-youngest starter on the team, Todd was still on a high from his first two weeks in the pros. He didn't seem discouraged that his batting average was so much lower than in college, but told us, "It's going to take time to adjust to seeing the ball out of the pitcher's hand at 80 mph."

That was an understatement! Charley told Todd about seeing Jim Rice standing on a side ramp at Dunn field, trying to help one of Todd's teammates with his swing. No one leaning over the stadium seats called to Rice or interrupted him. Fame was, indeed, a fleeting thing.

Todd's daily schedule went something like this. The team would get to the field at 3:30 for a home game at 7 p.m., and afterward they would go out to eat. The next morning, they would sleep in, get up around 10:30 or 11:00, do laundry, grocery shopping, or other errands, make phone calls, lift weights, or jog. If there was an away game, the team would leave on the bus in the morning and spend from two to five hours traveling. The buses in the New York-Penn League were fully equipped with air-conditioning and VCR monitors, unlike the Carolina League buses. We kept Todd supplied with paperbacks for the long road trips.

The players on the Elmira team seemed to be congenial, and none displayed "attitudes" because of their positions in the draft. Performance became a great leveler. Foreigners were appreciated for their humor, and Todd's Ivy League background was never ridiculed. In fact, he concealed it from his teammates as much as possible. He had discovered, along with Tim, that draft round meant everything, his being one of the highest on the team. That explained his starting position at shortstop every day. What counted was what happened on the field, and the players never scolded or turned on each other while we watched, knowing they might be in the same situation the next day.

We got to know Gerald Davis, George Scott III (son of the Sox first baseman in the '70s), and Bill Selby on the team. Gerald was a black kid out of Detroit, who had two children with his girlfriend. She came out to visit in early July. Gerald was released right after his girlfriend's visit, and the rest of the team regarded his release as an example for them. He had dared to question Manager Holt about his lack of playing time. As parents, we took this as a warning not to interfere, either.

We followed the Pioneers on the road to Utica that weekend, to see them lose two more. Todd began a batting slump, going one for seven with a walk. He was charged with three throwing errors to the right side of first baseman Jose Malave. By the second week of July, the manager had replaced Malave with another first baseman, who began scooping the throws out of the dirt.

After the Sunday game in Utica, Charley and I drove towards home as far as the Massachusetts state line, and were happy to find any motel with a vacancy sign and a vending machine for dinner. The players were given $15 meal money per day while traveling. Bill Enos had warned Todd, a junk-food junkie, to pay close attention to his diet. Concession workers at the ballparks doled out pizzas and hot dogs to the players after the fans had gone home. The players welcomed parents' visits for full-blown meals at local restaurants.

On Tuesday, June 30, 1992, the rookie team in Winter Haven was informed that players age 21 and over would be cut to three per team. Older pitchers on Tim's team were placed on the disabled list to avoid having to cut them from the roster, but that meant no playing time. One pitcher quit and headed home. Tim, at age 22, hoped to be re-assigned to the Florida State League in Winter Haven, but was left on the rookie team, along with catcher Jeff Martin, for almost the entire summer. The two became the leading hitters, consistently batting over .300, as well as the team "graybeards" (over 21 and able to drink legally). Although both Tim and Jeff were competing to advance, they got along well, both having attended college and both awestruck over Frank White. They were able to console each other through-out the summer while other players moved up. After a two-week visit from his girlfriend, Jeff moved his wedding plans up to the following winter.

The rookie team in Florida continued to win, and in mid-July, Tim asked Frank White to hit him grounders at first base, where he had played sporadically in college. He became the permanent first baseman, instead of a twice-a-week catcher. He was, nevertheless, discouraged, because he felt his strength in the field was as catcher. He asked us to send him his resume and some government service applications.

Back at home after our visit to Elmira, we received a collect call from Todd, a procedure he used throughout his career which saved money on his phone bills. Awakening hastily from a sound sleep, we heard, "I stink! I can't hit the side of a barn, and I made two errors tonight. It's been three games since I've had a hit," a dry spell which continued through the following two games. We shook ourselves awake to respond to our first long-distance crisis.

I learned over the years that we would be constant cheerleaders, a safe harbor in their storms. If, after all, we who had created this child couldn't reinforce his self-esteem, there would be no one else to do it. However, we also had to be realistic. Charley and I repeated the litany that Enos had professed to both boys in our home when he delivered their contracts. It went something like this:

"Baseball is a marathon. It's a series of disasters, and even the best hitters fail seven out of ten times at bat. Stay even emotionally. You'll have good days and bad days, just as anyone does in any other profession. You have to say to yourself that with some extra effort and hard work, tomorrow will be better. So you can't get too up or too down. If you happen to be one of the few who makes it to the majors, it will be hard work and dedication that got you there. Right now, everyone with you believes that he will be the one to make it, and you have to believe it, too. You'll always be playing on the edge of disaster, even if you do make it all the way, because there'll always be someone to take your place. That's life."

Over the years we added things like, "We have seen your team play, and we know you are the best defensive player on the team...Bill Enos had enough faith in you to draft you...Frank White told us he thought you had tremendous skills for someone your age...This is a job with a contract you committed to. Now, dig down and do the work you know you're capable of." The phone calls would usually end with specific hitting instructions from Charley, the same ones the boys had heard since Legion days. "Hit to the opposite field on outside pitches; bunt for base hits if you can beat it out (Todd); choke up with a shortened back swing if you're down with two strikes against you." And always, "We love you."

The weekend of July 4, 1992, we traveled to Pittsfield, Mass., to watch Todd's Elmira team play the Mets "A" team. We arrived in the late afternoon, thinking the game would begin at 7 p.m., the starting time for all weekday games. Because of the holiday, however, the game had started in mid-afternoon, and we missed all but the last few innings. My parents had driven up from Connecticut to join us. Red, white, and blue bunting covered the front of the wooden stands and a chicken mascot paraded wildly on the field between innings, delighting the kids by cavorting with the players' pants. There was a contest between innings where contestants threw a ball toward a hole in a board ten yards away. If the ball went through the small hole, the contestant would go home with a new car! Another contest had two fans spin around on the field with their heads down on top of upturned bats. After ten spins, they had to run across a finish line. This contest always made me avert my eyes, as we saw dizzy contestants stumble to the ground, and in one case, fall over the third-base fence into the first row of spectators. There were charcoal grills off the main concourse emitting luscious smells of hot dogs and hamburgers. And after the game, while players hung around to sign autographs, a lavish fireworks display began over the field.

During this game and the succeeding one, Todd went one-for-seven. He did, however, follow Charley's advice, hitting some hard balls to the opposite field (left field for a left-handed batter) that were caught. Giving in to the temptation to pull the ball over the right field fence the following week, Todd began his home run trot. Halfway around the bases he realized the ball had fallen off the top of the fence onto the field for a double. His first home run still eluded him.

On July 4th, pouring rain did not hamper the people of Pittsfield from persevering with their annual parade. From their rooms in the Hilton, our players had a bird's eye view. On road trips the team stayed at hotels ranging from the Hilton to the Radisson to Howard Johnson's to the Comfort Inn. We learned as we made more visits that parents got a team rate at the same hotel where the players stayed, as well as at specified motels when they played at home.

That first year, we stayed as far away from the team as possible, at our sons' requests, but nonetheless, one day in the lobby of the Hilton while waiting for Todd, Charley bumped into Elmira Manager Dave Holt.

On the field, Holt always appeared stoic, never showing emotion, and never saying a word to any of the players. Only once did we see him explode at an umpire and get ejected.

Charley introduced himself, and Holt proceeded to explain that this season was viewed as an orientation year. "We try not to put any pressure on the players their first year, and won't look at their stats from this short season. It's simply a time to build confidence."

After watching nothing but losses in Elmira, the parents of one of our catchers (John Crimmins) asked us what we thought. I responded, "It seems they need some help! Where are the batting instructors and infield instructors? They appear and disappear like genies."

Steve Braun, another batting instructor with Rice, and Rac Slider, an infield instructor, did, in fact, arrive the following week. They were rotating among the minor league teams. "What good is a week?" I wondered.

On July 20th, Jim Rice arrived in Winter Haven to instruct the rookie team. He pitched batting practice to Tim and Jeff Martin, encouraging them to become long-ball hitters like him. During his brief stay in Elmira with the "A" team, Rice had endeavored to change the batting stance of catcher John Crimmins, resulting in making Crimmins so off-balance that he fell over in the box each time he swung. Jeff Martin commented to Tim, "Five years ago no one could ever have convinced me I'd be taking batting practice with Jim Rice and hating it."

It was Tim's contention that Rice had a lot of weight in the Sox organization, but as a teacher, Frank White was more knowledgeable and could transfer the knowledge to his players. Unfortunately, White stayed in the background in deference, while Rice visited the rookie team in Winter Haven. Todd reported to us that according to Rice, "There was only one person who knew how to play left field at Fenway – me!"

The truth became evident abruptly to both boys that the reality of standing next to Jim Rice in the batter's box – a life-long dream - fell far short of expectation. Rice had proved himself human. He was an egotist, still searching for a ray in the spotlight, which got in the way of his instruction. This realization was essential in the boys' progression from eager recruits to seasoned minor leaguers, and helped them weather the disappointments and politics of the business. In succeeding years, I was able to joke with Rice personally at spring training, but could never forget the ego he displayed in his teaching.

"Have you heard from Todd?" we asked Tim over the phone. The boys had contacted each other once a week during the first month, and then it became every other week.

"No," said Tim, "and I'm pissed. I called him last. He was doing lousy. He had nothing to say and didn't want to talk. I refuse to call him again!"

A week later, none of us had had any word from Todd. Tim, the older brother, finally caved in and left a message on Todd's answering machine. After a road trip, the call was returned. Distance allowed Todd a measure of pride when things weren't going well. Neither boy ever asked us what the other's batting average or stats were.

Many of Tim's roommates in Winter Haven were Latino and did not speak English. Tim practiced using his college Spanish with them, particularly when he was behind the plate catching with a Latino pitcher. He sat with them at the picnic tables at lunch and began to teach them English. The Red Sox made no attempt to instruct these players in English, and a Spanish-speaking scout had left the team by early August. The foreign players were just grateful to be in the U.S., even if they had no transportation and could not communicate.

Our next call from Tim on July 23 reported that none of the players on his team had received their signing bonuses yet. "I need the $1000! The coaches promised us the money this week. Since Jeff didn't move into my apartment, Joe (Hamilton) and I are splitting the rent, phone, and electricity. So far, he's paid for both of us."

In succeeding days, we couldn't reach Tim because he was "sleeping." I suspected he'd finally found a social life and hadn't come home, since we had tried to reach him at all hours. At 6 p.m. two days later, he called to say he'd been on a boat in the late afternoons, with Jeff and a friend of Jeff's fiancée. Mothers have noses for this sort of thing, and our instincts are usually correct. We can see through excuses and storytelling. Although our children like to think they were born with all the knowledge they will need to encounter life's obstacles, mothers know differently. We try to teach, even nag, until we have run out of age-old adages. In the end, common sense implores us to give them our blessing and get out of the way. But it's no easy task!

"How's baseball?" Charley asked after we'd listened to a recitation of Tim's social activities.

"I went 0-for-3 and 1-for-2 in the last two games, with four RBI's."

"Stay loose and keep hitting!" Charley advised.

During their professional tenure, the boys' stats were published every Sunday in The Providence Journal, always a cause for my brooding and comparisons. Like mother, like son! Todd was batting .194, and when he called us, he'd gone 2-for-12 over a three-game period, with two strikeouts.

"What happened?" Charley asked.

"Well, you saw our umps and you know they're right out of umpire school. They're trying to make a name for themselves to work their way up in the system, like us. Their strike zone is too big. My third strike was so outside one time that the catcher had to lean out to receive the ball, and he started laughing when I was called out. But my eye is getting much better. I'm seeing the ball as soon as it comes out of the pitcher's glove now, and I'm going 2-and-2 and 3-and-2 in the count. The right field fence is only 285 feet."

"So you've been trying to pull the ball out over it, right?"

"Right. But I still think I'll be picked for the instructional league this fall. I don't know what I'll do about my courses at Brown, though. Besides, I want to see my classmates before they graduate, since I won't be there in the spring."

"Why do you think you'll be selected for instructional?"

"Because they take fifty prospects, which means all of the draftees, plus some additional kids who need extra work. Not everyone has signed yet."

The significance of an invitation to fall instructional camp was huge for the rookies. It was an indication that the organization wanted to invest six extra weeks of time and money in intense instruction at bat and on the field. Those who were regarded as future "prospects" with a major-league career ahead of them were chosen, and those who were not knew immediately that making it to the big leagues was a long-shot. The politics of coaches, scouts, agents, as well as bonus money paid to a draftee, entered into the invitations. Someone like Tim, whom we had observed working alone with the coaches in extra drills to prove himself, had a much lower chance of going to instructional camp because he had not been drafted or given a significant signing bonus. After this rookie summer, hot "prospects" would be chosen for inter-league teams in Arizona, the Dominican Republic, or Mexico to play in the fall.

"It would be an honor to be picked, Todd, but you can't count on anything in this profession," Charley advised.

"I know that. Carla (his Brown roommate's fiancée who had visited) said I looked thin."

"Aren't you eating at least two full meals a day?" I asked him.

"I'm trying to, and it's easier when there's a rainout. We don't cook much in the kitchen in our house. It's under constant construction."

"How's your back?"

"Great! I do exercises every day."

"Any lifting?"

"Not with the traveling."

Tim's games, in contrast, were always in Winter Haven Thursday through Saturday at noon. The lights on the field never illuminated any rookie games. Monday through Wednesday Tim's team traveled one hour to play, and Sundays were days off.

"Dad, look in today's Sunday paper and see what Steve Rodrigues is batting in Winter Haven. He was released from the Olympic tryouts, and reported down there. I'd love to play short with him at second."

"He's at .250. Don't worry about other players, just worry about yourself." Frank Castelli, Todd's Brown coach, would repeat this advice to Todd many times in succeeding months. In fact, he asked us to relate these words to Todd:

"Tell Todd the main thing he's got to worry about is his own confidence in himself. He shouldn't compare himself to any shortstop in the organization. He should be saying, 'I'm the one they should be watching out for, because I belong up there.' Then he'll surpass them all. He's got the tools needed to make it to the majors. The Duke University coach two years ago said he would be the best shortstop in his league if he were there, and the Virginia Commonwealth coach said he's got unbelievable hands.

"Point out to him that only in professional athletics does someone stick a microphone in your nose and put your name in the paper if you screw up in your first few years. In business you might get chewed out if you make a bad mistake, but superiors would answer for you, and you wouldn't be under intense scrutiny. In the minors, you're all alone, where everything's magnified, and for a pittance."

I wanted to end the phone call with Todd on a positive note. I realized that Coach Castelli was right. Everything was magnified in the media and most of it was negative, and it had not even been two months yet! I told Todd that he and Tim were mini-celebrities in our town in Rhode Island.

"You and Tim have been asked to be the guest speakers at the Cumberland youth baseball banquet and to participate in a Rotary Club celebrity auction. The girls would bid on spending an evening with you in November."

That got a rise out of him. "No way! I won't get up in front of two hundred people to speak, either. Let Tim do it. He's good at that."

"You're going to have to get used to it at some point, so why not in front of kids? Start doing public service. You've got to give back a little of what you received from the town."

"Well, I'm not hard up enough to have people bid on me for a date."

Tim did the speaking, and both boys ended up in the auction, along with Tim's friend, Derek Laffey, among others. Todd received the second-highest bid of the evening, although he promised the woman he would only take her to dinner and a movie, not to New York in a limo, as some of the male contestants offered. As it turned out, the girls were only out for a fun evening of bidding, and neither Tim nor Todd was able to make contact with his prospective date.

When I asked Tim what he thought of his celebrity status, he replied, "First of all, Mom, we entered that auction as a favor to you and your friend running it. No one on this team thinks of himself as a celebrity. We play at twelve noon in ninety-five-degree heat, and there are no fans – I mean none. I've gotten calls only from my good friends at Dartmouth, and you, of course, and Granny and Grandpa Plumb. Aunt Kathy and Uncle Norm called when they were down here in Disney World, though."

Tim took full advantage of his summer in Florida. He went boating on interconnected lakes around Lake Hamilton. He saw a waterskiing show at Cypress Gardens, a lake volleyball tournament, and ferreted out a bar somewhere on the edge of the lake. While he was out enjoying himself, Todd was in his rented house in Elmira, wondering what the Sox shortstop one level above him (released from Olympic tryouts) had done in his game that day.

The difference in their personalities was evident in 1978 on a trip to Marco Island, Florida. Charley and I had attended a management meeting there with the board of directors of Fleet Financial Group, and had arranged for the boys to fly down when the meeting ended. They were seven and eight years old at the time. As parents, we were nervous about their unaccompanied flight and had tried to anticipate every step, as we usually did whenever we gave the boys a degree of responsibility or freedom. We tried to guarantee their successes by providing guidelines, rules, penalties, or someone's supervision. That philosophy worked about 75% of the time.

The day of their arrival, Charley's secretary called from Providence to say that an ice storm had prevented the boys from making their scheduled connection in Atlanta. They would be on the next plane, and we should meet the second plane in Fort Myers when it arrived. What she was unaware of was that their connecting plane was held in Atlanta to accommodate all those who had delays. The boys arrived in Fort Myers at the original time, but we didn't.

When we blithely waltzed up to the entrance at the miniscule Fort Myers Airport, located amid fields of cattle, we could see a lone child pacing back and forth at the doorway. As we got closer, we realized it was Todd. His eyes were red and swollen; he was, after all, an abandoned child in a foreign state. And he was mad as hell. The boys had tried to place a long distance call to our hotel, but had been thwarted by voice recordings and incorrect change.

Feeling miserably guilty, we consoled Todd and asked, "Where's Tim?"

"He's in the restaurant having a hamburger," Todd replied.

7

Roller Coaster

By the end of July, Tim was batting third in the lineup on the rookie team, and Jeff Martin, the former Vanderbilt catcher, was batting fourth. Jeff started at the catching position, and Tim was at first base. Joe Hamilton, a draftee out of high school from Massachusetts, and Tim's apartment-mate, had hurt his back and was sidelined on the Disabled List. Tim reported that the first-round draft pick of the Sox that year, a center fielder named Tony Sheffield, ran in circles to catch fly balls, and would let the ball bounce next to him.

Alan Nero, a former Rhode Islander and sports agent who owned Coordinated Sports Management, had been pressing Tim and Todd to make appointments to talk about his representing them. Tim responded, "I have no money to give anyone. Nero's basically interested in Todd, and we'll wait and see what he does for (Wade) Boggs this year when Boggs becomes a free agent. Nero's going to have a tough time negotiating."

In reality, we learned that agents demanded no remuneration until players made the "AAA" roster, and then took a flat fee for services which included income tax preparation. Until then, they had little leverage within the organization as representatives of minor leaguers, but could gain access to free equipment from sporting goods companies.

As summer progressed, both boys worried about planning for their immediate futures. Tim became increasingly frustrated as he and Jeff watched rookie team-mates progress to Elmira, while they labored at noon in the sweltering Florida heat. Since there was no indication whether Tim, as a free agent, would receive an invitation to the Red Sox instructional camp, he didn't know whether to send resumes out to government service agencies or wait until the following spring. A job in the off-season would depend entirely on his making contacts among Charley's business network in Rhode Island and Massachusetts, since unemployment figures in Rhode Island had reached ten percent. Tim began to express his desire to attend the Army Language School in Monterey as a member of the U.S. military, or to apply to the FBI. He didn't want to turn 25 and find himself still stuck in "A" ball. Todd would resume his studies to complete the fall semester of his senior year at Brown, if he weren't invited to instructional camp.

I couldn't believe one of my sons would give up a dream so easily. In reality, I couldn't face giving up the dream, either, though I had a business to run and was the wife of a prominent businessman.

On the phone I said to Tim, "Be patient! You're playing every day, loving your job, and batting .300. You like Frank White and are learning a lot. You're only 22, so give it at least another year. There will be so many options open when you leave baseball that you can't predict right now what your future might hold." Giving up under difficult circumstances was never one of the options in our family.

Tim's response to me was, "Mom, you don't have a clue about what I've been through. Dad, at least, had four years in the military before grad school."

Then Charley jumped in. "But Tim, I was an officer, and if you enlist in the service just to get out of baseball, that's an entirely different situation. You have no assurance that you will get into officer's school if you are an enlisted man. If, a year from now, you're stuck in Elmira and don't think that you will progress above that first level, then I'd agree that you should leave. By age 25, you probably will want to do something else with your life. It's just too soon to make that decision. Remember, if you leave, no other team will be able to pick you up, and baseball will be over."

Charley received a call at work from Todd requesting his allergy records. He needed hay fever/dust/pollen/mold shots, as the cut grass on the field was creating a problem with his play. As a child, he had been bitten by a bee on his ankle, and within ten minutes had had an antihistamine shot from our pediatrician. Nevertheless, his face had become so swollen that for three days the distortion resembled the "Elephant Man," with tiny slits for eyes. Immediately thereafter, his allergies were tested, with resulting shots every week to build up his tolerance, particularly to bee stings. We planned to bring his records to Elmira the following weekend.

Todd reported he'd had only one hit in four recent games. It appeared we'd be cheerleaders again that weekend. Charley could think of nothing he'd rather do, but I could think of a lot of things! Still, Todd needed our support.

Charley and I each drove a car to Elmira on the last day of July '92, delivering Todd's car to him. Although he said he was among the highest draft round on his team (bonus money), he guarded his paycheck like a vault and wouldn't outlay for anything but a bike for transportation. Charley and I had provided our sons with Ivy League educations and agreed not to supplement their incomes. A couple of players on Tim's team had received $80,000 bonuses for signing, and were buying houses.

Todd's team record when we arrived was 14-28. After watching three innings against the Expos, during which Todd hit a line drive single, we had to abandon our seats and head into the concession ramps, due to a tremendous thunderstorm. There had been flooding along the Susquehana River and tornado watches throughout the day. The grounds crew pulled two tarps onto the field. One guy had only one free hand, while the other held a beer. The pouring rain subsided, and the players from both teams chatted on the side of the field, idly swinging bats, playing pepper, or kicking in a circle a small beanbag shaped like a soccer ball. I observed that the Red Sox players were full of camaraderie, many of them leaning on each other, hugging each other, or waving and talking to the five sets of parents who were visiting. The opposing team didn't roughhouse or display any physical contact. The personalities among teammates made a season bearable or not.

Eventually, the game was postponed and resumed the following night, before a second game was played. Todd's hit counted. Among the five sets of parents visiting were T.J. O'Donnell's folks. As T.J.'s father told us, "Todd and T.J. have both been stroking the ball, but they haven't fallen in."

Both T.J.'s dad and catcher John Crimmins' dad asked us about Tim. We replied that he was hitting .300 on the rookie team, to which each of the other fathers claimed his son had hit over .350 down there! There was still an obvious sense of competition among the parents at this early level, which lessened at higher levels in the minor leagues, as parents became a true fraternity.

The Crimmins had brought a busload of friends from the Boston area to Elmira on a previous weekend to see John play. They had sung throughout two night games, and hosted a party for the team and visiting girlfriends at the Holiday Inn. Todd had been no angel at Brown, but seemed astounded at the drinking capacity of some of his teammates, who were able to recover by mid-afternoon to report to the field. During subsequent spring trainings, we heard stories of arrests for drunkenness among the minor leaguers, and wondered how many were alcoholics.

While we waited for Todd after the two games, Clyde Smoll, the Elmira Pioneers' principal owner, talked to us about the plight of owning the club and maintaining Dunn Field. He explained that $200,000 had to be raised for renovations at the field so that it would comply with major league regulations for minor league affiliates. A total of approximately $700,000 would be poured into the stadium by private donations, city, state, and federal contributions, as well as by community and regional agencies. Over $500,000 had been netted, and of the $200,000 difference, $160,000 had already been raised. Smoll paid the City of Elmira $6,600 in 1992 to use the field, plus an equal amount for stadium improvements. The lease he agreed to with the county for the '94-'96 seasons called for him to pay $20,000 a year, as well as to give the county $.25 from each adult ticket bought, if attendance exceeded 65,000 for the season. The 54-year-old stadium held 5,000 seats in 1992. City officials were quoted as saying it cost about $75,000 a year for them to maintain Dunn Field.[6]

Smoll told us that he had thirty-eight home games in which to make his profits, and with ten straight losses in the '92 season, the highest ERA in the league, and lots of rain, his attendance was down by 9,000 fans. The previous year, in which the Pioneers had won the division championship, the team drew 79,414 fans. He said the fans and the players had been very patient with Dave Holt, the new manager. Each time the team went on the road, Smoll claimed it cost him $2,000. On a game night, he had twenty-eight to thirty people working. Baseballs each year cost him $6,000, and bats cost $7,000. We asked how we could contribute to the fund-raising effort besides the miniscule contributions we made during the games, and whether he had tried to hold day games on weekends to save the expense of lighting, and to get both a lunch- and dinner-hungry crowd. He told us he had tried that previously at Dunn Field, and only 500 had attended. It took three to four years for word to spread about day games, and Smoll claimed that with only thirty-eight home games, he couldn't afford the lost revenue.[7]

We detected an undercurrent of a love/hate relationship with the Red Sox in Clyde's voice. We knew Todd and some of the other players had been working at the baseball camp he held at the field, but they had been asked to quit by their manager because it might interfere with the team schedule. Smoll maintained his distance from the players and parents, quite a contrast to Sam Plumeri, whom we would view three years later in Trenton, N.J., as the epitome of a successful owner. Sam, the owner of the "AA" Sox franchise, held a steak-fry night and other freebies at local restaurants for the team. He visited the clubhouse before and after every game to fraternize with the players. If there were empty seats in his owner's box, he invited parents of the players to leave their "family" rows behind home plate to join him. The years Todd played in Trenton were sellouts with standing-room only during the team's run for the "AA" championship, and Sam Plumeri's marketing team sustained a sea of green hats on the fans throughout the stadium. The players loved him. Todd approached Sam for an off-season job one year, and several players attended his funeral many years later. Todd remained in contact with his son for business purposes.

In Elmira, Todd presented us with his stack of newly-printed baseball cards. He had a terrible, mean-looking puss in the photo. I guess that was meant to intimidate opponents. On the drive home after the weekend, I lingered over each player's card from the Elmira team. Charley recalled the cards of his youth -- Mickey Mantle, Ted Williams, Willie Mays, etc. How he loved them, studied and memorized the stats on the back, and traded them to complete a team. How he wished he had kept that collection! And now we were looking at a card that held our son's picture. Incredible! There were no baseball cards for Tim's rookie team.

Over a late-night dinner at a team hangout in Elmira, Todd told us he had saved $100 out of his monthly salary. This seemed unbelievable to us, considering he was only making $850/month! He had always been tight with his money, and was renting a $40/week room in a handyman's "do-it-yourself" house on a quiet street. Unfortunately, the owner had never gotten around to doing it himself, and the kitchen remained for the entire summer with half-finished countertops and cabinet doors hanging from one hinge. The rotted front stoop was in the process of being replaced with cement, but by the end of the season in early September, a gaping hole still existed and we continued to go around to the back. It was a dump, but I kept my mouth shut, knowing Todd was trying to be frugal - he still had a year left at Brown. There was one couch, a chair, and a TV in the living room. Todd and Mark shared an un-air-conditioned, open second-floor bedroom and bath, which they didn't seem to mind. They shared the expense of one fan. In fact, they were quite content to save their money and hang their laundry on a line behind the house to dry, after washing it at a nearby wash-and-fold.

Tim, on the other hand, received the same salary and had been unable to save a dime in Florida, a result of the higher cost of living and Tim's willingness to spend to have a good time. His weight was up to 230 lbs. on his 6'3" frame because of eating out, he had joined a health club, and did not lack for nightly entertainment. His furnished condo rental was expensive, and with utilities, phone, and only one instead of two roommates, he quickly used up his entire $1,000 bonus.

Todd's later employment in the world of finance was predictable. He knew where every penny went, and was saving for a new car to replace the hand-me-down we had delivered to him in Elmira. Charley offered to trade that one in and donate the difference toward a new car of Todd's choice (within reason) when he graduated from Brown, as we had done for Tim upon his college graduation.

"Did you enjoy your road trip to Canada?" Charley asked Todd.

"No, I couldn't wait to get out of there," he replied. "Sodas were $4 and three of us got a bill for $75 for chicken wings, beer, and hamburgers. The exchange rate was lousy. By the way, what should we do with my bonus when we get it? I don't want to touch it to live."

"It will go toward your last two semesters at Brown. By combining your assets, we'll start an investment fund at the bank to pay for them."

We reacquainted ourselves with Bill Selby from Mississippi, and met Quinn Feno and Doug MacNeil from Massachusetts. The latter two kept us occupied the remainder of the night with tales of Fall River, particularly of parties at Horseneck Beach attended by Tim and Todd's cousins, and of a party in Fall River attended by Tim and a Rhode Island friend. After that party, the two had no way to get back to our summer house, and ended up on Charley's parents' doorstep for the night. Fortunately, Tim's grandmother took pity on them.

Charley and I proceeded that night to our reserved room at the midtown Holiday Inn in Elmira. We'd requested a king-size bed, and entered room 129, which proved to be the Honeymoon Suite! The desk informed us there were only two king-size beds in the place, both Honeymoon suites. Our bed was round, complete with drapes enclosing it and a VCR mounted above. We stayed put for the next three days, and enjoyed!

Over a late brunch the following morning, I suggested to Todd that he keep a journal of his experiences, which might aid me if I decided to put our family's saga together while he and his brother played pro ball. He absolutely refused, citing pitching coach's Garry Roggenburk's team meeting regarding Bouton's book, Ball Four, in which Roggenburk's teammates were named for improprieties. The point of the lecture: whatever happened in the locker room stayed there! Therefore, Mom, no notes would be kept on fellow teammates. Todd shocked us, though, by saying he was keeping a log of pitches he'd hit or missed, and hints from batting instructors. I assured him that in many years, after he and Tim were well established in other careers, both of them would be the first to read my rough draft for approval. By then, there would be plenty of printed material on their own or their teammates' baseball histories.

In Ball Four Plus Ball Five, Jim Bouton described the departure of Garry Roggenburk from his Seattle Pilot's team in 1969. In Bouton's view, Roggenburk was a marginal player who had four years in on his pension along with his college degree, but didn't realize the consequences of his walking out on "the bullshit." "He said he had no interest in the game anymore, didn't enjoy it, and was through with it and was going home." No other team picked him up.[8] The consequences of such a decision are enormous for a ballplayer, since pro baseball is a tightly closed fraternity which blackballs those who turn their backs on it. Whereas in business, teaching, or other professions, one could leave an entry-level job and (assuming an adequate performance) move laterally or upward within the profession, there is only one track available in pro baseball. Minor league coaches, such as Roggenburk, had had some time in the majors and re-appeared when there was nothing else on the horizon.

Todd asked for our assistance in grocery shopping and laundering his clothes. Charley and I shopped for a gift for his 21st birthday, approaching in two weeks. We selected a set of golf clubs, since Todd seemed to enjoy spending his free time on the golf course as opposed to working out. We dropped him at the field four hours before game time.

One hour before the game, Charley and I headed to Dunn Field. In twenty-seven years of married life, my husband had arrived at every game he ever attended, either as a coach or as a spectator, at least an hour early. It would have ruined his night if he couldn't watch infield practice, and particularly if he hadn't seen Todd fielding and throwing. There is no doubt in my mind that Charley's tactical understanding and passion for the game, as well as his work ethic, were inspirational for his sons, if not a definitive aspect of their success. "If we didn't have to get here so early," I complained, "we would have had time to go hand-gliding in the foothills!" That was something I'd always wanted to try and it was available right out past the Elmira Mall.

"Next time," Charley replied, "you can go hand-gliding and I'll grab a ride to the field with Todd." So much for an idyllic weekend together.

Todd got a couple of hits that night, including a double; made a beautiful play deep in the hole; and then booted a double-play ball that cost two runs. Behind us, when he made another difficult play behind second base, an elderly fan said, "Well, he still owes us for the botched double play." I was glad Todd would have a number of years before he hit Fenway Park, because I wasn't ready to hear tens of thousand of fans booing my son!

Afterward, we headed with Todd for a pizza dinner, where Charley stressed Todd's ability to bunt for hits, his intelligent base running (running halfway between bases when a fly ball might be caught), and most importantly, methods of compensating for being overtired during a double-header (the cause of the error). Charley suggested charging more quickly on double-play balls and switching to a bat that was an ounce lighter, if he were tired. Todd's back problems had not reappeared, despite his taking the majority of assists in infield plays during two games that night.

During the last inning, a mother and son from nearby Gillett, Pennsylvania, had introduced themselves to us. The son, Lucas, had had Todd as an instructor for one day on the field in a baseball camp, and they'd invited him to dinner shortly before his birthday. Doreen sent tins of cookies to Todd regularly, and baked a birthday cake in the shape of a bat and ball. Later, she flew to Lynchburg, Virginia, to visit a pitcher she'd befriended from the Elmira team the previous year. Although Doreen wasn't outwardly captivating, she definitely was alone frequently with her two kids, while her engineer husband traveled. I recalled Susan Sarandon's character in *Bull Durham*, whose self-esteem was tied to her seduction of one minor leaguer per year. Todd seemed oblivious to any of Doreen's ulterior motives and continued to frequent her house with other teammates in tow for home-cooked meals. When he left Elmira, he corresponded with the daughter, Meghan. Eventually, the parents split. It was not until the following year that I became more fearful of "groupies." I wanted to believe that that first summer, Todd spent time after games at team hangouts, and then collapsed.

My weight was shot, eating pizza at midnight after gorging on popcorn, beer, and a pretzel during the doubleheader. Maybe the glider ride wouldn't have been such a good idea!

Helping Todd do some errands the next day (thereby paying his bills), I grabbed a box of Snuggle softener sheets off the shelf. Todd put them back, in favor of a box of Cling-Free. "They're $.10 cheaper," he told me.

We decided to celebrate his birthday by having a decent meal at noon at a local restaurant. Since every night game began at 7 p.m., Charley and I spent the afternoons trying to get some exercise around the parks in Elmira. We rehashed Todd's game of the night before, or the lack of communication between Sox managers and minor leaguers, as we wound our way along paths and back roads. Todd needed to inform the dean at Brown that he would not return for the fall semester if he were selected for the Sox instructional camp.

"Can you believe the lack of consideration that management has for these kids?" I asked Charley on our visit to Mark Twain's summer residence and museum. "They're like pieces of property without any rights!" We had plenty of time on the drive back to Massachusetts to mull over the treatment minor leaguers received, but more immediately, we needed to shove Todd's laundry in and out of the washer and dryer at the Holiday Inn.

Todd had a good laugh over the round honeymoon bed in our room. We called Tim while we were all together. He had moved out of his condo and was renting a single room at the Holiday Inn of Winter Haven, next to his buddy Jeff Martin, for $350/month. It was a fifteen-minute walk to the field. He'd apparently had enough of playing nursemaid to the 17-year-old roommate, Joe Hamilton, and splitting the rent two ways.

Tim told us of other dissensions on the rookie team. One of the pitchers had broken his fist by punching out another player. Another was released after he was discovered with drugs. Martin had slightly injured his hand and was placed on the Disabled List for a week, a welcome rest. This allowed an older pitcher to come off the DL, since only three players over 21 years old were allowed on the roster. Tim filled in, alternating at catch when he wasn't playing first base.

The two brothers spoke of a catcher from the "AA" level, already invited to the September-October instructional camp. No one else had yet been informed. Todd still felt he'd be included, as well as two other infielders from his team. Tim didn't know what his chances were, or even if he'd play regularly at first base when Martin returned to the line-up. "They tell us nothing," Tim said.

The game in Elmira that night was dead – a pitcher's duel with a 3-0 score in favor of the Blue Jays – until the eighth inning, when Todd got a single and was sacrificed around to put our first run on the board. He made an error on an easy ground ball, and seemed disgusted with his mental mistakes. In the bottom of the ninth, our batter was hit by a pitch. With two outs, Todd hit a screaming double down the right field line. It bumped up against the fence, to make the score 3-2. Seeing the third base coach's (Holt's) hand circling, Todd continued on, trying to stretch a double into a triple. The throw was on the mark at third, for the final out of the game.

Jack McGovern, a veteran usher in the ballpark, spoke for all the unpaid coaches sitting in the stands. "Why didn't he hold him up?" Everyone's a critic, especially those in attendance every night. I kept my mouth shut and never responded, even if I heard criticisms about our son. The team sat at the bottom of its division.

Naturally, Todd was disgusted with himself for not being more cautious on the bases. "If the coach gives an unclear signal or no signal at all, then you hold up. I'm a better base runner than that, and I don't want the reputation around the organization for blowing games. Everything good I do is wiped out. I make two outstanding plays, then I fumble an easy grounder. I get a double to score some runs, but I'm called out stretching it." I reminded him of the hundreds of routine plays he'd already made that season, as well as the spectacular ones, which was why he was starting every night. Charley's advice was more basic: "Get to the field early for extra practice in the infield."

Todd responded, "I'm the first one there every day." We knew from past experience that was probably true.

Todd's teammate Bill Selby put things in perspective for us. He told us, "The organization is very high on Todd. I saw this quote of (Ed) Kasko's in a baseball publication, where he spoke highly of Todd's build and ability. He'll be invited to the instructional league. Geez, he was their eighth-round draft pick!" (Bill never swore.)

Our last night in Elmira, we were able to completely relax during the Pioneers' game. Todd had been given the night off, having played consecutively for a week. After the game, we took Todd and Marc, his housemate who'd caught the game, to the all-night Perkins Restaurant. They discussed what players they thought would be invited to the fall Red Sox camp. Marc had already been told to report back to school in the fall. He would miss the first two weeks, as the Elmira short season ended on September 3rd.

Their small talk related to the maturity level of those on the team who'd been to college, as opposed to those who'd signed out of high school. "The pitcher who came in tonight in relief, Randy, is so down on himself that I wouldn't be surprised if he quit," Marc said.

Some of the rookie players we observed on a later trip to Winter Haven were so immature that they literally went into corners of the dugout and sulked if they weren't playing well. We often wondered how these players, so young and without a support system to bolster them, could advance in the system.

In A False Spring, Pat Jordan describes the older, more mature college players:

...These men were not so single-minded about their baseball careers and so,

unlike most of us, did not live or die with each base hit or strikeout. Instead, they approached the game, outwardly at least, with a cool and mocking cynicism that confused the younger players and served only to reassure us they would never make the major leagues with such attitudes. They even doubted themselves, and were not reluctant to speak disparagingly of their talents, or lack of them. They preferred to regard baseball as simply an extension of their college life that would lead to a more meaningful career...[9]

Todd and Tim were in the system to reach the majors, and took the journey seriously. But we all knew that when they left baseball, they would have meaning-ful careers somewhere else. This security did not prevent them from doubting themselves, like all minor leaguers except the number one draft picks.

The team would leave the following morning for a six-day road trip. Todd suggested to Marc that they stop at the bank before departing, since they were heading back to Canada.

We had just settled into bed after the drive from Elmira back to Westport, when the phone rang. It was Tim. I hit the speaker button.

"What's the matter?" we asked.

"They may place me on the inactive list tomorrow."

"How come?"

"There are only supposed to be three 21-year-olds or older on our roster in the rookie league, and we have four. Jeff hurt his wrist and they placed him on the Disabled List so the other three of us could play. Then the 21-year-old pitcher got hurt, so he went on the DL. Now he's all better and pitching well. Jeff's the leading batter on the team and I'm the second, but one of us will go."

"Can't they move someone up to Elmira or Winter Haven?"

"The f****** Winter Haven manager on the 'A' team above us comes over and picks the top draft choices for his team – the kids who are dropping the ball, not hustling, and batting .175. But the organization's got money invested in them. Meanwhile, Jeff and I have kept our mouths shut, not caused any trouble, and hustled our asses off. Frank (White) told the team that hard work would be rewarded. Well, so far only the young assholes are being rewarded.

"If I get put on the Inactive List tomorrow, I'll be so pissed off that I'm going to demand some answers of Frank. The trouble with him is that he keeps saying it's out of his hands, that others are making the decisions for him."

I paced the darkened bedroom, listening to our older son rant. It began to dawn on me that there was no "elbow room" for marginal or slumping players at the lower levels, unless they were high-round draftees. The cumulative effect was for players to constantly doubt themselves, thereby undermining self-confidence and credibility on the field. It was almost a self-fulfilling prophecy created by management for those with little invested in them, or those in a prolonged slump. A "hot" prospect with a big signing bonus was given individual instruction if he fell into a slump.

"Well, don't panic over something that hasn't happened yet," Charley advised. "If it happens, it sounds as if each of you will have had a turn sitting out."

"Yeah, but you're coming down next week, and I don't want to be sitting on the bench. It's just the principle of the thing. Damn, I'm the second leading hitter on the team among the regulars."

"If it happens, you certainly deserve some answers, but do it alone in Frank's office, and conduct yourself in a calm, rational manner."

"Dad, you know I will, but I'm sick of these head games they're playing. I don't need this. At least on a job you are promoted or demoted according to your performance. I don't need this shit anymore."

"Tim, join the real world. In business or government service, or anywhere, there are politics and ass-kissing, even in my job among top management. Don't panic and jump ship too soon. Next year in spring training you might find yourself on a more favorable team."

"Well, I'm just telling you that if I get placed inactive, and don't get invited to instructional camp, I'm going to think seriously about leaving after this summer."

"What would you do?" I asked too loudly into the speaker phone. I calmed my voice. "It's only a week. You know you've played well in the Florida heat, and you probably practice twice as much as other draftees, because that's your nature. But, Tim, you'd have to take your lumps in any job. Be patient!" My voice was getting loud again. I stopped speaking and started assessing the situation. The Careys were never quitters, and the journey to Fenway had just begun. If Tim left baseball now, it would take months for him to find a permanent position where he could use his Asian Studies background.

"Call us tomorrow night to let us know how you made out," Charley requested.

Charley's advice had been the same I would have given, but I let him do most of the talking. Would we ever get a rest? Does any parent? The ages of the children don't seem to matter – a parent still worries. We wondered if our sons were more frustrated than the minor leaguers out of high school who weren't performing well but had no other options. I decided that the perpetual analysis that Tim and Todd went through and the distraction of wondering if they were spending their time in a meaningful way was more detrimental than simply going out each day to play a boy's game.

The following night, again at 10:30 p.m., we heard from Tim. He had indeed been put on the Inactive List for a week to ten days.

"Did Frank White tell you why?" Charley inquired.

"Because each team's allowed just three 21-year-olds on the roster. He said again the decision wasn't his, and there was nothing he could do about it."

"Well, I suppose that parents' visits are the last thing on a manager's mind when they make decisions."

"Right, it makes no difference to them. I'm definitely beginning the job search this fall to replace baseball. Performance means nothing if they haven't invested big bucks!" It was heart-wrenching to hear Tim so upset that he would give up a life-long dream.

"Just play it out and see what happens," Charley advised. "We're sorry to hear the news. Try to enjoy yourself." Neither of us slept all night.

Following this conversation, Charley took a cue from Todd's teammates who were in constant touch with the scouts who'd signed them. Bill Enos reminded us several times when the boys signed their contracts to call him with any questions that might arise. We had never contacted him, since both boys preferred to speak to their coaches themselves, though Todd seldom did. Eventually an agent would go to bat for them, but the agent only became effective at the highest minor league levels, and his interest was not always synonymous with the player's. Explaining Tim's good performance and the confusion on the rookie team because of surplus 21-year-olds, Charley asked Bill to check out what Tim's future held. Bill said that he was aware of the rule, though totally disagreed with it. He promised to speak with Kenney, head of the Boston minor league system, and get back to us.

Another call at 10:40 p.m. in early August. This time it was collect from Todd, per usual. Charley woke himself up and said, "Where are you?"

"In Wellens, Canada."

"How's everything going?"

"Horribly. I haven't played since you left Sunday."

"How come?"

"Bob Juday's been playing short."

"How's he doing?"

"He was doing fine until tonight. He's been hitting, but tonight he made two errors. T.J. O'Donnell's played every game at second base, and he's the coach's favorite."

"Well, he's very intense. The manager is probably taking it out on you for being thrown out at third base on Sunday night, ending the game. He certainly won't take the blame for waving you home, and make himself look bad. Keep your chin up now, and be ready to play your best when you get in. You've got to be ready to grab every opportunity they offer you. Has the team won?"

"Yeah, we won two and lost one."

"Well, your brother's just been put on the Inactive List for a week, and he's pretty down. We hope he'll be playing when we fly down there. Why don't you call him? He's ready to jump ship."

"I'm ready, too."

"Well, you really have no complaints, Todd. You've played regularly till now. Frank White told Tim that hard work and performance would be rewarded, but that's not the case."

"It's not the case here, either."

I grabbed the phone. "Just don't get discouraged! You played well last weekend."

"Thanks for coming up, Mom. I really appreciated it."

"We love you."

Quietly he said, "Love you, too."

How could I respond to this? Both Tim and Todd were so discouraged that they wanted to quit! The bastards in the Boston office were playing with Tim like a marionette. I twisted and turned in the humid air through another sleepless night. I started to make up positive things to tell them. But the next day was Sunday, and their stats would glare from the pages of The Providence Sunday Journal again.

I hated baseball!

8

Winter Haven in August

<u>The Providence Sunday Journal</u> reported all the stats within the Red Sox organization each week. Todd's average was listed at .203, Tim's at .289.

By this time, almost mid-August, we were growing concerned about Todd's scheduled return to classes at Brown. Upperclassmen were to begin on September 8, and there had been no invitations issued to instructional camp. If he needed a leave of absence, paperwork had to be submitted through baseball liaison Ed Hu in the Admissions Office, as well as through a dean, who would then grant or deny permission. We had not yet paid the fall tuition bill, awaiting word. My parents would be visiting Todd on his birthday in Elmira, and would discuss it with him then.

Charley met with Alan Nero, a sports agent, over lunch in Providence. Nero represented Boggs and many other Red Sox from his office in Chicago. He was lobbying to represent Tim and Todd, although Charley felt it was too premature for them to have an agent. Nero expressed his frustration with the Red Sox management, saying they were just then releasing the bonus money for June signees, and refused to develop a sequential instructional program in the minors. Communication was practically nonexistent between management and minor leaguers in the organization, Nero claimed, which we could verify. No one was ever told why they were playing where they were, or what plans the management had in store for them. A simple thing like issuing instructional invitations well in advance of all semester deadlines didn't occur to them; nor did the discomfort of foreign players who couldn't speak the language.

Nero agreed with our point of view regarding Tim's leaving baseball. "He should definitely play it out through next summer. I will be calling both boys to talk to them personally, and will give Tim many examples of why he shouldn't be impatient so soon."

We received a return phone call from Bill Enos, explaining Kenney's position

Todd and Tim - Brown and Dartmouth.

regarding the rookie team. The rule concerning the number of 21-year-olds per team applied to all teams in that league, and there were no vacancies to move the 21-year-olds anywhere. So the rotation off the roster would continue, one at a time. There was no mention of where the boys' bonus monies were or when instructional league invitations would be issued. Enos asked Charley how Todd was doing, but Charley didn't bother to explain that he hadn't played in a week. Later, the boys selected Alan Nero from Rhode Island as an agent to represent them, but Nero delegated returning phone calls from his minor leaguers to Cecil Cooper in his office. There was seldom any definitive answer when an agent questioned management in regard to a ballplayer's concerns, unless he was a very top prospect or at the "AAA" level.

On August 12, 1992, we flew to Tampa and wound our way through central Florida to visit Tim in Winter Haven. At 1 a.m. we determined from the map that it would have been much easier to fly into Orlando, and wondered why the Sox organization had shuttled the boys through the Tampa Airport when they'd arrived in June. After several false starts down side streets and around lakes with no signage for the centrally-located Holiday Inn, we pulled in at 2 a.m. to find Garry Roggenburk (roving pitching coach) honored as "Guest of the Week" on the motel marquee.

The Chain-of-Lakes Stadium complex contained six ball fields, including the Sox spring training field with molded plastic seats, concession stands (all closed for the season), and a lake behind. The minor league buildings were flat, gray, one-story buildings on a perimeter field. It was 95 degrees with no one in sight when we arrived one hour ahead of noon game time the next day. During the game, around thirty fans showed up. The condos where Tim previously lived rose behind center field, their pool in full action.

After the game, we talked to the rookie team trainer, Harold, back at the Holiday Inn. He discussed the upcoming Red Sox move to their new complex in Fort Myers. The effect on the City of Winter Haven would be devastating, as already witnessed by the closing of one complex of garden apartments, previously rented to the ballplayers. Harold told us the town had been unwilling to put money into the upkeep of the Chain-of-Lakes clubhouse, describing the infestation of bugs and the lack of air-conditioning in the locker room.

Since Tim had rejoined the active roster, he had only been DH-ing.

The night we were airborne he went 1-for-4 as fourth batter, and the first day we watched he went 1-for-3 at bat, with two additional walks. He again batted fourth. Tim's friend from Vanderbilt, Jeff Martin, was catching, and hit his first home run. His girlfriend retrieved it behind the left field fence for him. The second baseman, Tim Davis, was a veteran 24-year-old. His wife was expecting a baby while Tim rehabilitated from a shoulder operation.

The Kansas City rookie team first-base coach was Spanish-speaking, a necessity since he chattered continually during the game to his almost-entirely foreign team. I asked Tim after the game if Boston had anyone among the coaches who could communicate with the foreign players. We had noticed during his game that Frank White asked Tim to speak Spanish to the teenage foreign pitchers that were brought into the game. Tim told us that the scout who spoke Spanish had by then gone home, but had been available for the summer. In addition, the third baseman was partially bi-lingual, so was asked to come to the mound with White and Tim to translate during the game.

Tim's weight was at 225. He looked solid, tanned, and happier than we'd anticipated from his phone calls. His extra pounds hindered his speed on the base paths, but he told us he was jogging at 8:30 every morning before practice. He was the most relaxed we'd ever seen him playing ball.

During the game, he acted as diplomat and mayor, standing by the water jugs in the full 95-degree sun, talking to all who partook, and often conversing with Frank White. He draped a white towel "Sahara-style" from under his baseball hat down his neck and looked like a player from Oman. After being a base runner in the eighth inning, he retreated into the dugout with his head under a towel that he'd immersed in the jug.

Later, he explained he preferred to stand in the sun by himself so he wouldn't have to listen to the 17-year-olds in the dugout discussing how they would spend their $80,000 or $100,000 bonuses. These were the guys Tim had described to us who dropped balls in the outfield or didn't hustle. The amount of their bonus money and position in the draft could be determined by their swagger. Tim, a free agent without more than a $1,000 bonus, said he often overheard Frank White expressing his frustration to other coaches over being in the heat teaching babies who couldn't play ball.

Throughout the entire game, White never stopped teaching from his dugout or third base box. This was in direct contrast to Manager Hold in Elmira, who never uttered a word.

Tim's game ended with Boston losing 11-7, due mainly to errors by the outfield and first baseman. Tim said it was the first time he could remember when he (DH), Jeff Martin (catcher), and Tim Davis (second base) had all been in the same lineup and the team had scored more than a few runs. The sloppy play we saw had prolonged the summer for Tim. After the game, the team retreated to another field to practice bunting with the always patient Frank White.

Back at the Holiday Inn where he was living, Tim crashed around 4 p.m. after we'd shared a pizza lunch. We agreed to pick him up around 8:15 p.m.

As we entered his room later, he was on the phone with the family that had housed him in Coldwater, Ohio, during his summer playing in the Great Lakes League. The Knapkes had been willing to house ballplayers for almost no charge all summer, to do all their cooking and laundry, to attend all their games, as well as their own children's games. They restored our faith in American good-heartedness, generosity, and family cohesiveness.

We tried somehow to repay them by packing lobsters and clams on ice for our visits, by buying groceries and beer, by pleading with them to come east to visit us at the beach. We knew that they were an extended part of our family, and Tim would always be part of theirs.

For many college ballplayers in leagues away from home for the first time, their living situations could make or break them. They lived in homes in the summer baseball towns for nominal fees, such as Tim's $35/week. Plunked down on Cape Cod, in the middle of Ohio, or elsewhere, they were trying to make a name for themselves by using wooden bats for the first time (instead of aluminum used in college leagues), while they upheld part-time jobs. The heavier wooden bats used in all the professional leagues wrought havoc with a batter's timing and gave him less power.

We were leaving Tim's room at the Holiday Inn that evening when we met some of his teammates from the Dominican Republic and Venezuela. In broken English the catcher told us that they had all been in the States since March, and were anxious to get home by the end of August. All of them remembered Todd from his brief stay in Winter Haven, saying, "Shortstop! Shortstop!" Tim was teaching them English in return for their teaching him to cook dishes from their native countries, mostly chicken.

After taking Tim to dinner, we did some grocery shopping for him. His needs for the mini-fridge in his room were minimal; his total bill was under $30, almost half that of Todd's. Back at his room, he arranged to watch videos with catcher Martin and Stephanie.

The following day, Tim still did not take the field. The first baseman had been drafted in the eighth round, so he would take precedence. Jeff caught his fourth straight game, getting two hits. We figured Tim would not see much action for his duration in Winter Haven. As DH, he walked, went 0-for-2, and laid down a perfect bunt along the third base line. He told us that when the lineup was posted, he grabbed his glove and asked Frank White for fly balls in the outfield, so he could get in the game. "At least I don't drop them," he told White.

"You are in the lineup," White responded, "as DH."

Tropical monsoons, thunder, and lightning began immediately after the game, two hours earlier that the previous day. Before they started, a photo session was held for Tony Sheffield, the Sox first-round draft pick and center fielder who had misjudged another fly ball that day. Tim was not afraid to speak up to the younger prospects with high bonuses when they started giving Frank White backtalk about their errors. "Shut your mouth," Tim told them. He had nothing to lose.

All three of us phoned Todd on his twenty-first birthday, before he went out to dinner with my parents, who were visiting him in Elmira. The news was no better from him. After being benched for a week during the Canadian trip, Todd was also DH-ing and alternating with Bob Juday at short. He hadn't had a hit in three games, and his average hovered just below .200. Charley reminded him to bunt for singles, which he'd done twice that week. Unfortunately, Kenney, the Director of the Minor Leagues for the Sox, had been visiting Elmira for two days in an effort to determine which players would be invited to instructional camp.

Charley passed along Garry Roggenburk's suggestion to Todd that he ask his manager what his chances were, since paperwork would have to be submitted to Brown to obtain a leave of absence for the fall semester, if he were chosen. Todd didn't seem inclined to inquire, probably because he was afraid of a negative response. He seemed very tired from a golf game, or he could have been depressed. Tim thought a month off from the pressure of swinging a bat would be good for him. I knew Todd would not voice his concerns or requests to anyone in baseball except Tim or his Dad. To approach a coach or Boston management, he needed confidence. Since the boys considered me an outsider in their world of sports, they listened to advice exclusively from their coaches, their Dad, or each other. I just hoped that Todd could get out of his funk with a couple of good performances on the field. The muscles under my right eye began twitching, and continued for four days.

After breakfast the following morning, we began an hour's odyssey to find a packaging store that would send Tim's birthday gift to Todd, as well as all the books home that he'd amassed that summer. Maybe he hadn't spent as much time socializing as I had imagined! Then Charley and I followed our normal exercise routine in the park.

Tim caught the game that day, and was the fourth batter. The Astros' rookie team was almost exclusively foreign, with a few exceptions. We noted that during our stay we had only seen black managers in the rookie league, valuable liaisons for the transplanted players.

When Tim Davis, the second baseman for the Sox, lined a single to the opposite field, Charley commented, "That's what I've been telling Todd to do! The outside pitches go to the opposite field, the inside pitches are pulled. Why is Todd so stubborn? When he gets home, he and I are going to have a serious talk. I'm going to lay it all out – either he adjusts his batting, or he'll be spending next summer back in Elmira."

"I'm sure that with his good defensive skills, they'll work on his hitting," I replied, defending my younger child.

"If his defensive skills were that outstanding, Juday wouldn't be alternating at short."

"Let's not write him off yet."

"No, but he'd better listen up when he gets home. Castelli tried to tell him where to hit in college, my father tried, and I've tried his whole career."

Sitting in the 95-degree sun, I realized that the fine line we tread as parents between ardent supporters and constructive critics was more tenuous for Charley. He had been their coach for nine years and had been an All-Star college player himself. But first, last, and always, he was "Dad."

For me, being a concerned mother meant learning when to keep my mouth shut.

This balance between support and criticism was a constant theme in my life during the seven years we followed two professional sons, then one. The stakes weren't as high prior to this, but during their pro careers, they wanted me to be a mother, not a coach. Sometimes I overstepped the line.

Back on the field, Tim got two RBI's in the 4-3 win for the Sox. He told us afterward that the thirty-odd family members, girlfriends, and friends in attendance were invited to a cookout under the spare batting cage. The food was provided from a fund raised by levying fines on the players for throwing helmets, swearing, reporting late, calling their own pitches, etc. We introduced ourselves to the catching coach, Doug Camilli. Camilli was one of Tim's favorite people in Winter Haven, and had caught for the Dodgers when Koufax pitched. He told us that Tim's hard work hadn't gone unnoticed, and that Tim was making good contact with the ball, even when thrown out. He inquired about Todd, and said he was surprised that Todd's hot hitting in Winter Haven hadn't continued in Elmira. "He's trying too hard," I told him.

"That's why we don't count the stats from the short season," Camilli explained.

We thanked Frank White for the cookout before leaving. He said it was, instead, two of the players we should thank for their excessive fines – Tim not included. He also asked about Todd. We told him and Roggenburk (visiting pitching coach) that we had talked to Todd the night before, on his 21st birthday. "He was only 20 when he was down here?" White asked. "Too bad he couldn't have stayed; he'd have gotten a lot of good instruction. In Elmira there's only one coach, and not much time for him to teach when they're not playing." I secretly agreed that the extra time spent with White would have given Todd's ego a momentous boost before he got promoted.

We departed for the Tampa Airport the following morning, after breakfast with Tim. This time we found the airport within an hour.

It had been a good visit with him. We were proud of his leadership, both on and off the field, as well as his adaptability. Charley and I wondered why he'd want to throw in the towel when he seemed successful. There was no doubt in our minds that he could play at the next level, even if his future in baseball was uncertain beyond that. We believed that the key to both boys' immediate future would be the interest, or lack of it, that the Sox organization showed in them through invitations to the instructional camp. Tim, however, had proclaimed his own agenda, expressing an interest in taking the exam for the Army Language School in Monterey, to study Japanese or Chinese. That would mean enlisting in the armed forces. We hoped he would harness his frustrations for a year, since he had a position as Computer Services Director awaiting him in the off-season at a private psychiatric hospital in Providence. We felt the Sox would undoubtedly invite him to spring training.

"We'll see if Camilli and Enos and agent Nero are all correct about this season's stats being meaningless for rookies," I mused on the plane home. I'd spent at least two hours making notes from our visit, and pondered whether anyone would ever look at them again. "Do you think anyone beside us will be interested in any of this?" I asked Charley.

"You never know. Everyone is always asking us questions about the details of the process and the boys' daily routine. Their story is certainly a unique one. In general, major league teams distrust Ivy leaguers because they have so many other options, so it's unusual that they took both of them. Anyway, we'll have our own record of what happened, even if no one else cares. I'm sure you'll discover your own motivation for completing the story."

The evening after we returned home from Florida, we placed a call to my parents, Evelyn and Walter Plumb. They'd just completed the five-hour drive back to Connecticut after seeing Todd. My Dad was 81, and Mom was 77.

The conversation always began with a grilling session from Charley.

"Hi, Evelyn. Did you enjoy your trip?"

"Oh, yes! Todd's team looks horrible, but he played wonderfully," a typical grandmother's response.

"Did he get any hits?"

"He got none in the first game, and one in the second game."

"What did he do at bat when he didn't get on base?"

"Well, he didn't strike out, but he hit grounders to the second baseman and the first baseman, and flied out."

"Sounds like he's still trying to pull the ball. I wonder when he'll try to hit to the opposite field. Where did his hit go?"

"I don't remember. Wait a minute," (Pause while she turns to my father.) "Honey, where did Todd's hit go?" (Returns to phone.) "Charley, Dad said it was a two-bagger that went up the middle."

"How did he play in the field?"

"He was perfect! No errors at all, but the second baseman made two. And there were only four hits that first game. Their pitching stinks!"

"Well, thanks a lot for the report, Evelyn. Did you have a nice birthday dinner with him?" Yadda, yadda…

An hour later, the phone rang. "Hi, Charley. It's Evelyn. I was just looking at my notes, and I forgot to tell you that Todd also bunted to move the runner over."

"Thanks, Evelyn. Now I'll sleep a lot better."

Two days later, the local paper from Elmira arrived. Charley had subscribed all summer for reports of Pioneer games. Todd had, indeed, only one official hit during the doubleheader my parents witnessed. The boys' bonus checks for signing finally arrived on August 18th, two and one-half months after they had put their signatures on the dotted lines.

Todd called at 10:30 p.m., after his game. Surprisingly, it wasn't collect. "Just wanted to tell you that we just heard that Jeff Martin's been called up here from Tim's rookie team."

"As a matter of fact, Tim called today to tell us the news himself. He said one of your catchers got hurt, and your second baseman's also out. So they sent up a shortstop from Winter Haven for the infield. Tim's happy for Jeff, but he's pretty bummed out. He's one of the oldest on the team."

"I can imagine. You should have seen the mess when Josh Smith, one of our reserve catchers, got hit directly in the face. He was squaring to bunt and had his nose broken in two places. I've never seen so much blood anywhere. They took him out on a stretcher."

"What a shame!" I responded. "He seemed like a nice kid, and it almost sounds like the injuries we used to see on the ice. Those hockey players usually ended up with crooked noses the rest of their lives."

"Will you be sitting out if they want to watch the shortstop from Winter Haven?" Charley inquired.

"I don't know. I'll let you know if I'm not playing, so you don't come all the way up here again."

"How have you been doing?"

"I went 1-for-4 tonight, with good defense, but last night was the worst game of my life."

"What happened?"

"I don't want to talk about it."

"Did it cost the game?"

"No. We were playing Welland (Canada). Remember Mike Gulan, from the Great Lakes League? He plays on Welland. He flubbed up, too. We beat them 21-5 the night before. The trouble is, Ed Kasko from the Boston office was watching. He's been here for a few nights."

"You can't do well every night. Who got all the hits the previous night?"

"I only got one. George Scott III, got three, Juday got two. Their pitching was horrendous."

"Have you heard about instructional camp yet?"

"Not yet. It's supposed to be the end of this week when they notify everyone."

"Did you get Tim's birthday package?"

"Yeah, that was great."

"You should call him. Jeff will be gone, and his other friend, Tim Davis, was sent home to rehab his shoulder. Tim's the only one left over 21 who hasn't been moved up. Let us know if you hear anything. We love you."

"I love you too."

Would we ever get another phone call with purely good news? When could we stop worrying? NEVER! I began to dread hearing the phone ring. Besides dealing with the boys' news, Charley and I had to face our friends and neighbors, who always asked us how the boys were doing. I would respond in the grocery check-out line that they were doing well, considering the tremendous adjustment of playing in the pros and the stress of performing well every day.

The next day, Charley came home from work to say he'd heard from Tim, and the news wasn't good. Despite a batting average around .300, his name wasn't included among those from his team posted for instructional camp.

"The poor kid! He's worked so hard. I hope he doesn't want to jump ship and enlist in the Army," I moaned.

"I think we have to be careful not to read too much or too little into these invitations. I don't think they have anything to do with contract renewals for spring training. I still think he should play through next summer."

"What did he say?"

"He was pretty upset, and anxious to get out of there. I told him he'd done his best, and life isn't always fair. I gave him my consolation and best advice, put the phone down, and went back to work. We're going to have to let him deal with it. We can't live their lives for them." I had my own career, but when I heard news from our sons, my focus became temporarily diverted. Somehow, Charley had tunnel vision when business was at stake.

"The Sox are totally mismanaged (outraged mother talking)! How much would they have to invest to send a good hitter and leader down to camp? They haven't invested anything in him so far. Instead they're sending the high-round draft picks with attitudes. I'll bet they didn't even consult Frank White! He's worked so hard, and outperformed all but three on the team. I just hope we don't get a similar call from Todd. I couldn't take it!" By this time, I was stirring dinner on the stove so fast it was splattering all over the place.

On August 22, we received a message on the answering machine from Todd: "Mom, Dad – I got invited to instructional camp! Give me a call when you can. Love you." THANK HEAVENS!

A follow-up call revealed that three positional players had been selected from the Elmira team: Todd, Bob Juday, and Jeff Martin, as well as six pitchers. There were obvious names missing: Bill Selby (3rd Team All-American and 12th round draftee); T.J. O'Donnell; all outfielders and catchers, besides Martin. Todd made two other calls: to Brown liaison Ed Hu, concerning his leave of absence; and to his brother to persuade him to give baseball another year. As of 2005, only three of the '92 Elmira team had made it to the major leagues, and none of the positional players invited to instructional camp were among the three.

A hurricane hit Florida. We were able to reach Tim, who was room-bound at the Holiday Inn in Winter Haven amid thunder, lightning, and pounding rain. Twice the connection went dead before Tim's voice re-appeared. He'd been playing first base, getting fewer and fewer hits since the list had been posted for fall camp. That all changed on August 25th.

That day he received word that he'd been assigned to Elmira for the remaining week-and-a-half, instead of flying home. Although I was ecstatic, Tim's reaction was that the organization was just trying to appease him, and it was too little, too late. Frank White simply told him, "You're going to Elmira at 8 a.m. tomorrow. Good luck." Tim thanked both White and Camilli before leaving. The following February he thanked Frank White publicly in The Woonsocket (R.I.) Call:

I owe a lot to Frank White," Tim says. "Really, I figured I'd be down there as a bullpen catcher. At first, he was playing the guys who were drafted, but after a while, he started playing the guys who were working the hardest. I have to thank him for giving me a chance, because everyone on the team was drafted higher than me.[10]

He ended his stint in Winter Haven with a .278 batting average over thirty-nine games, and a team high of 21 RBI's. We suggested that he try to enjoy himself in the New York-Penn League.

"I think I'll just surprise Todd," Tim said. "I can't wait to see his face when I show up."

At last, we'd had two consecutive phone calls with good news!

9

Tandem on the Team

A dear friend from New Jersey, now deceased, had followed the boys' academic and athletic careers from the time they were twelve. Over dinner after Tim was sent to Elmira, she said, "Ralph and I were always astounded at the time commitment you and Charley devoted to baseball and hockey. The message you were giving to the boys, when you were there day after day, was that they were worthwhile human beings, whether they won or lost."

I thanked her for the compliment and told her that professional baseball was proving to be a crucible to test the boys' self-worth. She continued, "When the times were tough, as well as when things were going well, you were always there. They learned to cope with failure, to keep things in perspective. I'm sure you are providing similar advice now."

I responded, "There is more at stake now, but they certainly have matured at ages 21 and 22. And they've had a lot of experience living independently." Charley and I held in high regard her three Harvard-educated, independent daughters who were pursuing careers in the arts and teaching and would lose their mother within several years.

Three days after this dinner, Charley and I arrived back at the familiar Holiday Inn in downtown Elmira. We learned that Tim was also registered there. At 6 p.m., we joined the line waiting to get into Dunn Field in the rain. When we entered, we saw Tim and Jeff Martin on the field signing autographs for the kids lined up in the aisles. Tim was all smiles. I gave Todd, Tim, and Jeff big kisses. Doreen Passmore and her son and daughter appeared at our sides and presented us with a giant homemade cheesecake to share with the boys. I refused to regard this woman in any other role than as a surrogate mom. Doreen had told Todd when he was down, "You need to believe in yourself! Once you get your confidence back, you'll do fine." To us she said, "You should have seen Todd's face light up when he told us his brother had just been sent up here."

During a rain delay, Tim told us that Todd seemed tentative in fielding ground balls, rising in a jerking motion when the ball came up into his glove, instead of in the smooth, continuous motion that was his trademark. Jack the veteran usher, congratulated Tim on his arrival, and told us both that he and Jeff should have been there much sooner. Jeff had hit two home runs for the Pioneers, and was so excited that he'd called Tim at 2 a.m. in Florida on the same morning Tim arose at 6 a.m. for the plane ride to N.Y. Jeff promised to keep Tim's pending arrival a secret from Todd.

A woman named Sophie introduced herself and asked how Todd liked the photos her husband had taken. When I professed ignorance, she explained that her husband had used up twelve rolls of film on the Elmira players, making an album for each member of the team. In subsequent years, we would receive enlargements of Todd from Sophie's husband, Bob Havens, a diehard fan who watched Todd play whenever he was within a 100-mile radius.

Alone, Tim told us that Todd had been picking him up for rides each day, but had never thanked him for the birthday gift, and didn't make any effort at conversation. "I'm clearly infringing on his territory," Tim stated.

"Absolutely," I confirmed. "This used to be his realm, but now it's yours, as well, and he's got to perform in front of big brother. Don't worry about him. Just enjoy yourself."

"Well, I confronted him in the clubhouse and asked him if he'd gotten the travel bag. He said he had, and it was nice, and he'd forgotten to mention it. I told him I didn't understand how it could be completely forgotten, if he'd just received it. He was embarrassed and walked away." Our policy as parents while the boys were growing up was not to interfere in their sibling relationship. We trusted the bonds they had formed over the years and let them work out their differences, unless actual fighting broke out.

Tim also revealed that Todd was treating Jeff in a slipshod manner, mimicking his southern drawl, even though they'd reported to Winter Haven on the same plane together in June. A month and a half later, Todd and Jeff would become inseparable at instructional camp in Bradenton, Florida.

Around us in the stands during the rain delay, I heard fans discussing the write-up in the program that Todd's brother had been called up to the team. One man in a Pittsburgh ball cap razzed, "The younger brother's no good, and the older one probably ain't either. The only girls lined up for his autograph were twelve-year-olds!"

Two old men in front of me discussed Tim's and Jeff's stats while in Florida, and a group of three debated Todd's merits and demerits. I headed to the ladies' room. Normally, I'd eavesdrop to confirm or deny my insecurities regarding the boys' status. That night, I didn't want to listen. I had a sibling relationship to worry about.

The remnants of Hurricane Andrew ('92) picked up, and the game was called off. At dinner afterward with catchers Jeff and Marc joining our boys, Todd told us about his first reunion with Tim. He'd been in the clubhouse prior to the game and heard someone talking about Tim. He thought it was in regard to the rookie league's heading home, and questioned the player. Within five minutes of being told Tim was on his way up, Tim appeared, sweaty and tired. He dumped his gear directly in front of Todd's locker, to observe Todd's surprise. Younger brother just stood there with his mouth open.

During dinner, Tim and Todd joked around and poked each other. The air had been cleared, and things seemed to be back to normal between them. There was much talk among the four players of abuse big-leaguers took from fans; of the Mets' trade of Cone, their pitcher; of the Yankees' decision not to hold an instructional camp; of the small number (35) invited to the Red Sox camp as compared to the Pirates. The Sox and Pirates would share the Pirates' facility in Bradenton. Many of Tim's high school and college friends had tracked Tim down, as well as Dartmouth Coach Whalen, who amused Tim with tales of his imminent marriage. Although he had called the baseball liaison at Brown, Todd still had not posted his letter requesting a formal leave of absence. Charley and I were astounded, since Todd was usually extremely conscientious about details. We got all over him about it.

The four players headed out on the town together. I had a hard time coming to grips with the realization that this was not a college visitation with our sons, but, rather, a dinner with four pro ballplayers, two of whom happened to be our sons. The odds of that happening again were getting slimmer and slimmer. Charley and I had perused a copy of the Red Sox publication Underground Baseball, featuring one minor leaguer from each level. Todd was featured from Elmira. I was ecstatic.

At 1 p.m. the following day, Tim and Jeff appeared from their room at the Holiday Inn, having just awakened. Tim announced that he was all packed to check out, as $50 per night was more than his budget could handle. The Sox paid for only his first two nights, but Todd's landlord had agreed to let Tim use a couch at his house.

Over lunch, Jeff impressed us with his knowledge of players' abilities, stats, and business deals. He told Todd what a good position Todd was in, having been the only shortstop invited to instructional camp with Naehring, Juday, and Steve Rodrigues, all second basemen. Jeff, however, felt his chances at moving up were slim, since Flaherty, Wedge, Hatteberg, McKeel, and Delgado were all catching at higher levels. It constantly amazed me that players and diehard fans could sit for hours discussing pitching, hitting, stats, lineups, promising prospects, trades, and plays on the field. An announcement had appeared reassigning the Winter Haven "A" team to Fort Myers for the following year, coinciding with the development of the new Sox complex there. In addition, there was speculation that the Elmira team would move to Utica, New York.

I had to listen intently during these conversations, if I were to catch the names of players and teams that flowed fast around me. When I asked a question which had already been answered in the deluge, the boys regarded me as an alien intruding on protected territory. There was no tolerance for "outsiders" who couldn't possibly understand the intricacies of a game as complex as baseball!

After lunch, we rushed back to a one-hour photo place in the Arnot Mall, where snapshots of our Winter Haven visit and the previous night's game in Elmira were waiting. The boys clawed over the photos, particularly those of Jeff and his fiancée. Stephanie had returned to college in Nashville, and had been calling Tim and Jeff's room at the Holiday Inn between 1:30-3:30 a.m., when she knew she would reach them.

At Dunn Field, at least two hundred townspeople from the nearby town of Addison were lined up outside the gates for the promotion of Addison Night. Jeff caught the game in a losing cause, and Tim, wearing #39, was at first base. He looked good in the field, but went 0-for-3 at bat, swinging late due to a lack of playing time that week. Todd was out of the lineup, with Juday playing shortstop. Tim was brought in to catch the last inning, and manipulated three easy outs.

The next day, Charley and I rode partway home to Massachusetts in total silence, deep in thought and upset over that morning's brunch with the boys. Todd had questioned us about withholding taxes, closing of his Elmira checking account, and investment of his bonus. He planned to live in a house off the Brown campus between the time he returned from instructional camp and departed for spring training. He also planned to inquire about a position with the Planning Office for the City of Providence, where he was to have begun an internship in September toward his Urban Studies credits. We hoped the first semester's deposit would be refunded from Brown. Also of concern was the fact that neither boy had received a copy of his contract from the Red Sox, nor had either received medical coverage cards. Todd pointed out that an agent would have taken care of these details.

It was difficult for Tim to enter our discussions. His bonus of $1,000 had been eaten up by expenses over the summer; he didn't feel he realistically needed an agent, as he had been excluded from instructional camp. Then he announced that he might want to enlist in the Army when he got home. I asked, "What's wrong with staying in baseball through next summer? You'll certainly be at another level next year, and you'll only be 23."

We'd been over this ground before. "I may," he replied, "but I'm not going to stay in baseball just to be fodder for your book. It's been harder than you can imagine to keep sitting on the bench and see my teammates move up ahead of me. I know I can perform as well as they do. I've always wanted to go into the military, and since there are no openings for Officer Candidate School, I can enter as an enlisted person and then qualify for OCS afterward."

Charley immediately replied, "Tim, I served four and one-half years in the military as an officer during a war. There was nothing glorious about it, between the oppressive heat and humidity and the Viet Cong posing as our barbers to ambush us, and the rats and sickness and nights spent in bunkers under attack. I wouldn't wish war on anyone, especially my son. If you had trouble dealing with baseball draftees out of high school this summer, how would you survive for two years as an enlisted person?"

"I don't understand your motivation, Tim," I intervened. "You would certainly benefit from the Monterey Language School, but if the Persian Gulf heats up again, you'll never see Language School. Do you think I want my flesh and blood there in a tank or an infantry line, when you have limitless opportunities open to you? I had a husband go into a war one year after we were married, and I certainly don't want to see my son do the same."

"Mom, it's my flesh and blood we're talking about here."

"Then I think you ought to examine what's really motivating you to want to do military service. Why do you want to put your life on the line? I can understand government service, but military enlistment as a private would not even challenge you intellectually."

"I can't keep on pleasing you people all my life."

"We don't expect you to, and that's not what this is all about. We've never tried to direct your ambitions! We certainly didn't know how much you wanted to attend the Military Academy when you chose Dartmouth. There never would have been a professional baseball chapter in your life if you had become an officer out of West Point. OK, so there are some outstanding catchers and first basemen ahead of you in the Sox organization. But you've only tasted a tiny portion of the baseball experience this summer! Give yourself another year! Maybe you'll want to pursue something in the psychiatric field, after you work at the hospital this off-season."

There was nothing more we could say to Tim, and vice versa. Like any mother, I wanted to keep my sons safe, even though they were no longer young kids. I wanted to keep them out of harm's way if I could, even if that was a rationalization for my unwillingness to let them go.

In the car, I tried to recall all the fields we had visited in pursuit of the dream Tim seemed so willing to give up. From the University of Maine baseball camp through all the New England states, New York, New Jersey, Pennsylvania, D.C., Maryland, Virginia, North and South Carolina, Florida, Louisiana, Ohio, Indiana, Arizona, Hawaii, and Canada, we had kept the faith. I wondered if we had seen Tim play ball for the last time. I had always believed that they would choose to play baseball, given the opportunity. Perhaps Tim's definition of himself no longer included the boy's game. But mine did!

Charley, however, had a different theory. "Perhaps he is afraid of the future," he proposed. "He hasn't ever failed at anything, and if he went through next summer with the Sox, he might not receive a new contract for '94."

"On the other hand, this Army bug of his seems to be some sort of defiance of us or maybe he's trying to follow in your shoes."

"I doubt that. He's already surpassed anything I accomplished at his age. Todd, on the other hand, has a lot of maturing to do. He's still going through mood swings based on his performance. He has a couple of good games, then a bad game, a night off, and his temperament is rotten because he's down on himself. He's got to stay even! He's got to adjust at the plate, and keep an optimistic outlook."

"What were you doing when you were barely 21 years old?"

"Nothing, compared to what he's accomplished. I was lucky to make it through college and find a training program."

"Exactly. He'll grow up with experience."

I wondered whether I was the one who really didn't want to let go of the dream. Maybe I was denying Todd's detrimental mood swings and Tim's actual status in the Sox. I had always provided motivations for the boys in their pursuits. What if all of that were over? Would I move on, along with them? With everything else to think about, I tried to block out the weight I'd regained over the weekend.

Back in Westport, we received two days of newspapers from Elmira describing two more consecutive losses for the Red Sox Pioneers. Todd had not played again; Juday was getting a hit per game. Tim played both games at first base or catch, without a hit. With a record of 28-42, both the Pioneers and the Carey boys were ending the season not with a bang, but a whimper. I wished Charley didn't sub-scribe to the damn newspapers!

On September 6, 1992, The Providence Journal carried a story revealing Frank White's intention to leave baseball to join an insurance company. Apparently the Sox had offered him the job of managing the Lynchburg (Va.) "A" team, but he had declined. We thought he must have become too frustrated with the rookies to continue and wanted to be closer to his family.

Todd left for six weeks of instructional camp in Bradenton on September 14th. He had spent a week with his former Brown roommates after they'd returned to classes. They would graduate that year. When I asked if they had said anything to him about missing his senior year, he replied they hadn't, since it was a great boost to Brown's reputation for him to do well. He had not yet met the new baseball coach at Brown, Bill Almond, who was replacing Castelli.

At the airport, Charley gave Todd $175 spending money. We knew we'd be giving Tim an equal amount for groceries while he lived in our Rhode Island house and worked at the psychiatric facility. Joe Hamilton, a Massachusetts June draftee with Tim, was on Todd's plane for instructional camp. Tim Smith, an "AA" pitcher and neighbor from Cumberland, would also attend. Tim Smith related the story to Todd that he'd been informed of his invitation by reading it in a Boston newspaper. Todd hung around the airline gate with us, and although Charley had said it all before, he said it again. "Do exactly what they teach you, and relax. You know you can perform."

"Just enjoy yourself!" I told him.

Tim told us that the night before he left, Todd had spent the evening throwing the ball against the basement wall and fielding the rebounds. While Todd was gone, I immersed myself in my business, working on as many as eight homes at once. I enjoyed what I was doing, but it was very difficult for interior designers to compete with the mill outlets that had sprung up around us. Tim worked forty hours a week while living at home, and was out at night. My life was back to some sort of routine, at least, without eating at odd hours and jumping in the car for baseball road trips. Still, it wasn't nearly as exciting.

10

Instructional Camp

On Thursday, September 17, 1992, Todd finally called us from Florida – collect, of course. He was in a dorm at Pirate City with seventy-five Pirate minor leaguers and thirty-five Red Sox players. He was rooming with the other Red Sox short-stop, Randy Brown, who played over the summer on the Winter Haven "A" team, a step above Tim and Todd's Elmira "A" team. They had bunk beds, no phone, and a rental TV for the room. There was a golf course behind the ball field, where Todd hoped to rent clubs in spare hours until he finished on November 1st. Randy had a car, and together each night they went to the mall fifteen miles away, since neither liked the cafeteria food.

The first two days consisted of hitting and infield workouts. The day he called, they had repeated the drills from 9 a.m. till 11:00, then bussed an hour to Port Charlotte to play a game at 1 p.m., which the Sox had won. Randy played the first five innings, with a couple of hits, and Todd played the last four innings with one at-bat. Buddy Bailey, the Lynchburg "A" coach, was in charge of the camp. Rac Slider was the infield coach.

I reported to Todd that Elmira would no longer be affiliated with the Red Sox, according to our local newspapers. Both boys received a letter from Clyde Smoll, owner of the Pioneers, thanking them for their efforts the previous season and listing all the players with their home addresses.

"So, how do you like it?" I asked Todd.

"It's boring! After 3:30, I have nothing to do."

The next day, the Cleveland Indians announced they'd be using the Red Sox Winter Haven facility for their spring training, since theirs was devastated by Hurricane Edward.

At our Cumberland home, Tim got a collect call from Todd. Tim was anxious to hear about instructional camp. Todd repeated, "It's boring," but divulged he was working harder than he'd worked all summer, attending morning and afternoon sessions, as well as games the same day. Tim had little sympathy, having followed practically the same schedule for most of the summer in Florida.

Within a few days, we had another collect call. I listened on the extension phone while Todd talked to Charley about the last four innings of the previous game. He had struck out against a lefty pitcher and grounded weakly to second. Steve Braun was giving him instruction to hit to the opposite field. Then I made a mistake a mother should never make. I popped into the conversation by asking, "Did you make any errors?"

"Oh, hi, Mom. It's so nice of you to ask how I am. I'm not even going to answer that question."

I apologized and shut up while Todd talked of his golf game, and how expensive it was to rent clubs for eighteen holes. He had gone to the beach in Sarasota on his day off.

Four days went by before we received another collect call. He was still alternating at short, and had gone 5-for-12 at bat over the week. He was very upbeat, reporting that lots of scouts were in attendance.

Predictably, Todd had given up golf – it was too expensive. The players were required to wear golf shirts to eat in the cafeteria, and Todd continued over and over to wear the one he'd brought, washing it nightly rather than buying another. Nero, the agent, had contacted him to sign a contract. Todd was partial to Nero because he was originally from Rhode Island. The players freely discussed their agents, and categorized Nero as being more self-interested than player-interested.

Todd's instructional team's record was 2-5. Tim Smith, our neighbor from Cumberland, had not pitched as yet. Jeff Martin, Tim Smith, and Todd placed a call to our Tim. The others reported that Todd was one of the few hitting the ball. They had hysterical tales of a country and western bar they'd attended with Bob Juday and Joe Hudson, where everyone was outfitted in jeans and cowboy boots. Todd seemed pleased with his performance on the field and wanted details of the festivities at a family wedding that eight of his cousins had attended.

Scout Bill Enos called upon his return from Bradenton to report on Todd. My mom took the phone call while visiting and gave us extensive notes when Charley and I got home. It was essentially the same we'd heard from Todd. All the scouts had meetings during instructional camp and checked in on their draftees. Todd was miffed that Enos hadn't made any effort to take him and Joe Hamilton to dinner, as the other scouts did for their draftees. Enos' reasoning: "I didn't want to single Todd out to embarrass him."

Dartmouth Coach Whalen called us, saying he'd also had a good report from Enos about Todd. I responded, "He needed this as a confidence-builder, since he didn't have a good summer."

Whalen informed us, "No one who hasn't been through the professional experience can understand what a tremendous adjustment it is to step into the pros and have the pressure of playing every single day. Look at Bob Bennett (Dartmouth pitcher drafted in the seventh round by Oakland that same June). He had three losses this summer before he could blink, but in instructional he's doing great, too."

On his godfather, Coach Whalen commented, "Bill Enos is like a dinosaur in the scouting business these days. The paperwork almost killed him. It's time for him to enjoy himself."

I replied, "Bill was surprised that Todd was rooming with a player competing for the same position. I guess Todd shocked him by explaining that the Sox had paired him with Randy Brown, and both were enjoying it." Just wait until one didn't play equally!

During the next call from Todd, he talked extensively with his brother. He'd played nine innings two out of three previous days, and five innings on the off-day. We could only speculate that Todd must have been playing well. His average sat around .300 in camp. He planned to sign with agent Nero, as soon as Nero's representative contacted him.

"I played against the Olympic shortstop today, signed by Chicago."

"I'll bet he was almost as good as you are."

"Yeah, sure, Mom!"

"Mrs. Smith said her Tim thought the cafeteria food was pretty good."

"It's okay, but I wouldn't call it good." Todd's brother didn't mention to him that he'd had to use Todd's car to get to work all week. His had been overheating, and Tim had not yet drawn his first paycheck. He knew this would drive Todd crazy, even if Todd's car was a '91 Chevy Cavalier.

Tim was the scheduling director for the professional staff at a private psychiatric hospital in Providence. He worked in his own office, setting up the schedules on a newly-installed computer system, and meeting regularly with the head nurses of all the wards. Only one psychotic women's ward frightened him, and he enjoyed observing and talking with the patients. "I met George Bush the elder today," he reported.

"You mean the president?"

"No, I mean some inmate who thinks he's the president!"

By October 1, 1992, the major league Sox had clinched last place in their division. Fleet Financial Group, Charley's employer, had season tickets at Fenway, and Charley had access to them. At that point in the season, however, even Tim was not interested in going. The tickets sat unused on our kitchen counter.

Cleaning out the beach house after we'd moved back to Rhode Island, I recollected the summer past. We had spent five weekends at ballparks, a wedding, or a business meeting. I needed some time for me – to do exactly what I wanted when I wanted. I was still operating my interior design business out of the Cumberland house.

I hoped Todd would move into a house in Providence with his former roommate when he returned from instructional camp. I didn't know how we'd all survive together again under the same roof. Tim was still living with us while he worked in Providence. Somehow, kids in the '90s kept coming home to roost.

When Todd called us on October 5th (collect), he sounded disappointed that we weren't going to make a trip to instructional camp. Since Randy Brown had sprained his ankle in the first inning of the game that day, Todd was the only remaining shortstop. He had attended a Tampa Bay exhibition hockey game. "The p.a. announcer was trying to explain off-sides and penalty shots to a bunch of southerners in the stands who have never put on a pair of blades," he laughed. "By the way, some of the guys here who have Nero for an agent got boxes of equipment. I guess he wants their business next year, but I could sure use some new gloves and spikes!"

"So how are things going?"

"Okay. I've been playing every day, and another second baseman's hurt, so Bob Juday's been at second every day."

"How's Bob doing?"

"He's doing okay, but his fielding isn't that steady."

"Who's hitting well?"

"It changes daily. Jeff hit a home run today. He's definitely our best all-around catcher. Hecker's still hitting well."

"How are you hitting?"

"I'm not hitting anymore. I've been working every day with Braun, and he's lowered my hands a bit. Also, I've been trying to hit to the opposite field. We have morning games now, with no BP. I'm not striking out, and in the end it will pay off. Right now I'm around .225."

"How are you doing in the field?"

"I've never played so well in the field, ever. I'm making the routine plays, as well as difficult ones, and Hecker's great at scooping the ball at first for me. I've only had two errors in three weeks."

"That's fantastic! How are your back and allergies?"

"Both are perfect."

"Are you having any *fun*?"

"Well, I've run out of money to have fun. We have our room and meals provided, but only get $10/day for spending money, and we have an 11 p.m. curfew, which everyone breaks. One night there was a bed check, and I didn't have any money to go out anyway, because I'd bought a shirt (!!) and some other stuff. So I stayed in. The coach's wife was here, so everyone figured there would be no bed check. They collected $750 in fines; $25 for the first offense, $50 for the second."

"You lucked out that night!"

"Tim (listening on the other extension at home), we went by the new Fort Myers facility. It's not near completion, but it's in the middle of a really bad section. The major league field looks beautiful, but the minor league fields are about three miles away and stuck in the middle of a limestone factory. To get there, you go by the projects with graffiti all over them. There'll be five fields and a minor league clubhouse at the end of a dirt road."

"I'm not surprised at anything the Sox do, despite their hype about the place," Tim replied. "Any major leaguers down there with you?"

"There's only Kevin Mortin, the pitcher from Pawtucket. Wait a minute, someone here wants to say hello to you." Todd handed the phone to Jeff Martin, who handed it to Tim Smith, who handed it to Mark Johnson, Tim's frat brother from Dartmouth, playing for the Pirates.

Harold Alfond invited Charley to attend the World Series in Toronto. Harold was a part-owner of the Red Sox and Charley's benefactor at Colby. Also in attendance in the World Series suite were Hayward Sullivan and Lou Gorman, Red Sox brass, as well as Coach John Winkin from the University of Maine. Tim and I watched the World Series together on television. Tim contradicted the announcer, Tim McCarver, when McCarver described pitching and catching duties and sequences of pitches. He gave me insight into hit-and-run plays and how to expand the strike zone, among other things. Todd called, and although he sounded lonely, he was heading off to the beach in Florida on his day off. We wondered if his friends were accepting collect calls the way we were.

The next time Todd called, I was the only one home. "Where's Tim? He's never home when I call!"

"He's at the dentist for the first time in a year and a half, and Dad's running errands in your car to keep it tuned up. As a matter of fact, here he comes now."

"Hi, Todd. How's everything?"

"I'm totally exhausted. I've played first base all week because Hecker's hurt and Joe diPastino went home. Juday's playing short, and Randy Brown should be back in action next week. That means I'll finally get a rest."

"How's it going?"

"I'm doing really well in the field. I've only had three errors the whole five weeks."

"How about your batting?"

"Jim Rice has been working with me every day, but I haven't hit this week. I'm just too tired."

"Are you striking out?"

"Yeah, sometimes. I'm too tired to worry about it. We start early in the morning doing warm-up drills, then go from infield practice to batting practice to inter-squad games. We're definitely all in better shape, but exhausted. The rumor is that after camp is over here, they make up the teams for next summer."

"Where do you think you'll be?"

"One team behind Randy Brown, wherever he is."

"If he hasn't played and you've done well, you might be in Lynchburg."

"I doubt it."

"Well, give it your best shot for one more week and leave them with a good impression. By the way, I sat with Lou Gorman at the World Series, and he said the Winter Haven "A" team will be moving next year."

"No kidding! Well, Daytona would be great, but Plant City would be another Winter Haven."

"I also asked him to send the contracts you and Tim signed, which we never received. The World Series game was fantastic! The Toronto dome has a noise level that's like being inside a sealed can. Gorman said he saw you play three or four times and you did well."

"Good."

"How's Tim Smith doing?"

"He's pitching every three days and doing fine. He'll probably be in New Britain ("AA") again next summer."

"When are you coming home?"

"I hope it's the night of October 31st, because that's one of the best nights of the year at Brown for parties. But we have a game that morning, so I may not get in till the 1st."

"When are you moving down to Providence?"

"The same day I get home."

"Granny and Grandpa Plumb will be there in Florida to visit you in four days. They're on vacation down there."

"Good. But I looked at the schedule, and we play away that day. We'll be back around supper, though."

"They'll find you. Any thought about a job when you get home?"

"I'm going to contact the City of Providence Planning Office, where I was supposed to have an internship."

"I saw the City Planner downtown the other day," Charley said, "and he said they're not hiring. Also, I read in the paper that he left the Planning Office right after I'd talked to him."

"With the holidays coming, I'm not worried. I can't wait to get home and just sleep."

"Tim's had a few days at Butler Hospital that were like a zoo. The weather's getting colder and the addicts, alcoholics, and psychos are coming in off the streets.

He gets five emergency cases on a busy day, and has to get extra personnel and secondary back-ups."

"I can't believe Tim is earning more than me for the first time in his life."

"He works hard for every penny."

"So do I!"

I entered the conversation. "Todd, Dad was with Harold Alfond in Toronto at the World Series, and Harold had been bidding on the Tampa-St. Petersburg baseball franchise as the new owner. Too bad he didn't get it! He said he would have asked Dad to be the general manager!"

"Would you have taken it, Dad?"

"Definitely!"

This didn't surprise me a bit. I knew Charley would have loved a career in baseball, though business had proven to be his forte. As GM in charge of a team, he would have continued chasing his own neglected dream, instead of his sons'. I would have loved the excitement, but not the risk and publicity.

Todd weighed around 180 pounds when he arrived home on Halloween night. He looked healthy, despite the rigors of camp, and more tanned than we could ever remember. "We all just went up to strike out in the game this morning, so everyone could catch a plane. The game was over in an hour.

"Even the umps wanted to get out of there. One of our opponent's runners went from first to third on a ball that was overthrown to me at first, just so he would make the last out coming into third."

Todd entertained us for hours, as he related tales of Jeff's cold feet upon receiving samples of his wedding napkins and invitation from his fiancée; of pages of dietary tips and exercises for the off-season from his trainer; of the hilarity at the dinner Randy Brown, Todd, and Jeff shared with my parents during their Bradenton visit; of his Dominican Republic teammate's visit to the local jail for shoplifting, from which the Sox rescued him for a scheduled operation on his arm. Within a few hours, Todd and his brother had left for the parties in Providence. Within twenty-four hours, two of Todd's Brown roommates had come to dinner, while Todd had done all his dirty laundry and moved all of his possessions into a rented house just off the Brown campus.

The next time we saw him, Todd asked us if we were charging Tim rent for living at home. We responded by saying we would not charge Tim, since we were paying Todd's rent in Providence.

"But I have to pay meals and electricity," Todd replied.

"Then come home to eat," I responded.

"By the way, Bob Juday's brother is also a pro ballplayer, and his Mom got an "800" phone number for the two of them during the season. You should think about that with Tim and me probably in different locations next summer. Besides, it would be beneficial for your business in the house, Mom."

The long-distance phone bills for my interior design business did not compare to the astronomical bills we received while the boys were in Florida and Elmira the previous summer. "I'll definitely think about it, Todd. More importantly, how about your employment until March?"

"My roommate on the Brown team suggested asking the Director of the Brown Sports Foundation for a 20-hour/week job. I know him real well."

"Dave Zucconi! Be sure to talk to him face-to-face. That's a great idea!"

Todd did end up working twenty hours a week for the Foundation, doing filing and errands. Tim, meanwhile, was up at 6 a.m. to work out at Gold's Gym, was at his desk in the Hospital by 8 a.m., and off to kick-boxing after work. He never ate dinner before 8:15 p.m.

In December, both boys flew to Nashville to attend Jeff Martin's wedding. Charley and I offered to pay the boys' fares. They stayed at the Martin's home, and were able to help Jeff with last-minute errands the day of the wedding. Jeff was extremely nervous, while Stephanie was reportedly extremely calm. Typically, Tim left his suit jacket at the Martin's house.

Three days before Christmas, '92, Alan Nero took the four of us to dinner in Providence and signed both Tim and Todd to one-year contracts. A former Rhode Island resident now based in Chicago, Nero had been in constant contact with the boys since June, particularly Todd. Nero claimed that the primary advantage to signing with a sports agent this early in their careers was to have someone who wouldn't let them get pushed aside if they were performing well, particularly since they were older than many of their teammates. In return for dealing with the Red Sox management, Nero would receive no income till the boys reached "AAA" level. Then he would receive a flat fee, with negotiated clauses for every bonus at elevated levels. The boys were supposed to receive some type of sports equipment, increasing at each level. Every promotional contract would be negotiated through Nero. However, none ever materialized during their careers.

Having just negotiated a successful $11 million deal for three years with the Yankees on behalf of departing Red Sox third baseman Wade Boggs, Alan would fly to Tampa early the next morning to have Boggs sign the contract at his home. During forty-five minutes of uninterrupted harangue about the history of Wade Boggs' tenure with the Sox, Nero talked about Gorman's lack of communication with his players; of Gorman's "writing off" players at an early age (never to give them another look); of his not informing Boggs and Nero where meetings would take place and not showing up on time; of his treating Boggs (a batting champ whose major league tenure consisted of ten years solely with the Sox) like a first-year minor leaguer after the "Margo incident." This "incident" happened when Margo Adams, Boggs' mistress on road trips, sued the superstar for $12 million for breach of "oral contract." His wife, who was creating new chicken recipes for her hero at home, later ran over Boggs with the car. Boggs claimed his wife was unaware that he had fallen out of the car!

Nero claimed that of all the major league teams he dealt with, the Sox held onto their money the longest before paying their players. It was his feeling that Mrs. Yawkey, primary owner of the Sox, was the glue that held the team together.

We asked Nero where Hobson fit into all this. He said Hobson was respected as a tough "AAA" manager, but had bowed to the egos of the superstars while managing in Fenway.

The most disheartening information concerned the Red Sox trainer, Dr. Arthur Pappas. Alan advised the boys to inform him immediately in the event of an injury, so that he could get an independent diagnosis under their Blue Cross/Blue Shield coverage. He cited the case of Marty Barrett, who later won a large settlement in court against Pappas, as well as the cases of Wedge and others who needed second opinions after Pappas' diagnoses. Prior to the Barrett court case, the consequences of not using Pappas to operate could mean a possible trade for the player.

I wondered how effective Nero would be in talking with Red Sox management on behalf of the boys, given all the bad blood during his prior negotiations with them. At the conclusion of the dinner, he urged the boys to keep a daily journal, something I'd encouraged so that I would have substantiation for my writing. At that point, my intentions were simply to create a family history. This had only made them protest more vehemently about my writing anything down. Alan cited the journals as possible proof of an injury and its treatment, should the need ever arise for a lawsuit. In addition, he urged them to call him or his associates toll-free at any time beginning with spring training, so that he could have updates about their progress, and would know where to visit them.

Nero impressed all four of us that night. That was, after all, what he was in business to do. The sad reality was that Alan seldom returned the boys' calls, delegating that responsibility to Cecil Cooper on the days Cecil was in the Chicago office. In retrospect, it was all a big crock! In late January, Nero contacted Tim and Todd and directed them to call when they'd received their new contracts, before they actually signed them. He promised to negotiate for an extra $50/month on behalf of the both boys, based on their maturity and Todd's experience in instructional camp. Nero dangled a carrot: if Tim performed well the following season, he'd have an opportunity to be Nero's player rep in Japan in the off-season (because of Tim's undergraduate degree in Asian Studies). Given the later influx of Japanese players in the major leagues, this position would have been a great opportunity. Although Tim did meet with Nero while he was living in Japan for two years, Nero never delivered on any of his grandiose schemes.

The boys' new contracts were for one year with a salary of $950/month, based on their assignment to a team at the conclusion of spring training. Minor leaguers received no pay during spring training, but had their housing provided at the Days Inn Motel. Meals were provided at the attached Denny's. During the playing season they would receive $15/day meal money while on the road.

After that dinner with agent Nero, I never spoke to him again. Things quieted down for a couple of months. I focused on my interior design work and enjoyed having Tim live at home, while he was working in Providence. We rarely saw him. Although Todd lived and worked in nearby Providence, Charley and I had to arrange ahead of time to meet him and his Brown roommates. We all relaxed around each other, and spring training was still at least two months away.

11

A New
Family Chapter

In mid-February, the Red Sox announced that the Florida State League had granted permission for the Sox to use the former Yankee field in Fort Lauderdale for their entry in the Florida State League. This team, the third rung up in the Sox farm system, would replace the "A" Winter Haven team. If the boys were assigned to Fort Lauderdale, they could live in the condo we owned one-half hour from the field, thereby saving a great deal of money. It would mean some arrangements on our part to insure that the place stayed intact, since we weren't there most of the time, and we would need reassurance that our condo neighbors would tolerate their lifestyle.

On March 4, 1993, we watched on NESN the dedication of City of Palms Park, the new Red Sox major league facility in Fort Myers. On hand were Ted Williams, Carl Yastrzemski, Dom DiMaggio, John Pesky, as well as the Sox management, and Fort Myers dignitaries. Almost 7,000 fans watched the Boston College Eagles hold the major league Red Sox to two runs in the Sox 2-0 win. The Eagles arrived right out of a blizzard in Boston without any prior playing time outdoors, just two hours before game time.

That day had been a memorable one for our family. Charley came up the stairs after work into the kitchen, where I was cooking supper. His face looked relieved, yet he had been under tremendous strain for several years as a Vice Chairman of Fleet Financial Group. "I submitted my resignation today," burst from him as soon as he cleared the stairs.

I didn't speak for a couple of seconds then told him what I was seeing. "Well, you look totally relieved, and if you're relieved, then I'm relieved," I answered, as I gave him a bear hug. I didn't dare think of the consequences of his resignation at that point, but I knew Charley never did anything in haste, and had probably been thinking through the consequences for several years.

So, his employment at Fleet Financial Group ended after almost twenty-one years. Charley was fifty-one years old. The Chairman had asked Charley and another Vice Chairman to report to three younger managers who were being promoted.

Since Charley had been cleaning up behind one of those younger managers for several years, he said, "No thank you." The other Vice-Chairman also resigned. We hired a lawyer to negotiate his severance package. We had always taught the boys not to give up until the very last out, and we wouldn't either. We hoped our future would be resolved by the time we arrived in Fort Myers to watch their spring training. At the same time we would be there, the Fleet Board of Directors and management team would be in attendance at their annual meeting nearby, a meeting we had attended for almost twenty years.

After that first day when Charley made his announcement to me, I got more and more enraged at the way he had been treated. He had, after all, helped build the company from a local Rhode Island bank to a bank/holding company that owned subsidiaries from Georgia to Maine and had offices throughout the world. There no longer appeared to me to be any loyalty in business, no standard of conduct by which an employer treated his long-term employees, especially those running the company. The chairman never spoke to Charley again, except to say "Hello" once in the parking garage. We were at the whim of the Board of Directors, as our lawyer negotiated with theirs.

Charley went back to his corner office next to the chairman's to clean things out. His secretary had scheduled appointments every fifteen minutes throughout the day for well-wishers to say "Good-bye." The line became so long that a policeman escorted Charley from his office when he was ready to leave, his boxes of personal items in his arms. The only token of gratitude he received was a gigantic "Thank you" board, with messages all over it from those who had taken his classes or worked for him. He had trained every commercial lending officer in the state of Rhode Island, and had helped create lending policy for national banking organizations.

A couple of days later, Tim and Todd drove in tandem to spring training, since they might be assigned to different teams directly afterward. Before they left, Tim said, "Dad, we really admire you for defending your track record and not backing down."

"It took a lot of guts," Todd agreed, "to live with the consequences." It was one of those touching moments that I would never forget, like the time Todd thanked us for everything we'd done for him after he signed his first contract. After three days, they called to tell us all went well on their trip south.

Charley was out of a job when we began driving south on Friday, March 12, 1993. Talk about stress! We had no severance package worked out for him and a

Tim Carey in spring training, 1993.

blizzard blanketed the entire east coast of the U.S. Dubbed "the storm of the century," it forced us to remain at my parents' house in Riverside, Connecticut, while eighteen inches of snow fell. The snow turned to rain, and as temperatures fell into the teens, a frozen cake glistened on which we could have skated as far as Virginia. Covering almost 2,000 miles, the storm stretched from Maine to Alabama. Since my parents' driveway was a half-mile long, even Superman could not have shoveled that block of ice! The storm proved an apt metaphor for the turmoil in our lives. We had to sit tight until help arrived.

A gigantic plow assured our escape three days later. All the while, our New York City lawyer, hired by Charley and the other vice chairman who had resigned, called incessantly. Both men had tied their fortunes to each other and were negotiating through one lawyer. There was still no deal for the two of them.

Monday morning we left Connecticut by 7:30 a.m. to drive south, without knowing how far we'd get on ice-encrusted highways, or whether Charley's twenty-year pension, salary parachute, and stock options were worthless. It took two hours to reach Newark, New Jersey, normally a 45-minute drive. We smacked into the middle of New York City rush hour, and encountered entrance and exit ramps that resembled the ten-foot-high tunnels outside our Colby dorms in Maine, midwinter. The temperature was 15 degrees when we left Connecticut and never got above 24 degrees as far south as Florence, South Carolina.

In addition to the normal pit stops, we had to find pay phones at appointed times to check the lawyer's progress in negotiations. These were the days before ubiquitous cell phones. By 7:30 p.m. on the second night, we were at our hotel in Fort Myers. Since the Fleet Board, management, and bank analysts were together in nearby Naples, they were anxious to release an announcement about Charley's and Bob's resignations, as well as the new organizational chart. Without a deal worked out for the two of them together, Charley and Bob expressed their intention to release their own version to the press on the succeeding day — their first ultimatum.

The stress continued until we arrived at the Red Sox minor league complex. Exhausted, we watched Tim and Todd work out together with the Lynchburg "A" team (the highest "A" team in the Sox organization) on one of five fields in the new complex.

There were 163 players in minor league spring training, all trying to be one of the twenty-five who would eventually make it to Fenway. That meant that if everything went right for at least a few years, one out of six or seven players on the field that day would be a major leaguer.

Then the rains came. The teams retreated to the indoor meeting rooms and batting cages. Charley hung out in a corner under an overhang, watching them bat. I caught up on my notes in the car and pondered how many trips we'd made down back roads, only to be rained out, snowed out, or tornadoed out. The time baseball parents spend hanging around during their kids' careers had to be in the hundreds of hours. We could have spent much of our idle time inside bars, but we tried to avoid that. Charley and I usually preferred to walk several miles, or relax at a pool with a book. I reviewed orders and billings for my interior design clients or caught up with my journal. However, we visited J.D. Penguins Bar in North Fort Myers one afternoon, and simultaneously felt dizzy. We thought we either had had too much to drink or were coming down with the flu. Then the bartender told us. "Don't worry, guys, the bar's revolving and no one can ever tell!"

Tim and Todd looked great in the field and at bat. Tim was playing first base and catching. We observed Todd's motioning to him during one drill to change his location at the first base bag, where Tim was still a novice. The players had all had three-hour physicals, and had been in the major league clubhouse the previous evening, two miles down the road. Tim and Todd were still on a high from the experience. "You wouldn't believe the size of Clemens!" Todd reported. "He's huge! And he's so thorough before he pitches, he watches films of the batters and looks at scouting reports. He's totally focused and doesn't mess around with anyone in the clubhouse."

Our routine during spring training was to watch the scrimmage games in the afternoon and treat the boys to dinner after the game. However, because of the crisis over Charley's unemployment, we had several pre-arranged dinners with business acquaintances. Every time we entered our room at the hotel, the blinking beacon awaited us on the phone. Our lawyer's familiar voice told us, "Still no deal." The Fleet management board meeting literally down the road from us was about to break up. An announcement of the "significant contributions" by Charley and Bob during their lengthy employment would appear in papers nationwide the following morning.

Like a rubber band stretched to its limit, my emotional fiber was going to snap at any given moment. I was in a constant state of anxiety, and minor tasks and daily chores, like filling the car with gas or returning a client's phone call, seemed monumental. I had tried to be the strong support Charley needed while his career and our financial future went down in flames. For three weeks, the chairman and his puppeteers toyed with our lives, pulling their strings to make us jump to the phone or review conditions of an agreement like marionettes. In order to face the incoming phone calls beginning at 7 a.m. and ending at 10 p.m., Charley and I increased our resoluteness and our commitment to each other, beginning and ending with time together in bed. We spent our days distracting ourselves by watching the boys on the field.

New commandments were added daily by the lawyers, which had to be signed, sealed and delivered. They included such tenets as, "Thou shalt never work for a competing bank," or "Thou shalt never divulge the terms of this agreement," or "Thou shalt never badmouth Fleet Financial Group." Not to mention having waited out a blizzard and driven 1,400 miles in two days, we awaited word about where our next dollar would come from and wondered whether the boys would still be employed in baseball by the end of that month. I was ready for aggression, even if it were only on the baseball field.

Unfortunately, too often Charley became my nearest target. We had always been totally supportive of each other, beginning in our college days when Charley was a senior and I was a sophomore and we helped each other study. Then through the Air Force days with the Viet Nam War, when he went off and we had only been married a year. We corresponded daily by letter and recorded messages on tape, and thank god, he came home intact!

Then we put each other through graduate school, and had kids. Charley changed jobs after eight months, relocating the family from Boston to Rhode Island, where he started as a vice president and ended up as a vice chairman. He had supported me through a second graduate program, while I changed careers. I had never doubted his judgment in twenty-eight years of marriage, and vice versa. This last crisis proved utterly daunting for both of us. While I had always been there for him and the kids, I didn't know how to handle the lack of income that we might have to face. My business certainly wouldn't support both of us, although, fortunately, our kids were almost through college and we were debt free. I was angry at the treatment he'd received, and so was Charley. We had to be careful not to direct our anger on each other, but we were with each other 24/7 and sometimes it happened.

During another rainy day at the minor league complex, I sat working in the car, then decided to walk two miles up to the new City of Palms major league field when the rain stopped. Without incident, I passed haunted low-income housing projects, corrugated tin businesses owned by whites, several black schools, churches, and recreation centers, as well as vacant lots filled with debris. Cement block houses were painted in melon, turquoise, or goldenrod. On a Caribbean island, I would have snapped them through the camera lens, but in the middle of bustling Fort Myers, they seemed only a reminder of the city's attempt to rescue the area from total disintegration. By the time I returned to the minor league fields at the end of the road, Charley and the boys were ready to go for pizza. Charley wanted to fill them in on our lawyer's negotiations, although Tim was totally independent financially and Todd needed just two more semesters at Brown. The boys warned me never to walk along that route by myself again, although the road was bustling with traffic.

The next morning, Charley and I walked for miles along the Fort Myers beach that lay ten miles west of the city and stretched all the way south to Naples. It was hard white sand and wide, with a pier reaching far out into the Gulf of Mexico. Honky-tonk motels, clam shacks, and T-shirt shops lined the edge of the roadway for miles. I felt like a blimp, having gained weight while we were housebound in Connecticut during the blizzard. Our eating habits during spring training revolved around the boys' schedules, so there were numerous snacks between breakfast and dinner, with no lunch in between.

We left our serene surroundings on the Gulf so that Charley could be at the boys' field for their game, as though he were a member of the team. It turned out there were merely double-session practices that day, so we observed the last session standing in the newly-constructed concrete tower that sat in the center of the five fields. Four of the five diamonds radiated outward from the tower, with the outfield fences defining the perimeter of the pie. The tower was supposed to be the exclusive domain of the Red Sox management, whose responsibility was to watch the players develop, but the sun had proved too much for us. There were still no bleachers anywhere, and only portable johns along the walkways. In desperation, I sometimes prevailed upon Molly, the Sox receptionist inside the minor league offices, to let me use the indoor facilities.

Rico Petrocelli fed Tim extra ground balls at first base, after the others left. Todd played shortstop for two inter-squad teams and reached base every time he came to bat. Back in our room at the Fort Myers Sheraton afterward, Charley discussed the eight-page severance proposal for an hour on a conference call. Still no deal.

We picked the boys up at their Days Inn in North Fort Myers, where the minor leaguers stayed. The married players got their own apartments. While the boys' meals were provided at Denny's, the major league team was housed at the Holiday Inn near City of Palms Park, and was given an allowance of $50/day for meals. Across the street from the stadium, a new two-story brown stucco apartment building, advertising "Two-bedroom units," was surrounded by a man-made pond and newly transplanted palm trees. Crack houses in the immediate vicinity of the stadium had been torn down for parking and batting cages.

The new City of Palms Park was sleek and eye-catching. It was built of square white cement tiles, bordered by beige brick in horizontal bands. Emerald green tiles accented access areas, ticket lobby, and gift shop, creating a dazzling south-Florida effect of contrasting sea and light. The cantilevered roof projected over individual molded green seats, without a back wall behind the top row of seating. Press booths perched in this open space at the center area of the semicircle behind home plate, above concession stands and the grand concourse.

Directly in front of the stadium, hundreds of palms had been planted, true to the City's name. Thousands of begonias and impatiens in pink and coral provided a colorful contrast to the startling white structure behind the trees. The parking lots had not been paved over; instead, for blocks on either side of the stadium, grass was sown for a soft berth under the fleets of vehicles depositing Red Sox fans.

Three weeks into the spring training exhibition games, Valentin had committed six errors at shortstop. Clemens came to his defense in the local paper, describing the unevenness of the infield and consequent weird hops the ball was taking. The next day we observed the grounds crew filling in the perimeter of the shortstop's station with mounds of dirt.

On March 20th, we had our first taste of prolonged, fantasy, 80-degree Florida weather at the minor league fields. Todd started at short for the Lynchburg team, playing the entire game against the Twins. He batted one-for-four (a double), and made beautiful plays in the field. Tim caught the second half of the Lynchburg game, talking to the pitchers, yelling plays to his infielders, and getting a hit to bring in the winning run during his only time at bat. Jeff Martin was a catcher on the team, as well as Todd's roommate from Elmira, Mark Senkowitz, who was on the disabled list. Jeff and his wife Stephanie, whose wedding Tim and Todd had attended in Nashville, joined the four of us after the game for Italian food. It was the perfect day!

The next day in March, we departed two-and-a-half hours before Tim and Todd's game against the White Sox in Sarasota, an hour-and-a-half drive. There probably had been only one infield or batting practice I could remember that Charley had missed in all of our years following the boys. That was in Pittsfield, Massachusetts, on July 4th the previous season, when we'd shown up at night for a day game! He loved sitting there, assessing the players' strengths and weaknesses, and it was therapeutic for him. He remained at every field until his sons had showered and appeared out of the locker room.

I really didn't mind the time commitment, since I often took the car after I dropped him off and ran to the mall, trying to return to see the first batter. Or I would read during infield and batting practice or catch up on billing for my business. One thing I did not do was bring my journals to the field! I loved watching while the boys were in the game, never knowing how long it would last.

During my "down" time alone, I planned activities that related to my design business, such as frequenting art galleries, antique shows, or designer show houses. Although my business was back in Rhode Island, I enjoyed seeing how designers in different parts of the country used faux paint finishes, accessorized, or accommodated the light. I tried to use the Boston Design Center once a week while I was working, visiting the show rooms and collecting samples before keeping appointments with my clients. In between I visited my vendors, since a designer's reputation was only as good as the people who produced and installed her products.

On days they weren't playing games, the minor leaguers spent hours in the batting cages and on the fields doing sprints and drills. On his day off, Todd was coached by Carl Yastrzemski in the batting cage. Yaz, the Red Sox left fielder for twenty-three years and Hall-of-Fame inductee who won three batting crowns and an MVP trophy, had turned into a chain smoker. Somehow he found enough breath to scream at the batter preceding Todd. By the time Todd got into the cage, he was scared out of his pants. Just then the TV promotional crew for the Sox started the cameras rolling. With a cigarette dangling from his lips, Yaz asked Todd, "Why don't you relax?" Yeah, sure! Somehow, Todd listened, learned, and executed. "See, I told you you'd be a good hitter!" Yaz leered.

We stayed at our condo on the east coast of Florida in between visits to Fort Myers. By the 30th of March, cuts had been made by the major league teams, creating a ripple effect throughout the minor leagues. We dreaded a phone call from either boy, but they remained on the Lynchburg team together until the 31st. During that final week when management was making cuts, players looked only at the floor in the locker room, never at each other. If they were asked to report to the coach's office, they could find their lockers cleaned out by the clubhouse manager by the time they returned. Few players who were cut chose to return to the locker room to say goodbye to their teammates. When given the bad news in the coach's office, most left by the back door, never to be seen again.

Todd had called us (collect) on the 28th of March, and reported that he'd had two hits that day, including a home run. He said Tim was sick with the flu, but had been playing well at catch and alternating at first base. When we reached Tim, he was indeed sick in bed and couldn't get warm. The previous night, he'd had a fever and had blasted the air conditioning on high. His attitude was, "I want to play every day, I don't care where." He knew that if he stayed on the Lynchburg team, he'd be a back-up catcher behind Jeff Martin, who'd been promised 80 percent of the duties behind the plate. First baseman Doug Hecker moved down to the "A" Lynchburg team from "AAA," so Tim wouldn't be playing first.

On March 31st, Todd called. "Bad news!!" he began. "I've been moved down to the Fort Lauderdale "A" team, a level below Tim. My Lynchburg manager called me into his office and said I'd done everything he asked this spring. I guess they want me to play every day in Ft. Lauderdale. I'm really bummed!" We commiserated, but really wanted him to get the playing time.

Manager DeMarlo Hale welcomed Todd to the Ft. Lauderdale team. Todd had been caught in the domino effect. Randy Brown moved down from shortstop in "AAA" Pawtucket to "A" Lynchburg, knocking Todd out of a position. Tim remained on Lynchburg, along with catchers Martin and Walt McKeel. Moral of the story: spring training meant shit, and you merely followed in the tracks of the fellow ahead of you at your position. The teams had been penciled in well before spring training. No matter where they sent you, though, you had to produce. Todd couldn't afford another summer like Elmira.

The roller coaster ride was in full swing, the boys on theirs and we on ours. On April 1, 1993, Charley signed a severance agreement with Fleet. He had seven days to rescind the negotiated settlement, which provided financially and medically for our retirement years. He was fifty-one and figured that with his experience in banking (23 years), he'd get a lot of other business offers and could still collect his pension. To say we were relieved would be an understatement! However, if we relocated, which was very possible, I had to decide whether to take an exam to get certified in interior design in another state.

In baseball, one boy was up while the other was down. Tim called at 8 a.m. on April 1st to tell us Manager Meleski had told him he didn't know where to place him — he remained on the Lynchburg "A" team, batting .400 as back-up catcher, and had thrown out eight of the last eleven runners stealing. He felt that Yaz and Rice were not really giving him much help in the batting cage because he was not a draft pick. "I can't figure out how both Jeff Martin and Walt McKeel are gonna stay on the Lynchburg team as catchers," Tim commented. "Martin's been promised 80 percent of the playing time and Walt's ego won't put up with sitting on the bench!"

I don't know whether players or their parents develop worse paranoia. We dissected, regurgitated, and diagnosed every word the managers said to our kids. In our minds, there may have been a series of at-bats or errors in the field that could make or break them. Later, we realized that the players had more staying power than we'd thought, particularly if money had been invested by the organization. We tried to find a rationale for what happened to the boys but, in reality, there were so many factors involved, that any rationale became impossible. Jim Bouton described the emotional roller coaster in Ball Four Plus Ball Five. To paraphrase, he said he was pitching well in spring training, then didn't make the team. The self-doubt crept in, and he had to start over…but with the knowledge that management didn't really think he was good enough. It was like "some crazy Dow Jones chart….In baseball you're only as good and as happy as your last appearance…"[11]

Tim described Jeff Martin as having become a royal pain in the ass during the course of spring training. There was tremendous pressure on Jeff to succeed, now that he had a wife. In addition, his father had had a series of strokes and had undergone angioplasty. Stephanie, Jeff's wife, reported to us that the first words out of his father's mouth on the phone were always, "How did you do at bat today?" It had gotten to the point that Jeff lied to his father to keep him from worrying. Nevertheless, Jeff exhibited insensitivity to his teammates, especially to catcher Mark Senkowitz prior to Mark's being sent down to "A" Utica. Jim Bouton described the difficulties in getting too close to teammates in Ball Four Plus Ball Five. He said that the reason players didn't form close lasting relationships in baseball was that the following week, one of them could be gone. So players held each other at arm's length, even though they roomed together and hung out during the season.[12]

When we arrived in Fort Myers for the last several days of spring training, we spotted Tim catching in the bullpen behind the minor league clubhouse. After he took a break, we asked him if Todd were discouraged after being bumped from Lynchburg down to Fort Lauderdale.

"Not really," Tim replied. "He knows he's one of their prospects, and they've guaranteed that he'll play every day, which he's doing. They'll bring him along slowly, one level a year, till there's nobody in front of him."

"There will always be somebody in front of him, and always somebody pushing him from underneath," Charley responded. We inquired about Randy Brown, the shortstop who'd been sent to the Lynchburg team while Todd was bumped down a level. Tim was honest in his assessment, then told us, "You can't be worrying about who else plays our positions. That's what Todd's going to have to learn, too."

We left Tim to watch the first half of Todd's exhibition game, plopping our lawn chairs just to the left of home plate behind the screen where his team had taken the field. We were soon surrounded by numerous golf carts bearing pitching and hitting coaches Slider, Wagner, Braun, Rice, Stange, among others, as well as by Red Sox management in charge of the minor league system. On the field, the team managers and coaches, used to audiences as former ballplayers, swaggered and strutted in their tight white uniforms before five of us parents.

The day did not bode well for Fort Lauderdale, beginning in the first inning. Todd made an error on an easy tag at second base, and our pitcher was wild. Our team finally came to bat after three runs had scored. The opposing pitcher, a tall, skinny kid with glasses who looked scared to death, was even more uncontrollable. We scored five or six runs, as everyone got a hit except Todd. The 85-degree heat began to get to the players and to us.

On another field, Tim caught the second half of the Lynchburg game. Without permanent bleachers, Red Sox management and coaches who had abandoned their golf carts because of the heat began to fill the concrete tower in the center of the five fields. It contained the only toilet, designated for personnel on the payroll only. When Tim entered his game, we gave up sitting and cut paths in the grass between Tim's and Todd's games.

Tim walked, then got a bloop single to the opposite field. When he was on second base, his teammate hit a double that looked catchable. Tim tagged up, then raced for third. Meleski, coaching at third, gave no immediate arm indication to Tim, then began screaming for him to run home. Tim was thrown out sliding. Immediately, two coaches descended on him to talk about his mistakes, and continued their discussion about him after he returned to the bench. Charley and I could hear everything they said, so we retreated to Todd's game. We had often described Tim as "obsessed" about staying in shape, but decided we wouldn't open our mouths again, as speed was essential. After both boys' teams had won their games, Tim spent an hour lifting weights and sprinting before joining us for dinner.

Back at the Sheraton Harbor Place in Fort Myers, we again received the $89/night rate offered to Red Sox families. The busloads of BoSox fans on vacation from New England were not in evidence, as the major leaguers had broken camp two days before, and their fans had departed. There were no longer any bulletin boards in the lobby announcing the schedule for pre- and post-game activities, and side trips to tourist attractions; nor polyester slacks with windbreakers and nametags, awaiting a whistle from their leader to board the bus; nor hookers, nor groupies hanging out at the bar, awaiting the young major league prospect or manager.

We picked up Tim, Todd, and Mark Senkowitz for dinner at the Days Inn. Todd was in a funk until dessert was served, probably because he'd had a bad game—no hits in five at-bats, and one error. Charley, instead, thought he was still disappointed at being placed down on the Fort Lauderdale team, while his brother remained on the higher Lynchburg team. My translation from Charley: "Pam, you babied him too much while he was growing up! You always gave him the benefit of the doubt and made excuses for him. He's sulking because he can't handle adversity!" Mark, meanwhile, was in good spirits, and seemed to have accepted his assignment down two levels to Utica. Because the New York-Penn League was a short season, Mark would remain in Fort Myers till mid-June doing drills every day and scrimmaging against the remaining Gulf Coast League teams. By that time, Utica's snow should have melted.

After the following day's games, my hair and ears were full of non-biting black flies. We had walked almost four miles in the morning along the Fort Myers marina and waterfront park, where thousands of kids participated in an Easter egg hunt. Just before reaching the manicured grounds of Edison's home, we could hear loudspeakers directing busloads to the pay station and entrance for the fascinating tour of the residence and laboratory of the botanist. Along our route were new construction sites, indicating a renaissance for downtown Fort Myers. The shell of the Riverfront Motel was being magically transformed into a deep-water resort of the future. Several years later, the shell of a motel remained. "Shooters" would sit out on the waterfront, attracting the singles crowd. I thought again about all the walks Charley and I had taken awaiting ball games — under the shadows of mountains around the residential streets of Scottsdale's desert; along a canal under volcanoes in Honolulu; around a Spanish-moss-covered park in Lafayette, Louisiana; bordering hundreds of acres of cornfields in Sandusky, Ohio; through industrial Elmira up past the college, where ravines spread out below us, reminiscent of Vermont. None of these footsteps would be included in a walking tour guidebook, but they had certainly given us a Charles Kurault view of America.

Tim had again caught the second half of the game that day, behind Walt McKeel. Walt had allowed two passed balls, but had also gotten two hits. Once the team hit Lynchburg, we were sure Tim would become predominately a bullpen catcher, like Velazquez whom Bouton described in Ball Four Plus Ball Five as a "poor devil," never to squat anywhere in the major leagues except in the bullpen. Several years later, Todd's good friend Dana LeVangie would accept the bullpen position in Fenway. The following day, the minor leaguers would disperse to their assigned teams, their equipment and clothing piled high in their cars, after playing their last scheduled spring training game. Within thirty-six hours, their summer league games would begin in the evening, and they would draw the first of their bi-weekly paychecks ($474, in Tim's and Todd's cases).

We had seen Tim's friends from the University of Maine, Plympton and Niles, pitch for the Red Sox while Tim was catching. Niles had gotten into trouble and the Rangers had increased their lead, so Tim talked at length with pitching coach Bibby when he came off the field.

We treated our neighbor Tim Smith to dinner with the four of us that night. Tim was a pitcher from Cumberland who had been reassigned to the "AA" Sox New Britain team for his second year. Our boys' history with Tim Smith went all the way back to Little League, when they opposed each other as Red Sox and Yankees, with both fathers coaching. Tim S. had pitched on the Cumberland/Lincoln American Legion team under Coach "Mac" Wright, while our Tim was the catcher on that team. In addition, Tim's father was our boys' orthodontist.

The stories among the three boys continued for two hours. Mostly, they concerned Lief McKinley, who appeared in the weight room every morning with his overnight bag, never having gone back to the Days Inn to sleep. Lief had either been with a different girl every night, or had fallen through black holes. The three boys predicted Lief would probably win the 50-man pool for the NCAA basketball playoffs, never having watched a game, never having read a news article, never having pronounced the names of the teams correctly. "Seton Hall" was transformed into "Set-on Hall," and "Tulane" became "Tu-Lane-e." Lief and Ironman Dan Collier, an Amazon with a lighted batting cage in his back yard in Alabama, would be sent back to Utica at the end of spring training.

Another player to bear the brunt of the joking at dinner was Kevin Becker, a high-school draftee from Ohio, pitching for Utica. The spring training bus rides were filled with Becker's non-stop yapping about the cops' radar machines set up on Ohio highways to resemble deer. The hunters popped the figures going 85 mph, then the cops popped them. This was the greatest entertainment Becker could ever imagine. Tim had played with Becker on the rookie team the previous summer, and because Tim happened to know more about snakes than Kevin, the Ivy Leaguer was required to answer every question that popped into Kevin's head all summer. "How many alligators are in that pond? Can we shoot them? How big are they?"

The boys also discussed the illogic of the assignments managers were making. We all knew by then that the managers were mere puppets of the player development personnel in Boston. We wondered if DeMarlo Hale would be as good as his word, and play Todd every day in Fort Lauderdale.

Todd planned to room with Bryan Brown in Lauderdale, and asked our help in locating an apartment. Using our condo after Charley and I had left to move north for the summer was out of the question for them. They wanted to be surrounded by bars and teammates, not "old fogies." Charley and I scanned and called every rental ad for a week. Since the Red Sox were using the Lauderdale facility for the first time, they had no listing of available housing for the players, as they did in other locations. It would kill Todd to pay $250-$375/month for rent (his half), when he'd only paid half that in Elmira.

Tim and Todd were amazed the day the major leaguers, who had been on their rosters a predetermined number of games, each received $75,000 for major league franchise sales and promotions the previous year. This included such things as T-shirts, hats, pennants, etc. Every major leaguer in both leagues got the same amount, depending on the sales of goods and promotions the previous year.

It was always mystifying to me how men could spend hour upon hour discussing the intricacies of baseball without interruption—stats, strategies, misplays, future potential. A New York Times Magazine article appeared the last weekend of minor league spring training that explored what major league baseball had become to the writer, Richard Ford. Entitled, "Stop Blaming Baseball," he said:

"...Baseball is about money, first and last (though maybe not in the middle), and when money's concerned, ethics and balanced, disinterested judgment go out the window."[13]

Period, exclamation point! Players were pieces of meat, to be traded to the highest bidder. The appeal for me, as a mother, was less in the dissection of the game, and more in what Ford demanded of the game:

"...Quit asking of others — people we don't even know and who don't want to be our models — what we don't ask of ourselves...We just need, instead, to go out to the ball park, have long, elliptical and serious talks with our sons and daughters about what constitutes a good person, what talent is worth in this world, who's a real hero in this life, how we dare to sit in judgment of others, and when these topics run thin, turn our attentions gratefully back to the game."[14]

Here's what I mean. Mothers huddled together in lawn chairs or on bleachers, sharing tales of sons' relocations and disappointments, as we watched our prodigies on the field. We never repeated tales of triumph to other mothers. We were a support group for each other, and the support grew stronger the more we got to know each other, at each level. At first, I regarded other sons as Tim and Todd's competitors, but later, when Todd had survived five years in the organization, the sense of competition diminished. We parents became inseparable, especially at games. Much of this camaraderie and cohesiveness resulted from the fact that we sat together in the "freebie" section, given passes by the players. But more than that, we had become involved in each other's personal lives. I met Dana LeVangie's girlfriend Traci, got invited to Trot Nixon's wedding, fed Hunter Hyzdu's new baby sister, and called Sheryl Brown when we were in New Orleans.

The fathers of the players retained more of a competitive distrust among each other than the mothers did. They still saw stats and abilities rather than human stories when they looked down on the field.

The last day in Fort Myers, the Pirates were visiting. Tim was on an unused outfield when we arrived, shagging fly balls hit by one of the batting coaches. He wanted to be prepared to play anywhere. He was the designated hitter the entire game for Lynchburg, going 1-for-2 with a walk and an RBI, jogging between fields to shag balls and then to enter his game to hit.

Todd, meanwhile, sat on the bench for the duration of the Fort Lauderdale game against the Pirates, while three players who had been bumped down from "AA" rotated in the infield. There remained two shortstops between Todd and New Britain, two levels higher. He would have to battle back to a higher level of performance by shrugging off the move down to Lauderdale.

I sometimes felt guilty about hoping that the players in competition for our boys' positions would screw up, particularly when we knew the boys and their families and liked them. Some mothers would make great sacrifices for their sons' careers, such as Brian Rose's mom. She watched her son every time he pitched in Pawtucket, Rhode Island, before working the night shift at a factory. Other moms endured emotional trauma, such as Ron Mahay's mother, who oversaw two operations on her son's pitching arm. Later, when I was more confident about Todd's abilities, I no longer worried about others competing for his position. But it took several years to reach that detachment. Certainly it would have been emotionally easier for me to stay away from the ballpark, to avoid the daily ups and downs. There were days when I was dying to go to the pool or beach, but I figured we only visited spring training for short periods of time, and who knew how long we would see our boys playing pro ball?

The players spent endless hours thinking up nicknames for their teammates, coaches, and opposing players. Just as Gary Bell became "Ding Dong," so Randy Brown would later become "Rat" (he had a thin strand of hair hanging down his neck). In Lynchburg, Bill Selby had become "Fat Ass." The players teased Bill that his mama's Mississippi dumplings seemed to have settled all in one spot.

They also spent hours engaged in mindless trivial pursuits, wasting time until games began. They chose "The All-Ugly Nine" from nearby fans, ran under the bleachers for peep shows, judged age contests among the spectators, hit grounders to a fielder four feet away for a game of "Pepper," played hackey sack, or in Pete Rose's case, bet on which raindrop would make it to the bottom of a window first.

Prior to departure for his new assignment, Tim returned some of our books he'd borrowed, asked us to mail some letters he'd written, and gave us hugs before driving to Lynchburg in tandem with infielder Bill Selby and catcher Jeff Martin. He planned to room with Bill Selby in Lynchburg in a $700/month condo.

After the Ft. Lauderdale game ended, the players ran sprints. Todd appeared, looking composed and relaxed. "How come you didn't play today?" Charley asked.

"I needed a day off. I haven't had one in two weeks, since you were here for the game in Sarasota."

"Well, we want you to keep a positive attitude and battle back at your position. It looks like you'll have a good team, and you never know when they might move you up again. When's your first game in Lauderdale?"

"Friday, but we don't know where we'll be living."

"You and your roommates are welcome to stay at our condo till you get a place."

"Thanks! The Sox will pay for our first four nights at a motel. Same for Tim."

"Either way, Mom and I will probably catch as many of your games as possible before we head north."

Charley had meetings, lunches, or dinners every day in Florida concerning possible future employment. With his pension assured from Fleet, he could be picky about the title, responsibilities, environment, and salary for his second career. All of my clients' projects were in hiatus until I returned north. But I was constantly on the phone.

12

Sophomore Season

On April 9th, Tim called from Durham, North Carolina, where his team was playing in the Bulls' Stadium, made famous in the movie *Bull Durham*. He said there had been 7,000 on hand for opening night, complete with a band and parade. The Lynchburg team won in extra innings, but, as expected, Tim didn't play. Jeff Martin and Walt McKeel were expected to alternate at catch. "I wish I'd been sent down to Lauderdale," Tim said to us. "At least I'd be playing, because I know I could beat those catchers out." Relegated to the bullpen to warm up the pitchers, he was doused with beer over his head from the outfield bleachers, where Duke fans reigned. They'd studied the program and had zeroed in on Tim's Ivy League alma mater. Duke was viewed in that territory as the Ivy League of the south.

"Please send me some sheets, Mom! The condo's two floors with two bedrooms, but we won't have any rented furniture till Sunday night, when we get back from our road trip. There are no towels in the place, either." Ever the good mom, I ran to a discount store, packed up two sets of sheets, towels, blankets, and pillows, and sent them two-day express. It cost me $75 to send the stuff!

Todd's first game in Fort Lauderdale was April 9th. There had been a terrible thunderstorm with a tornado watch prior to game time. After only a half-hour delay, the game began. Only about 500 people attended opening night. The Fort Lauderdale Airport was nearby, and city football and soccer fields immediately surrounded the ballpark. A Miami Herald reporter interviewed Charley and me about the irony of a Red Sox team playing on a field formerly used by the Yankees. I guess we were the only Sox fans they could find. The next day our quotes were in the paper.

Todd's team looked extremely impressive, beating the West Palm Beach "A" Expos 7-2, with Peter Hoy, a former major leaguer for 30 days, closing the game for the Sox. The Red Sox doubled, homered, made running over-the-shoulder catches in the outfield, nice blocks behind home plate, and turned two double plays. Both Todd and the third baseman, a local Fort Lauderdale player named Marty Durkin, charged two balls on the infield, getting the runner at first. In addition, Todd got two hits, including one down the opposite field base line against a left-handed pitcher.

After the game, Todd's roommate, Bryan Brown, his mother, and girlfriend set up a hibachi in the players' parking lot behind the clubhouse to grill Cajun sausages the women had brought in the car from Louisiana. They produced crayfish from a yard-long box. We munched on the delicacies, let Tim Davis' baby grow familiar with our new faces, and talked to personable and funny Lee Stange. Todd seemed very relaxed among the coaches.

Our condo was only forty minutes from the ballpark. The next day Todd called to say he and Bryan had been rejected by a landlord as potential renters. They were amazed to think someone didn't believe they were trustworthy tenants, particularly since they'd already put a security deposit down and needed the first and last month's rent up front. Certainly landlords had had plenty of justification for their low estimation of ballplayers as models of behavior. Todd was furious that he'd have to drive back to Deerfield Beach to retrieve his security deposit. Class "A" paychecks were still only $950/month, so the players investigated condos that ran around $750/month. Todd squeezed in a check of the bars in Fort Lauderdale, with the verdict: "Nothing special."

Charley flew out at 7 a.m. the following morning for various board meetings in Rhode Island. Todd called to say Bryan's mother would be taking them to look at another condo and then to Sawgrass Mills, a mind-boggling two miles of discount outlets. All the players who had not yet found housing were at the Wellesley Inn in Fort Lauderdale. None had been able to sleep well, including Bryan's mother and girlfriend. So we invited the two women to stay at our condo overnight, before they started their 14-hour drive home to Louisiana.

The following night there were only 250 in attendance at the ballpark, many of them cheering for the Twins' "Miracles," who'd previously been based in nearby Pompano. Gray-haired diehards who loved baseball and weren't mobile enough to do much else under the stars, as well as fathers with their kids, made up the majority of fans. Tickets were $3, or $4 if you bought box seats. Under the stadium foot-long hot dogs, soda, ice cream, popcorn, and Crackerjacks sold in the $1.75-$3.00 range. During the seventh inning stretch, organ music piped "Take Me Out to the Ballgame" over the loudspeaker. Throughout the game, BoSox hats, shirts, and Carvel cakes, among other things, were awarded to the lucky fan who could trample down everyone else on the inclined concrete ramp to reach the information booth with the first correct answer to a question posed over the loudspeaker.

There was a major league air to this stadium. The dugouts were painted the same color as the seats and built under the box seats. Total capacity was 7,000. The entire outfield fence contained local advertising, and trees were a backdrop behind left field. It seemed the Yankees had built a first-class spring training facility here. The grounds crew worked before and after the game, all in uniform, and were systematically trained to roll up tarps (or spread them) like a race team. Although the fans didn't have immediate access to the players, there were no poles nor any bad seats in the stadium. There was a definite feeling, despite the poor attendance, that the players had advanced a level. The town owned this stadium, and the Red Sox had leased it for one year.

Back at our condo after the game, Bryan Brown's mother shared with me Bryan's experience during a recent elbow operation under the supervision of Dr. Arthur Pappas. The Browns had not relied on Pappas' advice, but had sought a surgeon in Louisiana to perform the delicate maneuver of relocating the elbow nerve and removing bone spurs. Fortunately, the operation was a success for the outfielder. I sympathized. I knew in the event of a serious injury, moms and dads would have to pick up the pieces.

In the morning, Sheryl began her journey home around dawn. Todd and Bryan had also stayed overnight at our condo, and left to play golf on Hutchinson Island. In the afternoon, they moved their remaining belongings into the new place they had rented near the ballpark in Coral Springs. I didn't know how they would have the energy to play ball at 7 p.m.

Todd's substitute at shortstop, Nick Ortiz, played well at his position in the third game, and hit a single and a double. I sat with the third baseman's parents, Alice and Harry Durkin, from Fort Lauderdale. They had watched four sons play ball from Little League to the pros, and had to endure two errors that night by their son Marty.

Todd began to alternate at third base when Nick Ortiz played short. He hit the ball the first time above the shortstop's head. The shortstop timed a perfect jump and caught it in his webbing. The next time up, the second baseman went deep behind the first baseman to rob Todd again. His total production had been 3-for-12 at-bats.

I was convinced that hitting was simply a matter of confidence. Todd needed some "attitude." This opinion, of course came from someone who had never hit a hardball in her life.

Tim told us later that we need not have worried about Todd's developing some "attitude." "He can be a little shit sometimes," big brother reported. "The spring he was drafted at Brown, he acted like a big shot and treated the freshmen ballplayers like turds."

By the middle of April, we heard from Tim. He still had not had a phone installed in his condo in Lynchburg, nor had he taken the field in any game. He told us he was the only team member thus far who hadn't played a position. He was getting extremely frustrated, despite Manager Meleski's warning to be patient because three would be moving up to "AA." As Designated Hitter, he had gone 3-for-10. He expressed his intention to approach the manager to find out why he hadn't been in the games, and Charley reminded him to be professional during the discussions. "Selby and I get to the field two hours early every day and work our butts off. He and I are in the same position, and he's thinking of quitting. I even took fly balls in the outfield again, because Jose Malave has been whacking the hell out of the ball and will probably get moved up. Our Assistant Coach Marchese told me he had a golf game and had to leave, so Manager Meleski hit some fly balls to me."

"How's Jeff catching?"

"He's catching well, but still isn't hitting."

"I bet McKeel will be moved up, and then you and Jeff will share catching duties."

"That's not the way it works. They stick with one guy, no matter what. Randy Brown made six errors last night and is still starting tonight. But with nowhere for Randy to move up to, he'll stay here, and Todd will stay in Fort Lauderdale."

"Well, stay cool. Call us when you get a phone. We sent you a birthday package, but I don't think it will arrive till after you've left for Durham. We love you."

We wondered after that conversation how long the management in Boston stuck by their draft choices, even if they weren't getting a return for their money. Jeff, for example, had yet to hit in four weeks of spring training and two weeks of season play. The Sox were notorious for developing players slowly, even if they'd made a mistake with a couple of top draft picks. Like Todd, some took longer to develop than others, and we were grateful for their faith in raw talent. As a free agent, however, Tim would hover in the shadows until the catchers above him eventually failed.

Charley and I were avid moviegoers, and among others we saw that spring was *The Sandlot*. It was nostalgic and fun and provoked a discussion about the demise of baseball today among kids, particularly inner-city kids.

Charley grew up in Fall River, Massachusetts, the oldest of seven kids. He spent every day of the summer from dawn to dusk at a park not far from the family's three-family apartment house. There was only one way to play ball all day when 100 kids showed up. Each group of nine played the winners, so in order to keep playing, you had to keep winning. Like Benny Rodrigues in *The Sandlot*, only one thing mattered to Charley — the game! That dedication and single-mindedness got Benny to the majors, and Charley to "All New England" in college. Of course, it was also a means of escape, and one of the few forms of free recreation (except you needed an old glove) available to kids those days.

Our kids always had a "sandlot," because I was always home when they were young. They could go directly outside in our back yard. By the time they were five, they had an instant ball team among the neighbors. Our house was the first built on speculation down a dirt road that used to be a Boy Scout camp. Since it was a heavily Catholic area, each successive family that commissioned a house around us had numerous children. When the kids could get between bases in five strides, the sandlot moved from our backyard to the street in front of our house. As in the movie, *The Sandlot*, the game never ended, and took up where it had left off the previous day. As soon as Charley arrived home from work, he became the pitcher. When Tim and Todd came home from college, they'd pick up gloves and play catch between two house lots on the street. I loved looking out the window and seeing them doing what they'd done as little kids!

But I operated my design business out of the house and could keep an eye on the kids. In Charley's case, his mother was home with his six siblings. That seemed to be the key. Today, with both parents working, or only one caregiver living at home, the alternatives seem to be to allow the kids to stay at home, watch TV or play with the computer, and be safe; or to find a pick-up game, and deal with major safety issues. Many children are programmed into extracurricular activities after school today because the parents work and worry about supervision. They hope the activities will benefit the kids later on. As an educator, I believe a tremendous amount of childhood is lost by sacrificing "down" time and spontaneous interaction with peers. Kids need unstructured time to relax, create, read, or find interaction of their choosing. For most kids today, ball fields don't exist right around the corner. They need bikes, a dangerous alternative, or rides from moms. Charley and I never gave a thought when we grew up to biking across town five miles or more, and back at dinnertime. Today, basketball hoops are abundant in suburban driveways.

Those who graduate from the lots or streets go into organized ball. Little League has always been, and still is, run by fathers. In inner cities, single moms are the norm. All these factors contribute to the dearth of baseball teams, particularly in the inner city. Yet surrounding us in the theater in Boynton Beach, Florida, to watch *The Sandlot* were kids with their buddies — boys and girls as well as entire families, and fathers with their kids. The criticism that girls were excluded, even denigrated, in baseball movies seemed frivolous to our professional sons. Having played with female Little Leaguers, Babe Ruthers, and even ice hockey teammates, Tim used to advise his cousin Becky, "Don't be on the sidelines cheering for others. Be one of those they're cheering for." Spoken like a true son of mine! The hit movie, *A League of Their Own*, put an end to the criticism. Within a few years, audiences couldn't get enough of the female U.S. Olympic gymnastics, soccer, basketball, crew, softball, and volleyball teams.

There were two books published in the spring of '93 entitled Play Ball: The Life and Troubled Times of Major League Baseball by John Feinstein, and Coming Apart at the Seams: How Baseball Owners, Players, and TV Execs Have Led our National Pastime to the Brink of Disaster by Jack Sands. Yet the audiences filling the theater seemed heedless of the business aspects of the game. Outselling all other movies except *Indecent Proposal* for several straight weeks, *The Sandlot* glorified the childhood joy of belonging and acceptance, of achievement, of independence every day from Mom and Dad. I believe to this day that most successful youth achieve some degree of success as adults. The ball field, soccer field, or hoop court provided arenas for that success, as did a million other arenas.

In late April, the Fort Lauderdale Red Sox snapped a losing streak of seven games. In picking up their second overall win against the Chicago Cubs' Florida State team, Todd did not play. We saw a third major leaguer in rehab, Lance Dickson, pitch for the opposition. Since he was a lefty and Todd batted lefty, our alternate infielder and right-handed batter (Ortiz) started at short. In later years, Todd proved that as a lefty he could hit against a lefty pitcher as well as against a righty pitcher, but coaches stuck by the old adage.

Several of our friends had accompanied us to the games, and we were always grateful whenever Todd got a hit or made a nice play. He still had zero errors in the young season. A couple of times our friends were only able to see him warming up along the first base line, as Ortiz took the field in Todd's place.

Tim called from Kinston, North Carolina. Since no one on the Lynchburg team had yet moved up to New Britain, Tim still wasn't playing. He spent two nights in Durham visiting with a pro hockey buddy from home, Jeff Robison. Tim's friend from the rookie team, Tim Davis, had been bench warming on Todd's Fort Lauderdale team, and had gone home. He hadn't gotten any hits for the season, and with a new baby, was anxious to finish his college degree. The trick was to know when to say "when."

Breakthrough! Todd went 2-for-3 at bat on April 21st in a losing effort against the Cubs. He played third base most of the game, and made his first error of the season there. Then he moved over to short. After playing golf that day, he had spent a couple of hours alone with the batting instructor. Steve Braun had told him to concentrate on keeping his weight back, and to keep practicing his new swing from high to low. Todd had always had a perfectly level swing.

When we met after the game, Todd seemed most pleased that his hits had come off a pitcher that had pitched a game for Cal State in the College World Series (against Pepperdine). There were two University of Maine players on the opposition team, who'd been in the minors for several years. Charley and I couldn't believe that Todd had risen to such distinguished company. When one considered the weather that Ivy Leaguers contend with, as well as their academic demands, it was even more miraculous that so many played pro ball. There were four from previous Dartmouth teams playing that year alone. The centerfielder that night for the Cubs had been Glanville, the #1 draft pick two years prior, who was an engineering major from Penn.

Charley and I took off for four days to Key West, where we'd never been, while Todd's team was on a road trip. Charley had signed and delivered his severance package from Fleet, so he could take his time considering the numerous business offers coming in. With nothing to do but eat, sleep, make love, swim, walk miles and miles a day, enjoy the funky and historic sites, we felt like honeymooners. The world seemed very far away — there were no telephone messages, not even a clock in the room. Besides the bizarre sights of Duval Street, we immersed ourselves in the gingerbread architecture; in tourist stops, such as the Audubon House, Hemingway Mansion, Truman summer White House, the Maritime Museum; in glass-bottomed boat rides and spectacular snorkeling; and, of course, in fresh catches of the day. One day, a flotilla of medical supplies embarked for Cuba over nine-foot breakers. With the sunset as a backdrop, we watched a water battle among vessels off Mallory Pier, complete with a hosing of us spectators by the Coast Guard cutter. We happened to be visiting during "Conch Republic Festival," celebrating what we gleaned was an attempt by the Bahamians of long ago to restore their authority over the colony. The following day, we witnessed various Key West establishments participate in the bed race down Duval Street. Each bed was bedecked around an appropriate theme, and was pushed by the employees of the Hog's Breath Saloon, Fat Tuesday's, Sloppy Joe's, and a number of other saloons. A stopwatch determined the winner. T-shirts advertised each bar's famous concoction, "Two-for-One Specials," or a "Crawl down Duval Street" scheduled for the next day.

Charley's whole demeanor had changed. After a month of free time and exploration of employment possibilities, he no longer walked hunched over, as if on a forced march. Stress had been erased from his face, and the only time he consulted his watch was an hour before Todd's games. Most importantly to me, he had become demonstratively affectionate again and was pitching in around the condo with laundry, even vacuuming. The only thing I didn't want was his shadow behind me in the grocery store.

Perhaps the highlight of the weekend in Key West was an image of Charley I will carry with me forever. Each day we walked to a Cuban magazine store that carried newspapers in every conceivable language from all over the States. Charley was intent on following Todd's team, even if the papers were a day old. On our second day in Key West, I returned to the hotel pool, where Charley had a Florida paper spread over him. As I rounded the corner, he spotted me, and with a grin from ear to ear, he held up three fingers. Immediately it was obvious that Todd had gotten three hits in one game. Other than those daily papers, I never thought about baseball. I had a stack of books and design magazines to read.

Miraculously, Todd's hitting streak continued, and the Ft. Lauderdale team won two more games. Their record stood at 4-11. While we were gone, Todd had hit 6-for-11, with a slugging percentage of .545. The night we returned to our condo, his average stood at .327. He managed to hit in seven straight games, with only two errors during the season. We noticed a new swagger in his walk on the field before game time.

I asked Todd and Bryan if there were a chance we could visit their apartment. I even promised to bring groceries, and I figured if we made a future date, they'd have made it presentable. I had a suspicion that Bryan was a neatnik, like Todd. "He really cooks great meals," Todd said.

"Maybe he could give you a few lessons," I suggested. The boys put our visit off till after their upcoming road trip. No explanation.

Around 11 p.m. on April 26th, Tim called us in Florida. He and Bill Selby had left a message for Todd on the answering machine in Fort Lauderdale, which Todd said was incomprehensible because the two roommates in Lynchburg seemed to be in a drunken stupor. Tim had had a sit-down with Manager Meleski the previous week, at Meleski's instigation. Catcher McKeel had been pulled out of a game, and instead of giving Tim a chance, Jeff Martin was put in at catch, in addition to his normal rotation. Tim went berserk behind the scenes. As DH, he was batting .500. Eventually Meleski picked up Tim's vibes.

"What's the problem, Tim?"

"Why didn't you use me when you pulled McKeel the other day?"

"I have no choice but to play Martin and McKeel. I'm told by Boston every day what to do and who to play. If it were up to me, I'd play you."

"It looks like you have no confidence in me."

"Not at all. You call a better game than either of them, but my hands are tied. You've worked your ass off, and you're hitting the hell out of the ball. Do you want to go down to the Fort Myers extended spring team so you can play a lot?"

"No way!"

"Then just be patient. There's bound to be some movement up or down eventually."

Over the phone, Charley asked Tim how the shortstop Randy Brown was doing.

"I hate that kid! All he cares about is himself. When we lose, all he talks about are his two hits. He's whacking the ball, but he's made seven errors. Even Meleski is fed up with him. If Todd keeps hitting and has so few errors at the end of this season, he'll jump right over Brown to New Britain next year. And I told Todd that. All he has to do is hit .250."

"Well, I'm glad to hear you're hitting so well. But we knew you could. Keep your spirits up and be ready when they need you to catch. They'll have to acknowledge your hitting eventually."

"How's Bryan Brown doing?" Tim asked.

"He's in a slump. Of course, he set the league on fire for the first ten games. He couldn't keep up a .484 average."

Charley advised, "You have to stay even, and work through it. You can't get too high or too low."

That's the key to baseball right there!

Accompanying us to one of Todd's games was the security guard from our condo building, Elmer Palmer. Unfortunately, Todd's hitting streak ended with an 0-for-3 night, although he hit the ball hard each time and was flawless in the field. It was a close game, which the Sox lost to the Osceola Astros. After enjoying a few brews, Elmer began asking us, "Why does he put his hand on his hip between pitches? Big leaguers can't do that. Why doesn't he back up the pick-off throw? Why doesn't he crouch down more?"

I felt like asking, "How about those major league plays at shortstop, Elmer?" But I kept quiet, knowing I would see this man at the reception desk in our building every day we were in Florida.

A first baseman arrived the following night from our New Britain "AA" team. Unfortunately, Todd struck out twice and grounded out. He'd only struck out five times all season till then. His .304 average was plummeting. After the game, we waited in the players' parking lot. The game was the last thing on his mind.

"Well, my Cavalier let me down today. A fuse blew, and I replaced it from an auto parts store, but that blew the whole circuit. So I spent the afternoon at three other places, but they had no circuits that fit. So now I've got to get to a dealer, and we're leaving early tomorrow for Port St. Lucie."

Charley and I planned to drive 1-1/4 hours for that game, and asked Todd to leave us tickets. We left the car issue for him to solve. When they had signed their contracts, we resolved to step back from the boys' financial/daily concerns and let them deal. Occasionally, we offered small amounts to meet immediate needs.

"Sure. Oh, I got a packet from Brown today, and it said the tuition next year will be $24,000. Too bad I need to go back for two more semesters."

"Well, we invested your bonus money, so that should cover it. Tim called up right after he talked to you. He's frustrated. I guess he can't take Randy Brown."

"He's all right when you get to know him. He's really a lot different from the image he projects. I didn't have a problem when I roomed with him during Instructional Camp. He was hurt and wasn't playing."

Finally Charley asked, "Why don't you hit those outside curve balls to left field and choke up with two strikes on you?" I knew Charley was frustrated that Todd wasn't utilizing things Charley had taught him as a Little Leaguer.

"I usually do choke up, but every pitch I missed tonight was a ball I shouldn't have swung at."

Then the oft-repeated advice: "I'd like to see you bunt for some base hits. You were always an excellent bunter, and on the first strike with the third baseman back, you'll pick up some added hits for your average. Just don't get down on yourself!"

I piped up, "Keep your chin up, Todd. Bryan's got lower and lower when he wasn't hitting."

"That's right," Charley concurred. "Start a new streak tomorrow. We love you." A hug always followed these words.

The Mets' facility in Port St. Lucie was right off Route 95. It was an imposing, gorgeous stadium, with concrete ramps winding upward to the turnstiles, a cantilevered roof, and seating raised high above the diamond. Five minor league fields surrounded the outfield.

There were fifty Little Leaguers on the field for the National Anthem, standing next to the Mets "A" players at each position. The kids were in heaven, except those standing on the mound. The Mets' starting pitcher chose to remain focused in his dugout. It was a promotional night, but still only 700 people attended. Between innings, fans were drawn from the crowd for Frisbee tosses and basketball throws, all with prizes. A Chevy circled the field jammed with pitchers from the bullpen. When a player came to bat, his name and home town were announced on the p.a. system. On the giant digital scoreboard in Port St. Lucie his batting average was flashed, home runs this season, RBI's, and what he did during his last at-bat.

By contrast, the owners and staff in the Fort Lauderdale stadium didn't seem to possess any marketing skills at all. Five hundred fifty fans had attended the season opener, and that number had never been duplicated. There were no tickets passed out for promotional nights — Kiwanis, Little League, hospitals, or anything else. There were no "Bring a Parent to the Game" nights, duplicate tickets for kids, no billboards inside the main gate announcing that night's lineup. The only attempt we'd seen to publicize the game anywhere around the area was a wooden stand out on the main road announcing, "Red Sox Game tonight." Even the local Sun Sentinel paper didn't carry the starting times. When I asked the staff if they intended to get a publicity campaign underway, they said, "Oh, yes! Another grand opening is scheduled for May 8th, in time for Mother's Day." Meanwhile, April revenues were down the drain.

Todd's team lost to the league-leading Mets on a balmy Florida night under the stars. Although he got one hit and made no errors, he seemed to disregard Charley's advice from the night before to choke up on the bat with two strikes. It was easy

Tim and Todd, spring training, 1993.

to criticize from the stands, forgetting Bouton's comment in his book, <u>Ball Four</u>, that the hardest thing to do in any game was to hit a spinning, curving ball traveling at 80 mph. The second hardest thing to do, he pointed out, was to throw it.

Two days later, we poked along up the east coast of Florida, exploring Jupiter, Stuart, and Port St. Lucie on our way to Dodgertown in Vero Beach. I was always happy during these excursions for an excuse not to cook.

The Dodgertown complex lived up to its reputation as the most beautiful of all the spring training/minor league facilities in Florida. There had been no changes to the field since the "old timers" built it almost fifty years ago. Fifteen hundred were in attendance, mingling where the concession stands topped the bowl of seats built into the side of a hill. Driving into the complex, we passed housing for the major leaguers (in use during spring training), as well as a golf course and clubhouse. The turf on the field was like a magnificent putting green, and we felt as if we were in the middle of a recreational park. The minor league fields were down sandy roads surrounded by tall pine trees. Behind the left and right field foul lines, as well as behind the outfield, were grassy berms, where pitchers sprawled to watch the game, awaiting their turns on the mound. The pine trees formed a backdrop behind the outfield knoll, so there was literally no barrier into which an outfielder could collide when tracking down a fly ball.

Only seventeen rows of seating, all close down onto the field, formed the bowl, without a roof over anyone except the concessionaires. The press box was part of the seventeenth row behind home plate, a cement enclosure perched above, while the concessions were behind it under its roof and across the wide concourse. Hawkers roamed the crowd selling all kinds of eats, as they did at major league stadiums. Charley and his pipe were banished to stand out in the open air along the end of the concourse. Most unique of all, there were no dugouts on this field. The players sat on two rows of wooden benches directly in front of a wire fence and the first row of spectators. The whole atmosphere was a throw-back to early baseball days, and the fans loved it.

Prior to the start of the game, a lucky fan and companion were named "King and Queen" for the night. The ticket was pulled from a bin of stubs. I heard my number on the PA system and lo! I was the night's "Queen!" However, I never got to wear the crown, or sit in the air-conditioned press box seats, or tell the announcer that I was not only the "Queen for the Night," but the "Queen Mother" of one of the players! My intense husband, who would be too far from the action and couldn't smoke his pipe, declined the honor. I had to turn my ticket in and the announcer drew another. I had put up with Charley's pipe-smoking, only if our air conditioning was on or a window was open. Ceiling fans constantly operated when he smoked. But turning down the chance to sit in the luxurious press box in favor of smoking a pipe was really too much!! I sat down in the third row by myself, while he stood on the top of the concourse, smoke swirling around his head.

During the entire game, 500 Little Leaguers ran up and down the seventeen rows of seats. They were all dressed in uniform, having been granted free admission. They ate and drank themselves into oblivion all night, much to the chagrin of "serious" fans, such as ourselves. We saw no such promotions during all our nights in the Fort Lauderdale stadium.

Todd didn't start that night, only his third night off since the team had started its schedule almost four weeks before. The opposing pitcher was a lefty. Todd had taken part in a clinic on the field during the afternoon for the screaming throngs, and signed autographs before and after the game. The Sox lost 9-4 and would head to Fort Myers on the other coast of Florida immediately after the game, where they would play the following night. We drove two hours back to our condo. The travel in Florida was minimal for the team, compared to future leagues, where the distances were greater. But in those leagues, players stayed overnight in hotels.

The following evening on ESPN we watched a clip of major leaguers' errors since the start of the '93 season: players colliding in the outfield, letting balls roll through their legs, dropping pop flies, overthrowing the cutoff man, pitchers not covering the bases for put-outs. Ray Knight, former major leaguer, analyzed the problem. He blamed the increase in these fundamental errors on players being drafted who were first, great athletes, and second, trained baseball players. His second contention was that minor league coaches were no longer the great instructors they used to be. The latter contention was contrary to some of the experiences we witnessed over the years with our boys. In Dodgertown Stadium, we watched Coach Luis Dorante work with Ortiz after he came off the field, having committed an error that cost runs. He was showing Ortiz what to do in making a turn without breaking too early toward second for a pick-off. Later in Sarasota, Coach Tommy Barrett was tremendously helpful to Todd, and in Trenton, Manager Ken Macha never stopped teaching.

It amazed us that Todd had acquired at a young age so many of the skills that coaches assumed were present at this level. The boys had had excellent coaching early: Charley for nine years, James "Mac" Wright on the American Legion team, Tom Seavor at Mt. St. Charles Academy, Bruce Villeneuve at Cumberland High. Most important in Todd's pre-professional development was Coach Frank Castelli at Brown. Coach Castelli's successor at Brown, former major leaguer pitcher Bill Almon, said to us, "When Todd and Tim worked out with my team indoors this winter, I told my players to watch Todd's feet, to study how he moved. They could learn more by watching him than I could ever try to teach them. He is a natural." One image is worth a thousand words, but sometimes it takes a coach to embed it in your memory bank!

13

A Very Long Season

In Fort Myers, Todd's team played 13- and 15-inning games after rain delays, and arrived back in Fort Lauderdale at 5 a.m. on the bus on the third day, with a game to play that night. Their record stood at 7-16. Todd had had thirteen assists in the field in one game (outstanding!), but went only one-for-nine at bat. He reported to us that Mark Senkowitz, the catcher back in Utica, was the remaining catcher on that team. Two others, including John Crimmins, had quit. Neither of them had risen in the organization in three years.

Tim called from Lynchburg, and spoke to Charley. "He said he isn't playing at all, and hasn't even DH'd in a week, even though he was batting almost .400 as a DH. Martin and McKeel start every game at catch, even if they've made errors that cost runs. Tim sounded really discouraged, and claimed this was the last year he was going to be humiliated by sitting on the bench."

At the end of the first week of May, Manager Meleski called Tim from the dugout to catch the last inning of a game the Lynchburg team was winning by ten runs, thereby humiliating him further. Three of the team, including Tim, sat on the bench every day, even after they had accounted for seven of the nine hits during a game in which all three played. Mike Walsh (former head coach at Dartmouth, who'd recruited Tim) stopped by, and helped to lift Tim's spirits. "I told Tim he'll do whatever he's got to do," Charley reported.

In addition, Tim discovered by talking to his teammates that, almost without exception, they all earned over $1,000/month before taxes. Tim's salary was under that, and his agent, Nero, certainly wouldn't go to bat for him with the Sox management until Nero could earn a huge commission. Agents didn't earn a cent off players at the "A" level.

"You see," Charley told me during one of our walks together along the beach, "this is another example of bad management. What would it cost them to pay minor leaguers another couple of hundred a month? Instead, they want to keep them in their place and show them who's boss. All it does is breed animosity among the young guys."

Ever the businessman, he had a unique perspective on the business of baseball. Getting more agitated as we weaved in and out of the waves, he continued, "When these kids do, if they do, make it to the big-time, they remember how the management stuck it to them over their years in the minors. And they're determined to reverse the tables.

"Nero told us that Boggs earned a total of $6,000 from the Sox during his entire minor league career with them," Charley continued. "Can you imagine? On the phone I told Tim how proud we were of the way he was handling the disappointments this season." That last sentence lowered the tone of Charley's voice.

"I did lose my cool one day," Tim had reported to his Dad, "the day after the three of us who never play got seven hits, and none of us were back in the lineup. All three of us broke a few things in the dugout with Meleski sitting right there. He never said a word."

"Do any of the guys speak up?" Charley asked Tim.

"Once in a while somebody does, but it doesn't help. The guys can smell when they're going to get released. All I know is I'm sending applications out again for careers I've always wanted. Unfortunately, there are no openings in officer's candidate schools, and government service agencies want people with advanced degrees or experience overseas."

We drove down to all the Ft. Lauderdale home games. One night, our third baseman's father expounded upon the proper execution of a drag bunt. Harry Durkin, the father, believed that none of our Fort Lauderdale team seemed able to execute this properly. I learned that there were five steps in all, and Harry demonstrated each with a forceful grunt. "First, you square your shoulders to the pitcher before he begins his motion," Harry began. "Then you stick the bat out horizontal to the ground," etc., etc. The team had gotten a total of one hit during the game that night. "What's wrong with these coaches?" Harry asked all of us sitting next to him. "Why aren't they teaching these players to get hits by bunting?" Then, lo and behold! In the bottom of the ninth inning, our team's leading hitter executed one perfectly. Guess who it was? Marty Durkin.

On the evening of May 8, 1993, the Fort Lauderdale Red Sox literally and figuratively "reopened." As if by magic, there were about 1,500 in the stands for the Mother's Day weekend "Second Opening." Clowns juggled on top of the dugouts, creating balloon animals for the kids. Waitresses from Hooters Bar handed out coupons for "Ten Free Chicken Wings," and the first five hundred lucky fans received BoSox hats. In addition, the Sox beat the Vero Beach Dodgers 4-3, although Todd went 0-for-4 at the plate. He pulled the ball again, instead of hitting to the opposite field (left), and struck out twice. When Charley was upset, his jaws locked. They were locked after that game.

In the parking lot afterward, he gingerly opened the conversation with Todd, "Are you discouraged?"

"Yeah, a little bit."

"About what?"

"About my hitting, of course."

Then the lecture started from Charley. "Now, listen! Only three games ago you had a two-hit game. You can't get down on yourself because of two bad games, or you'll spiral downward." Todd stared off at the floodlights above the field while he listened.

"We haven't yet seen a shortstop with your ability at this level," Charley continued, trying to bolster our son. "You only have three errors on the season! You are a good hitter, and could bat .300 in this league. Listen, you're not batting smart." At this point, Charley was crunching down on his pipe while Todd stared at the pavement and moved his toe back and forth over the uneven asphalt. "You're getting on top of the ball and then trying to pull everything to right. I want you to promise me you'll concentrate on using all fields. And don't take so many first strikes!"

"Okay, okay, Dad!" Todd put up his hands in resignation.

"How about getting some hits tomorrow night for our last game before Mom and I drive north?"

"What do you think I've been trying to do?"

I gave Todd a big bear hug before he slumped his shoulders and headed toward his car. We slunk off to ours. I thought Charley had overdone it.

"I can't believe Todd's lack of confidence at the plate," Charley confided on our ride back to the condo. "He has such a fragile ego, after all the success he's had!"

"Anyone who went 0-for-7 would lack some confidence," I replied.

"Not a really good hitter. A good hitter would just shake that off and be anxious to get back up to bat." Charley always had an answer when it came to baseball. Which I, as a mother, knew nothing about! The only thing I knew was that when I played tennis competitively, I couldn't wait to beat my next opponent when I had just finished beating someone else. The first couple of successes were the key.

We did have a good ending after all, to our spring. Although the Red Sox lost to the Dodgers in an afternoon game, Todd got two hits, and every mother in the stadium received flowers for Mothers' Day. Afterward, the Durkins had seven teammates and their parents back to their house for a baked ham buffet. Their backyard had direct access to the Cardinal Gibbons High School baseball field, complete with bleachers, dugouts, and batting cages. Charley told Harry Durkin that if he'd seen that house when our boys were younger, we would have been living there instead of the Durkins.

It was fun being with the ballplayers. They were such gentlemen, and truly nice kids from all over the country. It was a real tribute to the Sox scouting bureau. Some had been in the minors for five years, and one had had Valentin, Plantier, and Naehring as roommates, all of whom had gone to the majors.

Charley asked Todd's roommate, Bryan Brown, why his girlfriend couldn't bring two friends from Louisiana to visit Todd and their third roommate, Les.

"Because I got the best one, and the rest can't compare," he replied. Bryan's girlfriend, Donna, later became his wife.

We finally were able to visit the boys' apartment in Coral Springs that day, our last day before heading north. We weaved in and out of traffic, trying to follow Todd from the Durkins' house.

At the apartment, Todd gave me a book by Tim Parks for Mothers' Day entitled, Italian Neighbors. Charley and I had a trip planned to Italy the following autumn. The apartment had been bombed for fleas, and was the smallest living space I'd seen three guys share. I asked him if any chicks hung out at the pool, since so many ballplayers lived at the complex. "Not really," was the response I got. That was typical of all the responses I got from my sons when I inquired about their love lives.

Where girls were involved, Charley and I were the last to get any details. We actually found out more about Tim's and Todd's romantic interests from their friends' parents than we did from them. We never met their dates until relationships had developed for at least three months. We never got a single fact from either brother about the other's love interests. Like true friars, they maintained their vows of silence for each other. I respected this allegiance, but it often drove me to play the "Twenty Questions" game with them. Usually before we got to twenty, they'd simply tell me, "Butt out, Mom!"

On our way north, we were able to see Tim's Lynchburg team play in Wilmington, Delaware, against the "A" Blue Rocks. Because of a fierce thunderstorm the previous night, the game turned into a double-header. Prior to game time, we spent some time with Tim.

The Blue Rock's stadium, amid industrial warehouses off Route 95, was barely completed, with carpet still being laid in the office area behind the ticket booths. Everything smelled new, from the carpet to the paint to the sawdust. It was a beautiful facility, with a wide concourse overhung by a roof that didn't quite cover the fans, and concession stalls on the first and third base line along the back of the concourse. Seating went directly to the field, where players signing autographs stood beneath the fans' feet. There wasn't a bad seat in the house. Corporate season ticket holders were treated to enclosed glass sky-boxes. Seating capacity was 6,000.

Fifty-one-hundred attended the double header to see the Blue Rocks defeat the

Red Sox twice. "Blue Rocks" — we couldn't figure out what the reference was. Did it mean "Cold Stones?"

Tim hadn't played the previous week, not even as Designated Hitter. In the second game, though, he was in the lineup as the DH and walked once, then drove in the Sox only run. He had had only twenty-three at-bats in almost thirty games. Jeff Martin had become the primary catcher, with Walt McKeel as backup catcher. Tim still hadn't approached the manager, instead throwing bats in the dugout when he'd had too much sitting. McKeel did catch the second game we saw, and got thrown out of the game after his first at-bat. Because Tim was listed as DH in the lineup, he couldn't go in to catch, so Jeff caught two games.

Tim was still talking about leaving baseball after that summer. He wanted to join the Army as an enlisted man, and then apply to officer's school afterward, provided there were openings. The thought of an Ivy Leaguer, not to mention my son, in the trenches for the Army made me sick, so I just listened and said no more. I knew the process of resigning from baseball and enlisting in the Army would take time and hoped Tim would postpone any decision until the season ended.

The Lynchburg team contained personalities far different from those on the Fort Lauderdale team one level below. This team contained many more individual egos. During infield practice, Randy Brown and Steve Rodrigues were hot-dogging for the crowd. They were clearly enjoying themselves, confident of being starters every night. Later Randy was introduced to us and inquired about Todd. Tim assured us it was only Randy's means of finding out whether Todd was having a season superior enough to send him to Lynchburg to replace Randy. Tim complimented Todd's "do-my-job," closemouthed approach, combined with his outstanding ability. In later years, we understood that Randy was as insecure as the rest of the players; his antics were part of a defense mechanism to shield his ego from damage. He and his family were genuinely caring people.

Jeff Martin seemed extremely relaxed during infield practice. He knew that he could fail as often as his .215 batting average indicated, but there would be no consequences. He was the chosen one.

At bat, Tim's shoulders were hunched, his hat pulled far down over his brows. He was intense, his only focus the ball. His body was full of emotional tension, like a coil ready to spring. He was one of only three bachelors without any long-term attachment on the team, so most of his emotional release was through roommate Bill Selby or teammates at a sports bar or crunching the ball. I didn't want to know about other releases.

When we departed for our home in Westport, Mass., Tim's team record stood at 14-16, while Todd's was 8-24. As we entered our house, the phone was ringing. It was Todd, calling to tell us he'd hit his first home run. We'd sat for one month watching him play, and as soon as we left, BINGO! He had relaxed since our departure. This indicated to me that it was a blessing Charley and I would be over a thousand miles away for his games.

His average had risen to.260, and he was frequenting the golf course.

The pressure to perform in front of us and hometown fans didn't bother Tim as much as it did Todd. Later, at "AAA," Todd would have his former coaches, friends, teammates, neighbors, and Charley and me at every home game. We decided he'd simply have to adjust, if he were going to the major leagues.

The next call came from Tim. He was distraught. During three previous losing efforts, Tim was the only team member <u>not</u> to get into a single game, either as a catcher, designated hitter, first baseman, outfielder, pinch runner, etc. Most of all, he was worried about being released. Tim had a rage boiling inside him, so Charley suggested that he take the manager aside privately. "Do what I did in business," Charley suggested. "Ask Meleski if you can call Kenney in Boston (head of the minor league system) to get some answers. Remain professional in your approach, but certainly start exploring other options. Mom and I could never condone your enlisting in the Army, after you graduated from Dartmouth. But the final decision will always be yours, and we will always support you."

My parents visited Tim when the Lynchburg team played in Maryland. In addition to their never seeing him get into the games after driving eight hours, they were also upset at the prospect of Tim's enlisting in the Army. Unfortunately, they broached these subjects at dinner in Jeff Martin's presence (Tim's primary rival at catch), which completely embarrassed Tim. Contrary to our belief that Tim had been overly patient, my mother felt that a bad attitude toward his manager might be contributing to his bench time. Tim's agent, Alan Nero, never returned his calls.

Fortunately, Tim kept his cool with my parents, but was unable to do so with Meleski. Behind closed doors, Tim asked the manager directly whether he felt his capabilities were equal to the other two catchers. Meleski told him they were, but Boston management was directing his every move. Tim knew that by not playing, he was losing his skills. "That's bullshit!" he shouted at Meleski. He sat on the bench in Maryland by himself, apart from the others, and was the last to board the bus for Lynchburg. Baseball had changed our gregarious, affable Tim.

It was the same old story. Two draft picks were ahead of Tim as catchers on his team. According to Meleski, someone would eventually be moving, and Tim would play. "Nothing personal," Nero told Tim when he finally returned Tim's call. "They like your work ethic, and want you to go up through their system. Unfortunately, someone will have to move or get hurt first."

"Just what they say to everyone," Tim sneered. The '93 amateur draft would be that week, so drafted catchers would be rotating in. To appease Tim, Nero offered the possibility of playing in Japan in the minor leagues. It didn't interest him.

A quote from <u>Fathers Playing Catch</u> seemed appropriate for Tim. It was a remark made by Steve Blass: "Growing up means ending what their lives have always aimed for."[15] Fortunately, Tim had many other directions to explore.

In a subsequent call to Todd, Nero expressed his concern that Tim would leave baseball before the season was finished. Todd assured him that wouldn't happen, as he'd been in touch with Tim also. Furthermore, none of us felt Tim would be released before the end of the season.

In Daytona Beach, Todd watched the cars drive on the hard sand below his hotel. He'd hit a triple and a double the previous night. "What did Nero report from Kenney about you, Todd?" Charley asked.

"Not a word. We only talked about Tim."

"How did Tim sound to you?"

"Not good. He wasn't himself, was very down. In ten days, he only DH'd twice. Meleski was giving him a lot of bull. My manager plays everyone. I told him to stick it out through the season, but in the end he'll do what he's got to do. First, he's got to get reliable information about his options."

Charley answered, "He wrote Governor McKernan in Maine to see if he could open up a spot in officer's school or perhaps a government position. There was a letter in response, which we forwarded to Tim. Perhaps he can help him. What else is new?"

We listened to a report on who'd been hitting for the Ft. Lauderdale team and who was now playing at higher levels. Finally getting down to what was relevant, Charley advised, "Todd, there are no other shortstops at this point, all the way up through Pawtucket (the highest level), who have only four errors like you. Randy Brown is the only other one with an average higher than yours. All you need to do is get a hit a game, and the pathway is open."

"Dad, my triple went to left-center."

"Great! Keep up the good work. We love you."

We had separate reports about Tim and Todd by the end of May. Harold Alfond, a part-owner of the Sox, reported that management in Boston was giving Todd extremely high marks. In fact, they expected him to be at "AA" by the end of the following season. Alfond also reported that the only information the Boston office had about Tim was that he hit well. If he never played, how could they have any information? Talk about a Catch-22! Nothing personal.

With Charley still considering career opportunities from New York State to Florida, we were able to travel. I could easily rearrange my clients' schedules, except for major installations. We drove twelve hours to Lynchburg over Memorial Day weekend to try to lift Tim's spirits. The traffic down the Blue Ridge Parkway was horrendous, and we were got lost coming down from the mountains into the bowl of Lynchburg. However, we saw some gorgeous colleges, including Randolph-Macon.

I loved having the freedom to take off and see different parts of the country. I kept a bag packed with cosmetics and makeup, so that I could just throw in a few items of underwear, a nightgown, swimsuit, and outfits for the ball field.

Tim was in the bullpen when we arrived, peering up expectantly. He was obviously happy to see us. Kenney, Director of Minor League Operations for Boston, had been observing the team all week. The night we arrived, Tim was not in the lineup. He claimed he no longer put pressure on himself, because he planned to leave baseball at the end of the season.

"This is no longer an acceptable career path for me. It's been a humiliating experience, and management should be humiliated with only 500 people at games, and the team in last place. Our first and second basemen and catcher are hitting around .200. The second catcher will strike out probably 150 times this season."

Meleski told Tim, "If you sit for two days, then DH and strike out occasionally, don't worry about it. I don't expect you to hit all the time. When you play, you can't expect to do everything."

During the game, we sat with Bill Selby's parents, who'd driven up from Mississippi. Bill and Tim were apartment mates in Lynchburg. The Selbys had been visiting for a week and clearly resented the fact that Bill didn't start every day. He'd been on a hitting streak for a couple of weeks and had won a game with a homer in the bottom of the ninth.

Pam and Bill Selby were tuned in to their son's moods and potential career steps. They attributed his sudden surges in hitting to the ups in Bill's engagement to Teri, and his slumps to the downs in Bill's engagement to Teri. They were very supportive of Tim and his frustration. After the game, they retreated to the boys' apartment, where they stocked the fridge and did Bill's laundry. Having already prepared fried catfish, Pam promised the boys chicken and dumplings next. Tim and Bill joked about whether Todd would still look like a minor leaguer if he made it to Fenway, because he hated to part with his money. The previous season, Todd had agreed to exchange cleats with Bill. But when Todd discovered his own cleats were worth more, he asked Bill to pay him the extra $20!

Tim gave us a quick tour around Lynchburg the next day, including the historical area downtown, and drove us to lunch. He had been a guest speaker at a grammar school class in the morning, and had spoken before two other grade levels. The one he'd enjoyed most, he said, was the high school class. "They got past the question, 'How much do you make?'"

"The Selbys are great people," he told us. "One morning I was awakened at 8 a.m. They were playing the guitar and singing downstairs. I asked them if they were having a hillbilly hoedown. Remember, Mom, when you used to come into our apartment at Dartmouth and immediately start cleaning? That's what Mrs. Selby does."

We all managed to rouse Todd on the phone in Fort Lauderdale around 11:30 a.m. Charley and I described the graduation functions we had attended as guests of his roommates and their families at Brown. Todd was clearly ambivalent about not graduating with his class. But I didn't care when he would wear the cap and gown, as long as it happened.

Todd's immediate concern was for needed rest during the rain that deluged Florida. He wasn't eating properly and needed a year-round weightlifting program to build his stamina. Tim's work ethic at the gym hadn't rubbed off. Charley and I had tried for years to convince him to expand his eating choices, and I had always cooked balanced dinners at home. As it turned out, when Dan Duquette became the General Manager, nutrition experts gave lectures to all minor leaguers during spring training. A staff member became responsible for developing a weight program for each player.

The kids on Tim's team seemed motivated, with their heads on straight. "Yeah," Tim agreed. "There are only a couple of screwballs who poured ice water over Coach Bibby when he was on the crapper, or someone like Randy who cries about not playing a game. I tell him to grow up and stop his bellyaching because no one could stand it. If anyone should bellyache, it should be me."

We spent an hour after the game in a restaurant listening to Tim's future plans for Monterey Language School, Army Intelligence School, Officer Candidate School, or clandestine government work. In our motel room afterward, I couldn't help expressing my feeling of helplessness to Charley: "I hope good things happen to that kid. He works so hard, he's so enthusiastic and motivated! It's hard to believe he's getting the shaft this summer."

"The idea that hard work isn't always rewarded is a tough lesson to learn so early," Charley answered. "But I saw it every day."

"Look what happened to you!" I exploded. "You didn't deserve what you got, either. As the kids say, 'Life can suck.'"

"Look, I hate those bastards at the bank, but our lives are comfortable. And our kids have the best educations in the world behind them, so they'll make it somewhere else, if they don't make it here."

Several days into our stay in Lynchburg in early June, Tim still had not started a single game in the field over the course of the season. Walt McKeel, who'd been in the system around four years, hit a double and a triple during one game we watched, and had become the number one catcher. Jeff Martin caught one out of every three games, and had struck out nine consecutive times before hitting a home run.

Unexpectedly, Tim and Walt McKeel had become friends. Walt amused Tim by trying to eat a 22-ounce steak, which he couldn't finish, burping like John Candy all the while.

"We hated each other at first, but now he no longer sees me as a threat." Tim related hilarious stories about "the pen." There were five considered permanent fixtures in the bullpen because they sat there so often. Tim was one of them. To amuse themselves during games, Maloney, a pitcher, sent messages up to the PA announcer with fictitious names. "Would Pete-Zerria, and Hugh-Jassole, and Stu-Pidassa please report to the press box." They devised a Jeopardy game, with two pitchers to a side while Tim played Alex Trebek. It was Tim's responsibility to think up questions in each of four categories, one for each pitcher's area of expertise. For verification of Tim's answers, the pitchers consulted their trainer or pitching coach Bibby. "If you see a bunch of guys in the pen jumping up and down, it's because they've won the game that day. Jeff, when he loses, goes in the locker room and sulks or throws stuff. All the wives and girlfriends know the results and congratulate the winner."

Speaking of families, we were amazed at the babies brought to the field every night to watch their fathers play. The minimal salary they lived on, with an additional stipend for being married, forced several couples to double up in an apartment, even if there was a baby involved. Some single players in Fort Lauderdale (salary level $50/month lower than in Lynchburg) shared apartments with married couples. It was a wonder the married players could concentrate at all, with the traveling away from the family, pressure to succeed, and odd sleeping arrangements.

Back in the bullpen, there was a fellow who was an institution there, inherited from the previous tenants, the Mets. He had no apparent affiliation to the stadium, except to clean up the locker rooms. His nickname was "Saladbar." One day he jinxed the Red Sox pitcher who had a no-hitter going, and the pitcher's effort was lost for the record books. The players, being superstitious and wanting some amusement, decided to put Saladbar on trial. The entire team was called into the clubhouse after the game, including the coaches and batboys. One impartial team member, Bob Juday (with "the best eye for a strike zone I've ever seen," according to Charley), was the judge, while Tim and two others from the pen served as witnesses. Saladbar pleaded his own case and was sentenced to supplying gum and sunflower seeds for the pen over the course of the home stand — unless he wanted to be banished forever.

I was half an hour late to pick Charley up for one day-game in Lynchburg. I'd driven about fifteen miles out of town to see Jefferson's second home, Poplar Forest. The tour guide was an elderly woman who prided herself on giving us every detail of Jefferson's visits to the home. I only got halfway through the tour before I had to excuse myself to get back. When I got to the Best Western ten minutes before game time, Charley was waiting at the highway curb, red in the face. We got to the ballpark just before the national anthem, and I apologized the entire ride over. After many innings of silence from my spouse, I told him I'd had enough punishment! After all, we had both gotten what we wanted that day: my partial tour of an historic home and his entire nine innings at the ball park. It took a meal with Tim after the game to unclench his jaw.

Steve Braun, the roving batting instructor, was visiting Lynchburg that week. We told him Todd had benefited from his instruction. "When he's playing in Pawtucket, you'll be next door to watch him," Braun replied. We parents clung to every encouraging word.

I purchased lots of Lynchburg T-shirts for Christmas gifts at half price from the souvenir stand. Ron Roberts, the assistant manager at the stadium, was very accommodating. He'd reserved our motel room for $40/night.

Kevin, in his thirties, was one of the umpires staying down the hall from us for the three-game series. Kevin would move on to his next assignment around the league after these games. He was trying to work his way up the umpire's ladder, just like the players. He said the majority of his road trips were four-to-six hour drives, whereas some of the Texas or Southwestern League distances were brutal. Kevin was from Cajun Louisiana, wore an earring, and was infamous for kicking a batboy out of a game after the batboy slammed some balls into Kevin's hand in disgust over a call he'd made against the home team. His license plate read, "Pro Ump."

As of June 15, 1993, major league baseball banned all chewing and smoking tobacco for every level of the minor leagues, but not the majors. This included all players, managers, coaches, and umps, with huge fines for those in possession. Of course, the idea was to save the young players, who had little money to contest the ruling legally, from mouth and tongue cancer. For many of them, the addiction would be hard to break. Bob Juday had a difficult time talking to us before game time because of the wad in his mouth. Major league baseball sanctioned the managers' right to go into the players' bags and lockers looking for tobacco. No doubt there would eventually be court action if the managers tried this at the major league level.

It was a disgusting habit, and most women found it difficult to understand. Chewing the tobacco necessitated spitting out the juice. The spittle stained the players' cleats brown. I guessed that chewing was part of the macho image, and perhaps part of the boredom of waiting in the dugout to get in the batter's box or take the field. When major league baseball outlawed tobacco in the minor leagues, sunflower seeds took tobacco's place. Soon the players were ejecting spent sunflower shells from their mouths like missiles.

We golfed in the mornings in the foothills of the Blue Ridge Mountains, and discovered new areas of the sprawling Lynchburg metropolis. After the game, Tim gobbled down his meal with us so he could meet the guys and their dates at 10:30

p.m. He'd neglected to send a check for his estimated income taxes, had not responded to a wedding invitation, nor sent a gift. I bought him and Bill an answering machine, since Tim would be expecting calls from the Army and foreign language programs. A friend of Tim's, Blake Taylor, cut her forehead open on Tim's Jeep door after they left us, so he spent most of the night in the emergency room.

The major league draft had been held that day, June 3rd. The Red Sox first round pick was a high school outfielder and football player, Trot Nixon. Trot's bonus for signing was a record $890,000. Trot would become Todd's teammate for four years and would eventually play the outfield in Fenway Park. Trot invited Todd to his wedding in North Carolina several years later, and vice versa.

About an hour before game time on June 4th, we waited in our car in the parking lot in Lynchburg, as a thick black cloud roared quickly towards us. There were frequent violent thunderstorms in that area, but there'd been no warning of anything more serious. The Selbys sat next to us in their truck. We were all waiting for a reporter who'd requested interviews with us for her article in Baseball Underground, a Red Sox publication distributed outside Fenway Park. The subject of the story would be "The Parents of Summer."

Just when the reporter's car pulled in next to the Selbys', the sky turned black, the wind began gusting at 75 mph from the north, and hail hit the windshield with such force that we thought it would shatter and blow in. Forty-foot trees surrounding the parking lot began cracking and snapping, though we could see nothing but white ice out of our windows. When the winds began rocking our Lincoln Town Car, we buckled our seat belts and hoped we wouldn't tip over into the Selbys' truck.

As the storm subsided, we sent word into the clubhouse for the boys to meet us back at our motel. That was easier said than done. Electric and phone lines littered the streets, and huge tree limbs lay everywhere — on houses, cars, trailers. It looked almost like the devastation of Hurricane Bob in our area of Massachusetts in '91.

We were convinced we'd sat through a tornado in our vehicle. When we reached the Best Western, we discovered there was no phone or electricity. As it turned out, there was no power for forty-eight hours. After the boys had threaded their way through the maze to our motel, we carpooled to the mall just behind us. There, a generator cranked power for Morrison's Cafeteria. The food line stretched the entire length of the corridor between the stores. No one had power in the surrounding area.

The following day we surveyed the damage to the Sox field. The fence behind home plate had collapsed onto the field, pulling the lights and netting down with it. A batting cage was crumpled like paper. During the height of the winds, Tim had observed the tarp that covered the field blowing into the air like a giant tent. No clue where it landed! The cylinder on which it had been stored remained airborne twenty feet high, hung up on an electrical pole. Surprisingly, the press box remained on its perch above the stadium, its flimsy walls still intact.

The next day, we drove with the Selbys to Appomattox. It too had been damaged, and there was still no electricity there. We didn't have to pay anything to enter, since weather experts verified that a tornado had hit. Trees that dated back to the Civil War had been uprooted, but miraculously, none had fallen on the historic buildings. The paper reported that fourteen counties had been hit. The Bulls-Sox games would be moved to Salem, Virginia, two days later.

Meanwhile, the Bulls were staying at our motel, and to pass the time they went to the mall, played catch, and sprinted in our parking lot. Tim's team did the same on the dry spots of the Lynchburg field. The clubhouse that had housed their team during the height of the storm had minimal damage.

The Bulls' bus was a far cry from the broken-down Lynchburg team bus. We'd noticed in Wilmington that the side of Tim's bus was dented in. He said their driver was certifiably insane, trying to go through openings where the bus couldn't possibly fit (with the team aboard), and constantly getting lost en route to out-of-town fields. The Lynchburg owner insisted on leasing the cheapest possible equipment and the bus had no VCR or seat belts. When the driver reported to his company that four new airbags were needed over the shocks, he was told to replace only one. The bus that took the team to Salem looked like something from the Red Foxx junkyard on *Sanford and Son*. Tim then revealed that Todd's bus driver almost drove the Fort Lauderdale team off the road one night crossing Alligator Alley between the east and west coasts of Florida. The driver had fallen asleep at the wheel, and only when Manager DeMarlo Hale lurched forward in his front seat did anyone realize they were riding the shoulder!

We called Todd from Tim's apartment, because Tim's phone was working and our motel still had none. We also showered there, using his electricity. The Fort Lauderdale team had spent the morning in Homestead, Florida, picking up garbage that had collected around a ballpark and recreation center during Hurricane Andrew. A year later, Charley and I would pass through Homestead on a return journey from Key West. After twelve months, buildings remained crushed, and ubiquitous blue roofing paper remained where tiles had ripped off. The insurance companies were slow to pay their policy holders after two devastating hurricanes within two years. Many of the inhabitants of Homestead moved on after the Air Force closed its base.

Manager Meleski had issued new edicts regarding fines. If any player on the team were caught chewing tobacco, he would not only pay his own $100 fine, but also the Manager's $100 fine. If any pitcher stormed off the mound directly into the clubhouse after being removed from a game, he would pay the maximum fine of $499. All members of the team were fined $2 if infielders had a bad infield practice prior to the game. The manager and coaches used the fines to provide beer for the clubhouse after games, perhaps even to pay their own cart fees at the local golf courses. In Elmira, N.Y., Manager Dave Holt had used the team's fines to buy cases of Coke and sandwiches for the team's road trips, while Frank White in Winter Haven threw a barbeque for the team while we were visiting in '92.

On the bench in Lynchburg, Manager Meleski distanced himself from his players. He protected his rear flank in the event the team had a losing season. In fact, he seldom backed up his players when quoted in the local paper. Instead, he blamed one or the other for a loss, and pitted players at the same position against each other. "I'm not saying he's (McKeel's) #1, because I'm not really sure myself," Meleski said. "Ever since Martin became #1 he's really gone backward. He's struggling a lot at the plate right now."[16]

In contrast, the Fort Lauderdale team displayed a more relaxed attitude, knowing each player would get in the lineup on a fairly regular basis. Todd was one of the few playing every game.

Neither Tim nor Todd condoned my taking notes back in our motel room on any of these anecdotes or daily activities. Both boys were worried that I might jeopardize their careers. Todd had been warned by Garry Roggenburk and others on the staff not to tell "insider" secrets. I assured them that I would not publish any of these "secrets" as long as either of them was still playing, and I would send them my rough draft before anyone else saw it.

We moved on to Salem, Virginia, for the re-scheduled games against the Bulls. There was far less damage down there, while the radio reported two days later that the Lynchburg area still had 20,000 homes without electricity.

In the first game, Tim was the DH, going 1-3, driving in a run with a double, and barely missing a home run. His average stood at .287 after the game, but he was not in the lineup for the second game. We watched him throw his glove in frustration. He went off by himself along the outfield fence, where he hung on with his head down between his arms, knowing that no effort on his part would make any difference. I couldn't just sit in the stands and watch him get humiliated, while his teammates rotated onto the field. I got up and walked along the upper concourse. He had played an excellent game as designated hitter.

Manager Meleski phoned the results of every game immediately to Kenney, Director of the Minor Leagues, in Boston. So we knew Kenney was aware of Tim's performance. We didn't know if Kenney was aware of Tim's frustration. Damn, he was only a cheap free agent, not a draftee, so what did they care?

As the Sox got behind in the second game, Tim had a number of pitchers to warm up in the bullpen. This helped divert his attention. Bob Juday's mother recounted her older son's recent release from the Pirates. Then both she and Pam Selby told us how much their sons admired Tim for his work ethic and maturity in handling his frustration. Bob Juday and Bill Selby were both excellent hitters, yet they were both platooning at third base for this team.

After the game, we advised Tim to be ready in case Walt McKeel moved up to "AA"; to get from this experience whatever he could for the remainder of the season; and to pursue his alternatives. We had seen Tim play for the first time in six games.

The girlfriends and wives all sat with us in Salem. What a circus! There were cliques of those who clearly got along, and cliques of those who gossiped about everyone else. Kim, a thin, blond girlfriend, was offended because a pitcher's fiancée had commented on her crooked toes. The two reported on who was dating whom, including bachelors like Tim, and who went to a bar while the girlfriends were away. Fights the previous night, heard through thin apartment walls by team roommates or neighbors, could decide ball games. Girls passed the players' babies back and forth to amuse the infants. One pitcher's son, a real hyperactive kid who was seldom restrained by his mother, ran up and down the cement steps of the ballpark until he finally tripped on the plastic Zorro cape that flapped over his shoulders and under his feet. I decided Tim was better off without a girlfriend, although he lacked the close support system that the others had daily. Waiting on the periphery of the steps after every game were four or five young teenage "groupies," who followed the team from Lynchburg wherever it went.

Charley and I had foregone college reunions, funerals, first communions, wedding showers, and high school graduation parties to follow the boys. We were, indeed, "the parents of summer." This suspension of our activities in favor of mini-vacations to watch our sons play professionally would have been idyllic, if they had both been playing regularly. But anxiety over Tim's frustration dominated our days in Lynchburg. I realized we were not just summertime parents, but parents for all seasons, all years. It was almost impossible to separate my own identity from what was happening to them during the seven years this saga proceeded.

Via overnight express we sent copies of Tim's Social Security card, birth certificate, and college diploma to him. He informed us he was applying for Army ranger school, as well as officer's candidate school. He also intended to take the test for the Army language school in Monterey, California — comparable to a Master of Arts degree in an Oriental language. I had no doubt my fears would be realized and he would be accepted for at least one of these Army programs. After all, he was an Ivy League graduate, honorary society inductee for campus leadership, workaholic, and fitness freak.

He had not heard from Todd. I called Todd's answering machine and left a message that if he had any empathy at all, he'd call Tim. When Todd was doing poorly, he didn't communicate with the family.

Our security guard at the Florida condo sent us the dismal box scores once a week from the Fort Lauderdale team. Todd had had one hit in ten at-bats, and had made two recent errors; still, he had the fewest on the team among the regular starters, and would be voted "the best defensive shortstop in the league" at the end of the season.

Charley couldn't get enough of the game. He continued to watch the tube as the major league Red Sox slid from first place in their division to fifth by mid-June. In addition to the broadcasts, he absorbed every word written in the Boston, Providence, and New York papers. It engrossed him while he pondered career offers.

...Sportswriting can take the boys' game and find in it ambition and failure, success, and aging... In baseball's diamond and numerical order, writers find a grid against which to set phenomena of time and the times – like aging, like the behavior of owners. In baseball, history writers find connections with the past that most Americans, most of the time, ignore or deny.[17]

Both boys called Charley within five minutes of each other on Father's Day, June 20, 1993. Tim had some good news — he'd caught his first two games after two-and-a-half months, because Walt McKeel was injured. The team had won both games, Tim going 2-for-10 with an RBI. "Some of the pitchers have told me they'd rather have me behind the plate than either Walt or Jeff," Tim reported. "Meleski just said he knew it all along. I knew I could do it, too, so screw the big shots in Boston! I can now get on with my life. I never even had to throw anybody out, because we led all the way. My average is still around .275."

Charley gave Todd another pep talk. Todd reported on his disastrous week, as did his stats: his batting average down to .219, and errors above ten. He had played the most games on the team, fifty-seven, and had a sore arm. Since there was no other shortstop to back him up, he could not rest. Charley emphasized the fundamental skills he had as a hitter, and where to hit the ball so pitchers would start pitching inside to him, rather than outside.

"I'm really making contact, but they're not dropping in. I've only struck out twenty-three times in 215 at-bats. Braun is here and says there's nothing wrong with my swing. My manager says he sends good reports on me every night, and knows my arm's sore. I told him they should bring (Lou) Merloni here to relieve the infielders. He just signed with us and is on the rookie team."

"They'll start falling in, if you continue hitting," Charley responded. "Just spray the field and start practicing your bunting again. Don't worry about your defense. That's always been your strong point."

I insisted on talking. "Do you have any days off without games?"

"We have four days off coming up over the All-Star break, which will be the only time all season. I'm going to the beach to forget baseball."

"Great! Hope you called Tim," I reminded him.

"I'll call him next. I talked to both grandfathers to wish them a 'Happy Father's Day.'"

By the time of the All-Star break, Todd had raised his average twenty percentage points. Both of his roommates had been elevated to the "AA" team in New Britain, so Todd asked another teammate to move in with him to share the expenses.

At the same time, Jeff Martin was elevated from Tim's Lynchburg team to "AAA" in Pawtucket, where the second catcher had broken his hand. Tim asked if we would mind picking up Jeff and Stephanie from the Providence Airport and allow them to live in our Cumberland house during the assignment. Of course we didn't object, since Charley and I were down at our beach house. Jeff then called to ask our permission but didn't know his flight times. It wasn't until the following day that we learned from Jeff's mother that the young couple had already arrived. The Sox were paying for their room at the Comfort Inn, and had given them a rental car. I had re-arranged some drapery and furniture installations and Charley had rescheduled some committee meetings for a board of directors in order to meet Jeff and Stephanie at the airport and bring them to our home. We never heard from them. Jeff was a big-shot and couldn't be bothered.

We assumed Tim would start catching in Lynchburg and tried to follow the labyrinthine reasoning that allowed Boston management to elevate Jeff two levels to "AAA" with a .159 batting average and 50% strike-outs in his total at-bats. Our conclusions went something like this: the catchers in New Britain at "AA" were real prospects, and needed to catch regularly. Since the slot in Pawtucket was temporary and encompassed primarily bullpen catching, they dipped down to "A" Lynchburg. Walt McKeel was still needed in Lynchburg to catch regularly.

Most of this theory was shot to hell when we read in the local paper the following morning that Jeff had DH'd in Pawtucket's game the night before, striking out twice in his only two at-bats. We did prove to be right about one thing: Tim caught a game almost immediately in Wilmington, DE, before 6,500 fans, and Lynchburg won. One of his fraternity brothers at Dartmouth, Joe Tosone, was signed as a free agent by the Expos. That made four Dartmouth teammates who were playing pro ball, an extraordinary number for the Ivy Leagues!

In early July, Todd received an unexpected raise of $200/month. There was never an explanation, and we didn't want to ask Tim if he had received the same raise.

In subsequent games for the Lynchburg team, with Kenney and minor league administrators in attendance, Tim continued to catch. Defensively he did beauti-fully, but he went 0-for-9 at the plate, striking out five times. However, behind Jose Malave and Bob Juday's bats, the team rose into first place in its division.

Tim and Bob Juday showed up for extra batting practice. Jim Rice, assigned to Lynchburg as a roving batting instructor, appeared behind the cage in street clothes with a can of Coke in his hand. He had a golf game scheduled, and watched Bob Juday hit. When Tim got into the cage, Rice turned and walked into the clubhouse.

In the first week of July, Tim had a busy schedule. He arose at 5 a.m. one morning to take his Cumberland High friend, Derek Laffey, to the airport. The next morning he arose at 4 a.m. to drive to Richmond to take the Language Proficiency Test for the Army's Monterey School. The following day, another 4 a.m. wake-up to return to Richmond to find out he'd scored in the 98th percentile. Thus began months of application procedures for officer's school. Thank goodness, he had abandoned the idea of ranger school! Other options Tim discussed: returning to school for a master's; playing ball in Japan; calling his contacts for advice about entering the FBI.

"Tim, do you truly see yourself as a Rambo or a LeCarre super spy?" I grilled him. I guessed from his responses that he really did. Tim had always been ex-tremely adaptable in any surrounding, and I believed he could become anything he set his mind to. Still, he was six feet three inches with blue eyes, and I doubted he could blend into a foreign population.

Alan Nero intimated to Charley that Tim might be able to try out for five minor league teams in Japan. We knew Tim had had enough of the minor leagues for the rest of his life. Meanwhile, I worried every day that he would go ahead and enlist in the Army.

Five days before my fiftieth birthday in July, Charley had a surprise party for me at a restaurant on Federal Hill in the Italian section of Providence. He had planned the dinner party for months with the help of his former secretary at Fleet. I believed that I was attending a dinner party celebrating the anniversary of our neighbor's large company, and was in total shock when I walked in and saw sixty-five relatives and friends! Tim and Todd sent me a dozen yellow roses. A lawyer friend of ours was the MC and had arranged a senior citizen's transit pass, an AARP newspaper subscription, and an application at a senior citizen's home. Those were the least offensive of the presentations. The next day we departed for our last trip to see Todd play that season.

Fort Lauderdale in July was a constant 86° to 90°, day and night. Todd did not keep track of the calendar, since his life consisted of simply getting up every day to go to a gym (a new routine), then to the ball field. When told by teammate Marty Durkin that we were in the stands, Todd said, "No way! They're not coming down till the 15th."

"Today is the 15ᵗʰ, Todd!" Perhaps he was in never-never land because he had the night off, with an opposing lefty pitching.

The team was an entirely different one from the one we'd seen in May. After the All-Star break, ten rookies who had signed in the '93 draft replaced those in Fort Lauderdale who had been released, sent down to Utica, or up to New Britain. The night we arrived, Lou Merloni was playing short. He had been a college rival, playing for Providence College, while Todd played for Brown. Lou played well, going 2-for-4 with a .260 average, and making every play in the field. He still chomped on his gold chains while he stood in the batter's box.

Todd came in to pinch hit in the bottom of the ninth and drilled a ball 375 feet to right center, which the right fielder caught at full speed over his left shoulder. The Sox eventually lost 8-5.

Just as before, we sat with Harry Durkin. His son Marty had played in only five games out of nineteen, since the rookies were brought up. Marty was a switch-hitter, with four years of experience. He had trouble fielding at third base. We had so many rookies playing for our team that the scouts in attendance at each game were going crazy. The scouts felt the Sox were making a mockery of the league, since almost every organization except the Sox had their topmost "A" players in this league, while we had our rookies. However, our rookies were doing the job. The Ft. Lauderdale Sox were 5-1 in their last seven home games.

At dinner at 10:30 p.m. after the game, Todd seemed totally relaxed and more confident than we'd ever seen him as a pro. He explained that when Lou Merloni had first joined the team, Todd had begun to DH and had sat out several games. Finally, he went in to talk to Manager Hale. He told Hale that he wanted 400 at-bats and 75 games out of the season. It was highly unusual for Todd to speak up, as he usually took what was dished out to him. Hale told him he shouldn't worry, because he'd be playing the next fourteen straight games and the organization considered him a promising prospect.

"If I bat .250 by the end of the season and keep my errors under twenty, I should have a shot at being on the 'AA' team next year," he told us. This new-found confidence sounded like a recording of what Tim had been telling him. Wherever it came from, I welcomed it!

Todd appeared anxious to return to Brown in September. His tuition bill had arrived. He had yet to select courses, which necessitated a call to the registrar's office. He'd already told his agent to inform the Sox that if he were invited again to Instructional Camp, he would decline. I seconded this decision, since those invited for instruction in the fall were mostly rookies.

Todd returned to shortstop in the field, while Merloni played third. Lou had a tough game against the Mets, but Todd could have helped him by calling him off a pop foul and taking it himself. Instead, Lou called for it and dropped it. There was definitely still tension between the two players, because they had competed against each other for three years in college. Despite John Graham's 4-for-4 night (U Mass-Dartmouth), and Todd's double to the 400-foot mark in center field, the Sox lost 5-4. It was great to see a few more fans showing up — there were 1,000 at that game—and it was great to see Todd so confident, hitting first pitches and telling the rookies where to position themselves. Now he was ready to progress.

Charley considered it a fun night just to be in any ballpark, especially if one of our boys were playing. That wasn't always true for me. The following night a transformer twice short-circuited all the lights, and numerous pitchers gave up hit after hit for our team. It was such a bad night that at one point the taped music started playing right in the middle of a pitch to the batter. Nevertheless, 1,800 fans stayed for the duration. I thought about all the movies I wanted to see in the theaters!

Todd was now one of six remaining veterans on the Fort Lauderdale team. He was clearly the most consistent player, and we hoped if he kept his average around .250, he would move up a level before the season ended.

Over the course of the next week, we witnessed three 10-inning games by the Fort Lauderdale team. Todd looked abominable at bat and superb in the field, then reversed himself and slammed the ball. At that point in early August, he had 23 RBI's, 77 hits, 2 home runs, 325 at-bats, 85 games played. He was striking out less than one in ten times at bat, which was fantastic, as well as providing his usual reliable defense.

Tim sent us his new baseball cards, one in a catcher's crouch and one in a first baseman's stance. They came out really well, as did Todd's, and I carried them with me at all times. People I didn't know asked me for them when they discovered I had sons playing pro ball. I usually found a way to weave that fact into my conversations or left my wallet open when I paid for items. The boys' photo together on the same field in Elmira flashed through the open insert.

Tim sounded different on the phone — more relaxed about his future. Charley and I were urging him to take time to enjoy himself before making any serious decisions. He was enjoying his tenure as a ballplayer actually participating on the field, since catcher Jeff Martin's departure for "AA." We suspected he might have decided to give it another season, since he no longer mentioned the Army. When he missed the team bus to Prince William, Maryland, I wondered if he had met a girl. He had to drive himself up there from Lynchburg, with a fine imposed. He also left his address book, with his entire accumulation of addresses and phone numbers, in the Lynchburg post office. It sat there until he returned from the road trip. He announced his intention to stay in Lynchburg an extra week after the season ended, "to hang out with some of the guys." Eventually he casually mentioned he was dating someone there who had a young daughter. I refused to begin worrying about Tim's becoming the dad for a ready-made family. Although he was outstanding with young children, particularly his cousins, he had enough other issues to deal with first!

Todd's team seldom stayed overnight if the bus ride were two hours or less, even if his team were playing the same team on the road for two consecutive nights. Todd often got home in Ft. Lauderdale around midnight or later. It was a much more grueling schedule than Tim's in Lynchburg,

Tim and Todd, Elmira, N.Y., 1992.

where road trips were usually four days because of the greater distances.

On this trip to Ft. Lauderdale, I finally learned from Harry Durkin why the Sox taught each new player to swing down, instead of on an even plane. The theory goes that unless you're a pure power hitter, stats prove you will fly out more times than anything else by hitting with a level swing. By swinging down on the ball, the hits will fall through the holes in the infield. But stats can prove anything you want them to.

Todd, being very critical of everything, particularly when it related to his mother, noticed I was getting a little pot belly. Charley and I attempted to walk three miles every morning in the heat (or play golf), and swim laps every afternoon, before going to the ball park in Ft. Lauderdale. Dinners at 10:30 p.m. and pretzels, peanuts, subs, or pizza before/during/after ballgames for twelve days were not conducive to losing weight. I knew I could lose some of it when I ran around the tennis court back in Massachusetts.

Our last game in Fort Lauderdale that August was at 11 a.m., in front of 2,000 campers. After sitting behind them for three hours in 95° heat, watching food fights, asking them to sit down instead of running up and down the aisles, getting insulted by having them tell Charley his pipe was bothering them (in a smoking area) or getting reported for smoking to an attendant (whom we knew well by this time), I had a blasting headache. In addition, I was exhausted. I vowed never to attend another day game in the minor leagues.

We celebrated Todd's birthday a couple of weeks early, and said our goodbyes to some of Todd's teammates back at the Durkin house. The Durkins' hospitality and baseball stories were inexhaustible. The thing that puzzled all of us most was the apparent scrimping by the Sox. The Lauderdale team still had not been sent a second catcher since Delgado went up to "AA," so Assistant Coach Luis Dorante, a former catcher, doubled as player-coach. The team had no permanent pitching coach. Scouts had reported to Harry Durkin that when infield practice was taken, the players came onto the field in plain white shirts without a name or number. The scouts felt the Sox were thumbing their noses at them, indicating, "You figure out who the kids are."

14

Promises Kept, Promises Broken

In August, we drove twelve hours once again from Westport, Mass., to Lynchburg, Va., to bolster Tim's spirits.

He had caught the previous eight nights straight, but wasn't in the lineup when we arrived. Jeff Martin, just back from his stint in Pawtucket, was catching, while Walt McKeel was nursing a displaced vertebra. Jeff had collected a lot of confidence among the "AAA" players, although he'd gotten very little playing time. He presented Bill Selby and Randy Brown with boxes of bats the "big guys" didn't want, but nothing for Tim. We wondered whether we'd see Tim play during the week we were visiting, since he was now the third catcher again. The Lynchburg team had lost every away game during the month of July, putting them in the basement of their division.

While we were awaiting the players after the game, I approached Stephanie Martin, Jeff's wife, who stood just ten feet from us. After she and Jeff had arrived in Pawtucket, where we'd offered to pick them up at the airport and install them in our primary residence for as long as they needed, we'd never heard from them - not once after their plane landed. "Did you get the message I left at your motel in Pawtucket?" I asked her.

"Jeff got it. Don't worry! The Pawtucket organization treated us royally and we were able to stay in the Comfort Inn with a car for as long as he was assigned there. We got to see a lot around the area - Newport and Fenway and Faneuil Hall in Boston. We went to Horseneck Beach, but it had the red tide one day and was disgusting."

"Well, I'm glad you got around so much. We wanted to take you to Brown, where Todd goes, and the Emerald Mall, in case you needed anything."

"You mean Emerald Square? Oh, we got there. Jeff might be headed back up there, because they told him if Pawtucket makes the playoffs, he'd be back. But we're glad Tim got a chance to play down here."

"Yes, so are we." Never a "thank you" from the young couple!

Tim no longer discussed government jobs or the Army or baseball, just that he needed a break after the season was over. Charley and I foresaw an ideal solution for him - entering a graduate program in January, 1994, if he left baseball. But we never mentioned it to him.

On August 3, 1993, we watched an exciting game with Tim at catch. Apparently Joel Bennett, the starting pitcher, had written a note to Manager Meleski, requesting Tim as his permanent catcher. Joel had the most strikeouts in the league (177), and didn't want Martin or McKeel behind the plate. McKeel had been given the okay to start within a few days, his cracked vertebrae having healed.

True to form, Bennett struck out nine Blue Rocks before leaving in the eighth inning with the game tied at 1-1. Bill Selby, Tim's apartment-mate, had hit a home run in the first. Tim went 0-for-3, but was hitting deep fly balls. He blocked every ball behind the plate and threw out their only runner trying to steal. In the tenth, reliever Joe Hudson pitched "tough" with two men on, striking out their remaining batters.

In the bottom of the tenth, Tim led off at the plate with a sharp line drive single to the opposite field. I was jumping up and down in my seat and screaming my head off! Bob Juday went in to run for him, was bunted over by George Scott, and scored on Steve Rodrigues' hit to win the game. Tim had saved the day!!Over lunch the following day, Tim filled us in on how disrespectful the managers and coaches were of their players in Lynchburg. Pitching coach Bibby gave no instruction to pitchers who weren't on the "upward" track, and actually put up with backtalk from these pitchers. The manager did not make players aware of his plans for them unless they asked. This lack of communication existed because those at the top of the Sox organization treated even their most highly paid major-league stars as adversaries. Such personnel policies started in Boston and trickled down, with the exception of Ken Macha, the highly respected, communicative, Trenton "AA" manager hired in 1995 and promoted to "AAA" in Pawtucket in 1997. Macha became the Oakland A's Manager from 2002 – 2005. Since most of the coaches and managers had played minor league ball, they learned to be in adversarial positions early on. Furthermore, they did not want to jeopardize their status with the head office by sticking their necks out for kids who did not later prove to be major league material. The cycle could not be broken unless the manager had the guts to treat his players with respect. If the players were respected, they in turn respected the manager. Winning teams usually resulted. For managers, this often meant bucking the Red Sox staff in Boston.

Only George Scott and Tim were left without a position. Nothing had changed since June. The following night, even George was in the starting lineup in center field. Infielder Bob Juday, with another two hits, had claimed left field. Tim and second catcher Walt McKeel remained on the bench.

Mark, Chris, Jeff, and Scott Knapke from Coldwater, Ohio, arrived in time for that game in early August. They'd driven ten hours to visit Tim for the weekend in Lynchburg.

The Knapkes had housed Tim during his summer in the Great Lakes League, and were like a second family to him. Mark, the dad, had come down with the flu the day before. By the time we finished dinner with Tim after the game, Mark could hardly hold his head off the table. Fortunately, it rained the next morning and part of the afternoon, so everybody slept. Mark, it turned out, would return to Ohio with pneumonia.

Relaxing around the pool at the motel after the clouds disappeared, I had an interesting conversation with Chris Knapke and Pam Selby. Since we collectively had six sons and one daughter, we discussed the changing mother-son relationship as the boys matured into men.

Pam Selby felt that boys, unlike girls, often look to their mothers for guidance in the romance department. Pam was much more actively involved in the day-to-day details of Bill's life than we were in Tim and Todd's. Like all of us, she hoped Bill would eventually settle down with a girl totally devoted to him who'd be a model of "old fashioned values." This included church participation for the Selbys, since Bill was one of five players who kneeled to pray in a huddle on the field prior to every game. Tim felt they had a perfect right to worship as they wished, but the ball field was not an appropriate place for such a gathering.

"Let's face it," Charley chimed in, "no mom ever finds a girlfriend/wife perfect for her son!" There may have been some truth to that, but I didn't want any friend of Tim or Todd's to ever feel uncomfortable in our presence.

Pam also took Bill's baseball triumphs and defeats personally. As a parent, it was hard not to, knowing that careers were at stake. Later, we learned that one series of games or even one season did not make or break a player.

During our final game in Lynchburg, with our team trailing in the ninth inning and no outs, Bill Selby came up to bat. He hit into a double play. One out later, the game ended. We never saw Pam Selby again. She'd retreated to the pickup to await Bill, who'd gone one-for-sixteen during our visit and who, his parents felt, was destined for the same Lynchburg team the following year. Their son's mood later in the condo, Tim said, reflected the gloom of his parents. The pressure that parents unwittingly exert on their children can be enormous.

I felt betrayed by an ally and knew I would never have treated other parents rudely because of a son's performance on the field. Tim had not played in that game at all, and yet Bill had played the entire game. Our final words for Tim as we departed were, "Just enjoy this last month and store up the memories."

Shortly after our arrival back in Westport, we got calls from both boys within half an hour of each other. Tim had caught Joel Bennett that night, collecting a double to drive in the team's only runs. He was named "Player of the Game."

Manager Meleski stated publicly in the newspaper that he was intent on putting an end to players' striking out in crucial situations with men on base. Tim confronted Meleski to ask him about his constant criticisms in the press and his lack of praise for team members. Meleski told Tim that he would only be catching Bennett, while others would be filling in at first base, including Selby, who'd never played there before (Tim had played first base in college, as well as catch). Tim retorted, "I don't even feel like a member of the team any more, and any threats about writing bad monthly reports to the management in Boston don't mean anything to me! I've worked harder than most of these guys, and played the least."

The next call from Tim revealed that Meleski had acted upon Tim's suggestion to let him play first base. In a game as first baseman, Tim had gone 2-for-4 at bat. Out of his mouth came the newly-expressed thought, "Even if the Sox don't want me, maybe someone else will. All I need is exposure." The roller coaster ride was in full swing!

It was another five games before Tim took the field again. During the one game that Tim caught, Charley's brother Michael and his family were able to watch him in Wilmington, Delaware. They were vacationing in the area, and sat through an hour-and-a-half rain delay. Tim was really pleased to spend some time afterward with family.

Todd had not called in a week, so we attempted to reach him. He had obviously taken off for parts unknown. Tim reported that Todd had gone 7-for-9 at bat in the early part of the week, before getting sick again and having a dry spell for four succeeding days. On August 22, 1993, his stats were exactly as they had been when we had left Florida three weeks previously.

He finally reported in after hitting his third home run on August 27th, and going 3-for-5 the previous night. Todd had a pattern of not contacting us unless things were going really well or really badly. His average was in the .240's and his next hit would be his 100th that season. He'd added only one error in another week, finishing the season with only eighteen.

On August 31, 1993, his lease ran out for the apartment in Coral Springs, so he and his remaining roommate, Derek Vinyard, asked to live in our condo for the last five days of their season. They made arrangements with our neighbors to pick up the key after they returned from their road trip. We learned that some of Todd's teammates had been invited to attend instructional camp in the fall, while Todd planned to return to Brown. Meanwhile, Bryan Brown, Todd's former apartment-mate who was now on the "AA" New Britain roster, had been included among minor league players to conduct clinics in the Cricket Oval in London. Major League Baseball was trying to promote professional baseball in Europe. Unbelievably, catcher Jeff Martin, still batting .165 in Lynchburg, was also part of the roster of travelers. Obviously the Sox management knew something we didn't. In Westport, applications began to arrive at our house for Tim's positions overseas.

Tim finished the season with a whimper, Todd with a bang. Todd's final batting average was .250, and he was voted "Best Defensive Shortstop in the League" by the Florida State League Managers. He had had enough of the heat, and had no desire to return to Florida for instruction until spring training.

After Tim's last home game, he had not ascertained exactly where he'd be staying. His apartment lease had run out, and he'd locked all of his possessions in the car at the ball field during the team's last road trip. A security guard patrolled the parking lot. During his exit interview with Manager Meleski at the end of the season, he recounted his disgust at the manager's treatment of him, as well as what he considered the most humiliating episode he'd ever endured from Meleski. During one game only he and an outfielder were left on the bench because of a rash of team injuries. The attendance was at its capacity 7,000, and the game was being televised. When Bob Juday got spiked running the bases, Melski told Tim to stretch and warm up to take the field at third base, replacing Juday. When the team took the field, Tim grabbed his glove and headed toward third base. He was called back to the dugout and the remaining outfielder took the position. Tim controlled himself so that he could walk straight through the dugout into the clubhouse, where he changed clothes and immediately drove away from the field.

In his meeting with Meleski, the manager told Tim, "I have submitted outstanding reports about you. I couldn't have gotten harder work from anyone, even though you weren't playing. Of course, you have to work on your throwing arm and your hitting, but over the last month you have been my best-performing catcher."

"If I've been your best-performing catcher this month, why haven't I played?"

"You know it's out of my control. I don't call the shots for the lineup. Boston does. But you never stopped working hard all season and seldom complained."

The last night of the season, Bennett pitched. After Bennett's request to use Tim exclusively behind the plate and the glowing report from Meleski the night before, Tim sat on the bench while Jeff Martin caught. Halfway through the game, Tim asked Doug Hecker if he could go in for him at first base. Hecker knew Tim had been taking ground balls in the infield, and was glad not to jeopardize his end-of-season stats. So Tim took the field at first while Meleski notified the umps of the change.

Tim had called his agent, Nero, several times within the last weeks of the season, without getting any response. He had hoped to get enough exposure so that Nero would press the Sox for his release, and another team could pick him up. This was not going to happen. Tim had gotten little exposure, and much test of character. His batting average remained stuck around .220. He had plans to take further tests for Army officer's school, as well as to attend a tracking/survival school in New Jersey. "Baseball is not do-or-die for him," Bill Selby was quoted as saying. "He can almost take any direction he wants." [18]

"Baseball is more of what I enjoy than it is what I am," Tim responded.

Todd arrived back at our house in Rhode Island from Ft. Lauderdale at 3:30 a.m. on the morning of September 7, 1993, thirty hours after he'd departed in his restored Chevy Cavalier. He slept for five hours in his own bed, showered, and made it to Brown in time for his first classes of the semester. No accidents, no breakdowns, no speeding tickets. Charley and I hadn't slept for two nights, worrying.

Over a relaxed dinner after his first day of classes, Todd said he felt good about his accomplishments that season, but was afraid to think in terms of "AA" the following year. He said Hale, his manager, had been in a tough spot with so many leaving the team (to move upward) and being cut, as well as all the draftees coming on board. The scuttlebutt in Ft. Lauderdale was that the Lynchburg, Va., team in general had performed poorly, and there would be only a few of those team members moving up a level the following year.

What bothered Todd the most at that moment was feeling so awkward at Brown. "I feel old," he commented, "without my own classmates there."

He had selected four courses, two of which were senior seminars in urban studies. One of the seminars demanded a commitment to working part-time in a city planning office. His Sox teammates were getting married, taking several months off, picking up part-time jobs, or attending Instructional Camp. "I don't plan to pick up a baseball until winter workouts with the (Brown) team," he said.

No word from Tim until after he'd taken the Army officer candidate's exam. He scored 110 out of 120, and had to submit five references, as well as an essay. Although he had scored extremely well, as he had on the Monterey Language School exam, the recruiter told him his grade-point-average at Dartmouth was going to be a detriment (around 3.0). The appointment he had received to West Point prior to his attending Dartmouth was meaningless.

We watched the Sox play on TV with Todd. I commented on Greenwell's level swing that produced a home run and made the observation that Todd's swing used to be like Greenwell's, an even extension of his arms, but was now a downward chopping motion.

"In the first place, you don't know what you're talking about, because Yaz and Braun both told me I had a perfectly level swing. Secondly, if I ever swung in college with my wrists perfectly level, I didn't deserve to play pro ball - I wouldn't have hit a thing! What they changed were my hands, not my swing. The swing starts high, but then levels off."

What do mothers know?

On October 4, 1993, Todd returned home from a week in London. Todd had been asked to replace the New Britain "AA" shortstop on the trip, who sustained an injury prior to departure. It took Todd all of one hour to get our permission and then to call Brown to arrange permission from his professors.

At the same time, Charley and I were in Italy on a long-awaited wandering. All of us had torrential rains across the continent, including flooding and bridge washouts in Italy. However, the rains didn't dampen any of our spirits, and Todd did lots of unanticipated sightseeing. In addition, he was paid $950! The minor leaguers only got to play one game in the Cricket Oval, and all the clinics were canceled due to inclement weather. The Mets had superior pitching and bombed the Sox recruits in the one game they played. Todd was lead-off hitter for Pawtucket "AAA" Manager Bud Bailey. Although he never got a hit, he made good contact, and made a lot of plays in the field without an error. Since he was one of a few "A" players invited to participate, we asked him about the caliber of the "AA" and "AAA" players.

"Well, some of our guys played well, and the pitching at higher levels is definitely more refined. They can pick their spots. But the infielders didn't seem superior. In fact, our first and third basemen cost us runs on errors. Our 'AAA' catcher was nearly thirty years old, and Jeff (Martin) only played a short time. Bryan Brown only played a little in the outfield. The only impressive players were the pitchers."

Was this Todd talking?? What a difference in attitude a year made!

Tim had talked to his buddy Walt McKeel, catching down at the Sox instructional camp in Florida. Some of the coaches had returned from the London trip to instructional camp, so Walt had scuttlebutt to report to Tim. Apparently all that management had wanted from Todd the prior season was durability over the long 120 games. They weren't looking for a particular batting average at that stage of his development, or even a cap on his errors. Rather, they were looking for consistency over the four months, and, according to the reports Walt had heard, Todd had performed beyond expectations. It was inconsistency over the long season that would plague Todd later.

When I asked Tim what Walt had heard about Tim, he replied, "Are you kidding? Not a word! I wouldn't be surprised if Jeff Martin skips to 'AAA' next spring."

"Would you go back to Lynchburg with Meleski next spring?" I asked Tim.

"Unless a better rookie pushed me back to Ft. Lauderdale." We assumed Walt McKeel had had a great influence in persuading Tim to return to baseball.In mid-October, with my parents visiting for the weekend (we celebrated Charley's and my father's birthdays because they were one day apart), we attended the Brown University Parents' Weekend baseball reception. The only familiar faces were the junior and senior players and their parents. All the Almons were there - Coach Bill with his family; his father; his brother, all of whom collectively coached the Brown team. Todd circulated among upperclassmen and some of the newer players.

The media reported in late October that the Sox management fired three coaches from their '93 major league staff: Pitching Coach Rick Gale; Third-base Coach Rick Burleson; and First-base Coach Al Bumbry. The pitching staff had finished second in the American League in earned-run average, so Gale's firing was a surprise. Butch Hobson, manager in Boston, claimed he knew nothing of the firings beforehand. The minor league managers would not communicate with their players if the Boston management didn't even communicate with its manager at the major league level.

Underground Baseball published the article "Parents of Summer" in its October 3, 1993, issue. It featured both Tim and Todd's pictures. Tim was disappointed that it mentioned how little he played last season, but there were only three paragraphs about the Careys. They were positive paragraphs, emphasizing Charley's and my role as cheerleaders and advocates of a balanced lifestyle. The Selbys were quoted at length, surprising us by stating that they wouldn't mind if Bill went back to Lynchburg the following year, instead of moving up, to give him time to develop.

That off-season, Tim coached a baseball camp in Rhode Island during the day. He got his bartending license and began working at a banquet facility/restaurant in Massachusetts at night. The owner of the place trusted Tim, and often called on him to close up at 1 am. After counting the cash and checking on the inventory in three ballrooms, Tim often sloshed into our house in his beer-filled sneakers and flung himself on his bed without undressing.In late December, 1993, agent Alan Nero made a date to take both Tim and Todd to dinner. On the appointed night, Nero sent a rep from his office, Scott Pacino, instead. Alan was pursuing a contract with a Providence College player who'd just signed with the Orioles. Tim and Todd were astounded that Pacino didn't know their names, nor did he have any background information on either of them. Both had to recount their short histories with the Sox. Nero's contract for the upcoming year would be arriving within the month.

Right after the New Year, Charley and I began driving to Florida. After considering many possible job offers for nine months, he had decided to set up an investment banking subsidiary as part of a law firm in Fort Lauderdale. We planned to make Florida our permanent residence by putting our Rhode Island house on the market that spring, and would move from our small "get-away" condo to a larger unit in Delray Beach. We retained our home in Westport, Massachusetts, to escape the Florida heat in the summer. The boys would not begin driving down until March 4th, stopping with us before reporting to spring training on March 8th in Ft. Myers, on the west coast of Florida.

By the end of January, their one-year contracts had arrived from the Sox. Tim's salary had increased per month from $950 to $1,050; Todd's had increased per month from $1,100 to $1,200. The contracts were only binding for the months the

boys were actively playing baseball. According to agent Nero, they had no re-
course to ask for more. Our advice to the boys was, "Make a copy, sign it, and
send it in." Tim was obviously disappointed, as he had started at $850/month two
and one-half years previously.

Both Tim and Todd were working at Dave Stenhouse's baseball camp (former
Brown University coach) in Warwick. They kept in shape each day with neighbor
Tim Smith (Sox "AA" pitcher), new Sox major league Pitching Coach Roarke, Sox
major league pitcher Ken Ryan, and other "AAA" players from various teams.

The staff at the baseball camp apparently knew that our Tim had contemplated
leaving baseball for Army officer's school. They tried to convince him to stick
with baseball, despite past humiliations. We all believed the processing of his
application for Army officer's school would be completed by the middle of March.
From a baseball field to the desert.

In early February, 1994, Lou Gorman was made president of the Sox organization. He had been the general manager. At that time, Dan Duquette of the Montreal
Expos was named GM. With his track record in Montreal over a short period of
time, he provided hope that the "ole boy" style of management promoted by the
Yawkeys and Haywood Sullivan would be replaced by more effective and personal communication skills. In short, that the Red Sox would be managed more like
a business. Within a couple of years, we would regret wishing for such cut-throat,
impersonal techniques.

The boys began to receive calls from other agents while in Rhode Island in mid-
February. Norm Peters, an agent in Worcester, Massachusetts, had hired Dartmouth
grad and Pirates' minor leaguer Mark Johnson as a paralegal in his office. Mark had
suggested to Norm that Tim and Todd weren't pleased with their agent. Norm was
active in real estate and banking in Worcester. Many agents pleaded their cases to
Tim and Todd during spring training in order to get them to sign contracts. They
provided welcome free dinners.

Nero did report back to Tim and Todd in February regarding his meetings with
Player Development Director Kenney. Kenney's report on Tim was simply that
the management had never expected McKeel to remain in Lynchburg for the entire
previous season, but injuries necessitated it. Therefore, a logjam had built up and
Tim didn't get the playing time they'd anticipated. So they couldn't predict where
Tim would be next season, and Nero didn't press for more.

Kenney's report on Todd, by contrast, was glowing: "He's a prospect with
major league potential, provided he has a good spring training." Spring training, I
had already discovered, never really changed where a player was assigned after
he'd been "penciled in" by management in the late fall. The party-line was always
the same: "Players control their fate by their performance." But if an organization
had paid many hundreds of thousands for a player, it would certainly give him

**Todd signs autographs
in Florida.**

more playing time and promote him faster than players bought in the bargain basement! Tim and Todd finally spent two and a-half hours with Nero. He never produced his contract for the upcoming year. Instead, the boys conducted a civilized gripe session. "All you need is some power hitting," Nero repeated to Todd from the Boston office. Nero explained that Player Development Director Kenney predicted that Todd might jump from whatever assignment he received this season to the 40-man major league roster the following season. Management compiled this roster in the spring to protect its younger players so no other teams could steal them. Only 25 could remain on the roster for actual major league games.

To Nero, Tim outlined his frustrations of the previous season, as well as the fact that Nero wasn't speaking up for them with management. Both boys had expected baseball equipment through Nero from various sporting goods companies. Nothing ever appeared, with the exception of gloves. Tim told the agent, "I'm not going to deal with your representatives any more, because they don't know who we are. I'm only going to deal with you, Al, and if I can't reach you, I'm going to keep calling and calling."

Nero recognized their legitimate complaints, saying he had spread himself too thin because of contacts with the Japanese leagues. "The White Sox are starting an exchange program with Japanese players. If the Red Sox don't play you, Tim, we could ask for a release, and I could promote you with White Sox management so you might go overseas."

"That would be ideal," Tim responded. "I'd even go to Taiwan, where it's easier to make the teams. Let's see what happens after spring training. With my background in Asian Studies, I'd love it."

"Well, I believe you'd have been the best-hitting catcher on the team in Lynchburg last season if you'd played. I still intend to talk to Kenney again about both of you in the next couple of days. You should both go in to his office during spring training and introduce yourselves."

Promises! Promises! Nero's new interest in Tim and Todd was an obvious reaction to the news that Todd might be on the 40-man roster within a couple of years. And Tim would be a good contact for Nero to access Asian players as clients, if Tim went overseas.

15

An End
and a Beginning

On March 4, 1994, we saw our first major league game during spring training '94. We wanted to just sit and relax! The Braves played the Red Sox just 40 minutes away from us, in West Palm Beach, Fla. It was about 85 degrees without wind, and the game was a sell-out with 10,000 people. Despite having gotten our tickets several weeks earlier, we sat in the front row of the bleachers. That meant that for the first one-and-a-half innings, a parade of people marched directly in front of us to their seats. "Please move quickly!" we told the latecomers. Just as we started to get really testy, the stream thinned out. Two innings later, the procession started back past us for dogs and cold drinks.

A new face appeared at short, alternating with Valentin. His name was Richardson, and Duquette had just signed him. This pattern would repeat itself over and over in upcoming years, often with two backup players at every infield position at every level of the Sox. It was survival of the fittest! The major leaguers split into two squads during exhibition games, so two additional shortstops would play that same night in Ft. Myers against Boston College.

Tim appeared at our condo in Florida one day after Todd, having also driven his car down from Rhode Island. He had passed his black belt test in karate before departing. He had picked up Walt McKeel in North Carolina on the way down, so all three stayed with us before going over to Ft. Myers. Both Tim and Walt were nervous about being released by the Sox after spring training.

Once settled at the Days Inn over there, Tim called. He and virtually the entire Lynchburg team had been working out on the "AA" field, with the exception of Walt and Jeff Martin, who were catching with the "AAA" squad. Todd was disappointed because he was with the "A" Lynchburg squad. One hundred ninety players had reported to spring training for six squads, including the major leaguers. Players were being cut daily. Sixty new lockers now graced the minor league clubhouse, but by mid-March, the total number of minor leaguers was still at one hundred and thirty.

We waited until March 17th before driving over to watch minor league work-outs. By 1 p.m. when we arrived, the fields at the complex were empty. Todd had given us our marching orders: "Do not come around to our rooms at the Days Inn. The spaceshot working at the front desk will ring us for you." Who'd want to walk in on the mess, anyway?

We checked into the Sheraton Harbor Place in Ft. Myers, and turned around to see Manager Mark Meleski behind us. Charley and I introduced ourselves. "Ski" said he was happy to be working with Todd, and the main thing was that Todd play every day. He did not mention Tim. We figured Tim would move on and be better off.

Over dinner, Todd said, "I try to ignore him as much as possible, knowing how he told Tim one thing and did something else. He tried not to take any responsibility for whatever happened. But he did mention Tim to me, and was genuinely complimentary. He said the last month of the season, Tim was his best catcher, and neither Martin nor Walt (McKeel) deserved to be anywhere but back in Lynchburg this year. That doesn't explain why Tim didn't play the last month."

Tim told us, "I really hope I can stay with this New Britain ('AA') team. The core of the team is all of us from Lynchburg, but there are some guys from last year's New Britain team, too. Everyone gets along great. The whole coaching staff deserves respect and doesn't pull any punches, even with the bonus babies. Manager Pankovits has spent a lot of extra time with me at first and third, hitting me grounders. I can always ask Todd if I have any questions.

"Right now there are four catchers, but DelGado's one of them and his arm is hurt. I'm hitting well, but my arm isn't sharp. Yesterday, Juday, Selby, and I did our drills for forty-five minutes, waiting for Scott Bethea to finish in the batter's box. He broke his bat, and asked to take mine, which I gave him. Then we helped him pick up all the balls so we could get our turn. Finally he said, 'Just let me have twenty more pitches.'

"When he said that, I threw my bat into the cage and yelled 'Bethea, I don't care if you did play a national championship. We've waited patiently and now it's our turn!' At that, Manager Pankovits came striding over and I thought I was in deep shit. Instead, he yelled at Bethea to get the hell out of the cage and let somebody else have a turn."

Todd had been quiet during most of the dinner. Finally, he said that first-round pick Trot Nixon (center field) was on his team and when Nixon batted, Yastrzemski, Braun, and the Sox management usually watched. Pitching Coach Bibby loved the audiences so he could ham it up. In practice one day, Bibby said to Nixon, "I'm going to throw so hard at you, I'm going to have you peeing in your pants." If you got a hit off Bibby in batting practice, he might throw the next one 90 mph past you. He could hold seven balls in one hand at the same time. Of course, if he didn't think a pitcher was on the fast track, Bibby would ignore him, without instruction. If the same pitcher had a good game, Bibby would be quoted in the paper as having "worked with that fellow a lot lately." Todd followed Nixon in the batting order.

The boys had already seen many old friends who came to visit during spring training: Coach Barnard (Tim's first Assistant Coach at Dartmouth); Harold Alfond (Charley's benefactor at Colby, philanthropist at Colby and the U. of Maine, owner of Dexter Shoe Company, and part-owner of the Red Sox who was not awarded the Tampa franchise); Dartmouth and Brown friends; as well as Tim Smith's parents from Cumberland. Tim Smith was pitching with the "AAA" squad. The different levels of squads alternated home and away games, so it was almost impossible to get the Cumberland kids together during spring training. The fact that there were three playing pro ball from one small Rhode Island town was unbelievable. The boys had all been teammates on the American Legion squad, and their success seemed a tribute to "Mac" Wright's coaching.   The best baseball story of the evening was about "Whitey" Crimmins, who'd been released the previous year as a catcher in Utica, but was invited back to spring training in '94. On the first night in camp, he and another catcher went to one of the clubs that was off-limits to minor leaguers (Sox rule). He proceeded to get wasted. The second catcher refused to drive back to the Days Inn with Crimmins behind the wheel, so Whitey was on his own. At 3 a.m., the shrill phone awakened their third roommate.

"Where are you?"

"I'm in jail, and I have to pay a $500 fine. Can you guys raise some money?"

"Christ! Walt's not back yet, and I thought you guys were together. What the hell did you do?"

"I got caught speeding."

"Speeding, my ass! Not for $500!"

Turns out ole Whitey decided to pull a few spin-outs in the police parking lot; and then drag-raced two police cars to the end of that parking lot. When the cop threw Whitey's keys on the hood of his pick-up and the keys scratched its mirror-like surface, Whitey punched out the cop. Without bail, Whitey spent a couple of nights in prison with a roomie 6'6". Finally, the Sox put up the money and sent John's parents a release form to sign. They figured Whitey had gotten his paycheck. The backbreaker was that Whitey hadn't shown up for court hearings in three other states. Sadly, the Sox offered no program at this point for their young players who had alcohol, drug, or steroid abuse problems. Charley and I were always guessing about who used steroids. A huge increase in body size from the previous season was usually a clue.

At that point in the boys' careers, everyday stuff like errors and strikeouts seemed to matter only when I was actually sitting at a game. The best words of wisdom were offered by Tim Smith, who said, "You just have to do your job and can't worry about who's going to move up or down around you." Charley and I believed that Todd was equal to the task of some day making the big leagues. The '94 media guide listed him as having the best defensive average of any shortstop in the '93 Florida State League. We believed his hitting would improve with experience. "At a cookout for all the teams," Tim Smith told us later, "even our coaches were afraid to approach GM Duquette. Seems he has his own little circle of honchos, and everyone else is outside the clique." Although he was perfectly serious, Tim usually made his comments with a dry humor. Like the story he told about playing his first year of junior varsity basketball at Cumberland High. Seems his insulated mesh uniform had rubbed all the skin off his nipples, and then he'd sat on the bench, where he'd frozen in his insulated shirt. When he re-entered the game, he ran down the court holding the shirt away from his hard, frozen nipples.

Both Tim and Todd had "T. Carey" on the back of their uniforms, which didn't help scouts or coaches. "That's typical of the Red Sox," Tim Smith's dad commented. "They have the worst communication problems in organized baseball. And it carries right up the ladder from their dealings with minor leaguers to the GM. If they were in any other business, they'd be out of business!" The Sox minor league complex had undergone a transformation since its inception in '93. Two of the five fields sported new aluminum bleachers on crushed stone, and wind screens around the home plate fences to shield batters from dust and wind. Still, the complex emanated a "strictly business" atmosphere to the fans, as if they were the last thing on the management's mind in its design. There still were only two portable johns on the concrete walkway through the center of the fields. The permanent toilets under the central tower were reserved for players and coaches. On each field, there was a roped area behind the Sox dugout for the golf carts belonging to Duquette, Kenney, Kasko, and owners, so they could watch games unimpeded. The fans could either sit on the aluminum bleachers in the hot sun (only a couple of saplings), or pull their lawn chairs onto crushed stone behind the home plate wind screen. At least grass had replaced the mud surrounding the walkway.

Back at the Sheraton Harbor Place, I shared an elevator with Jim Rice. I introduced myself and said I had two sons playing for the Sox, Tim and Todd Carey. Rice's face broke into a wide grin. "Oh, the Carey brothers! I've got them," he said.

With the boys that evening, Todd went berserk when he learned I'd spoken to Jim Rice. "You always have to stick your nose in, don't you? You have to be in the middle of everything. Why can't you just stand there and not say anything?"

Tim just laughed and said, "Rice won't forget, and we'll never hear the end of it."

I concluded that my role was simply to stick my head in the sand until this baseball saga had played itself out. I could rejoin the world when and if Tim and Todd graduated to the big leagues! As much as I might try, I would never understand the game in their eyes, because I had never played. They ridiculed the aqua golf slacks that I wore as being too flashy, my aviator sunglasses looked "goofy," and I was too loud at dinner, though no liquor was served! Minor leaguers (and their parents) were to speak only when spoken to, and were never to draw attention to themselves!

Todd had a new golf shirt on at dinner with the logo, "Gateway Country Club."

"Where did you get that shirt?" Charley asked him. "It's nice."

"Bryan Brown and I were invited to play golf with Aaron Sele right after practice and I didn't have any golf shirts with me. So I was forced to buy a $30 collared shirt to get out on the course."

"You'd better wear that shirt every chance you get," Charley told him.

"Yeah, well, the course was gorgeous, and cost about $60 a round, but we get in for almost nothing."

"Can we go with you some time?" Charley requested.

"You'll have to practice a whole lot first," Todd joked.

The boys described how major league Manager Butch Hobson had come to speak to the "AA" and "AAA" players in their minor league clubhouse. Hobson's every other word was a swear, and he kept thanking the teams for listening in his good-ole-boy 'Bama accent. Then he revealed that he had no direct control over roster positions, and in his estimation, anyone with a batting average around .200 did not deserve to be there. Hobson felt he had no authority. It seemed unbelievable that the major league manager struggled with the same helplessness the minor leaguers faced daily.

March 20, 1994, was another beautiful day in the high eighties at the minor league fields. Todd had the afternoon off, while Tim again caught the first five innings of the "AA" game and held the Pawtucket "AAA" team scoreless. Bob Juday's parents joined us, and confided Bob "would do anything not to have to play for Meleski again." The Pirates had released Bob's older brother the previous summer from "AA," and I asked how he'd adjusted. "He's finishing up his bachelor's degree at Michigan State and is assistant to the baseball coach there. The scouts have approached him about rejoining baseball. His wife told me about it and broke into tears. 'I can't go through that rejection again,' she said. 'We have already started our lives over once.'"

The players' wives who lived with their husbands spent most of the baseball season in limbo. They never knew if they would have to pack up and move to a different level (state) overnight. Many of them in the lower levels never accompanied husbands to the assigned destinations, preferring to stay in their hometowns with children or careers and make periodic visits.

The minor leaguers had had a bed check at the Days Inn the previous night around 12:30 a.m. The fine for being out after midnight the first time was $25; for second-timers it was $50; for the third offense it was $100. Meleski knocked on Bryan Brown and Todd's door, then the door next to them. He stood midway between the rooms in the hall, and when Bryan opened the door, no one was visible. Bryan slammed the door shut just as Meleski stepped in front of it. The manager thought Bryan had purposely slammed it in his face. Thankfully, Todd was in bed.

Catching Coach Geren had a worse experience at Tim's door. The former Yankee and Padre catcher had the misfortune of pounding on the door after a rookie had awakened Tim on the phone. When Coach Geren appeared at the door, Tim assumed that it was the rookie harassing him and Tim Smith again. "Now what the f*** do you want? Oh...Sorry, Coach, I thought you were the drunk that awakened us before."

The next morning, Geren apologized. "I didn't realize until some of the kids told me that I was making so much noise," he stated.

"That guy really knows his stuff," Tim said. "His only problem is that he's a rookie coach and is trying too hard to succeed. He'd keep us out on the field until 6 p.m. if he could."

Todd's Lynchburg "A" squad was on the road the following day, and Tim had the day off from catching. He was in the batting cage through the middle innings of the "AA" game, with Jim Rice throwing to him. As Tim had predicted, Rice didn't want to let it pass that I'd introduced myself. Thank goodness it wasn't Todd in the cage! He was more easily embarrassed. Rice yelled to Tim, "Did you give your mother my message?"

"No," Tim said quietly.

At that Rice yelled at him, "It's probably because she's your mother. If it was your sister or your girlfriend, you'd have told her!" He left the pitcher's mound and trotted toward me. "Don't worry! It was all good," he said.

"Tim told me not to talk to the coaches," I laughed. "It's against his rules." I got a couple of extra photos of him with Tim and walked away.

The domino effect started that day. The major league team had reassigned catcher Hatteberg to "AAA," so Walt McKeel was sent all the way down from "AAA" to the "A" Florida State team. Jeff Martin remained as backup catcher at "AAA." We hoped Walt got his career on track. Management wanted him to improve his hitting. Two years later, Walt would hit consistently over .300.

Tim's roommate in Lynchburg the previous summer, Bill Selby, had been sent back to his old team, Lynchburg. These changes occurred so frequently that there were always surprises whenever we arrived at the minor league complex. We still firmly believed that teams had been predetermined well before spring training. The

"AAA" squad still carried seventeen pitchers; Tim Smith was fighting for a position as one of its relievers. Yet even that late in spring training (March 21st), another pitcher signed on. Apparently Duquette had a grand scheme in mind, which consisted of "survival of the fittest." He had decided that one of his major objectives that season was to sign a bonafide major league right fielder, and within a week he got Murray from Montreal. He could have traded sixty minor leaguers for one Murray, which would have given the remaining minor leaguers more game time. Naturally, that's not how it worked.

Four days later we drove the three hours across Alligator Alley again. Todd sauntered over after pre-game practice. Alex DelGado, another "AAA" catcher, introduced himself. "How's your arm feeling?" Charley asked him.

"Pappas operate here," he said in broken English. He pointed at an eight-inch scar in the shape of a "v" on the inside of his elbow. "But I said before he cut - the pain here," and he pointed to the outside of his elbow joint. "Chips still floating. He do it again."

"How long has it been since the operation?" Charley queried.

"Four months. Injury from throwing too much."

The temperatures had been in the nineties or above all week, and I sat under one of the five scrawny, year-old trees for protection during Todd's game. It was too upsetting to think that management was going to cut sixty more kids of the 130 there, so I began reading a book.

Todd shared the left side of the infield with Lou Merloni, the Providence College shortstop. The two used to be rivals, but now the only time Lou gave Todd fits was when he hit dead center down the fairway with a three-iron, even off the tee. Merloni and Selby alternated at third. As fifth batter, Todd knocked a double out to the fence in his first at-bat.

The Texas Rangers eventually figured out our pitchers, and the game became tedious. Todd's team made basic mistakes: Todd awaiting the pick-off throw at second base from his pitcher, who was oblivious; a teammate attempting to bunt for a single, with two men already out.Back at the hotel, Todd's Ft. Lauderdale manager the previous year, DeMarlo Hale, and Pitching Coach Al Nipper stood at the elevator with us. This year, unlike previous years, each team had a pitching coach on staff. "I don't know Tim, but I know Todd was a class act, and Tim's coaches all say the same about him," DeMarlo said.

"Thanks!" I responded. "He sure enjoyed playing for you, and we know you gave him tremendous confidence last summer."

"I saw a great improvement in his play," DeMarlo said. "He was just real steady. My only regret was that I had to keep playing him without any rest. He never got injured like the other kids, but he got pretty fatigued by the end of 120 games! He asked me how the guys would get chosen for the London trip, and the next thing I know, I see his picture over there."

The following day, March 26, 1994, the temperature soared into the nineties again. We pulled our lawn chairs against the wire cage of the Pirates' dugout. Throughout the game against Todd's team, the Pirates' minor leaguers had a conversation something like this:

"What the f*** pitch dhat?"

"Who know, mahn? That honkie pitcher no f***in' good. He no goddamn secret!" Swears were strung together, six or eight at a time, and the Latinos spoke in jive. Amid this chatter was a constant clearing of the sinuses, with resultant globules ejected through the wire fence near our feet. It didn't take us long to move into the glaring sun.

At one point during the game, the Pirates' next batter stood in the first base coaching box. He called to his bench for a replacement, so he could take his place in the on-deck circle. His teammates were Latino; not one of them moved. The red-headed, freckle-faced batter called "Time out" and went to stand in front of his dugout, pointing to the first base coaching box with his bat. Again no one moved. There was palpable tension between the white and Latino teammates, and no apparent managerial control. Finally, the batter grounded out and took over in the first base coaching box.

It was amazing to me how athletes found nicknames for each other that stuck. I guessed it was because of the hours they spent sitting around trying to occupy themselves. An entire team might discuss one nickname for days before they reached a consensus. "Stumpy" Allen pitched the last couple of innings for the Lynchburg team. "Stinky" Stenkowitz was catching for the New Britain team. The kid whose last name was Dzafic was nicknamed "Eye Chart." But Todd was still "T.C." and Tim was "Timmy."

Todd came over after his post-game drills. "Do you know where Tim is?" he asked.

"No, we thought he'd come watch your game with us after he finished his workout," we replied. "We thought he had the day off."

"He's the bullpen catcher for the big league game today."

"What? Why didn't somebody tell us? Let's go catch the end of it!"

Charley and I scrambled three miles down the road to the beautiful, sold-out City of Palms Park. It was the bottom of the ninth when we arrived, and we raced through the main aisle that cut the seats horizontally, as the ever-ready zoom lens camera bumped against my hip. At the extremity of the third-base bleachers was the Sox bullpen. There was Tim in his full catching equipment. He stood talking to the weight coach for the major leaguers, a Harvard graduate. He wore a major league uniform, and I took advantage of the photo op. He must have gotten a lot of practice warming up the major leaguers, as the Sox pitchers had twelve runs scored against them that day.

"The 'AA' and 'AAA' players were all stretching on the field," Tim told us at dinner. "I was on my stomach with my name facing upward on the back of the uniform. Coach Berardino was standing right over me and started screaming, 'Carey! Carey!' I couldn't believe he was screaming like that. Joel Bennett yelled, 'Coach, you're standing on his toe, and he can't answer you!' He wanted me to get over to the major league field, since I was scheduled to have the day off." Tim tried to act as if his assignment that day were nothing special, but I was pretty excited I'd finally seen one son in a major league stadium, even if it was in the bullpen!

During dinner Todd entertained us with a story about the loudspeaker system at the minor league complex. He said Coach Berardino prided himself on two things: racing around the fields in his golf cart to direct the placement of the tarps and the roped-off areas, and making announcements over the P.A. system. "Were you there this morning for the announcement that will live forever in Red Sox history?" Todd asked Tim.

"I don't think so," Tim said.

"It was hysterical," Todd said, and he started laughing uncontrollably. "We were in pre-game warm ups and suddenly the microphone started crackling. Charley Wagner's voice came on (a former pitcher and coach in his late seventies, who still looked and dressed like a movie star). 'Murphy (clubhouse manager)! Get the hell in this clubhouse! Someone's stolen my shorts and I'm sitting here bare-assed. Get over here this minute!' All five fields cracked up."

On March 27, 1994, twenty-one minor leaguers were released or sent down to teams below. Among those released were Todd's former teammates Marty Durkin (whose parents had invited us to their home in Ft. Lauderdale) and Les Wallin, who had been in the system for seven years. The two had joked during spring training that pretty soon they'd be able to replace the waitresses that were serving them. Todd's roommate in Ft. Lauderdale, Bryan Brown, packed up and went home to Louisiana. Jeff Martin, the catcher, moved back down to the "A" Lynchburg team. Tim and Dana LeVangie continued to catch for the "AA" New Britain team. Tim looked very tired, as the heat soared again into the nineties. His roommate from Cumberland, Tim Smith, went from "AAA" to "AA" for his third straight year.

Back at the Sheraton Harbor Place, we packed into the elevator with ten "little people" with blue heads, hearing aids, all in their seventies and eighties. They were adorned in sequined splendor and black tuxedos for an evening in the ballroom with their group of five hundred. After the elevator stopped at several floors to pick up more of them, the "straw who broke the camel's (or elevator's) back" stepped on, and the elevator refused to budge. The 5'4" woman in the front with the carrot-red hair whispered, "We must have gained weight while we were here, or else there are some very large people in the back." She tried to swivel her head inconspicuously to catch a glimpse of us. The rest followed her lead, and in unison caught a glimpse of Tim and Todd. "Oh, do you play for the Red Sox?" the audacious carrot-top inquired.

"Um-hum," my 6'3," 220-pound and 6'2," 185-pound sons murmured.

"My God, look at the size of them!" the blue-heads exclaimed. "They play for the Red Sox! Look at them!"

With four days of spring training left, the papers reported that the Sox had signed a new utility infielder, Greg Litton, to a minor league contract. I guess they didn't have enough of them! GM Dan Duquette would exclusively control the minor league system after March 30, 1994, deciding the fates of over thirty more minor leaguers by the end of spring training.

On the last day of March, Tim played against Michael Jordan's Chicago White Sox "AA" team. Jordan impressed with his size and speed, but his game expertise left much to be desired. "He tried to drag bunt several times in the wrong situation, and couldn't execute," Tim reported. "So I asked him, 'What are you doing?' while I was at catch. He wasn't concentrating and flied out. One of his friends came up to bat and hit a foul that I snagged against the ground. I heard Jordan scream from the bench, 'He didn't catch it! It hit the ground!' I would have been dead meat if Jordan had wanted some friendly contact. His physique is incredible (6'7")." Michael had purchased a bus for his "AA" team so that he wouldn't have to endure the un-air conditioned buses with no VCR equipment that the rest of the league tolerated.

On April 1, 1994, the era of the Carey brothers in professional baseball ended. Some April Fool's joke!! Within forty-eight hours and three days before the end of spring training, Tim moved from his "AA" New Britain team, down to the "A" Sarasota team (Florida State League), to a final release. It came as a total surprise to all of us.

Sox catcher John Flaherty left "AAA" for the Detroit Tigers that day, which left an opening for a catcher at the highest minor league level. After Tim caught the "A" game in Sarasota, Manager DeMarlo Hale called him aside to the end of the dugout. Tim assumed he would receive the news that he was needed again at "AA"; perhaps one of their catchers had been moved up to replace Flaherty. Instead he heard, "I'm sorry to have to do this, since I've only had you with me one day and don't really know you. And I've heard good things about you. But I have to tell you you've been released." Tim was the only one released that day.

He marched into Ed Kenney's office, the director of Minor League Operations. Kenney told him to take a seat, then stared blankly at him. Tim took the initiative.

"I've been released today."

"I know."

"I'd like to know why! I have better stats than any catcher in Sarasota or

Lynchburg, and equal stats with LeVangie in New Britain. DelGado ("AA" New Britain) has only played two games this spring."

"We don't feel you have major league potential."

"Then I guess stats and hard work don't mean a thing."

"Maybe another club will pick you up and prove us wrong."

"Yeah, maybe, with only two days left in spring training!"

Tim exhibited the calm of a Buddhist monk as he walked out of the office and over to Todd's game on another field. He wanted to say goodbye to his brother and former teammates. Todd didn't know what to say, so Tim told him about the meeting with Kenney. "Meleski says you got a really bum deal," Todd told him later.

"Yeah, well if he'd stuck his neck out and played me last summer, they might have seen a little more of my potential." Tim had gone from catching in a major league bullpen to catching a game against Michael Jordan to a total baseball void in five days.

Charley and I received the news on the phone in our condo. We each got on an extension. "What the hell happened?" Charley asked, incredulous.

"Kenney told me I had no major league potential. No warning, no word from anybody first. I already called Nero."

By this time I had sunk down to the kitchen floor, with the phone cord wound round and round my hand. "What did he say?" I asked, trying to keep my voice from quivering with rage.

"He's going to call me tomorrow if the White Sox have a spot for me here or overseas. But the rosters are pretty much set by this point."

"Come on over here to the condo and relax for a while," Charley advised. "You know, no one's job is secure. Look what happened to me! At some point, even the major leaguers have to face that this is going to happen to them. Todd has to get used to the same idea. Luckily, your life doesn't focus just on baseball."

"That doesn't make it hurt any less," Tim responded.

"No. We know you are hurting right now, and it's a totally irrational decision. But the bottom line is they had no money invested in you, and they're going to protect their investments in other catchers. Remember, every business is a shitty business!" Charley knew how to make the boys deal with realities. This time he was gentle.

I don't know who hurt most, Tim or us. I knew I would never forgive the Sox for the way they had handled him. He drove across Alligator Alley to stay with us. Todd must have been hurting, too. He called that night to make sure Tim had arrived safely and to find out his plans. "I don't have any plans right now, at least not until I hear from the Army. I'm just going to relax for a while and not think about baseball." A minor leaguer signs his contract for a year at a time. When an organization drafts him, it has the right to keep him under contract for six years. If the organization releases the player within those six years, any other club might pick him up. The minor leaguer is at a total disadvantage, since each contract is, in effect, "one-way." It allows the organization to release the player at any time without upholding the salary stipulated.

On April 5th, Todd arrived in Lynchburg, his assigned "A" team. Mark Senkowicz, his former Elmira housemate, was also on the roster in Lynchburg. Since Mark didn't have a car, he asked Todd to drive his belongings up. Mark's belongings arrived in Lynchburg, but Mark didn't. At the last minute, the organization sent him back down to Utica, his third year in the New York-Penn League.

While Tim lived with us in Florida, he pursued an instructorship in scuba diving (still no word from the Army). We received a desperation call from Todd in mid-April. He had prolonged a downward spiral. His voice cracking with emotion, he asked to speak to his brother.

"Tim's not in," Charley told him. "Can I help?"

"No one can help. I can't get a hit, except for one home run. And in less than two weeks, I've made five errors. I only made eighteen all last season."

"Well, what's the problem?"

"I don't know," Todd answered haltingly. "I've got to speak to Tim." This was the same brother who was slow to call Tim the previous season because he was afraid he wouldn't measure up to Tim's standards.

"Well, I'll have him call as soon as he gets in. You know you have to believe in yourself. You've seen the shortstops at higher levels, and you know your skills are just as good as theirs. Get some confidence! Get some attitude."

"It's pretty hard to have an attitude, Dad, when you stink! I thought I could tear this league apart, but now I don't know if I belong here. I don't know if I belong in baseball."

The boys would not believe anything I could say in this situation. They thought I knew diddlysquat about playing sports, particularly in the pros. They were probably right, since my only competition had been on cheerleading squads through college or on interclub tennis teams in Rhode Island. It was better to let Charley have the floor. "Todd, believe me, you do! I'm sure Tim will tell you the same thing. You know you do. You've got to get tough and overcome your emotions. It will come together."

Todd's conversation with his brother lasted forty-five minutes. His older sibling was the only one Todd wanted to confide in. Tim was the only one who had been in the same meat grinder.

"Why has this happened?" I asked Charley. "It's like he's regressed two years, back to his rookie season in Elmira. Then he was so scared, and he pressed too hard. He had such a great spring training this year!"

Another night without any sleep.

Former coach of Brown University, Dave Stenhouse, sympathized. "I can remember when I was real discouraged and wanted to quit," he said. "My dad talked me out of it, and I went on to the major leagues. You should be real proud of your two boys, and any way I can help, I will. I'll be sure to call Todd." We appreciated his support, but it didn't assuage our worry.

"The only thing I can attribute this turnaround to is the mass exodus of Todd's friends and Tim at the end of spring training," I told Charley. "His uncharacteristic errors and lack of confidence at bat started almost the day after his friends were sent down and Tim was released."

"He's probably looking over his shoulder thinking, 'I'm supposed to be tearing up this league, and if I don't, maybe I'll be next.'" Charley responded. "I thought he'd have a mental toughness by now that would carry him the rest of the way. But I guess not. Tim's release must have affected him more than he'll admit."

"At least he's still playing every game." I tried to look on the bright side.

"Well, he'd better snap out of it soon, or he won't be playing regularly."

Charley started subscribing to the Lynchburg paper, which arrived in our Florida mailbox daily. The third one we received reported Todd had gone 0-for-4 in one Lynchburg game, and his errors were a total of seven. Charley and I tried to focus on our lives in the present, with so much up in the air! His young investment banking company had not signed a single deal, and we were on the last year of full salary from Fleet before his pension kicked in. We had put the condo in Florida up for sale, but hadn't received one offer. Keeping it shipshape for realtors with 23-year-old Tim living there was getting on all of our nerves. He had not yet heard from Army officer's candidate school, despite several follow-up calls, and was reluctant to pursue leads in Washington until he knew about officer's school. He spent his time working out, studying scuba diving, preparing equipment, diving, or watching television on the sofa at night. We planned to put our primary residence in Rhode Island on the market when we returned two months later.

Charley and I revisited Key West for a long weekend. I reminded him of our glee when we had been there the previous year and had read in the paper that Todd had had three hits in one game for Ft. Lauderdale.

On April 24, 1994, we finally reached Todd. We had not heard from him in almost ten days. He was playing every third day, but his spirits had improved, and he seemed to have put things in perspective. The bench rest was taking some pressure off.

I asked him not to shut us out again, no matter what happened. I figured he had been afraid of our disappointment in his performance. He had one hit in about thirty at-bats.

Always the mom, I played the cheerleading role. "We are proud of you, no matter what you do. How many sons have reached your level in baseball? We'll always be here for you, in baseball or out of it. It's not your first slump, and it won't be your last."

"Have you been able to isolate the problem?" Charley asked.

"Well, I'm not worried about the fielding, and neither is Manager Meleski. The fields are horrible - all bumpy and uneven. But my hitting stinks. Braun arrived in town today, and started working with me. My swing was so screwed up, I had to start over."

"I hope you begin to hit to the opposite field instead of pulling the ball," Charley said. That line was like a recording.

"Dad, I've gotten so much advice from so many people, I have to listen only to Braun. Oh, and thank Tim for the book he sent me."

"Okay. What's it about?"

"Having a positive attitude in baseball." Brotherly advice he would heed, we hoped!

"When do you think you'll play again?"

"Well, hopefully in two nights. Tomorrow a lefty is pitching, so I won't start. Schaefer is the new director of Player Development for the Minor Leagues, replacing Kasko. He saw me play and said I looked really uncomfortable out there. That's when I sat. He saw Dana LeVanie catch, liked what he saw, so Jeff Martin's been sitting out."

"Yeah, well Schaefer's the one who saw me play one day, and I was released right after that," Tim told his brother. Not too encouraging!

Todd's calls became increasingly depressing for us during early May. He called to wish me a "Happy Mother's Day," and his voice kept cracking. "I'm hitting again - I've brought my average up to .200, and my third home run went to the opposite field. But I haven't gotten into a rhythm because I'm playing every second or third game. I made a couple more errors, and lost some confidence fielding. Last year DeMarlo (Hale) let me play through a slump, so I came out of it quickly. Now, I'll have to go 3-for-4 if I want to be in the lineup every night. Every time a lefty pitches, I sit. Last year, my stats were better against lefty pitchers than righties."

"Maybe you should talk to Meleski," Charley suggested.

"I plan to. But he doesn't stick to his word. Just ask Tim!"

"You've also got to look at it from his perspective. Juday's hitting when he plays in your spot. He makes things happen. How's his fielding?"

"He has errors, too. His natural position isn't shortstop."

"Well, it's futile to worry about anyone else. All you have to do is set your goal at getting one hit in every game you play, and he won't be able to keep you out of the lineup. Extrapolate the figures for the rest of the season," Charley the mathematician advised. "You've played almost fifty games, and you're batting almost .200. If you go 1-for-3 and there are 100 games left, figure it out. You don't have to pound homers. The best news is that you're hitting to the opposite field. Don't worry about not playing every game."

"I didn't sign on to sit on the bench. I could go back to finish school."

"Imagine how Tim felt last year, sitting all the time. He had to block Meleski out of his mind, and perform when he got the chance. Work on your fielding by taking extra grounders. We've never seen you look uncomfortable in the infield."

"I've just lost my confidence. I can relate to Tim, because it's very depressing to sit down so much," he replied with a cracking voice.

Meanwhile, Charley and I had to contend with Tim's frustration because he hadn't heard from the Army. We had not yet sold our Florida condo, but had bought a bigger one that would become our permanent home in Delray Beach. My parents had listed their home of forty-eight years in Riverside, Connecticut, but it had been on the market for a year. They planned to relocate near us in Florida. There was one bit of humor from Todd: "Mr. Keiser came down from Cumberland to one of my games because his father died near us. I had to go the bathroom during the game, and the walkway was up next to the grandstand. Mr. Keiser grabbed my hand, shaking and shaking, and kept talking and talking, and I had to go to the bathroom. The game kept going, and there were two out for the other team, and I still hadn't gone to the bathroom. Finally I told him I had to get back down on the field. At least he saw me hit a home run."

Charley was morose and sullen for a period during mid-May, when we hadn't heard from Todd again in over a week. A large part of Charley's psyche had been tied to baseball from pre-school through college, and then again while he had coached the boys. To have a son play professionally and not be closely involved in his progress was stressful for him.

As for me, I relished being so far away from baseball that I didn't have to pack up for the ballpark or worry about Todd's performance every night. There was enough else to be concerned about. I certainly didn't miss the depressing phone calls. Charley finally decided to take the bull by the horns and reached Todd after an afternoon game. Though he was still alternating at short, he'd had three hits the previous game, and hadn't posted any further errors. No explanation why he hadn't called."At least he's come out of his slump," I said, trying to sound reassuring to myself and to Charley.

"You don't come out of a slump with one good game - you do it with consistency," Charley responded. "The kids who will play are the ones who bat consistently. What a great fielding talent sitting on the bench!"

Of course, Todd didn't like the twenty questions when we talked to him. That probably explained his reluctance to pick up the phone. "How have you been playing? Are you hitting? Have you hit to the opposite field? How's your fielding?" Charley and I were like sponges soaking up the information, but to Todd it seemed an inquisition.

Charley drove from Florida to Westport, Mass, for the summer, while I flew. He stopped to watch Todd play in Lynchburg. Todd was playing every night again and was back to his old vacuum-cleaner form at shortstop. His average was .222. His dad reported he was hitting hard line drives and not pulling the ball to right or striking out.

Todd planned to speak to Bob Schaefer, Player Development Director for the Minor Leagues, who'd be visiting Lynchburg that week. That is, indeed, what he did, privately, in a clubhouse office. Todd had matured a good deal in two years, and opened the discussion by asking about his status with a rookie shortstop aboard in Lynchburg.

Surprisingly, Schaefer responded by assuring Todd he'd be playing regularly, lefty pitchers notwithstanding, and that the rookie shortstop would only be a backup. He remarked that Todd had shown great improvement since the beginning of the season, and he fully expected Todd to be playing "AA" in New Britain by the end of the season, or certainly the following year. The meeting concluded with Schaefer reasserting that management believed Todd was a major-league prospect.

Over the course of the next week, Todd's batting average rose ten percentage points and he held steady in the field without an error. It was amazing what a little reassurance had done for him! But on June 1st he called us to say he'd had a terrible game.

"What's the problem?" Charley asked.

"If I knew what the problem was, I'd fix it, Dad."

"How's the hitting?"

"I didn't get a hit today. I hit the ball hard in the Wilmington series, but got no hits. Today I didn't even hit the ball."

"What about your fielding?"

"I don't want to talk about baseball any more. Oh, did I tell you I had to speak to all the elementary school kids at the anti-drug game? It was an afternoon game at home, and Meleski had asked me to go down on the field to speak over the microphone. I didn't want to do it, but then I changed my mind. At first I was nervous, but I only spoke for a few minutes and Blake said she heard me clearly. Her class was there. The good thing about it was that none of the kids were paying attention, anyway."

On June 3, 1994, the papers reported that in the first round of the draft, the Sox had selected an All-American shortstop, Nomar Garciaparra. In addition, the paper stated that when he eventually signed, Garciaparra would be playing in

Lynchburg. At that moment, Nomar was playing in the College World Series for Georgia Tech. We wondered if Alan Nero would help Todd, in case Nomar were assigned to play Todd's position in Lynchburg. Nero hadn't been able to obtain a single offer from other teams for Tim, though he had been full of promises to send Tim overseas, or to have him picked up by the White Sox.

Todd remained undaunted by the news that Nomar had been drafted. With no apparent motive for a phone call to us, Todd wriggled Charley's reaction from him. Then he said, "It won't bother me. First of all, he won't be in Lynchburg until he gets some playing time under his belt at the lower levels. Even Trot Nixon had all of spring training before he reported here his first season. One thing I know for sure is that I won't stand for sitting on the bench. I'll ask to go down to Sarasota to play every day."

"Have you been playing?" Charley asked.

"The team had a day off yesterday after my bad game, and then a lefty pitched. So I haven't played in three days."

"Have you talked to your agent? Tim thinks that would be a good idea."

"It probably is. I called him, but he was in Japan. So I think I'll call Cecil Cooper in the Chicago office."

By June 12, 1994, Todd's batting average had dipped to .199, the lowest on the Lynchburg team. He had added no further errors. Charley and I decided to visit Lynchburg to lend some moral support.

It was definitely a love-hate relationship I now had with America's pastime. Since Tim had been released in April, I hated the game - the injustice to the minor leaguers (with money always the bottom line); the mismanagement, lack of communication, and even lies; the cut-throat competition; the treatment of individuals like pieces of meat; the emotional upheaval over and over for kids in their late teens and early twenties; and most of all, the turmoil it caused in family life. Certainly, our kids had achieved a level of competition few in the U.S. had realized, and they had learned valuable lessons at an early age. But Tim's life was still unsettled, without a permanent job. And who knew what lay in store for Todd. We wondered if we'd find the new draft pick out on the field taking Todd's place in Lynchburg, after we'd driven twelve hours in mid-June.

When we arrived there for the second year in a row, Todd's dazzling white uniform down on the field again gave me an immediate rush. It was the "love" part of the game that is addictive, especially for parents of the minor leaguers. I could explain some of the rush through pride in my son and the excitement of seeing thousands of kids all dressed in their Little League uniforms, hoping to be out on the field some day. We met some of them, in whose classes Todd had spoken. Another part of the rush was the intensity of almost 3,000 fans chanting, singing, and even booing. The Sox won, and Todd got a hit with an RBI against the Frederick, Maryland, Orioles.

But the nagging uncertainty would always be there while Todd played professional baseball. The faces of those who'd been sent down or traded or released, like Tim, remained behind. After the game, Todd discussed with several teammates the ineptitude of Meleski, putting one lineup on the field for opposing right-handed pitchers, and another for lefties. The team was at the bottom of its division, same as the previous year, and Meleski often sulked after losses, not speaking to the team. "John (Graham) and I haven't faced many lefty pitchers this year," Todd said, "even though last year we both hit well against them in Florida. So tonight in the last inning, I had the hit-and-run sign against a lefty, and I foul-tipped it. The catcher threw our runner out. Meleski sulked. I had spent three extra hours hitting this afternoon in 95-degree heat."

"And it paid off, Todd. You almost beat out that drive up the middle and you had a nice hit to the opposite field. I'm sure the new management sees the players' discontent with Meleski," Charley remarked.

"Yeah," John replied. "They do. I think there will be a lot of staff changes next year."

"The rumor is that I'll be sent down to the Florida State team when Garciaparra reports here," Todd said. "He hasn't signed yet."

"How do you feel about that?" Charley asked him.

"It's better than sitting on the bench behind him. I just want to play, and I will if I'm in Sarasota. At some point, this kid would jump over me anyhow."

"Don't you think there's a possibility that you'll be moved up, rather than down?"

"Randy Brown's having a decent year at 'AA.' I talked to Cecil Cooper (Nero's associate), and he said after Garciaparra signs, he'll talk to management about my prospects, and put some feelers out elsewhere."

Jubilation prevailed at the June 15, 1994, Lynchburg game. The Sox had four homers, including one by Todd, and beat the Orioles again. Todd went 2-for-4 at bat, with a line-drive single up the middle for another RBI. After his homer, the diehards at the top of the stands bought Charley and me a beer. One of these men, Frank, always led the crowd in "Take Me Out to the Ballgame," from the top of the dugout during the seventh-inning stretch. Word got down to Todd that his parents were celebrating with a couple of brews in the stands. We had found an instant relaxation technique to increase our enjoyment watching this Lynchburg team!

After the game, however, Todd was calm and reserved. He said he was disgusted with his fielding. He'd collected his thirteenth error during the game, bobbling a ball then gunning it to first base, a play that he could usually count on because of his strong arm. "My fielding this year has been disgusting. I can only blame about four of my errors on the field conditions. Sometimes I make a great play on a ball, then I don't get it to the bag in time. Tonight was a perfect example of an error that shouldn't have happened."

"Don't worry about your fielding. It will resolve itself. You are putting undue pressure on yourself because you had such an unbelievable year in Ft. Lauderdale. You can't expect to do that every season."

During dinner in Lynchburg after the game, we met Bill Selby's fiancée, Terri (later his wife). We had heard secondhand the saga of their dis-engagement the previous season, when Tim had lived with Bill. Tim had not been able to understand a player's spending half his bonus money on a diamond engagement ring. I kept my mouth shut, knowing love does strange things to common sense.

Another story introduced during dinner revealed Meleski's character. On a five-hour road trip to Wilmington, Delaware, the team bus always stopped in Maryland after the first few hours. Meleski told the team to be back on the bus within fifteen minutes. Despite long lines at the food counters, everyone managed to board within fifteen minutes except pitcher Shawn Senior. One of the team discovered he was missing, and yelled up to Jack, the bus driver. Jack backed up, stalling for time. Manager Meleski, however, was determined to teach the team a lesson. "Let's go!" he commanded to Jack.

"We can't go! Senior's not here!" the shouts came from the back of the bus.

"He's only one f***ing minute late!" Shawn's teammates began screaming in unison.

"I said to go!" Meleski repeated to Jack. And the bus crawled out of the rest stop.

By the time a distraught bunch of players arrived at the Wilmington Stadium, they saw an even more irate player and his father pull up beside them. Luckily, the Senior family lived in New Jersey, so Shawn's father had driven to Maryland to rescue his son and deliver him to Delaware. What if the player had been from California? Shawn had it out with Meleski right then and there in the parking lot, and the next day was sent down to Sarasota. We hoped it would be the coup de grace for Meleski, provided the media picked up the story. They did, indeed, but Meleski stayed in Lynchburg.

We detected a positive character trait that had recently emerged in Todd. One of the Lynchburg outfielders, Dan Collier, was a huge "down-home" 'Bama boy expecting his first child. His recreational activities consisted of fishing, hunting, and harassing his teammates. The latter caused the Lynchburg players to make snide comments about his mental capacity, but sarcasm was often lost on Dan. When Collier stood on the dugout steps in the first inning of the June 15th game, he criticized John Graham, leadoff batter, for hitting the first pitch for a single. "Oh, that's good, Graham!" Collier yelled. "Leadoff batters are supposed to let us see some pitches up there!"

"Shut up, Collier," Todd spoke up from the dugout. "Leave the kid alone. If he wants to hit the first pitch, let him get on base! It's none of your business!"

"F*** off, Carey. It's not your business, either."

The next evening, we had a two-hour thunder and lightning delay that came off the Blue Ridge mountaintops. We talked with other players, parents, and our sons on the field, and watched while the ballplayers amused themselves palming a small rubber ball - the kind you squeeze to improve hand strength - in a circle until someone missed. The hours they spent doing nothing were remarkable. We sat through an agonizingly long game that ended around midnight. While some of the Sox collected four hits apiece, Todd barely boosted his average to .213. He was picked off first base after his single, adding to his funk when the game ended in a 14-12 loss.

"The kids say that Meleski wants me out," Todd told us.

"Why is that? Have you crossed him?"

"No. He knows I haven't performed up to my potential, and he wants to share in the glory of a first-round draft pick when Nomar gets here. I've just got to keep my bat going, wherever I am. At least I started badly and progressed, not the opposite."

"You can't keep on worrying about anyone else's performance, or who's coming up behind you. You're still only twenty-two, and have plenty of time."

"It's easy to say, 'Don't worry about being replaced,' but of course it's on my mind all the time, Dad." Charley and I spent another afternoon golfing on the Blue Ridge foothills to get our minds off baseball.

Todd's uncertainty about the future began to display itself in the field. In a trouncing by the Salem Pirates, Todd retained his confidence at bat, walking twice and getting one hit. But he added an uncharacteristic two errors during the game. His were among seven errors the team made that night. We began the twelve-hour drive home the next morning. In an emotional parting, my only words of advice were, "Believe in yourself, no matter what happens next. We know and you know the talent you have. And we'll always love you and be there for you." The team would go on the road for six days after we departed.

I viewed part of my parental role as a cheerleader and president of our boys' fan clubs, always and forever, no matter how old they (and I) became. That was not to say that I didn't point out deficiencies that needed work or change, nor to say that I didn't discuss past and future actions realistically. If someone like Todd, with considerable success in hockey, baseball, academia, and personal relationships, lacked self-confidence, I wondered how the kids who had not tasted such success in their youth, or had no-one to bolster their self esteem, would make it to the major leagues.

I felt chided by a nagging voice in the back of my mind, "You're only trying to define your self-worth through your sons." I guessed that was an inescapable reality as a parent, but minus their successes, I certainly didn't regard myself as a failure. I had achieved two Master's of Arts degrees, taught high school and run a successful business, as well as sustained a fantastic marriage for twenty-nine years. I had become president of every club, organization, and team I'd ever joined. It was when our child had his own expectations and felt he had failed to meet them that my role became critical to bolster his self-esteem. In the stands I continued to cheer unabashedly through the years for Todd and his teammates.

Weeks passed, and Todd remained in Lynchburg while Nomar Garciaparra, the new draft pick, negotiated his bonus and contract with the Sox. Todd dug down, held his average at .230, and increased his home runs to eight.

On the fourth of July, when at least thirty of our friends and relatives came to the beach and back to the house afterward for our annual cookout, Charley and I really missed Tim and Todd. The older our nieces and nephews became (we had eleven on Charley's side of the family), the fewer appeared at the beach every year. It had been years since Tim and Todd had been able to join us on July 4th. I think they missed the gathering, too. If they were unable to call on that day to speak to everyone, they would call us the following day to find out who had attended and what tales we could relate. Todd, of course, was still playing ball every night. The biggest crowds of the season always came to the stadiums on July 4th to watch the fireworks after the game. Tim had observed the fireworks over the ocean in Delray Beach, Florida, from our condo, where he lived by himself while completing his instructor's certification in scuba. He still had no word from the Army.

On July 16, 1994, we arrived at the Wilmington, Delaware, Blue Rocks' stadium with an entourage of grandparents, aunts, uncles, and cousins, including our 8-month-old nephew, Jake. They'd come in a rented van with a stroller, picnic baskets, Barney CDs, diapers, etc. Todd's Lynchburg Red Sox were in town for three games. The team had checked into the Hilton instead of the downtown Holiday Inn where they normally stayed. Naturally, we were all booked at the Holiday Inn.

The weather was around 85 degrees at 7 p.m. game time. We all enjoyed an exciting game, which the Red Sox won 6-1. Todd went 1-for-3, walked, and laid down a beautiful bunt. He made lots of routine plays in the field, with one error. Afterward, we followed the team bus north to the Hilton, where Todd joined us for an 11 p.m. supper. Baby Jake went back to the Holiday Inn instead. He had lasted through eight and one-half innings before falling asleep. It had been a long day for all of us, starting in Massachusetts.

Sunday was a day game at 2 p.m. in 90-degree heat. There had been 5,400 fans the previous night, but there were less than 5,000 on Sunday. It would have been hard to find better family entertainment for an afternoon at $4-per-person admission. Every inning featured Bluewinkle, the mascot moose. He danced through the stadium, throwing Frisbees into the crowd; rode around the field in an auto; and refereed a hoop-shooting contest as well as a dizzy-bat-race on the field. The most popular audience participation game featured young cheerleaders from the crowd (aged five to twenty-one) who stood on top of the dugouts to lead the dancing and swaying for the song, "YMCA." Our niece made Charley get up and learn how to jive! He had remained motionless, smoking his pipe when permitted, until Casey got him moving. Motionless also were the Red Sox bats, collecting only four hits against outstanding off-speed pitching by the Blue Rocks. Todd looked particularly listless at bat, weakly grounding out, then striking out twice. He made one outstanding play deep in the hole at shortstop. At the bus, he thanked the Massachusetts relatives for traveling to see him. However, a dead battery in the rented van delayed their departure.

Charley and I met Todd back at the Hilton where he was staying and went out for a leisurely dinner to discuss his finances, change of residency, and his car registration associated with the possible sale of our Rhode Island house. Todd planned to visit Kristie, a friend in South Carolina, over the All-Star break. Kristie was an equestrian who owned her own horse.

We were a dejected group that arose early the next morning to drive back to Massachusetts. Todd had had one hit in ten at-bats during the three days we visited Wilmington that July. We hoped he would have fun during his three days off, and get his mind off baseball. We planned our last trip to see him in August.

On July 21, 1994, Nomar Garciaparra, the Georgia Tech shortstop, finished negotiating terms and signed a contract for a reported $850,000. He was assigned to the Sarasota team in the Florida State League. This unexpected event was a boost for Todd's state of mind, indicating a vote of confidence by the management. He would remain in Lynchburg for the remaining five weeks of the season.

Charley and I spent up to three days each week during July and early August sorting, packing, and removing our belongings from our primary residence in Rhode Island, still unsold. The beach house absorbed all the casual stuff, but we left the boys' two rooms in Rhode Island intact for them to tackle. We shipped a lot of furniture and accessories to Florida. A month later, my mother and father would move after forty-five years from their Connecticut house to Florida. I anticipated a lot of hustle when we returned from Lynchburg. I planned to fly to Florida to meet my parents' moving van at their new home, while they took the auto-train down. Both Charley and I had attempted to keep our businesses going - my interior design business and Charley's investment banking business in Ft. Lauderdale. It proved to be too much for my business. I learned interior design was something you couldn't run part-time, even with conscientious supervision and outstanding workmanship. When Charley and I became permanent residents of Florida, I decided not to take another state exam. Instead, I freelanced for relatives and friends.

The Lynchburg trip in August didn't provide much of a break from stress. When we arrived, Todd's average stood at .226. He had hit eleven homers with thirty-four RBI's, and had posted twenty-two errors up to that point, four more than the previous season. In the first game we saw against the (Baltimore) Frederick, Maryland, team he hit a blooper over the shortstop's head to shallow left, which bounced out of the shortstop's glove as he circled backwards. Our hometown scorer didn't credit Todd with a hit, but instead gave the shortstop an error. In his next at-bat, he hit one to the center field fence, which the center fielder tracked down. Next, he reached base on a Frederick error, and finally, left the bases loaded in his last at-bat. We met the Stickels from Rhode Island, who had made a point of spending two nights in Lynchburg on vacation so their kids could see Todd again. He and Tim had coached their son Steven at the Rhode Island Baseball Academy.

Tim's former roommate, Bill Selby, had moved up to "AA" New Britain after batting .310. Dan Collier from Alabama had had an accident in the dugout, where he'd been standing when a foul ball caught him directly in the jaw. How appropriate was that? He went home to have it reset and wired shut. Meanwhile, his baby's delivery was imminent. There were now four living in Todd's two-bedroom condo unit. Brian Bright was sleeping on the floor with the cushions from John Graham's sofa-bed. Forty-nine players had been on the Lynchburg roster at one time or another that season.

The quote of the year had to be what Schaefer, Director of Player Development, had said to Todd on a previous visit. "Are you enjoying yourself yet?" he asked. Todd had shrugged his shoulders in response. How could he answer a man who'd circulated to the media that Garciaparra might jeopardize Todd's position in Lynchburg? How could he answer, when none of the team respected Manager Meleski? The players were dead tired and had learned in Kinston, North Carolina, that five of their cars, including Todd's, had been vandalized in the Lynchburg parking lot while they were on the road. One player's car was missing. On the trip back from Kinston, the bus driver had run out of gas. The players had slept alongside the road outside Danville, Virginia, from 3:00 to 4:30 a.m. while the bus company sent another bus from Lynchburg. The team had arrived back at their parking lot at 6 a.m., the same day we arrived, with a game that night. Having fun yet?

I began taking reading material to the nightly games. Todd had gone 2-for-24 over the week prior to our arrival and seemed unable to turn the trend around. His errors went to twenty-three. "I don't feel tired physically," he said, "but it's been a long, stressful season, and I'll be glad when it's over. I'm not relaxed, and haven't gotten into a groove the way I did last year. I've been pressing too hard, especially since Garciaparra signed. I certainly had more fun last year."

"Why don't you try to take a lesson from Mike Bordick (Oakland-Baltimore-Toronto major leaguer)?" Charley suggested. "He always gets one hit a game, occasionally two, but never will he go 0-for-4, or 0-for 5. So he's got a base for his average on which to build. If you could get up and just try for a single, then the pressure is off for that game. If you hit a home run after that, fine. But now you're going up thinking you've got to hit a homer every game." In the succeeding four games, Todd went 4-for-12 at bat.

The third day that we were in Lynchburg in '94, Todd was tested for drugs. At the beginning of the season, all rookies were tested, and once a month thereafter, the players were selected at random. By the end of the season, the entire team had had a turn. The system hardly seemed methodical or comprehensive. Thankfully, that was one test result we never worried about. If any player were caught, we never heard about it or the consequences.

It still surprised us to hear tales of bigotry among the Lynchburg teammates. One player from Massachusetts was a hothead about gays and black women. "We tease him," Todd said, "because he gets so worked up if his masculinity is questioned, or if someone suggests that he have an interracial date. Sometimes he's ready to fight. He's worse than any redneck on the team. It gives New England a bad reputation." The following night, this particular player got caught twice in-between bases with men on. He had slugged three hits. Running off the field, he reminded me of a bulldog whose forehead led his chin (or lack thereof) forward, as if he were trying to break loose from an imaginary leash. He displayed the same approach in his personal dogmas.

Despite meeting many wonderful people in Lynchburg, we hoped this would be the last season we'd be watching one of our sons play there. At the end of the week-long home-stand, Todd's average hovered around .224, almost exactly where it had been when we arrived.

Todd began expressing the wish that he would get demoted to Sarasota, just to begin playing for fun again. Charley abolished that thought from his mind. "To want to go backward just to have fun is ridiculous. Why don't you try to relax now that this season is winding down, and you'll enjoy yourself?"

I added, "There are a lot of people in this town that have tried to help you and are pulling for you, Todd. They believe you've got a bright future, and Dad and I do, too. Why don't *you* try to believe it?"

We headed home to Massachusetts behind the team bus, as we were planning to watch them play in Frederick, Maryland, on the way. When we got to Frederick, we heard the most unbelievable minor league travel story of the boys' careers. The Lynchburg bus had no air conditioning on a 90-degree day for the four-hour ride to

Frederick, and the windows would not lower. The day had started well, when stadium officials picked up the players at their apartments. That way they wouldn't have to leave their cars in the unlocked Lynchburg stadium lot. After an hour on the stifling bus, players had stripped to their boxer shorts and were causing such a commotion that the driver (the same one that had run out of gas at 3:30 a.m. in Danville, Va.) stopped to phone back to the Lynchburg bus company. However, he also took his time in the air-conditioned rest stop, buying himself a soda while the players sat sweltering on the bus. After passing into Maryland, he pulled into a truck weighing station. The bus, without permits for overweight poundage in Maryland, was detained forty-five minutes and the driver was fined $700. None of this was even necessary for passenger buses. Since the driver was black, the players were afraid to open their mouths, for fear that Coach Bibby, also African-American, would interpret the insults as racial slurs.

Because of the ordeal the players had been through, Meleski agreed to have the players board the bus later from the hotel, at 5 p.m. The game started at 7 p.m. Fully dressed in their uniforms, the players again mounted the steps to the sweltering bus for the one-mile ride to Keys Stadium. Thirty minutes later, they found themselves lost in downtown Frederick, their uniforms completely soaked. Even after such outrageous trips, the Lynchburg owners and GM continued to contract with a bus company that did not maintain its buses or supply maps or directions for its drivers.

The major league strike had begun, and 6,000 fans attended Todd's "A" game that night, including one of his former Brown roommates. After performing well, Todd's face lit up when he greeted his good friend, Salim Haji. He towered over Salim in his spikes and his increased shoulder span from weight-lifting. He presented autographed balls to Salim's two young cousins, and was buoyant afterward at a 10:30 p.m. dinner, despite being dead tired. He was obviously pleased with his at-bats during the last few games, drawing walks and getting at least one hit per game. "I'm not swinging at bad pitches anymore, the way I did in the first half of the season. Schaefer told me to take a strike, just to get a look, and that's what I've been doing."

"You aren't off balance at the end of your swing, either," Charley said. "That's because your stride is shorter when you swing, and that's important. Even when you were young, you used to take too big a stride."

"I didn't realize Schaefer had actually been instructing you," I said.

"Yeah, he tried to make me whip the ball with my wrist during infield practice, too," Todd added. "But I don't want to do that because of wear and tear. Marchese is the infield coach, but he doesn't teach us anything. Braun, the roving batting instructor, teaches us a lot. He's always had confidence in my swing."

What a turnaround!

Charley and I spent the next day touring Gettysburg in light rain, while Todd slept. Our road trip ended with an agonizing drubbing by the Frederick Keys. At the end of the second inning, we were losing 10-0. Todd looked like he was sleepwalking. He took first strikes, which often got him down in the count 0-2, and he ended up striking out twice. After the game Todd said, "I don't want to hear any criticism tonight, Dad."

"All right, I'll butt out," Charley responded. But he couldn't help himself. "There's a reason why you performed the way you did tonight, and it stems from a lack of concentration. You've got about twenty-one games left, and you don't want to start a slump now." Unfortunately, it was a tense goodbye. Todd was displeased with himself and aware that Charley was disappointed. We hoped he'd be playing the next day on his 22nd birthday, when my sister and her husband would attend the game in Maryland. In my continual role as caregiver, I jumped out of the car before we departed to give Todd a birthday hug and hiss, and asked him to call us once a week. I whispered to him, "We love you!"

Todd struggled along the remainder of the season, having flashes of brilliance and signs of total lack of concentration. In an article in the Woonsocket Call on August 18, 1994, a feature article highlighted Todd's season and the stress of pro ball playing. It quoted Manager Meleski as saying Todd had gotten off to a rough start, and it was essential for a shortstop to be consistent. Meleski pointed out that Todd had great lapses in consistency over the season. About the only positive thing in the article by Scott Cole were the stats Todd had put up for homers and RBI's.[19] The second article directly beneath the first was a follow up on Tim, who had been awarded the Call's "Student-Athlete of the Year" honor his senior year of high school. After reporting on Tim's release from the Sox and the fact that he was living and working in Florida, it stated he was considering enlisting in the Army.[20] In actuality, Tim returned to Rhode Island within a week of the article's publication to teach in private schools while interviewing for federal service jobs. Still no word from the Army.

Todd's season ended September 4, 1994, with 13 homers, 42 RBI's, 363 at-bats, and 28 errors. His average finished at .234. Like moths to a flame, Charley and I had been drawn to the fire early each Sunday morning in the stats of The Providence Journal.

With the major leaguers on strike, the "AAA" Paw Sox had reached the International League playoffs and had gotten extensive local TV time and newsprint. This included interviews with GM Duquette and Schaefer. Todd showed great interest in attending the Paw Sox playoff games at home, while Tim showed no interest in seeing any of them. Pawtucket lost in the first round. Todd returned to Brown to complete his coursework for his Bachelor of Arts degree in Urban Studies.

16

The Strike

On Friday, September 16, 1994, the major league professional baseball season was officially canceled, without any agreement between owners and players. There would be no World Series. To fill in the gap, we began to watch the PBS series of nine documentaries entitled "Baseball," produced by Ken Burns. Our Colby classmate and Pulitzer Prize winner, Doris Kearns Goodwin, was interviewed in the second of the series, having been a reporter covering the games at Fenway during her tenure as a professor at Harvard. I saw photos of Ivy League fields in the 1800s where our boys had played. I could draw an almost mythical connection between baseball and American history.

On the same day, the press announced Duquette's wholesale firings of seven minor league instructors, including New Britain Manager Pankovits, Lynchburg Manager Meleski, Utica Manager Holt, Lynchburg Infield Instructor Marchese, as well as three pitching instructors. Bibby retained his job in Lynchburg as pitching instructor.

However, there would no longer be a Red Sox affiliate team in Lynchburg. The city of New Britain, Conn., had severed ties with Red Sox management and within a few days in mid-September, Trenton, New Jersey, became the new Sox "AA" affiliate. Eventually, Sarasota did become the highest "A" team in the Sox system, and a team was added in Michigan; another in Lowell, Mass., replaced the New York/Penn League short-season team. By December, 1994, the Sox hired Ken Macha as the new manager of the Trenton "AA" affiliate.

The Providence Journal announced the trade of our Cumberland neighbor and "AA" pitcher Tim Smith to Seattle, as well as the trade of Todd's roommate in Ft. Lauderdale, Derek Vinyard, to the Montreal Expos. [21]

Charley predicted the Sox would switch Todd to third base during spring training, because his weight had reached 195 pounds on his 6'2" frame. Nomar Garciaparra had been playing successfully at shortstop in the Arizona League during the off-season. In mid-October, Kevin Kennedy of the Houston Astros became the new Sox major league manager to replace Hobson. Tony LaRussa from the Oakland A's had turned the Sox down.

Charley and I traveled back to our permanent residence in Florida in early January '95, while the boys stayed in our Rhode Island house, still on the market. We were sorry to learn that Rico Petrocelli had resigned as "AA" batting coach. He'd been hired the previous month along with Al Nipper, pitching coach for the "AA" Eastern League affiliate. Todd got along well with Rico and greatly respected him, a key element to Todd's self confidence. Apparently Dan Duquette was bringing in all his own people at every level.

While the major league strike continued, another rumor persisted that the minor leaguers would have to report in February, to fill in the major league slots. We welcomed this, if Todd were involved, because it meant we would see more of him in Florida. He had graduated from Brown University in December, '94, and was interviewing for management-trainee positions in banking for the off-season. He received an offer from Citizens Bank in Providence the week of January 23, 1995. I knew Todd's natural abilities, aside from sports, were in the math/finance realm, and he had loved Charley's world of analysis and deal-making.

The owners ran public ads and did everything possible to find "replacement" players during the major league strike. Anyone 25-years-old and under could show up, either in or out of shape, for team tryouts. Major league teams began to call on former players in their thirties, including Mike Stenhouse, outfielder, and Carl Allaire, shortstop, from Rhode Island. The burning issue for the replacement players became whether to cross the major league picket lines. Tim expounded on the issue. "Minor leaguers have never benefited from the major league players' union. Our pay was under the minimum wage; we got no pensions or benefits besides health care. Management treated us like shit, without any communication about our future. Every month we had to pay dues to the union, right out of our paychecks. So the option to play on a major league field is very appealing, especially for the exposure in front of scouts and other owners."

There was no decision about moving the "AAA" players up to fill in the vacancies during the strike, and this was late January. I could see that the owners wanted it both ways - they wanted to keep the minor league structure intact, so when the strike ended, their talent would be in place with the depth at each position that they'd paid for. But the reality was that a replacement player would have to walk right past national heroes standing on a picket line. And the replacement players would run the risk of getting beaned with a fastball, if they ever came to bat against the striking players, once it settled.

The Sox invited Todd to report to spring training on February 23, 1995. The stated purpose was to have the "AA" and "AAA" players work out together, thus leaving the 40-man major league roster intact. The major leaguers, of course, were still in limbo and couldn't report at all. No one received a contract in the minor leagues until early February.

Todd signed for the same amount per month as the previous year: $1,200. That amount would jump to $1,500/month if he made the "AA" roster, with an additional one-time bonus incentive of $2500, if he made a higher level. Todd immediately called Kenney in Boston, the Director of Minor League Operations, to ask why he hadn't received a raise. Kenney responded by saying all salaries across the board were frozen until a settlement was reached in the major league strike and major league ball park income started flowing again.

Todd had been working out every day in the Bryant University field house with Carl Allaire, a 31-year-old replacement player and former "AAA" shortstop for Detroit. He helped Todd with his fielding. During batting practice they pitched to each other. Todd had also been in contact with Ron Roberts, manager of the Lynchburg stadium, where the Pirates would base their "A" affiliate. The '95 Sox teams were as follows from the bottom up:

Rookie Team	-	**Ft. Myers, FL**
"A"	-	**Utica, NY**
"A"	-	**Battle Creek, MI**
"A"	-	**Sarasota, FL**
"AA"	-	**Trenton, NJ**
"AAA"	-	**Pawtucket, RI**

Congress proposed a repeal of the anti-trust agreement for major league baseball on February 15th to break the strike. Even President Clinton wasn't able to move the owners off ground zero. The players' union had supported the repeal.

Speculation in the New England papers swirled around Red Sox minor leaguers who might constitute a replacement team. Todd's name appeared. By February 23, 1995, when he reported to spring training, the Sox had signed only ten replacements to minor league contracts. Todd figured these players were "expendable." Approximately 170 minor leaguers were on their way to Ft. Myers as the reservoir from which a replacement team would be selected.Todd amazed us by expressing an interest in being a major league replacement. He felt that only those minor leaguers who were "hot prospects" would be exempt from the replacement team. Todd sensed that he was "expendable" after Nomar Garicaparra signed, so if he were selected, he'd consider accepting the $115,000 minimum salary guaranteed, once the season started. He figured he could invest it. Since there would be tremendous resentment against the replacements once the strike broke, he figured he'd be forced to leave baseball. The management might even cut all the replacements. These were weighty problems for a 22-year-old to consider.

Charley and I tried to point out to him that many people within the Sox organization confided to us that Todd had major league potential. In addition, Frank White had been impressed enough with Todd's fielding on the rookie team that Frank had wanted to work with him all that summer, instead of sending him to Elmira. I truly believed his potential had not fully surfaced. If he did, in fact, become a legitimate major leaguer, his salary would far exceed $115,000. In addition, a banking position awaited him in the off-season. We couldn't understand his jeopardizing all of that so soon, even if he gained excellent exposure as a replacement. He promised to call his agent, as well as us, should the dilemma present itself. Meanwhile, he had once again settled into the minor leaguers' home at the Ft. Myers Comfort Inn. Minor leaguers would receive their first paycheck in April, after managers listed their team rosters.

It was disturbing to hear Todd talk about the use of steroids in baseball. He mentioned that he'd been tested during the first week of spring training for AIDS, and said testing for addictive drugs was done randomly during the season without warning, and seldom repeated. "There's nothing in baseball to prevent players from using steroids. They're easy to obtain, and the testing system is easy to fool," he explained.

Some major league clubs threatened to ban minor league players from spring training camp if they refused to play in exhibition games, thereby forcing the club to sign replacements from outside their minor league system. The Yankees became the first club to do so on February 23, 1995.

Each club, it seemed, was handling the situation differently. The Red Sox would invite each minor leaguer individually to play major league exhibition games, and would guarantee a spot back on his original minor league team, once the strike broke. Of course, major league players and their union would ostracize the minor leaguer, should he ever be elevated to major league level.

In The Palm Beach Post on February 27, Rick Lancellotti, a 15-year minor league veteran and Marlins' replacement player at age thirty-eight, said:

'....the union wants fans to believe major-league and minor-league players live under one roof, when it's actually a house divided. The average major leaguer makes 1.2 million a year.' Lancellotti estimates that the average minor-league salary (for the months played) is $10,000, with Class 'A' players making roughly $4,000, and Class 'AAA' players about $30,000.

'I'm starting my seventeenth year and I have no pension,' said infielder Nick Capra, thirty-six, whose 1,769 games in the minors dwarf his forty-three major-league appearances. 'Baseball had never done anything for me.'

The owners want minor-leaguers to play exhibition games because ...participating 'is an important part of your career development.' The players' association is calling those who play 'scabs.'

Lancellotti points out salary and licensing as obvious places major-leaguers could tap to give minor-leaguers a pension and incentive bonuses....

Several in camp remember two years ago when minor-leaguers asked for two percent of licensing money, but union chief Donald Fehr said, 'We are not a charitable organization. [22]

It was a frustrating time as a parent, and a confusing time as a minor leaguer. Neither management nor the major league players' union was sympathetic to minor leaguers, unless they were top draft picks. A byline in The Palm Beach Post the same day reported that Boston General Manager Dan Duquette had told players to decide by February 28th if they would play in exhibition spring games, "although he left an out for top prospects, such as shortstop Nomar Garciaparra, by saying less-experienced minor-leaguers aren't ready for the games." Garciaparra had played steadily from July until Christmas, first in the minors, then in instructional camp, then in the Arizona League.

True to his word, Duquette had all the minor leaguers fill out a form the following day, asking whether they would participate in major league exhibition games. Only Ryan McGuire, Doug Hecker, Trot Nixon, and pitcher Chad Amos would not participate. Papers in the Boston area reported that five pitchers had said they would not engage in the games.

Todd had discussed the situation with Charley before agreeing to play. "I really have nothing to lose, because I may never make the majors, but if I do, it won't be for several years. By then, nobody will remember who did what. Besides, the management is threatening to send everybody home who doesn't play. They probably won't, but I certainly want to play ball. All the guys are going to sign."

"I completely agree with you," Charley responded. "Spring training exhibition games are a whole different issue from replacement games during the season. If the possibility of replacement games arises, you'll need guarantees for the rest of the season. What did Alan Nero say?"

"Naturally, he came down on the side of the players' union, because he represents so many major leaguers."

"That's certainly where his bread is buttered."

"Our first games are Friday, and they'll split us up. One game will be against Boston College on NESN."

"It would be great to watch you on TV! I'll be back in New England for four days of meetings, starting tomorrow," Charley said, "so call me to let me know if you'll be playing in that game."

On March 1, 1995, the press reported that the players' union had held meetings with minor leaguers at various spring training facilities around Florida. Officials of the union and big-leaguers in attendance said that if the minor leaguers played in exhibition games during spring training, they would be considered scabs. The minor leaguers voiced their interest in the formation of a pension plan and limited benefits, but major league union officials informed the minor leaguers that they should form their own union to prevent any illegalities if the union represented them.

The Red Sox solved the problem by beginning their exhibition games with two distinct squads of minor leaguers. The major leaguers traditionally opened their exhibition games against Boston College on NESN. One squad chosen to play against Boston College were the anointed "prospects," while those who would play against the Twins were viewed as "expendables." Todd would play in the Twins' game, along with a few of the other minor leaguers, and all the replacement players. He had signed a pledge to play exhibition games, against his agent's advice. "They certainly have let us know where we stand," was Todd's reaction.

His brother suggested Todd contact his agent to "get a release from those assholes." Then he could negotiate a trade. It was difficult for Charley and me to keep our equilibrium amid numerous calls from Ft. Myers, but we frequently reminded ourselves of our blessings. We had relocated to a beautiful new residence in Florida, and although Charley's investment banking company was in its fledgling stages, he had his self-respect and a relief from stress, the value of which was immeasurable. In addition, we had enjoyed an unforgettable trip to Italy the previous June, and were planning a 30th anniversary trip to Spain. My parents had relocated to within five miles of us in Florida, and were still active in their eighties. Charley's parents remained in Massachusetts, but were active in their seventies. We were able to split the year between residences in Florida and Massachusetts. Most importantly, both boys had obtained their college degrees, and Todd would begin an internship at an upstanding financial institution during the off-season.

Charley told Todd, "I think you are putting too much emphasis on this splitting of teams. You know they're going to showcase their top draft picks on the televised game. You've got a golden opportunity to show what you're made of, so go out and produce! At least you'll be making $80 per game!"

Todd took the field at third base during the second half of the game against the major league Twins, just where Charley had predicted his future would be. "The play of the game" was how one of the Boston papers described the stab Todd made deep in the hole between third and short. "It wasn't that great," Todd said later. "But I did hit a double off the wall in only two at-bats. Kennedy (the major league manager) was in charge, with two assistants. Rice was the batting instructor. Kennedy's very organized and all business."

"Was he intimidating?" I asked.

"Only if I let him be. But I'm out here to enjoy myself, since I've got nothing to lose."

"Well, that's a great attitude, Todd. Keep having fun. Are you playing tomorrow?"

"No, the other squad will play tomorrow." Wily as they could be, management instead kept the squad of "prospects" off the field for the following two days, hoping the strike would break. That way none of their future major leaguers could be viewed later as scabs by the union. Todd's squad played instead.

Todd's third game, in which he played at shortstop for the second half, was televised on the New England Sports Network up north. Tim taped it for us, with a narrative. "The first time at bat he went after the first pitch and got jammed for the first strike. The next pitch was off-speed, which dropped in for a strike. So he was behind 0-2, and he hit the next one sharply, but right at the shortstop. But you could tell from his body language that he was disgusted to even be out there with replacements" (who, as former players, were out there just to fill in during the strike).

"Well, he shouldn't be. This is his chance for some real exposure, if he can perform well."

"There was an article about him with pictures on the front page of the sports section of the Providence Journal today. It reported on his first two games, and quoted him as saying this is a chance to show some talent, or perhaps get traded. Actually, the article was positive about his position and his attitude. He sounded very confident."

"Did he discuss the dilemma of the minor leaguers during the strike?" I asked.

"No, nothing too involved or controversial."

"What's new with you, Tim?"

"I have interviews coming up and might accept a position as coach of the JV baseball team at Cumberland High. It pays $1,500. I started Japanese lessons in Cumberland with a native Japanese lady for $20/hour. My bartending and karate instruction have increased, so I'm pretty tired."

"That's all great news! We're sure you'll do well in the interviews. Let us know when you hear the outcome. And don't get overtired."

The second squad of "prospect" minor leaguers began playing exhibition games on March 6th, while Todd's squad played in the major-league City of Palms Park in Ft. Myers. We got immediate calls from relatives and from Tim, who'd watched Todd's game on NESN. Todd began to play shortstop and to hit well. Legally, agent Alan Nero couldn't represent those on strike, as well as the strike-breakers, so Todd had no contact with him. During the second week of March, Tim received an offer to teach English in Japan through a California-based school franchise. I was overjoyed for him! It seemed an ideal situation to showcase his talents. As it turned out, one of the schools in Fukuchiyama City, Japan, needed a teacher in late July, so Tim scheduled his departure for July 8th.

On March 10, 1995, we drove to Ft. Myers with my parents to watch Todd play. He had played the day before we arrived, and was not in the lineup when we got to City of Palms Park. The other squad beat the Twins 7-0, with fourteen hits. Over the PA system we heard, "Tomorrow we will feature this year's Red Sox 'AA' Trenton team against the Sox 'A' team. There will be no admission charged."

When we saw the "AA" lineup for that game, we were puzzled. Todd's name wasn't included. "They're just trying to get everybody to play," Charley explained. "It doesn't mean these are the only kids that are bound for Trenton. Everybody's mixed up right now." Afterward, we talked to some of the minor leaguers on the other squad: Nomar Garciaparra, Walt McKeel, Jeff Martin, Lou Merloni. At dinner with Todd, I began, "You look great, Todd, and have certainly performed well so far this month!"

"Yeah, a lot of the guys say I'm like a different person here this year. I'm not so intense, pressing too hard, because I'm having a good time. There's not so much at stake."

"Have you thought at all about whether you would begin the major league season as a replacement, if you were asked?" Charley queried.

"I have no trouble with the decision to play in Fenway Park as a replacement and leave baseball. I'd take the $115,000 and invest it."

"Well, if you're considering playing once the regular season starts, you'd better have some clear-cut demands. You know management always catches players off guard when they want signatures on the dotted line."

"I've already thought about my demands. I'd want all my money up front, because some of the replacements who were signed to minor league contracts haven't been able to collect the $5,000 out of Kenney that they were promised as a signing bonus."

My son had suddenly become an adult! He was making life-altering decisions at age twenty-two and I knew we would support his thorough thought-process. "And what about finishing the rest of the season, if the strike breaks?"

"If I play in Fenway and collect my $115,000, I wouldn't care about going back to the minors. There'd be too much resentment, and what would compare to playing in Fenway?"

I played the devil's advocate. "Why would you want to give up a chance to be a legitimate major leaguer through the normal channels? Then you'd be making a minimum of $115,000 for as long as you were in the majors. Even if you don't make it with Boston, you might somewhere else."

"Mom, you live in a dream world concerning your sons in baseball!" Todd replied. "If I'd been a hot prospect, I'd have played at 'AA' by now. Say I might have four or five years tops left, since I'm twenty-three. That means one or two years at 'AA' and also 'AAA,' and a very short career in the majors. In one season as a replacement I could earn five times what I'd earn at 'AAA' and I'd still have a professional career afterward."

"So you're ready to kiss baseball goodbye?"

"I didn't say that. I still love the game, and I'm going to play as hard as I can every time I take the field. Besides, I'm having a lot of fun this spring. The only reason I might never be a replacement player would be on philosophical grounds. I don't know if I could cross the picket line."

"Just keep all your options open in baseball," Charley advised. "You're still on an upward track."

"By the way, I was paid over $700 today."

"Boy, that sure beats not getting paid at all for spring training," I said.

"And we get $80/day meal money to eat anywhere," Todd responded. "The caterer does a good job with the lunches they bring in to the field after practice." Then he mentioned he'd forgotten to pack some shirts to wear out at night. I gave in and shopped for him the next day, despite his windfall.

By the following weekend, the 170 minor leaguers in camp would divide into teams that would practice on each of the minor league fields. Todd would be living with Randy Brown in the Sheraton overlooking the Ft. Myers harbor. There were just too many players, including the replacements, to house them all in the Days Inn in North Ft. Myers.

The whole situation became more confusing for the minor leaguers as March progressed. Todd felt the Sox management had done an admirable job mixing and utilizing all the players, to avoid a media incident involving anyone's being sent home.

We were confused by the fact that Todd was still in the major league dugout, but wasn't playing. We had not seen him take the field in a major league uniform over two weekends. We theorized that management might be trying to protect him from eventual jeopardy with the players' union.

"I can't figure out why they're not playing him," Charley said. "If he weren't up to the caliber of the replacement team, they'd have dropped him to the minor league field. There are forty-five still available for the replacement team, with four deep at every position, and they can only have thirty-two. It would be nice to see him play on the major league field just once."

Todd traveled to play an exhibition game on the former Yankee field in Ft. Lauderdale, where he'd played for the Sox on their Florida State team in the summer of '93. My parents watched, as he went into the game as a pinch runner. In the 5-4 win over the Yankees, Bob Juday collided against our catcher, Jeff Martin, chasing a foul ball. Jeff's shin guard broke Bob's jaw and cracked one tooth. Bob was hospitalized in Ft. Lauderdale, where his jaw was wired shut. He lost most of the season.

On March 19, we finally saw Todd take the field in a major league uniform in Ft. Myers' City of Palms Park. He played the entire game at third base, and NESN carried it live. He had one hit and a walk, and made several routine plays in the field. The Sox beat the Twins 3-0, with the infielders accounting for seven hits.

At dinner, Todd said that Duquette had offered all forty-five players in the dugout that day replacement contracts. The offer consisted of the following:

$5,000 up front for signing

$5,000 if the player made the thirty-two man replacement roster

$625/day pay plus $60/day meal money on the road ($115,000 salary over the entire season, if the player was in every game)

$20,000 severance pay if the major leaguers returned from their strike

Guarantee of a place in the minor league system for the remainder of 1995 if the strike ended, and increased salary of $1,000 per month added to the player's current contract.

Although Todd was disappointed with the offer of money up front, Charley and I were not surprised that management would risk as little as possible financially. "A lot of guys are upset by this offer, and they're going to walk over to the minor league fields tomorrow and not participate as replacements. They don't trust management, and they wanted the $20,000 up front. Mo Vaughn told Lou (Merloni) that when the strike is settled, none of the replacements better be around. Mo also said that it would all be forgotten in a few years. I don't know if I'll still be playing in a few years."

"With Juday hurt, your chances are excellent to make the replacement roster," Charley pointed out. "You can play different infield positions, and would get tremendous exposure. You'd also have $10,000 in your pocket. Don't put too much stock in Duquette's telling you that he's not out to screw you. He's a businessman covering his ass so that stadium seats are filled."

"Well, I just want to appear versatile in their eyes. Whenever they need a pinch runner or a sub in the infield, Kennedy points right to me. But I still want to play regularly if I sign."

"One thing's for sure: if you are playing the first game in Fenway for the Sox, we'll be there!" I said. "Your dad and I have always been opportunists. We believe in seizing the moment, and this is a good time to show them what you've got. Let me tell you a story that you've probably heard before. After we bought our first house in Wenham, Mass., and you'd just been born, Dad came home from work at New England Merchant's Bank in Boston one day and said, 'I have an opportunity at Industrial National Bank in Providence.' We bought and sold that first house in eight months, but Dad ended up as a vice chairman twenty years later, when Industrial National had become Fleet."

"Well, I'm not afraid of the consequences, or of losing friends among the players. Most of them would give their eye teeth to be in this position. I'm just sorry to unload all of this on you."

"We wouldn't want it any other way, Todd. We're glad we're here to be able to discuss the options with you. You *are* fortunate to have so many options. Give us a call tomorrow night when we get back to Delray. By then you'll have let them know your decision. And please contact Alan Nero to inform him of your decision, even though you have no formal contract with him. You'd better sever ties in writing, if you don't intend to sign with him again."

Tim later told us that Todd immediately called him from the Sheraton. The boys still relied on each other, especially regarding baseball. "Grab the opportunity!" was also Tim's advice. "But you can't blame the guys for doubting that they'll ever see their $20,000 severance pay," Tim reminded us.

Charley started biting his fingernails again.

Todd signed the replacement contract the following morning, along with forty others. He played at short and third base in late innings for the remainder of the week. Eight of his peers had declined the offer, and went back to the minor league fields on strike. Jeff Martin decided to hold out for major league monies someday, now that he was a married man. He was on strike and walked to the minor league fields. The next day he walked back to Todd's field, unable to resist the financial enticements for the replacements.

On the last Friday in March, we traveled to the west coast of Florida for the last time. The replacement Sox had Todd at second base for the entire game - a position he hadn't played since high school. He went 1-5 at bat, and made a nice play by charging the ball hard behind the pitcher to get the runner at first base. He also turned a difficult double play.

While my father retrieved his dentures at the hotel before we took Todd out to dinner, Todd revealed to us that management had informed no one as to when the final cuts would be made for the replacement team. There were still forty-some men in the dugout, and the final roster would consist of thirty-two. The replacement players had been paid for the last time. Those going to Fenway would live in the Copley Square Marriott for the first month, and would be paid $625/day. Their cars would be shipped north on carriers, since the first five days of their schedule would be in Minnesota and Kansas City.

Privately, Todd told Charley that in batting practice Jim Rice had been all over him. Todd controlled his anger, but inside, felt like throwing the bat at Rice. Later, Jim apologized to Todd and explained that Kennedy wanted Rice to work Todd hard, since he'd either be starting in replacement games, or coming off the bench.

Aloud, I queried Charley as to why Todd hadn't mentioned the incident in front of me. "He doesn't want to get your hopes too high," Charley responded.

"And you don't have high hopes for him?" I retorted.

"I don't get as upset as you do if things don't work out," he said. "Everyone has to learn to make adjustments in life."

"I would hope that because of the events of the last two years, I have demonstrated that I can adjust to change," I quipped. "Let's see - you lost your job, we moved our residence 1500 miles south, and one of our sons will soon be living in Japan."

Todd described a meeting two psychologists held with the replacement players. The object was to provide a resource for those with families. The Sox management was finally entering the 1990s. "They stressed that if things aren't going well at home, they won't go well on the field," Todd said. "Then they said that adolescence is the most difficult time of all for a child, and they asked how many of us had adolescent kids. Only 'Pookie' Bernstine, who's thirty-four, raised his hand."

The next morning, Todd was among several of the Sox players who participated in a benefit golf tournament for a children's hospital. "I saw Duquette playing with Coach Thurston (baseball coach from Amherst, who recruited Todd to play there). I asked Duquette later if that's who it was. And I told him to say 'Hello' for me."

"Good. Sounds like Duquette is no longer unapproachable," I commented. "Do you still trust him?"

"At this point, I have no reason not to."

In the succeeding two days of spring training, Todd played entire games at second base and shortstop, with all the major league coaches in attendance. He had posted no errors in the field during the entire month, but his batting remained tentative. Twice during one of the games, Rice called Todd over to remind him of something about his batting, while Todd was in the on-deck circle.

The local TV station in Ft. Myers announced that because of the strike, attendance at major league stadiums had been one-third the average of the previous year's spring training. We had been among 1,500 to 2,500 fans over the three-day weekend in stadiums that held 8,000.

Charley and I had gotten to know Randy Brown quite well, and really got a kick out of him. Wherever he was, Randy was able to attract attention. He wore arm bands, sun glasses, and high stockings on the field; off the field he wore gold chains and tee-shirts that proclaimed, "Property of the Red Sox." Running down the third base line chasing a pop foul from his position at shortstop, he would roll over the tarpaulin stored nearby. In a double play, he would end up somersaulting over the runner who was trying to take Randy out of the play. Yet we discovered Randy was as insecure as the rest - and from Texas, no less. His father had suffered a fatal heart attack while dining in a restaurant with his son the previous summer in New Britain, Conn., after an "AA" game.

We were able to catch a final game of Todd's when his squad, one of two still playing exhibition games for the Sox, came to the east coast of Florida to play the Expos' replacements. The Braves and the Expos shared the minor league fields and stadium in West Palm Beach. The Pawtucket coach, Bud Bailey, accompanied our squad. We had a cheering section of eight with us. When Todd belted a double off the center field wall his first time up to drive in a run, we all let loose. He was third in the batting order! He hit two more deep to center and left center, which were caught; then he walked. At third base, he was flawless. The majority of replacement players for the Sox had remained in Ft. Myers that day, so Todd's squad consisted of many "AAA" and "AA" regulars in the Sox system. Charley and I started playing mind games, trying to guess what management was up to, an activity we should have learned over the years was futile.

Afterward, I asked him what management was telling him. "Nothing," he replied. "They don't know what will happen with the strike from day to day. The replacement team is flying to Minneapolis for the Sox opener in three days, but we still don't know who'll make the roster. There are so many infielders down in minor league camp that I might be sent home," he concluded.

"Not a chance!" I contradicted. It made me furious to hear him lack confidence at the end of this spring training.

"He's just playing mind games with himself so he's not disappointed," Charley explained to me later.

"If they never play one game, at least he'll get $5,000 for signing the paper at this point," I said. "And if there is a replacement roster, the owners will have to pay each player another $5,000. The owners would be stupid to shell out any money if they could avoid it. If the players play just one game and the strike breaks, then they'd have to deliver another $20,000 severance pay to each player."

"Right," Charley agreed. "Plus daily fines if the court ruling goes against them."

On March 31, 1995, Manhattan Circuit Court Judge Sonia Sotomayor ruled that the owners had not negotiated in good faith, and enforced an injunction against them. As a result, the Player's Union voted to return to the ball fields. Of course, the owners could still vote to lock the players out, and would appeal the decision within days. With the ruling, there was the possibility for the major leaguers to attend training camp for three weeks, then for Opening Day to be re-scheduled around April 26, 1995. We assumed the owners wouldn't put replacements on the field for a mere three weeks. The scenario unfolded minute by minute.

In the final exhibition game on April 1, 1995, the replacement team belted fifteen hits. Todd sat out. We could not even guess what would be happening to him in the following twenty-four hours. Our only safe conclusion was that his future lay at third base. Management always won the mind games we played with them.

The following day, the bubble burst. Without an agreement with the owners, the major leaguers headed to their spring training camps, and the season was scheduled to officially open on April 27th. The Red Sox had never listed a replacement roster, and no "official" replacement game was ever played as part of the major league season. Todd had benefited from major league coaching, and had gained exposure and confidence. Monetarily, he had gained the promise of a $5,000 signing bonus payable on April 15th, and $1,000 additional salary per month during the season. To major leaguers, this kind of money was peanuts, but to minor leaguers, it was huge. The owners had saved themselves $5,000 for each player by never listing a replacement roster, and $20,000 severance pay for each replacement.

But there were still just too many players. Replacements that looked promising signed minor league contracts; those minor leaguers who had purposely sat out during exhibition games, as well as the top "prospects" on the forty-man roster all had to be placed back on minor league teams. Todd was one of eight infielders assigned to "AA" in Trenton, including first-round draft pick Nomar Garciaparra at shortstop. At second base were Lou Merloni and Pat Murphy. At third base were "Chop" Pugh and Bill Selby. Todd foresaw bench time all season. His most recent roommate in the Sheraton, Randy Brown, would play shortstop at "AAA," along with Tony Rodrigues. Todd could not have done more that he did during '95 spring training. His batting average ended around .280, with zero errors over the month.

Tim and Todd in New Haven, Conn., 1995. Todd was with the Trenton Thunder. Tim was going to Japan to teach.

17

Another Roller Coaster Ride

Todd did not play until the fourth game for the Trenton Thunder. Garciaparra played every game at shortstop, and Lou Merloni was playing second base. In Todd's first start, he hit a home run and reported to us he was pleased with his defensive play. He was very happy to be playing for Manger Ken Macha, who demonstrated a new breed of communicative, positive coaching that demanded instant respect. In addition, he was an excellent role model, getting to the field early, jogging each morning to keep in shape, and providing support not only for his team, but also for his pre-adolescent son and daughter.

Tim and an entourage of friends were finally able to watch Todd play when the Thunder traveled to the refurbished Yale stadium in New Haven, Conn., to play at the Rockies' "AA" home stadium. Tim and Todd had both played there against Yale. Charley and I had sat on splintered wooden seats, while a hidden employee posted the numerals on the scoreboard in the outfield at each half inning, just like at Fenway. The Rockies had invested millions in, among other things, an electronic score board and new locker rooms. The Brown and Dartmouth teams had had to shower and change across the street, at the Yale Bowl. Yet the aura of tradition had been retained. This was, after all, where President Bush the elder had captained his Yale team.

At 7 p.m. game time the third week of April, it was around 50 degrees. Only Tim and his friend stayed for the entire game to see Todd get two hits and make some fantastic plays at third. "He and Ryan McGuire look very comfortable," Tim reported, "both at bat and in the field. The first time up, Todd struck out against a leftie throwing junk. But he adjusted nicely for the rest of the game." Of course, Tim thoroughly enjoyed seeing his old buddies on the team - Walt McKeel, Jeff Martin, Doug Hecker. Two of Todd's suite-mates from Brown and a frat brother of Tim's from Dartmouth partied afterward with the Carey brothers. Since the next day was Tim's birthday, Todd remembered to give him a couple of gifts.

"I could tell that Todd really wanted us to go down to New Haven," Tim told us. "He called me three times in a row, leaving messages asking whether we were going, and how many tickets we'd need. The last message was to call him as soon as possible.

"When we got there, I was talking to the guys on the team for a while. The game was about to begin, so I yelled to Todd, 'Nice talking to you, bro!'

"'I'll see you after the game,' Todd said.

"We all stayed overnight in New Haven, and twelve of us went out together. Todd was really happy." Always the big brother, Tim's primary concern about his relationship with Todd overshadowed any feeling of regret that he wasn't out there on the field.

During the day, Tim was coaching his Cumberland, R.I., junior varsity baseball team before heading to his bartending job at night. One of the youngsters who used to live next door to us was now his first baseman on the J.V. squad. Tim had filled every moment of his life outside of baseball, instructing karate and working out at the gym. I knew it wasn't all challenging work, but kept my mouth shut. The experience of living in Japan would immerse him within a few months.

On April 21, 1995, the papers reported that the Sox had sent two "AAA" players from Pawtucket camp over to major league spring training: Randy Brown and Ron Mahay. Both had signed replacement contracts and, with only a few days left in the major league exhibition games, management re-opened the wounds of the players' strike by sending the two into the lions' den. Less than three weeks had transpired, but management claimed the major league club needed bodies to rest those who'd played every day. So Randy and Ron made the '95 team picture. It was much later when we found out how the major leaguers had treated the two strike-breakers.

As for Todd, by April 21st he was leading the Eastern League in batting with an average of .433. He still had made no errors.

Exactly a week later, on April 28, 1995, the Sox hit all of us below the belt. Charley and I had arrived the day before in Key West with our friends, the Laffeys, from Cumberland. We received a call at 11:30 p.m. from Tim.

"Todd's been trying to reach you, but he didn't have your number at the hotel," he said.

"What's happened?" Charley asked frantically, groping for his glasses and turning on the lamp on the nightstand.

"After he played in the game for Trenton tonight, the manager told him he was being sent down to the top level 'A' team in Sarasota (replacing Lynchburg)."

"What?" Charley jumped up, wide awake. "How come? He's batting around .350 up there now, and has only two errors in almost two months."

"That's right," Tim confirmed. "He's been playing third base two out of three nights, but now Selby's coming off the forty-man roster and will replace him. There are too many kids in Trenton, and they've got to keep a spot open for Juday when his jaw heals."

"I can't believe this!" Charley exploded. "Todd's had the best spring of his life, and Selby's batting just over .200. What did they tell him?"

"Macha didn't tell him anything. He was just relaying orders, and he's only seen Todd for one month. But Todd called Bob Schaefer, who told him they wanted him to get more at-bats down in Florida."

"How did Todd sound?"

"How do you think he sounded? He was bullshit! There's no logic to this - there never is. He asked to be released or traded, and Schaefer said, 'No.' So Todd told him he might quit."

"Well, we'll call him right now. Thanks, Tim. I can't believe this is happening! Was anyone else sent down?"

"Just him. And two kids got traded."

We were stunned. Todd's batting average was in the paper the following day at .340. All the other players who'd been on the Sox replacement team were playing at either "AA" or "AAA," if they were still around.

"How are you feeling?" Charley asked Todd when he answered at midnight.

"I don't know if I want to subject myself to this shit any more," he said. "I have a professional career I can pursue."

"But that doesn't start until September," Charley reminded him.

"Well, there's nothing more I could have done to prove myself," he said. "I belong at the 'AA' level and I have played as well and batted as well as Brown and Rodrigues in 'AAA.'"

"That's exactly right. What did Schaefer say to you?"

"He said they wanted me to have more at-bats. And that he hoped I wouldn't quit, but he'd give me a few days to report down there. Big fucking deal! It's a two-day drive anyway."

I interceded for the first time to give some shelter in the storm. "Why don't you come to stay with us so we can discuss it? That way you'll have two days to think about the decision on your drive down. Did you talk to your agent?"

"It's Friday, Mom. I can't reach him over the weekend."

"You should leave an urgent message at his business number before you make any decision," Charley suggested. "Just remember that if you quit now, you'll never have the option of playing again. We'll leave Key West and meet you at our place in Delray."

The next day we made the five-hour drive back with our friends. We had discussed management's move over and over in the car. There was still no plausible explanation any of us could come up with by the time we'd arrived.

Around 6 p.m. on the day we got back, Todd and my parents all walked in the door together. Todd was calm and thoughtful, but dejected. He told us his team-mates were totally shocked by the news. Selby and Mahay had joined the "AA" roster in Trenton, one of them taking Todd's spot. Privately, Charley and I hoped he hadn't given up.

I knew enough not to talk baseball to my son. I was still an outsider in that world. In his room behind closed doors, Charley advised Todd to consider this a mere obstacle in his path, such as we had had to face when we were married for one year and Charley was sent to Viet Nam; or when he was released as vice chairman of Fleet. Todd had exhibited a self confidence that spring that we'd never seen on the field before, and in the bedroom he verbalized his belief in himself to his dad. Charley told him to keep on believing in himself; that if he reported to Sarasota with a chip on his shoulder or with self pity, he should give the game up.

"I can't do that yet. I know I can play, and I still want to play."

"Then go out and prove it all over again." How fortunate for Todd that his dad had been a player himself!

The next morning Todd drove to Sarasota. In his first fifteen trips to the plate, he hit three singles and three doubles, with no errors in the field. He played two out of three nights at third base. My parents accompanied me up the east coast of Florida to watch him in Vero Beach, while Charley was away on business. We arrived back home at 1 a.m., but Todd had appreciated our support.

"He certainly doesn't belong on this team," I told Charley by phone. "The kids are younger, and they make so many errors. Todd's a loner on the team. He talks mostly to the coaches on the bench. I felt really bad for him, because he looked so out of place. But he seemed extremely focused. Greg Patton and his wife and baby got sent down to the Michigan team, when Todd replaced him."

Back in Trenton, Dana LeVangie had taken Todd's spot in the Morrisville apart-ment. Dana had been rotated down from Pawtucket, making a total of three catch-ers in "AA" Trenton. The players became phantoms, disappearing in the middle of the night to other teams. Dana took care of Todd's details, such as the landlord and the phone company.

The emotional roller coaster that Charley and I had been riding had taken a toll on my stomach. I was popping Tums for acid. I also had deja vu, having seen Todd play on the same Dodgertown field in Vero Beach two years previously, for the Sox "A" team based in Ft. Lauderdale. I knew how much he'd progressed, but there he was, back in the Florida State League! I suddenly hated baseball, espe-cially Dan Duquette, and the way management treated minor leaguers. I wondered whether Todd would meet the same fate as his brother. Only time would tell.

On May 15, 1995, Charley and I traveled diagonally across the state of Florida for five hours to Clearwater, where Todd would play two games over Mothers' Day weekend. The two-lane highway we chose was the antecedent of the more southern Alligator Alley, now four lanes to accommodate the cross-Florida traffic following the expansion of the Naples/Marco Island/Ft. Myers areas. Route 70, instead, was dangerous, bearing large trucks and car carriers in our lane, which we had to pass as we whizzed by cattle farms, citrus groves, and an occasional remnant of the Seminole tribe. By the time we crossed the bridge over Tampa Bay, we were both exhausted and in foul moods. I downright hated baseball, and resented following the Florida State "A" team again. The only thing I did not resent was the lifelong commitment of time, emotion, and energy that I had made to my sons.

Finding the stadium proved easier than in a lot of other cities, and we postponed checking into our hotel on the Gulf of Mexico in favor of dinner at the closest restaurant to the ball park. Everything at "Hong Kong," in downtown Clearwater, tasted wonderful after the long ride.

Todd looked great. He had rented an apartment in Sarasota previously held by Shannon and Greg Patton and their baby. The Pattons had driven on to the Sox affiliate in Michigan when Todd replaced Greg. Todd would have no roommate, and put down $500 on the new place (first month's rent).

It was directly on a private, members-only golf course and had a pool. Todd had convinced the landlord to let him borrow a TV, as well as to introduce him to some club members. The apartment came complete with linens. Shannon Patton had left him baked goods.

After we'd talked to him, we settled into our box seats at the side of his dugout. There were only 1,200 in attendance, but Todd had, as always, left tickets for us, and I began to feel more positive. The temperature was in the low 80's at 7 p.m., without a cloud in sight. Was there a better way to spend an evening than sitting outside in the balmy air with Charley? The game was secondary. The stat sheet inside the program lifted my spirits even further. Todd's batting average had remained at .333 with three doubles, and four RBI's. He'd made two errors in two weeks.

Unfortunately, in a 6-0 loss to the Phillies' affiliate, he made two more errors at third base while we watched. For the first time since March 1st, he looked unsure of himself defensively, and let the ball play him. He stepped back when he should have charged the ball, and stepped into it when he should have backed up. In his defense, the infield dirt was so hard that the ball ricocheted as if it had hit Astroturf. The infielders had no idea whether it would bounce over their heads or skid through their legs. Our infielders had a total of five errors. One fan knew we were Todd's parents and asked, "Is he new to the position? He doesn't look a third baseman." I bit my lip.

Batting sixth, Todd hit a shot over the right fielder's head for a double the first time up. The next time, he walked, then hit a rocket to the center field fence. The outfielder caught it to the left of the 400' marker. He went 1-for-3 at the plate and seemed content with his designation on the team as an "AA" veteran. We even got laughter out of him as he recounted stories of catching fish in the Waterway near his apartment, while manatees swam right up.

Tom Barrett, the Sarasota manager, was really fun to watch. Like his brother, Marty, he was short in stature, but exhibited boundless energy and enthusiasm. He motored out to the third base bag to coach his runners at the top of every inning, and ran off the field directly toward the player he wanted to speak to at the end of the half inning. In one game in Ft. Myers, he ran across the grass behind the pitcher's mound to argue with the umpire, and slid the last ten feet, landing on his ass with the umpire over him. He jumped to a standing position to begin shouting in the ump's face. "Don't ever do that again!" the ump warned. "I don't want to be shown up."

"I have a groin pull, and didn't want to stop short," Barrett immediately countered. A good example of "thinking on your feet," or your ass, as the case may be!

The kids really wanted to play for Tommy, and respected him for being on the field every day at noon to work with them in groups of three or four. "He takes more ground balls than any of us," Todd said, "and loves doing it." I had seen Barrett consult Todd back in Vero Beach regarding another infielder's throwing motion. After the game, the team had to do sprints on the field, and there were complaints from the prima donnas. As a result, Barrett uncharacteristically exploded at the team in the locker room, screaming swears and spewing pizza he'd been eating. He even had tears in his eyes, because he took the game so seriously. Afterward, he apologized to the players.

We found out that the reason Charley and I had been coughing at the Clearwater beach that day was because of "red tide," which polluted not only the Gulf water, but also the air. Dead fish lay strewn across the sand for lack of oxygen.

Sunday morning, Mothers' Day, we drove down to Sarasota to pick Todd up at his new apartment so we could have brunch with him. Despite having assured ourselves that Todd had settled in well, on our minds was the news of Charley's mother's third stroke, of our house remaining on the market in Rhode Island after one year, and of the prospect that Charley would part ways with his investment banking partner in Ft. Lauderdale. My interior design business was dwindling, as I devoted less and less time to it. We read in the paper that Ron Mahay, one of the other two 23-year-old replacement players along with Todd, was being moved from Trenton up to the major league roster because of an injury there. Mahay had a superb Fenway debut, but it was difficult for me to swallow that all of those Todd had played with on the replacement team were on "AA" or higher, while Todd remained at "A." Then Charley gave me a good talking-to.

"We have known Todd's potential, but let's admit it! Up until this year, he hasn't shown it. They have given him every chance over the last three years. Bill Selby hit .310 over the season last year in Lynchburg, but Todd only hit .235. Naturally they want Selby at 'AA.'"

I had an easy target for my frustration: politics. "I'm sure Kennedy's managing Mahay on the replacement team helped promote him to Fenway."

"Well, it sure hasn't helped Todd that he played for Kennedy as a replacement!"

Management had previously fed Ron Mahay and Randy Brown "to the lions" when they put them on the major league roster with five days of spring training left. The reasoning was that the confrontation between major leaguers and replacement players should take place in the Boston locker room before the season started, rather than during the season. Management wanted the public to believe these two replacement players would allow the major leaguers some rest after an intense month of spring training.

The confrontation had, indeed, taken place in the locker room. ESPN had interviewed Randy Brown and Ron Mahay afterward, and Randy only reiterated what minor leaguers had claimed all during the strike: they had no union, hence no bargaining position, and were accepting an elevation to the major league roster for an interim period only because they had no other choice. They wanted to further their own careers, and viewed the strike as past history.

When Joel Bennett pitched in Pawtucket a couple of weeks after coming off the major league roster in early May, he met Tim for dinner. Tim had been the catcher Joel requested each time he pitched in Lynchburg, before Tim's release.

The story circulating among the players was that during warm-ups on the day Randy and Ron were up in Fenway, the team surrounded the two of them in the locker room. The story continued that Roger Clemens accused them of fucking with the major leaguers' families by being strikebreakers, and told the rest of the team to ostracize Randy and Ron. Surprisingly, it was Mike Greenwell who stepped in before it got really physical, reminding the team that all of them would have done the same thing, maybe with the exception of Clemens, who never really experienced the minor leagues. Of course, this was all hearsay. What was absolute fact was that no other team had put replacements in such a tenuous situation.

Unfortunately, Clemens was scheduled to appear on the Sarasota team within two nights of our being there, for rehabilitation of his shoulder. Todd was now the only remaining replacement player on the Sarasota roster, after the release of Chris Antosazek. "The team has been told by Barrett not to even talk to Clemens, not to ask for autographs or anything," Todd told us. "He's supposed to be here to concentrate on getting his shoulder ready as quickly as possible."

Our baseball sojourns were always an adventure of discovery - geographically, emotionally, and physically. Charley and I loved having time to be alone together, as well as to explore the towns where ball parks took us. We always found interesting aspects of American culture to remember, including historical sights, museums, and cuisine. I had a few favorite dishes from the Ft. Myers Sheraton, McGregor's Country Club Restaurant (now Smitty's), and Peter's La Cusina. Some of them were real treats, since I hardly ever ate them because of high cholesterol: grilled chicken over penne pasta with a tomato, olive, caper, basil, garlic, parsley, and gorgonzola sauce; lobster bisque; and crepes filled with mushrooms and crab. In Punta Gorda, on the Charlotte Harbor, we savored New England scrod, shipped fresh to Florida. At Monte's in Vero Beach I tried linguine with Maine clams and sausage. To work all of this off, we religiously walked between three to four miles every morning, and swam or played tennis or golf in the afternoon, if Todd had a night game. Emotionally, the roller coaster ride continued. At each stage of being a parent we looked forward to the next stage and thought, "If we make it that far without any catastrophes, we'll be home free." In high school, we fretted over the boys' drinking and driving, their getting into colleges, their remaining drug-free. When we escaped relatively unscathed, we thought we could relax. But we realized when they were in college that what they didn't tell us was potentially more disastrous than anything they'd done in high school. The problems increased in their ramifications, and we would never, ever, be "home free" as parents, no matter if our children were fifty. Besides, then grandchildren might come along to worry about.

For my farewell game on May 21st, we watched Todd hit another home run and a single in a 4-1 win against the Twins' Miracles in Ft. Myers. He also got into a heated argument with the home plate umpire over a called third strike. Since the team was staying overnight in Ft. Myers before returning to Sarasota, we were able to have a very late dinner with him. Todd was still pretty irascible until his meal arrived, because of his dispute with the umpire. At least he was finally clean-shaven after sporting the "scruffy" look during our visit.

Charley was planning to drive back to see Todd the following weekend, while my sister visited me at our condo. "Do you mind if I bunk with you on the pullout couch in your apartment next weekend?" Charley asked Todd.

"Of course not! Bring some sheets and a blanket and pillow. A pitcher just got sent down to our team on a trade and asked if he could live in the apartment on my couch. I explained the apartment was only two rooms and too small. I don't mind living by myself - I kind of like it. On the road, no one has been assigned to room with me yet."

I reminded him, "Just remember when you were sent down here unexpectedly and needed a place. Three others took you in until the Pattons left this place."

"I guess Bob Juday's jaw has healed and he was sent back to the Trenton team today," Todd said, ignoring me. "That makes eight infielders up there. I don't expect that anyone will play very much except Nomar."

"What they should do is clear out some bodies from 'AAA,'" Charley suggested. "No one is producing up there at bat, and some of those infielders have been around quite a while. If you keep hitting home runs, Todd, you won't be ignored" (he now had four in three weeks).

"I ask Tommy (Barrett) after every game to tell Schaefer I want to be traded," Todd told us. "But Schaefer is either away or not in his office, and Tommy leaves messages on his voice mail. Schaefer hasn't been down here yet."

"Well, when he comes, I want you to sound like a broken record. Keep asking to be traded so you can play at a higher level. But you must keep up the hitting! Then you know they won't release you, and you certainly won't sit on the bench."

When we drove north for the summer on June 1, 1995, Todd's average remained at .302 after one month in Sarasota. He had five homers, sixteen RBI's, and four errors. Charley had bunked with Todd for two nights the previous weekend.

Todd in Trenton, 1995.

"You'll never believe what Kenney tried to do!" Charley related. "He called Todd from Boston to get his Trenton contract revised to a Sarasota contract. Kenney wanted him to settle for $1,200/month, as opposed to the $1,500 salary he's had since he was assigned to Trenton. That doesn't include the extra $1,000/month for being a replacement player.

"'Why would I do that?'" Todd responded to Kenney. 'I already played up there for a month, and besides, I was a replacement player helping you guys out.'

"You can't try to take money away from Todd! Kenney said he'd heard how well Todd was doing in Sarasota, and thought he'd be back up in Trenton before long.

"'I should be back up there now!' Todd told him. Todd thinks Kenney is a front man who backs down when confronted. There's really no room for Todd to play in Trenton." Our focus over the upcoming month was diverted from baseball. Charley's business partner in Florida was in the hospital for high blood pressure and chest pain; we had to select a new realtor who would be more aggressive in selling the Rhode Island house; we planned to attend a thirtieth Colby reunion in Maine and to celebrate our thirtieth wedding anniversary in Spain. In early July, Tim would be leaving for two years in Japan. We'd decided to have a surprise farewell party for him at our beach house on July 4th. I'd invited ninety relatives and friends, and was still trying to locate his '92 Dartmouth classmates.

On the drive north from Florida we stopped at Kiawah Island, South Carolina - a delightfully low-key golf, tennis, and beach resort 21 miles south of Charleston. Wonderful! Charleston was a walking paradise of history and art. When we returned to Kiawah Island in 2005, the multi-star, elegant, Sanctuary Resort had replaced the casual Kiawah Inn. But the wide, wide beach and magnificent golf courses remained.

18

Back Up Again

The day we arrived back in Westport, we learned that Todd had been called back up to Trenton the same day. In typical fashion, the Red Sox bungled the communication. Todd had bussed with the Sarasota team from there to West Palm Beach for a four-game series. After he'd arrived, Tommy Barrett informed him that he was to report to Trenton and be dressed for the Tuesday game, two nights hence.

"Coach, I have to get back to the west coast to get my stuff in the apartment in Sarasota and pick up my car. Why didn't you tell me before we got on the bus?"

"I just got the call now, Todd, after we got here. They want you to get a plane back to Sarasota today."

After calling my parents who were going to watch the four games in West Palm Beach, Todd flew back to Sarasota, arriving at 9 p.m. He packed his belongings and did some minimal cleaning, then signed out with his landlord early the next morning. By 8 a.m. he was on his way to Fayetteville, North Carolina, for the night. Unfortunately, Hurricane Allison, the first of the season, was sweeping across the Florida Panhandle toward Georgia. For two days, the storm stalked Todd as he drove north.

By the end of the week, when his Trenton team reached Norwich, Conn., on a road trip, we finally heard from him. He'd moved in with Ryan McGuire in Trenton, next door to the apartment he'd had during the month of April. He expected to be bouncing around the infield as a backup. In four days, Todd played two games at second base.

On the day Charley and I were to leave for my thirtieth Colby reunion in Maine, the Cumberland High junior varsity team that Tim coached was in its final state playoff game. Ever the baseball mom, I agreed to postpone our departure for my reunion until after the game. So we began the six-hour drive to Colby at 4:30 p.m., after Tim's team lost 9-6. As we left, Tim, Molly, and Coach "Mac" Wright left to watch Todd play a night game in Norwich. When Charley commented, "I wish we could go with them, instead of to a reunion," I totally lost it!

"Are you kidding me?" I yelled. "I've waited five years to see some of my Colby friends, and we've already missed this evening's dinner. Can't we devote some time now to my activities?" It was a pretty silent trip north for the first hour!

As we departed for our trip to Spain, Todd's average was published in The Providence Journal at .300, with two homers. When we returned around July 1, Todd was sharing second base with Lou Merloni and Mike Hardge, who'd dropped down from Pawtucket. Out of four consecutive days, Todd and Hardge played once each, while Merloni played two - not a good omen. Todd's average had dropped to .250, since he had had only two hits in his last twenty at-bats while we were away. Garciaparra, playing every day at short, had made the All-Star team, and was batting .257. Bill Selby, batting in the .280s, was playing every day at third base for Trenton. The team led its division, and was blessed with the addition of three players from Pawtucket. On July 3rd, Ken Ryan, a major league reliever, also dropped to Trenton.

Duquette was showing no tolerance for anyone who didn't produce, yet was still acquiring players. On any given night, we could tune into the major league Sox game on NESN in New England and see a newly-acquired face on the field. As of July 30th, forty-six names had been on the major league roster at some time during the season. Only three players were at the same position as the previous season: Vaughn, Valentin, and Greenwell.

The average attendance at major league ball parks around the country had dropped twenty percent after the strike had ended. There were only two exceptions - one was Fenway Park. Doris Kearns Goodwin proclaimed on national TV, while writing Wait Till Next Year, that baseball players could no longer fulfill the function of providing a nostalgic bridge to America's history, primarily because the majority of Americans could not relate to the salaries or the strike. Minor league stadiums were filled.

It was difficult having Tim's surprise farewell party without Todd there. Many of Tim's Dartmouth classmates had come from five states to say goodbye, not knowing if they'd see him while he lived in Japan or whether he'd choose to stay overseas longer. "I still feel uncomfortable playing second base," Todd said on the phone from Trenton. "There are double plays that I should be making, but I'll turn the wrong way. It's just because I haven't played regularly. At least I'm not making errors. Our pitcher, Orellano, and 'Pork Chop' Pough were on the All-Star team. Orellano was the winning pitcher in that game, and Pough got the homer to win the game, making him the MVP. Jeff Suppan just moved up to Boston from our team, to start against Kansas City. Al Nipper, our pitching coach, went up there with him."

"That proves you're not too far away, Todd. It also proves they have absolutely no pitching, to have to dip down to Trenton. It's hard to believe Boston is leading the league by four games. Did you have a good time in New York during the All-Star break?"

"It was great! Dave Murphy took the train down from Providence, and I took the train up from Princeton. We stayed with Cubby (Tom Crain) at his NYU Med School apartment. How's Tim doing?"

We proceeded to tell Todd about Tim's adventures, first outside Osaka, where he stayed with his supervisor before being driven to Fukuchiyama City, with its rural population of 200,000 in the mountains outside Kyoto. Tim loved this new location, and rented a two-bedroom apartment from the school where he'd begun teaching English immediately. On weekends, he helped coach baseball for the local public school teams. The Japanese pitcher for the L.A. Dodgers, Hideo Nomo, had been forgiven for abandoning his culture, and was a national hero in Japan after the All-Star game here. When Tim took out his pictures of his Red Sox days with his brother, he was an instant hit. The young children, who had never seen a 6'3" blond, blue-eyed, 220-pound American, actually dropped their book bags on the street and stared. Some approached him to feel his arms and legs, whispering, "Atsui! Atsui!" ("thick").

On July 25th, the Trenton Thunder began a four-day road trip to New Britain, Conn. The team had had a day off before heading north, and Todd appeared tired from his "relaxation" at Sea Island on the Jersey shore. He didn't play the first night in New Britain, while Hardge played second base, and Ryan McGuire, Nomar Garciaparra, and Bill Selby completed the infield at their usual positions. The infielders contributed homers, triples, and doubles. At this level, there were no slouches on the roster. Later, Fenway fans would recognize some of these names as if they owned them. But the higher up the ladder a player progressed, the less secure his job became.

Ken Ryan, for example, and Greg Blosser had bounced from Fenway Park down two levels to Trenton. We had watched Ken struggle with the Trenton team, but by the time we saw him in New Britain, he'd shrugged off his, "Why me?" attitude and closed two games with velocities in the low 90s. We were surprised, though, by his appearance. At 6'5," he slouched like a much older person, and was graying at the temples.

Todd played the second game that we watched in New Britain, giving Nomar a rest at shortstop. During infield practice, he exhibited the confidence and authority of an "AA" player, as he scooped, whipped, and barehanded the ball. The infielders were clearly enjoying themselves, and their enthusiasm was infectious. The team loved playing for Macha, and were one game out of first place in their division on July 26, 1995.

Todd had picked up the "AA" strut. As he walked to and from the bullpen to swing the bat before the game, his hat was slung low, just above his eyes, while his shoulders remained erect, his head high. Only his butt swayed.

I must admit I still didn't understand the intricacies of many plays on the field. In situations with men on base, I saw the infielders move to their predestined positions as the ball was hit in some unorthodox fashion, and I questioned Charley as to why one fielder covered the play instead of another. Most of the time, he replied with a one-liner that indicated I should have known the answer.

The temperature had hovered around 90 degrees that week in New England, with a dew point and humidity near 100%. The rain and fog came and went, dousing the field. There was no relief from the sweats. We arrived back in Westport, Mass., at 1 a.m. after the Saturday night game, and took off again in the morning for Sunday's midday game in New Britain.

It was "Kiddies Day" for the noon game, and at least forty buses sat in the parking lot. As a lesson in sportsmanship for the day campers in attendance, the two teams had a brawl in front of home plate. After an incident in Durham, North Carolina, earlier that season, any minor leaguer who left his position on the field during an altercation would be fined at least $200, and would be suspended for two days during the season. Obviously no player wanted to remain standing on the field if his teammates cleared their bench, so twenty-three of the Thunder's twenty-five players ended up with fines. Players rotated two at a time to miss their games— probably the games in which they wouldn't be in the lineup, anyway. Baseball players were not known to be ferocious fighters. I seldom worried about these altercations, even if Todd piled on in the fracas. Two days later, in Trenton, six members of the Thunder got fined again for their part in a barroom brawl that left the SoHo Bar "in shambles," according to the AP report. Fortunately, Todd was not among them. Manager Macha put all barrooms in the Waterfront Stadium vicinity off-limits to the team.

After the noon game in New Britain, Todd's apartment-mate at Brown, Dave Murphy, drove Todd and Trenton first baseman Ryan McGuire to Rhode Island. They toured the Brown campus and the Pawtucket "AAA" stadium, and met us at our beach house. It was the first time in the four years since both boys had begun playing pro ball that either had come home during the season. Ryan McGuire was batting .350, and played first base every day. We really enjoyed his company and his subtle sense of humor.

After a huge breakfast and a trip to the beach in the morning, we drove the boys back to Beehive Field in New Britain to rejoin their team. Todd would again be playing shortstop. Charley and I spent a couple of hours in the 90-degree heat at a public golf course, awaiting game time. Todd hit a homer, a triple, and a single for four RBI's that night. He'd missed the hitting cycle by one hit: a double. His errors for the season remained at six, and his home runs stood at ten. He had raised his average that night almost ten percentage points. Too bad the Sox were loaded two-deep at every position all the way up to Fenway. Duquette's grand design still appeared to be "survival of the fittest" - to load up talent throughout the system for the least cash, then see who would survive after a couple of years. After the game that night, two reporters interviewed Todd, including one from The Providence Journal. A Fall River native and Detroit scout, Skip Lewis, was in attendance, as well as three of my high school classmates from Greenwich, Conn., whom I hadn't seen in over thirty years.

Admittedly addicted to our son's games, we were on the road to Trenton a little over two weeks later for a week's home stand. When we arrived, Todd's average stood at .262. He'd only played once in six days, and had served his two-game suspension. Merloni was playing third base, with a batting average also in the .260s. Todd had had a homer and a triple off a lefty pitcher in New Britain, but Macha didn't play him in Trenton when a lefty pitched. He was still trying to find a position for Bill Selby, who had twenty-seven errors but was batting .297. The night we arrived, Bill was playing second base.

After a win over the Portland Sea Dogs that night, the Trenton Thunder was in sole possession of first place in its division. Seven thousand three hundred filled the beautiful new sphere called "Waterfront Park" along the Delaware River. Parks and glass-fronted brick buildings surrounded the area, reminding us somewhat of the Wilmington, Delaware, area surrounding the stadium. Three blocks away in Trenton was the state penitentiary.

Todd talked to us mainly about his conversation with Macha and Kenney regarding placement in a fall/winter league. We had never seen him so enthusiastic about playing ball, to the point that he was willing to forsake his management trainee position with Citizens Bank in the fall. It was clear to us that rooming with Ryan McGuire had had a tremendously positive influence on him. Ryan was extremely focused on his baseball career - to the point of obsession, almost - but that had made him the team leader in batting (.341). In addition to being confident and intense, he held Todd's baseball ability in high regard, and it had rubbed off on Todd. The prospects who played fall and winter ball would undoubtedly move up in the organization, and Todd really wanted to be included.

"Kenney didn't say one word positively or negatively," Todd told us. "He only said they're just beginning to talk to the winter ball teams, and there'll be a place for all the major leaguers, either in Puerto Rico or Venezuela. I think the slots for the Sox in the Arizona League will be filled before they get to my name."

The following day, Charley and I re-explored Princeton University campus and museum. We hadn't seen the campus since the boys had played baseball there as Princeton's opponents, and we thoroughly enjoyed the walking tour, restaurants downtown, and extensive museum open to the public without charge.

Aaron Sele pitched the second game against the Portland Sea Dogs in a 3-1 losing effort. He was down from the major league team, rehabbing his shoulder. His curve ball absolutely would not break over the plate. Todd played third base, seeing little action, both in the field and at bat. He beat out a bunt for a single, something his dad had been begging him to try during his pro career. He'd always been the best bunter on his teams until college, when he started to jack everything over the right field fence so the scouts would notice him. Once on base against the Sea Dogs, he got tagged off the bag at second, when the succeeding batter hit a line drive to the second baseman.

The day before Todd's birthday, 7,200 attended a Sunday afternoon game in 95-degree heat. Under the overhang in front of the grand concourse that housed the concession stands, fans stood three-deep to watch the game. It was 30 degrees cooler there than out in the molded plastic seats. Vendors sold ice cream and Pepsi with ice bags around their necks, or wet towels over their heads. Thankfully, we'd brought hats and got Trenton Thunder golf towels to wring cold water over us. By the last inning, when the sun had shifted and our team was losing 6-1 to the Sea Dogs, most of the crowd had left to head to their cars.

While we were there that week, the attendance at Waterfront Park in Trenton set a record for all "AA" ball parks across the country that season (409,000 by season's end). Every home stand was sold out, with standing-room-only tickets still being sold. Completed in 1994, the ball park was comfortable and fan-friendly, with lots of attendants at every aisle, lineup boards visible as soon as you scaled the top of the entry steps, huge toilet facilities on each side of the concourse, vendors hawking their goods in and out of the seats, games on the field in which fans participated between innings, and a huge electronic scoreboard in full color, complete with sound effects. Hanging above the concourse were air-conditioned sky boxes. Fans lined up outside the doors of the souvenir shop to gain admittance, while staff monitored the "one out, one in" system. As parents of ball players, we got a 40% discount on the hundreds of dollars of paraphernalia we purchased over our two years in Trenton. Fans loved the souvenir shop not only because it was air-conditioned, but because they carried home a piece of their division-leading team. Packages of baseball cards for the team were available inside; Todd's 8" x 10" action photos were on sale for $5 each, as were his teammates.' I was afraid to monitor how Todd's photos were selling. During the game, one could see whole groups in green Thunder T-shirts across the ball park. Those who hadn't worn a head-covering to the game quickly bought a Thunder hat for the heat. Too bad the minor leaguers didn't get a percentage of the sales, as the major leaguers did unilaterally for sales at every park! The marketing in Trenton was a stroke of genius.

The fan following could be attributed in part to the fact that the Thunder was in first place in its division. But part of the reason could also be attributed to the high prices of major league tickets, which led to declining attendance at major league parks around the country. A family of four could afford to go to a minor league game (tickets between $3 and $7.75 each). Together, they'd have a great time with mascots in the stands (sometimes the Phillie Phanatic or Famous Chicken even made guest appearances from major league fields), kids' contests, and promotions where fans vied for free fill-ups of propane, pizzas, or even a trip, a car, or a house. And still, they could partake in the American ritual.

Another of Todd's Brown University baseball campers and his dad, residents of Cumberland, came to Trenton to see Todd play. The two males were making a week's tour of minor league ball parks. Doreen Passmore and her children, who had befriended Todd when he played in Elmira, planned a trip to see him over a weekend. In addition, there were the groups of players' families who came. Lou Merloni's parents filled a van with six other couples, sharing rooms at the Best Western in Princeton. We got a parents' discount there. They arrived at the pool en masse, shouting between balconies for room numbers and refills of beer. They also made their presence known at the ball park, where Lou's dad invited season ticket holders to accompany them out to eat. Fortunately, the van they had traveled in had air-conditioning, but it had been so cramped that there was no room for extra baggage, such as baseball hats. So the entire group purchased a set of Thunder hats to watch the game in the heat.

We met Judith Blahnik and Phillip Schulz at the ball park. They were two authors selling their 1995 publication, <u>Mudhens and Mavericks</u>, which describes each minor league field around the country with a short history, and itineraries for families to follow on baseball outings. They gave us their theory on the attendance records at Trenton. "Not only are we in the vicinity of a major metropolitan area," Judith said, "but all of us can relate to the struggle of the minor leaguer." They wrote about the struggle we knew all too well: the minor leaguer was paid little, told practically nothing as to his daily status, suffered the indignity of being sent to and from teams without warning, tolerated long road trips after which he was to perform brilliantly, and yet, he dreamed the dream of all of us -- some day, if he were one of the lucky few, he might make it big. In the introduction, the authors describe the unique player-fan relationship in the minor leagues: how fans nurture and support their players by showing up every night, getting to know them on a first-name basis, charting their progress, hoping their heroes will move upward and carry a bit of the hometown glory with them.[23]

On the field, Todd played short while Nomar began his two-game suspension. Todd fielded well and got two hits during three trips to the plate, one going to the opposite field. But in general, the team looked lethargic in the heat. For three days in a row, they had collected half the number of hits as the Sea Dogs. Todd let a ball get by him thrown to second wide of the bag by Ryan McGuire during a run-down. Fortunately, neither was credited with an error.

Ryan had been voted the Eastern League's "Outstanding Player" in June. His average stood at .335. When we went back to their apartment, Ryan was sound asleep. Bill Selby and Dana LeVangie lived across the hall. "When we first stopped at Dana's apartment," Dana's mother told me, "Todd opened the door and invited us in, with a toothbrush in his mouth. I wasn't sure I was at the right apartment, but I guess they're all in and out and back and forth." The apartments consisted of two bedrooms, a kitchen, bathroom, and living/dining room area. Every year, the ballplayers' apartments looked exactly the same, until they blended into one another in a blur in our minds. If any of the girlfriends came to stay, each player had privacy. Assuming, of course, a third roommate hadn't been invited to move in.

All we heard about Todd's love life was that he'd been to the beach on the team's day off with a girl who did sonograms on pregnant mothers. "She has a hard time dealing with some of what she sees on the monitor," Todd said. After dinner with us one night, he asked Bill Selby to grab a ride home with Dana instead of in his car, since he had made plans.

Ron Mahay's parents from Illinois were also in attendance during the August home stand. Almost immediately upon the Mahays' taking a seat in the stands, a Thunder staffer named Fran introduced herself to the Mahays and us. During succeeding innings, she took photos of all of us and began to bring the Mahays free drinks. By the second game, she had positioned herself in the seat next to them and kept them cool by wringing out water from Thunder golf towels she'd found in a storage room.

Her behavior seemed straight out of *Bull Durham*! It reminded me of the groupies that followed the Lynchburg team from park to park, and were in their mid-teens. I had had a nightmare one night while visiting Tim in Lynchburg that he had eloped with one of them.

We commented to Todd about Ron Mahay's lack of confidence at the plate in Trenton, after his spectacular appearance in Fenway Park for five days. Ron's dad had told us that the manner in which the major leaguers had treated him after the strike broke had been a "learning experience." Back down in Trenton, he was batting .220.

"You know he stutters, don't you?" Todd asked us.

"Yes," we replied.

"Well, Joel Bennett tells a story about the first day Ron and Henkel (pitcher) were put on the major league team with Joel. Bennett was sent to the outfield to shag fly balls with the other two, and went up to Ron to introduce himself. Ron, of course, stuttered, so when Joel left Ron, he went over to Henkel to introduce himself.

"'I can't believe how that guy over there stutters!' Bennett exclaimed to Henkel.

"'You bet-t-t-ter bel-lie-e-e-e-eve i-i-i-t!' stuttered Henkel in reply. 'An—an-an-an-d so d-d-d-d-do I!'"

Another struggling Thunder player was center fielder Trot Nixon. He'd been leadoff batter for three games against the Portland Sea Dogs, and had yet to reach first base, swinging wildly so that his body spun completely around on strikeouts. It was Trot's first full-length season after being drafted in the first round in '93, then missing most of the '94 season with a congenital back problem. With all the hype surrounding him, Trot put tremendous pressure on himself at the "AA" level.

The Trentonian was the tabloid whose novice reporter covered the brawl in the SoHo Bar. She alleged the Thunder players sucker-punched the husband of a woman in the bar.[24] "She never interviewed one player, coach, or manager when she first published the story. And her story was what the AP report picked up," Todd told us. Every day the paper's front page ran a sex scandal or a full-length sex kitten photo.

Ed Zambrano, outfielder, had come to Trenton from the '94 major league Chicago Cubs team. He still posted a .000 batting average after six games for the Thunder. "This is about the time of year that the Venezuelan kids want to bow out, so they can recuperate before starting their Venezuelan winter ball. They think this league is practice for that, since they can get up to $5,000/month down there. What they don't realize is that if they can make it big in the States, they'll get that as a small percentage every month. Some of them fake injuries or just don't try very hard this time of year. The lucky ones get sent home, but I doubt that will happen here, since we're in a pennant race."

On August 14th, Todd's birthday was announced on the PA system during the night game against the Sea Dogs. The Thunder mascot, Boomer, cavorted amongst us. Todd had the third highest average on the team at .270, after Selby and McGuire. Although the Thunder split the series with the Sea Dogs (who led the other division of the Eastern League), the Sea Dogs had outhit the Thunder in all four games by a margin of 2-1.

After the game, the Sox put Ron Mahay on waivers. During the waiver process, he was unable to play for three days, and another team could pick him up.

In the pool at our Best Western the next day, Ron's mother attempted to find some logic to the action by the Sox. "Ronnie was a mess last night, when he found out after the game," she said. "None of us could eat or sleep. Ron feels so helpless, with no control over his life. His great performance in Boston when they needed him meant nothing. So he called his agent this morning to see what the process involves. After three days, if another team doesn't pick him up, he could remain right here in Trenton. The first thing his agent asked him was for the real story about the brawl in that bar. Ron said he was outside when it started.

"This kid batting .220 right now isn't the same kid who performed in Fenway for five days. Somehow, he's got to convince himself that if he could perform under that kind of pressure, he can perform in Trenton day-to-day at 'AA.' After all the shoulder and shin operations he underwent with the Sox, I hope they stick by him now." Baseball certainly is a mind game.

Meanwhile, Ron's dad tried to help him deal with the mechanics of baseball. "His dad thinks he's changed his swing by moving his elbow," Mrs. Mahay explained.

"Where was your elbow when you were hitting this spring?" Ron's father asked his son. "And where is it now?"

Todd's birthday was also VJ Day (Victory over Japan). On that day in 1995, the Japanese Prime Minister formally apologized for the Japanese actions during World War II in front of 100,000 people in Tokyo. Tim said the bombing of Pearl Harbor was never included in any Japanese history books. Actually, the Japanese had never claimed any culpability during World War II until Todd's birthday in 1995. Still, the Japanese population considered Americans to be barbarians who used the atom bomb on two of their cities. The Japanese actually called Tim "gaijin" to his face ("outsider") when they assumed he couldn't understand them. Although they were helpful and polite in his presence, their hypocrisy was de-signed to "save face" in front of their peers and superiors. The Japanese behavior changed only when they got to know the "gaijin" as individuals. The same way we treated foreigners.

Nevertheless, Tim seemed to have adjusted well there. He was introduced through his boss, the owner of the Japanese school, to other Japanese karate students who rented a hall together and practiced kendo (complete with pads, guards, and bam-boo sticks). Tim was a first-degree black belt in karate. He was coaching baseball and had met a Buddhist monk, who explained the beliefs of his religion. Tim eagerly awaited a vacation to explore Kyoto and Osaka, as well as Todd's visit after the Thunder season ended.Amid night games between the Thunder and the Rockies' affiliate, the New Haven Ravens, we spent an enjoyable afternoon with Todd exploring the region surrounding New Hope, Pa. It was an arts and crafts community not too far from Trenton, with wonderful galleries, restaurants, and live theater.

We were having a hard time understanding some of Manager Macha's strategies on the field. Todd hotly defended his manager. "Macha is the most knowledgeable manager I've ever played for!" Todd claimed. "He never lectures us. Even when they doubled me off second base in one of the games this week, he didn't criticize me. I approached him to explain how I froze."

After the second game he came out to greet us. "Well, I have some bad news and some good news. Before the game tonight, Macha told Lou and Trot Nixon that the Sox had found places for them in the Arizona League. He told Bill Selby and Ryan (McGuire) that they had places in the Mexican League. And he said he had a message from Bob Schaefer for me. Schaefer's been talking to the Puerto Rican and Venezuelan Leagues to find me a spot. Nomar's going down to Instructional to work on the weights, then he'll probably take some time off. He might be in Fenway by the end of next season."

"Todd, I have only one suggestion," Charley said. "Please don't leave this to chance. Take the bull by the horns and call Schaefer yourself tomorrow morning. Then it will be off your mind and you can stay focused on the next twenty games. You're putting up some good numbers this season, so finish with a bang."

"All I know right now is that I'm not ready to sit behind a desk in a bank for six months, when I could be playing ball. I want to continue."

The next morning, Garciaparra was in the headlines of The Trenton Times sports page, in a write-up by Brian Dohn (August 17, 1995). He'd made a spectacular play deep in the hole behind Todd at third base to throw the batter out at first. There had been only a smattering of applause from the standing-room-only crowd. Yet many big league shortstops couldn't have made that play. "'I didn't hear anything (in the stands),'" Nomar was quoted as saying. "'It just shows me that they (fans) don't know... So I'm out there for myself and my teammates, rather than the fans.'"

With Nomar in the lineup, Todd again played third base against the Ravens. One game out of first place in its division, the team began to pull out crucial wins. Lou Merloni, especially, worked hard to manufacture a run here and there. Against the Ravens, he hit a double, stole home, then tied the game at 3-3 in the eighth with an RBI single. In the bottom of the ninth, Todd led off with a single and his buddy, Ryan McGuire, hit a sacrifice fly to move Todd over to second base. With one out, Ben Shelton (DH), hitting .208, got the big one to score Todd. The throw to home was behind him. It was the kind of game we wanted to see!

Afterward, we took Dana LeVangie, Bill Selby, and Todd to dinner. Ryan couldn't join us; he had to meet a new agent. We listened to funny stories about the previous season in Lynchburg, such as Steve Rodrigues' and Scott Bakkum's pouring a bucket of ice over pitching coach Bibby as he sat on the toilet naked before taking a shower. Bibby stormed off the seat like an enraged bull, looking for the culprits. Another story had Stratton, a pitcher in the bullpen, using a syringe of gasoline to make a trail up to the heel of new pitcher Thad Rollin. Rollin was sitting on a bench engrossed in one of the mindless games that go on in the bullpen during a contest. The opposing left fielder watched the antics from the outfield, as suddenly a trail of fire snaked its way toward Thad's heel. He never saw it or smelled it for several moments, then shot up in the air when his sole began to smoke, and stomped around to extinguish the smoldering. The left fielder was in hysterics, with one eye on the batter at home plate.

On August 17, 1995, the major league Sox were ten games in front of the Yankees for first place in their division. Still, age-old disappointments in August and September made Charley refrain from raising his hopes for a pennant title. The Pawtucket Sox were in first place in their International League division, and the Thunder was one game out of first in its Eastern League division. Perhaps Duquette's philosophy was working.

Our last game of the Trenton home stand began on Friday, August 18, 1995, at 7 p.m. It ended Saturday morning, August 19, around ten minutes after midnight. The marathon game lasted seventeen innings. The only time Todd got in the game was to pinch hit for the catcher in the bottom of the twelfth inning, when we were down 5-3. He grounded out, moving Trot Nixon to second base. Todd was the only non-pitcher who didn't play in the field. Ryan McGuire also sat out until the twelfth inning, after which he took left field instead of his usual first base.

In the seventeenth inning, Lou Merloni, having contributed three hits, two errors, and a spectacular catch at third base, crowded the plate to lead off. Hoping to alter the New Haven lefty pitcher's view of the strike zone, Merloni was hit on the shin. Selby bunted to move the runner to second, and first baseman Ben Shelton was intentionally walked. A wild pitch put Merloni on third base for batter Greg Blosser. Blosser hit a sacrifice fly to center field to win the game. The Thunder remained one game out of first place in its division, but the first two teams in each division would make the playoffs.

Immediately after the game, at 1 a.m., the players boarded a bus for the eight-hour drive to Canton, Ohio. There they were scheduled to play a doubleheader the same night they arrived. Since Todd had rested during the marathon game, we surmised he'd be back in the lineup in Canton. Mahay had gone off waivers and would also be eligible to play in the outfield. There was still no word from management regarding Todd's playing winter ball.

Neither Charley nor I had any words of wisdom for Todd before his bus departed. During the five games in which we'd watched him play, he had pulled every ball to right field except two. His average stood at .270. "We had such a nice week with him," I commented, "I'm glad we didn't discuss baseball as our parting thoughts."

It was another week before he heard from Todd again. When he called from Bowie, Maryland, it was to tell us he'd hit a grand slam the previous night. He'd played first base. Still batting .270 with nine errors for the season, he was playing every night all around the infield. Ryan McGuire played left field on the nights Todd played first base. The infielders were doing all the hitting.

"Any word on winter ball?" Charley asked.

"Schaefer said he'd make a conference call about me. I'm at the top of their list, but it's getting late, and I'll probably have to take somebody's place to get a slot.

Puerto Rico is out, since so many major leaguers want to play there. So I'm hoping for Mexico. I told him I have a bank job waiting, but I really think it would benefit me to play this fall. I'll have to know around playoff time, since I can't start at Citizens and then leave. Schaefer agreed it would be beneficial for me, but Kenney's the one who places us. Maybe Schaefer will put the pressure on him."

"Any word on playoffs?" I asked.

"We're two games out, but well ahead of the third place team, so we're in it for sure. It will go down to the wire Labor Day weekend to see who gets home field advantage."

"Please let us know as soon as you find out," I requested. I would have to postpone our friends' visit to us at the beach. I knew Charley would never miss Todd's playoff games, and I wasn't about to entertain alone!

"Sure. Oh, Tim called to find out the playoff schedule. He's really anxious for me to visit him in Fukuchiyama before I start work or go off to winter ball."

We drove to Reading, Pa., on September 5, 1995, to watch the Southern Division "AA" playoffs. The last game of the regular season on Labor Day had decided first place. Reading had the same number of wins as Trenton at the end of the season, and in a head-on-head comparison, Reading had the edge. Thus, they got home field advantage for the first two games of the series, and for the fifth game, if it came to that. The Reading team had played its last game of the regular season in Portland, Maine, a longer trip back home by two hours than Trenton's trip back from Canton, Ohio.

Todd had a sore throat and was generally worn down. He'd played second and short the last week of the regular season, still versatile as a utility infielder. He'd heard nothing about winter ball, and planned a trip to Japan before beginning work in Providence in mid-October.

Trenton lost the first game in Reading, with a lack of offense behind a strong performance by our knuckleballer, Jared Fernandez. Todd played first base, while Ryan McGuire was in left field. Todd's average had registered .272 at the end of the regular season, with eight homers. However, he went 0-for-2 in the first playoff game. In the seventh inning we were three runs behind with two outs and two on. When a Phillies' left-handed pitcher came in to relieve, Manager Macha pulled Todd for pinch-hitter Ben Shelton. Shelton walked, loading the bases, and Dana LeVangie followed with another walk, scoring a run, to make it 4-2. Ninth batter Trot Nixon, also a lefty batter but a first-round draft pick, came to the plate batting .160 after a previous strikeout. Nixon struck out again. The game ended 5-3 against us two innings later.

Afterward, Todd told us that Macha had informed the team in Canton that it was Division Co-champion. No word of congratulations arrived from the Trenton GM. "If we had been winners in the Florida State League, we would have had corks popping," Todd said. A reporter from a Princeton paper picked up on the players' malcontent, and the GM appeared in subsequent playoff games with a few cases of beer on the team bus.

The second game of the playoffs in Reading began badly for the Phillies. With three errors, they fell behind in early innings 5-1, but crept back against our lefty pitcher Orellano (league strikeout king), with homers. Our runs increased to six with a homer by Ryan McGuire, but in the eighth the Phillies tied it at six, then won it on their fourth homer in the bottom of the ninth. Each team used at least five pitchers.

Charley and I sat in total disgust during that game. Todd, a lefty batter at .272, was not in the lineup that night against a righty pitcher. Instead, J.J. Johnson played left field. He had just appeared from the Sarasota team. Ryan was back at first base. Selby, Garciaparra, and Merloni (with three hits that game) completed the infield. It seemed to us that management was making a statement to Todd by not placing him in winter ball and by playing a recruit from "A" Sarasota in a playoff game. In addition, the third game of the series, although back in Trenton, would showcase a lefty pitcher for the Phillies. The odds were that Todd would sit on the bench.

"What a shitty way for them to treat Todd at the end of the season!" I exploded to Charley. "He did everything they asked of him!" I waited with Charley outside the stadium for Todd, before his bus departed for Trenton. I knew he would feel humiliated.

"What was Macha's reasoning for not putting you in the lineup tonight?' Charley quietly began.

"I don't know," Todd responded.

"Well, you've had a fine season and have helped them get to this series. I would think you'd want an answer. You deserve to be in the lineup without any doubt."

"I know why I wasn't in the lineup," Todd responded. "Because they think more of J.J. Johnson than they do of me."

"Todd, I find that hard to believe," I retorted. "J.J. just got up here from Sarasota. You're being treated like a piece of shit, if you don't mind my saying so, and you deserve some answers." I knew as soon as I finished that I shouldn't have said that!

Todd lashed out at me in his frustration. "Well, I do mind if you say I'm like a piece of shit. You knew when I got back on this team who would be playing," he snarled at me. "And it certainly doesn't help to have you squawking at me about how I should be treated. Now cool off in the car and head back to your hotel."

"Todd," Charley said quietly and reasonably, "all we want is for you to get some answers and to stand up for yourself. I don't think you have an answer about tonight's lineup, and it's doubtful you'll play tomorrow night if a lefty pitches against you. You've had a fine season and are entitled to get some information."

"The only thing Macha said to me before the game was that there were still vacancies for fall and winter ball and he couldn't understand why I hadn't heard from Kenney. I told him Kenney hadn't even returned my phone call before we left for Ohio. Maybe there's nothing to tell me."

"That's not the point, Todd. Common courtesy demands a return call, if only to tell you he's still working on the situation or that the situation's dead. It's typical of the way this management treats its minor leaguers. You should remind Kenney you chose to play replacement ball to help them out when they needed it," I suggested.

"Do you think they care now who helped them and who didn't? Todd got his $5,000," Charley quipped.

"Well, I plan to call Kenney tomorrow from Trenton before the game," Todd said.

"Just keep bugging him if you can't reach him or can't get an answer. Tell him you have to know before September 21st when you leave for Japan," Charley suggested.

"We didn't mean to take our frustration out on you, Todd, but we hate to see you jacked around," I said, looking into his hazel eyes. "I certainly never intended to put you down!" I had abandoned my role as cheerleader that Todd obviously needed. I gave him a big hug and shoved off to the car, feeling no better than I had during the game. I hoped we had prodded him to become more aggressive in seeking answers. Charley and I wondered if, over the years, we shouldn't have schmoozed up to the management stiffs in Boston that we knew. Who knows - Todd might have had some answers if we had!

Charley and I remarked at the cohesiveness of the Trenton team over the course of the season. Winning always seemed to bring a team together, but, in addition, the personalities comprising the various ethnic groups on the Thunder complimented each other. It seemed extremely unusual. Mike Hardge, with his natural wit, was the one who pumped the team up, even when he sat on the bench. The Australian pitchers wore ready grins and a devil-may-care attitude. Wes Brooks was an outgoing personality around us parents, while the Southerners like Selby were gentle and courteous, until they swore loudly on the field. The Spanish-speaking players were the most unobtrusive, blending in as necessary, and quietly doing their jobs. The exceptions were the Venezuelans preparing for winter ball back home. The Mormon, Jared Fernandez, exhibited a quiet wiliness with his knuckleballs, and his wife Marcy always looked forward to a brighter tomorrow. "The Mayor" Lou Merloni, affable and intense, always seemed to have an inside edge. Lou received the "Fans' Award" wristwatch in Trenton that year, as the crowd chanted "Lou, Lou" in unison to the electronic scoreboard.

On September 7, 1995, the third game of the playoffs began in Trenton's Waterfront Park, as the drought and heat wave of August continued. As we'd predicted, Todd was not in the lineup. The Phillies had a lefty pitcher starting against us. Then a lefty reliever came in. I couldn't understand Macha's rigid thinking, when Todd batted just as well against lefty pitchers as against righties. A right-handed reliever came in, but still Todd did not get into the game. Merloni, Garciaparra, Selby, and McGuire were our infielders again. Delgado caught for us and Australian Brett Cederblad pitched. Jeff Martin had not caught a single game of the playoffs (batting .217). Manager Macha had told Jeff he was a liability at the plate, since he had struck out a lot that season.

In the stands, Stephanie Martin and I vociferously stated our disgust at the team's performance, while her husband and my son sat on the bench. The score rolled to 12-5 against us before it was over. Charley sat in complete silence. We couldn't believe the season had come to such a disastrous ending, both for the team and for Todd. We just wanted to get home. When we said good-bye to Todd, Charley asked what Macha had said to him after the game. "Not much," he answered.

Todd leads a baseball clinic for students in Cumberland, R.I.

19

The Fun
Finally Begins

By the end of September, Todd was in Japan. He spent ten days in Tim's apartment in Fukuchiyama City, in the mountains outside Kyoto, and attended classes Tim taught. The staff members arranged for Todd to visit various locales and attractions in the area. The thing he enjoyed most, he said, was meeting the people who were central to Tim's life. Almost two weeks after his return, Todd began work at Citizens Bank in Providence as a management trainee. He had never heard from the Sox about playing fall/winter ball. The paper announced that the Sox had assigned Randy Brown from the "AAA" team to the Arizona League.

My family met on Amelia Island, Florida, (sans Tim and Todd) to celebrate my mother's eightieth birthday and our upcoming Rhode Island house sale. Todd moved into the Westport house while he worked at Citizens Bank, since Charley and I had vacated for the winter season to our Florida condo.

The American League playoffs of Cincinnati versus Atlanta and Cleveland versus Seattle were so outstanding that they made believers of those fans who had deserted in disgust after the strike. By the end of October, the Braves had won the World Series and, as announcer Bob Costas said, "It reminded us of why we were fans in the first place." There couldn't have been a more exciting month of baseball.

Charley and I flew north for two weeks in October to pack the Cumberland house prior to the sale. We looked up Todd and Tim's teammate, catcher Dana LeVangie, who was working in a restaurant near Westport.

"I called Ryan McGuire in California," Dana said, "and got his dad. His father said Ryan was playing ball down in Mexico, living in a two-bit town, and staying in a tiny motel infested with cockroaches."

"That's Mexico," I said.

After reporting on Todd's trip and job, we suggested he and Todd connect again. "I still can't believe they didn't place him in winter ball," Dana said. "Randy

Brown's probably there because Todd had to start work. Schaefer told me at the end of the season that they would always have a place for me in the Sox organization, if I wanted it. That doesn't mean I'll be a major leaguer. I could be a bullpen catcher forever."

On October 25, 1995, after signing six additional minor leaguers to contracts, including two third basemen and one first baseman, the Sox sent disposition letters to their players. "You are hereby notified of the action indicated by an 'x' in box 12 on the above date," Todd's form letter read. The line, "Your contract has been transferred to our affiliate" was completed in box 12 with the words, "Pawtucket Red Sox of the International League."

Charley interpreted this letter for me. "It means that they (Sox) either have confidence in his ability, or have received some interest from another team in picking him up." I was thrilled with the possibility that Todd might be at "AAA," but knew the reality was in the number of infielders already there.

Todd was pleased. He explained that this action by the Sox protected him from being drafted at the "AAA" level, but another team could draft him at the next level, a major league roster. It meant the Sox still felt he had potential. However, because of the number of "prospects" among the Sox infielders, the likelihood was that there would be a number of them sitting on the bench or bumped down to the Trenton "AA" team.

"Either way," Tim said on the phone from Japan, "it's a step in the right direction. He'll have a lot more leverage in bargaining if he can play in Pawtucket at least part of next season. A big indicator will be whether he's invited to major league camp when spring training starts."

As it turned out, Todd did not get invited to spring training with either the major leaguers or the "AAA" players. The disposition letters certainly weren't binding. By the end of January, he still hadn't received a contract, so he tracked Schaefer down in Florida. When asked about Todd's future on the field in '96, Schaefer responded that Todd would start off in Trenton and would play every day either at third or at first base. Once again, there was no word from agent Alan Nero, except a package of gloves and a box of cleats.

Todd's reporting date was March 8th, almost a month later than the pitchers and catchers reported. Dana LeVangie, Trenton catcher, hoped to work into a coaching position with the organization. He was willing to catch anywhere, without a formal contract assignment.

Around January 8, 1996, the Sox announced the trade of Todd's Trenton roommate, Ryan McGuire. Boston had put him on the forty-man major league spring roster, but then traded him to Montreal with Trenton pitcher Shayne Bennett and major leaguer Rheal Cormier. In return, Boston received Wil Cordero, among others. From Japan, Tim reported seeing a news article describing the Red Sox infield of the future: Vaughn at first; Cordero at second; Garciaparra at short; Valentin at third. The Sox, as of early February 1996, had not agreed to the $6.5 million Vaughn was demanding, and there was the possibility Valentin might go into arbitration. Nothing was set in stone in this profession.

Ten days into February, Todd received his minor league contract at our condo in Florida (Todd's permanent mailing address). The contract designated salaries for Todd: $2,000/month - AAA, $1,700/month - all other levels below.

If Todd were assigned to Battle Creek, Michigan ("A"), for example, his $1,700/month would be more than any draftee's on the same team, because of his years in the system. Similarly, a "hot prospect" like Garciaparra would be receiving more than the stipulated $2,000/month when he started at "AAA," despite his brevity in the system. A first round draft pick's contract covered all bases.

On February 12th, Todd's assignment arrived in the mail for the "AA" team. Several days previously, he had attended both the Pawtucket and Trenton team press conferences by invitation, along with other teammates. "Better than sitting on the bench in Pawtucket," was Charley's comment after he'd heard Schaefer's promise to play Todd every day in Trenton. Todd knew he had to turn in a great year so he'd be valuable for a trade or for advancement, but he usually did well when he had faith in the manager. That assumed, of course, that he'd play.

"Just remember, Mom," Tim lectured on the phone from Japan, "don't ask Todd any questions he can't answer. How did you expect him to answer when you asked him why Selby got invited to pre-season camp and he didn't? He has no control over the situation, so don't put him on the spot like that. His only support group is you two, me, and Murph. He did have a good year in Trenton because he had two good friends on the team who really believed in him - Dana and Ryan. Let's hope he gets some kids on his team that he is comfortable with. At least he has confidence in Macha."

When we drove across the state to spring training in Ft. Myers on March 15th, 1996, we met Rico Petrocelli and Molly Walsh, the jack-of-all-trades who held the minor league system together. They were in the front office of the minor league complex. "There are 185 in minor league camp, with more being signed," Molly told us. "There are going to be a lot of disappointed kids before this spring is over."

The players had all had physical exams, including blood work, miscellaneous inoculations, HIV testing, body fat measurements, stress tests, as well as drug, family and sports psychology counseling sessions. "When I walked into that Indian doctor's office," Todd told us, "all he had in front of him on the desk was a pair of surgical gloves and three jars of petroleum jelly. Thank God he never got to use the jelly on me!"

With all the costs involved in signing so many to camp (housing, food, transportation), Duquette was beginning to feel the money pinch. Major leaguers received $80/day meal money during spring training and lived in the Sheraton Harbor Place. Minor leaguers received $15/day meal money and lived at the Days Inn in North Ft. Myers. Breakfast and lunch were provided for all the teams. Of course, Duquette was still signing major leaguers from other teams for big bucks, like Kevin Mitchell. The Sox already had a power hitter in Jose Canceso, and had finished next-to-last in defensive play in the entire league the previous year. Still, Duquette signed power-hitter Mitchell. Dana LeVangie said, "Duquette decided that there were too many balls being hit out of City of Palms Park during batting practice every day. Look who he's signed – big hitters Mitchell, Canseco, Zinter! I'll bet if you stood by yourself outside the center field fence during major league practice, you could collect forty balls. So Duquette wants to save money by using these balls marked, 'North East League,' whatever that is. Kennedy negged the idea."

"Yeah," Todd joined in. "Macha was using the ball machine today at batting practice. He'd move his arm in the pitching motion and then hit the button on the machine to release the ball. Collier was batting, and you know how Dan prides himself on his physique and his ability to put the ball over the fence. He has his own private batting cage under the lights and a ball machine at home. He had already struck out twice today, because Macha was faking him out with his motion. He put one right by Dan, and Collier hit another one off the fist foul. Macha finally laid one in for Dan to hit, and he put it into the swamp behind center.

"Macha yelled, 'Don't you know we're supposed to be saving our balls, Collier?'"

The following day, as we proceeded to the dusty back fields of the minor league complex, I inquired out loud to Charley, "Do you think we'll ever be watching Todd play a major league game?" This was our fourth year trudging back to minor league fields far down the road or across the tracks from where the big leaguers drew thousands every day. I knew in my heart that as long as Todd played this game, we would be finding the fields where he played.

"You're asking questions again that can't be answered," he replied. Always the pragmatist, always rooted in the here and now, he refused to even speculate. "All I know is that there's no way the coaches can get a fair appraisal of all these kids in such a short time."

Charley and I had concluded long ago that the management's chances of finding a "diamond in the rough" or "oldie but goodie" among 185 minor leaguers were minimal. The psychology was to keep those on the roster off guard, always pressuring them to perform because there were so many to take their places. The rosters for each minor league team were "penciled in" well before spring training, and in the front office of the complex we requested a copy of those tentative rosters. Todd's name appeared under the Trenton team.

The attendance at City of Palms Park still had not recovered from the strike. Capacity was 6,990, and the Ft. Myers News Press published a comparison of attendance rates:

Year	Dates	Total	Average
1993	15	95,893	6,393
1994	15	96,135	6,409
1995	8	24,957	3,120 (Strike)
1996	13	77,077	5,929

Todd debuted at third base in spring training for Trenton against the Twins. He went 2-for-2 with a double and a single, and played another game at shortstop against the Red Sox Pawtucket squad. There were seven infielders on the Pawtucket bench, while the temperature at the complex was 87 degrees. Todd had a walk and a dribbler up the first base line in the second game, before coming out again after five innings to give his teammates a chance to take the field.

One day after another, we saw lots of old friends not only among the ball players, but also among the spectators - wives, children, parents, friends from home sitting on the aluminum bleachers at the dusty fields, keeping alive their dream of someday seeing their favored one in the major leagues. The first day we attended, Pat Darcey, one of Tim's friends from Cumberland, stopped by to see Todd. We had already missed Harold Alfond, a "passive investor" in the Red Sox ownership and benefactor of Colby and University of Maine. Many of the ballplayers inquired about Tim's whereabouts, including Walt McKeel, Dan Gakeler (now a pitching coach for the Sox), Bob Juday, Wes Brooks (released that week), Randy Brown, and Lou Merloni.

The Trenton owner, Sam Plumeri, and his wife, Josephine, became familiar figures to the Trenton players and to Charley and me. They took by far the most active role during spring training of all the minor league owners we observed. They watched every game from under a covered golf cart while they were there, and spoke to each player individually. After the games, win or lose, Sam would go into the clubhouse and mingle with his team.

Also in evidence were many of the players' agents, who spent most of their time at major league City of Palms Park with their stars. Todd's agent, Alan Nero, had sent two members of his office, Cecil Cooper and Scott Pacino, to spring training. Todd was not willing to renew his contract with Nero unless he also got a contract with a glove company to provide infield gloves for him. The procedure was that minor leaguers with big reputations rode "the coattails" of some of the contracts of the big stars. Wilson and Rawlings began to approach Todd.

At dinner Todd asked if I were still making notes for a book on baseball. When

I replied that I was, he retorted, "This is my life you're talking about here, and you know I don't want you to do this! Then you wonder why I don't tell you much." He was obviously feeling vulnerable enough, without Mom divulging locker-room secrets!

I assured him that there would be no manuscript until well after his career in baseball was over, and he might by then have a family who would enjoy the history. He seemed to think that writing and publishing were synonymous. "I promised you and Tim long ago," I said, "that you would be the first ones to read and approve it. Besides, this is the story of my experience as a parent, and is entirely from my perspective." That didn't seem to satisfy him much.The following Friday we drove across Alligator Alley from our condo on the east coast of Florida to Ft. Myers again. We drove directly to the minor league fields for the 1 p.m. Trenton game, but Todd was nowhere in sight. The first thought that runs through the mind of a minor leaguer's parent when she can't find her son is that he has been released. The second thought that occurred to me was that the Sox had moved Todd upward to the Pawtucket roster. As it turned out, he was sick with the flu and was back in his room at the Days Inn. We were sure it was the first game he'd missed for illness or injury during any season. When we went to check on him, he did, indeed, have a fever, aches, and pains.

"We had a meeting the other day in the clubhouse to warn us about the pitfalls of gambling," he told us, smiling. "The FBI made a presentation and then we watched a video. The featured speaker on the video was a guy who brought in $25 million a week for the N.Y. crime family through gambling. He'd arrange for prominent sports figures to get heavily into debt with prostitutes or gambling habits, then would tell them he'd clear the debts if the players fed him information about who was on the injured list, who was in a slump, who was starting or not starting, etc. If there were a close game and the player came to bat in the ninth inning, he was supposed to strike out or hit a grounder, depending on the point spread. At the end of the video, surrounded by FBI agents, in walked the informer. He's in the witness protection program. He admitted to us that he'd stashed untold millions in cash that government authorities haven't yet discovered." The Sox management was using scare tactics to prevent gambling from becoming an addiction at the minor league level.

On Sunday, March 24th, Todd had a large audience at the minor league complex. Two friends from the private psychiatric hospital in Providence where Tim had worked were in attendance. In addition, my parents were there, and one of my Colby classmates, Jay Gronlund, and his family and friends had driven up from Naples to see Todd. Todd still felt miserable from the flu, and stayed in the game only three innings at short against the Twins. He batted third, walking twice, before coming over to all of us for a brief, "Hello," on his way to the batting cages.

Something that impressed our friends, which Charley and I now took for granted, was seeing major leaguers in rehab take the field as minor league players, or former "legends" walking around as instructor/coaches. Carl Yastrzemski rode around on a golf cart, while Rico Petrocelli spoke to our guests, and Steve Braun introduced himself after complimenting Charley on the great spring Todd was having. "He seems very relaxed and confident," Steve said. It was most important that Todd become a starter during the regular season that year. By March 25, 1996, eleven infielders still remained at "AAA" for four positions. Lou Merloni, playing half the game at short and half at second base, had a good day for Pawtucket, with two hits and some excellent fielding plays.

Before returning to spring training the following weekend, I went to see Todd's Trenton roommate, Ryan McGuire. The Sox had traded him to the Montreal Expos, and their minor league training facility was a high school complex in Lantana, Florida, near our condo. Ryan was playing first base for the Expos' "AAA" team when I arrived. His face lit up when he recognized me. Ryan's car remained in California until he arrived in Ottawa ("AAA" home field for the Expos), where his dad would deliver it.

Ryan had lost ten to fifteen pounds from dysentery during the Mexican fall league, and he looked gaunt in the face. After asking all about Todd and Red Sox minor league camp, he said, "Tell Todd he doesn't know how lucky he is! This organization is so cheap. Look at these fields we're playing on! Look at our bus (a converted school bus)! None of the coaches say anything to us, and everyone here talks highly of Macha in Trenton. He's very well respected." When I asked if he'd be playing first base, he said, "I don't know. I'm one of three first basemen, and they really don't know me or what I can do. I'm a new face to them. They don't tell us anything. The Sox facility is a first-class operation."

I drove across Alligator Alley alone to pick Charley up at the Ft. Myers International Airport upon his return from Providence. The minor leaguers would be breaking camp and heading north to Trenton on April 1st. The "AA" and "AAA" Sox teams were still in the clubhouse after their inter-squad game when we arrived.

The atmosphere was tense and morose as players walked past our car with their heads down on this last weekend. No one dared look at anyone else for fear one of them would be cut by the end of the day. The "AA" and "AAA" rosters had changed considerably since the previous weekend, in an attempt to begin to solidify some of the lineups. Management, however, was up to its old tricks of waiting until the last day or two before releasing players, as they had done to Tim two years previously. This, of course, prevented other teams from picking the players up because, by then, their rosters were also set.

We met Chris Edwards, the reporter from The Trenton Times, who'd followed the Thunder team all during spring training. "You wouldn't believe the changes," he told us. "All around Todd this mess has been swirling this spring, but he's known all along where he was going, and he's been relaxed and confident. They have to reduce the 'AAA' and 'AA' rosters to twenty-three players, down from twenty-five during last year's strike. There will be a lot of kids released during the next couple of days. Unfortunately, I have a deadline tonight for our Sunday edition, when we publish pictures of everyone on the roster. The starting five pitching rotation is set, but the relievers haven't been notified. If I send in the wrong names, I'll look like a fool. And there isn't room for pictures of all the 'possibles.'"

Joining Todd on the infield was his old college rival and former Thunder team-mate, Lou Merloni, sent down from "AAA." Dana LeVangie moved back to the Thunder team at catcher, with Walt McKeel. The Sox sent Jeff Martin to the independent affiliate in California; they would not release him. The story went that Schaefer came up behind Jeff during the "AA" game and called him aside. When Jeff walked up to him, Schaefer asked, "Nervous yet?" It sounded like a terrible way to needle a player who was already on the edge emotionally! Later that year, we got to know Bob Schaefer as one of the most humane of all those in the Sox management team. The story just didn't ring true to the Schaefer we came to know. It was a trying time for wives and parents, as well as for the players. No one could make any plans for living arrangements without assignments. During the worst winter up north in decades, the snow and 30-degree temperatures continued. Players would have a tough time adjusting in a matter of days to Pawtucket, Trenton, and Battle Creek, Michigan. Lowell, Mass., would replace the Utica, N.Y., location for the short season, beginning in June.

Back at the Sheraton overlooking Ft. Myers Harbor, John Valentin rode the elevator with us, and later, Jim Rice sat behind us at "The Taste of New York" restaurant. The major leaguers boarded a bus at 6 a.m. the following morning for the airport and a flight to Atlanta, where they played the Braves in an exhibition game on March 30th. Minor league catcher Alex Delgado, as well as Bill Selby and Don Sadler (minor league infielders) accompanied the major leaguers. Remaining behind at the minor league fields were major leaguers Kevin Mitchell (soreness in the right knee); Stan Belinda (disabled list); Vaughn Eshelman (disabled list); Joe Hudson; Eric Gunderson; Bryan Eversgerd; Nomar Garciaparra; Alex Cole; Alan Zinter; Phil Clark; Felix Jose; Rich Garces.

Spring training had provided some memorable moments for the fans at City of Palms Park. Canesco, relegated to being a DH and kept away from the outfield, had hit a prodigious blast of an estimated 535 feet on March 14th. Kevin Mitchell, paid $3,000 per plate appearance rather than the guaranteed millions up front, had finally emerged as a hitter during the last week of training. In two games he had hit four homers. The most memorable quote was from Mike Greenwell: "We've got one guy who can catch one barehanded (Mitchell). We've got one guy who can hit one off the top of his head (Canseco), and we've got one guy who runs into the wall with his head (himself)." The biggest surprise had been pitcher Brad Pennington, signed as a free agent the previous November, who gave up zero earned runs in eleven spring innings.[25]

After the Trenton game on March 30th, the team ate lunch and had batting practice. Todd advised us to leave immediately after the game, because no one could predict which players would be called aside to be released or re-assigned. He had been a regular starter at third base. "You really shouldn't be here this weekend, and don't plan on it next year. It's too humiliating a time for the players. Mom, I don't want you sitting in the stands taking notes on who's walking by with his bag over his shoulder, accompanied by a member of the management." The fact was, my notebook never accompanied me to the field. I kept it either locked in the car trunk or back at the room. After we left Todd, I made my notes.

It would be April 1st before the final cuts came, making it virtually impossible for another team to pick up the released players. Randy Brown, a "AAA" player, as well as Tony Rodrigues and Paul Carey (no relation), were asked by Schaefer to stick around for another week in extended spring training until a spot opened up somewhere. They would still be collecting "AAA" pay, but at least one of them had few other realistic possibilities to pursue. Randy had packed all his belongings in his truck and had checked out of the Days Inn, when management asked him to unpack and stick around in limbo. Bill Selby and Dan Collier had been living at the Holiday Inn until Selby played his major league exhibition game in Atlanta. Re-assigned to "AAA," Bill ended up sleeping on the floor in another player's room at the Days Inn, since there were no more rooms available. Hecker and Mahay would stay on the Sarasota "A" team and retrain as pitchers instead of infielders.

The March 31st game against the Pirates was by far the best we'd seen Todd play during spring training. He played first base for the entire game and had four hits, including a double to the center field fence. Afterward, we asked him if he had yet made an error during spring training. "No," he responded. We left the field immediately after the game. Don Sadler had played in Atlanta with the major leaguers, and returned to shortstop for Trenton. He hit well, but Charley predicted that if he played the entire season at shortstop for Trenton, he would make a minimum of forty errors. The next day, Sadler played short again and proved he could make flashy, difficult plays. His speed was incredible.

It was hard to know who had made the Trenton roster and who didn't. The only missing faces at Todd's last spring training game were an unnamed player #55 (all other Sox players had their names on the back of their shirts), and Bob Juday. An excellent hitter, Bob Juday had fought back for a roster position after getting his jaw broken the previous spring. His family from Michigan was very supportive of all the players. Bob had an older brother released from "AA" during another spring, but it never got easier. The director of field operations, Bob Schaefer, circled like a vulture in his golf cart all during the games. We said goodbye to Todd in front of his bus, wishing him luck over the next couple of months until we saw him on our drive north over Memorial Day weekend. Within ten days we would be visiting Tim in Japan.

On April 5, 1996, Todd's team opened in Trenton. The Yankees had been snowed out in Cleveland, and the Red Sox had lost four straight. We didn't hear from Todd until the following day, and he seemed panicky.

"We won the first game and I played first, but I went 0-for-4. Then in the afternoon today, a lefty pitched against us, and I only went in for the second half. In the first game I hit the ball well, but not today!"

"Well, maybe you were pressing too hard," Charley said. "Why don't you go to a movie tonight and forget about baseball? You'll start hitting, don't worry!" My roller coaster ride had begun again. It was incredible to us that Todd had had such a confident bat at spring training and yet began the season 0-for-7.

By the time we left for Japan on April 10, 1996, Todd's team had only played five additional innings, due to inclement weather. "I played third base for the only five innings we played," Todd told us by phone, "and I went 2-for-3. Dana and I found an apartment about twenty miles closer to Philly this year, in Bensalem, Pennsylvania. It's going to be $100 more a month than last year. Dana had to go on the Disabled List because Delgado came down from the majors and they didn't want to move the Pawtucket catchers around. Someone had to be taken off the roster to keep it at twenty-three."

Tim coaching in Japan, 1995.

20

Breakout

We left for Japan in good spirits. Within a week, we had toured Tokyo, where Tim met us. He accompanied us back on the bullet train to Fukuchiyama City in the mountains west of Kyoto. We explored Kyoto and Fukuchiyama, meeting all of Tim's associates, observing his classes, and watching his karate drills in preparation for a tournament. His fluency in Japanese after nine months astounded us. He was comfortable and happy in his sixth-floor apartment, which he rented from the school. It was an extravagant living space by Japanese standards, with a kitchen, bedroom, a living/dining room and a TV room. He never stopped smiling the entire time we stayed in Fukuchiyama. For two hours on a drive to Kyoto, he conversed easily in Japanese with Fugitasan, his karate instructor, while Charley and I sat in the back seat dumbfounded. We had completely reversed roles with him; Tim led us by the nose, ordering for us in restaurants, arranging for drivers and guides, and introducing us to everyone in his environment. His students were clearly enamored of him. On his birthday, after several cakes and celebrations, we found a message from Todd on Tim's machine.

"How's everything going?" Charley asked when we returned his call.

"Not well, I'm still not hitting."

"Well, are you contacting the ball, or are you striking out?"

"I'm hitting the ball, with nothing to show for it."

"They'll start to fall in. Keep your chin up, and relax. Don't press too hard. Try to hit to the opposite field, instead of pulling the ball."

I had heard this mantra over and over through the years, and so had Todd! It tore Charley up to hear that at such a critical point, with an unbelievable spring behind him, Todd lacked confidence at bat. Whatever Todd confided in Tim, Tim kept to himself. When I got on the phone, it was to divert his thoughts to a different realm, and I described our adventures in detail. We planned to leave Japan for Singapore and Bali within a few days, so Charley terminated the conversation by assuring him we would reach him over the next week from Indonesia. Charley always carried the boys' team schedules with him wherever he went.

Singapore - a pulsating, clean, modern city of high-rises; a confluence of Indonesian, Malaysian, Asian, and United Kingdom cultures; a shopper's paradise, with designer boutiques as far as the eye could see along Orchard Road; a don't-look-down gondola ride over the harbor to a fantasy island.

Bali - terraced rice fields; volcanic mountains; Hindu stone carvings ahead, sideways, and behind; tropical rain forests with 300-foot river gorges; women carrying baskets of food on their heads to be blessed each morning in the nearby temple; rice being cut with sickles, then threshed in the field over baskets by barefooted women in triangular straw hats and sorted by women on the sidewalks over plastic sheeting with the family dog lying in the center; ikat sarongs and bright silk dresses with cummerbunds; hawkers stalking us along the beach and fishermen with more triangular hats waist-high in the Bali Strait; pagoda temples and gates adorned with replicas of Hindu gods dressed in black and white checked cloth shirts with parasols.

After we left the Bali highlands, our paradise on the beach consisted of a two-bedroom air-conditioned pavilion with Westernized bathroom and open-air pavilion for cocktails, lounging, and dining; coarse golden sand; a free-form pool with waterfall; all in a private compound with a staff of three assigned to do our cooking, laundry, and housekeeping. For $100 a night!

Two days before leaving for home, Charley started calling Todd's apartment. Unable to reach him because of the 12-hour time difference, Charley finally left a message that he would try again the following day. When we succeeded, we woke Todd up a 1 a.m. It was a heart-wrenching conversation.

Batting a published .154, he told Charley he had tried everything, and nothing was working. He was striking out one out of four times at bat. During the thirteen days we'd observed spring training, he'd struck out a total of once. How I wished I could transport him by magic carpet to the empty bedroom in our pavilion for a much-needed trip to fantasyland! My dream world allowed me to tune out his misery for a moment.

"I wish I could help you, Todd," Charley said. "All I can tell you is to try to hit to all fields, rather than pulling the ball. You had a fantastic spring, and it will come back at the plate. Believe in your ability, just as we do. Are you playing every day?"

"Yes."

"Well, at least Macha still has faith in you. Where are you playing?"

"All over the infield."

"Keep your chin up. We love you, and know you have the talent to hit the ball."

When I got on the phone, I began to describe our surroundings on Bali, to get Todd's attention off baseball. When he responded, his voice was cracking.

During a slump, a player focuses on what has gone wrong. Defeat is acceptable at the plate two out of three times, but not five out of six times. As the nervous and muscular systems go through the sequence of past failures, the mind overtakes the body. The mind reinforces the likelihood of failure and a further decline in confidence follows. Visual distractions begin to eliminate concentration on the pitcher, and the slumping batter's average flashes in digits ten feet high on the scoreboard. Teammates become distant, not wanting to say anything to hurt him, knowing at any time they could be in the same situation.[26] It would be up to the Trenton batting instructor, Harold "Gomer" Hodge, to help Todd work out of it, not up to his teammates. But still, a deathly hush might fall over the crowd every time he came to bat. Our hearts ached for him, halfway around the world. We were helpless. Todd alone would have to come to grips with the situation, and pass through this phase in the endurance test that is baseball.

"If he has such a fragile ego after four years, perhaps he doesn't have the total package to go any further," Charley said, trying to prepare me for the worst scenario. "He hit .275 at the end of last year on the same team, and should have management eating out of the palm of his hand. But, for whatever reason, the opposite has happened."

By the time we returned from our trip, Tim's former roommate, Bill Selby, had replaced Tim Naehring in Fenway, who was rehabilitating on the Trenton team. Bill hit two home runs within a week of his debut at third base. "Now that's what I'd call taking advantage of an opportunity," Charley said.

I expressed doubts to Tim over the phone about Todd's ability to raise his seasonal average so that he might attract a trade to another team. Tim blew up at me. "Why are you so negative?" he yelled. "He's only had fifty-some at-bats. It's a long season, and he had a good year last year!"

"Tim, I express my doubts to you in confidence. You know Todd will always have our total support."

The first week of May, Todd said he was hitting slightly better. From Tim we received a secondhand account of a meeting Manager Macha and Director of Field Operations Schaefer had had with Todd.

"Todd was in a great mood when he talked to me," Tim reported. "Macha and Schaefer told him he was one of the best players on the Trenton team, and they had complete faith in him and would continue to play him. Whatever it would take to get him back on track, they would stick by him."

On May 22nd, we began our trek from Florida to Massachusetts. The car was laden with clothes, golf and tennis bags, computer and printer, my notebooks, Charley's files, etc. Todd, like a phoenix risen from the ashes, had resurrected his average to around .270. We were really proud of him for not caving in. On May 20th, Charley's father, one brother, and a twin sister saw one of his night games in New Haven. Todd added a homer that night to his team's barrage of the Colorado Rockies "AA" affiliate, the New Haven Ravens. Todd added seven more RBI's on that road trip, bringing his total to twenty-two. His homers stood at five. He had the fourth highest average by late May, was tied for second in home runs, and was third in RBI's.

We had a fabulous stopover in Charleston, South Carolina, on the way home. It was one of the most uniquely preserved, charming, walkable, and livable cities we'd ever visited in the U.S. Nearby was Kiawah Island that we had thoroughly enjoyed on another drive home. We planned to return to the area again when we could.

We stopped over in Trenton during a home stand for the Thunder on our way to Massachusetts. Visiting parents and opposing teams stayed at the Novotel in South Brunswick, N.J., at a special rate. It was not as convenient as the Palmer Inn in Princeton, where we had had a Red Sox discount the previous year. The Novotel was eight miles further north, and although it was modern and large, the visiting Marlins' Sea Dogs from Portland, Maine found they could not afford to eat in the restaurant there on their meal allowances. The Dogs' bus driver made shuttle runs to local malls so the team could eat at fast food chains.

Charley and I walked our usual four miles along a corporate park ring road, going back and forth three times. It took us a full forty-five minutes during Princeton rush hour traffic to get to Waterfront Park in Trenton.

We met Todd prior to the night game against the Sea Dogs on May 24, 1996. His average stood at .266. He'd had a day off prior to our arrival, and had played golf with Manager Macha. "I'm getting sick of him," Todd said, meaning Macha had probably been in Todd's face about his early performance that year.

Instead of our bringing Todd luck, the opposite happened. He tried hard to perform well, since we hadn't seen him in two months. He grounded out three times all over the infield. During an eighth inning rally, our team came back to tie the game. Randy Brown and Walt McKeel got hits, and we went ahead by a run. With two men on base, Todd came to bat. He took three gigantic home run swings, then sat down.

It was especially hard for Charley to watch his performance at the plate. He had taught Todd his fundamentals, even before he became the boys' Little League coach, and when he saw that Todd didn't choke up after getting two strikes, he couldn't believe it. We saw Don Sadler, Randy Brown, and newly-acquired Tyrone Woods all hit homers that night. In addition, Holifield beat out two bunts for hits. Todd had had the patent rights on those in college, but gave up while trying to impress the scouts.

At third base, Todd took sole possession. Lou Merloni was out with a broken wrist until mid-summer. Tyrone Woods, who had Mo Vaughn's stature without his agility, played first base. Randy Brown was at short. Greg Patton had been called up from Sarasota, Fla., to back up the infield. His wife drove with the baby through the night, as she had done the previous season from Sarasota to Michigan. The team was in first place in its division, and at $5 per ticket, the games were sell-outs, with standing-room-only sold at the ticket windows.

Afterward, we took Todd for a late-night Italian dinner, where he ordered plain cheese pizza. That was Todd's taste in food - PLAIN! No ketchup, no mustard, no pickles, no lettuce, no onion. When he was growing up, we'd have to wait in the McDonald's for his PLAIN hamburger, while five families bypassed us to pick up their meals.

We talked about everything except baseball. When he told us of all the relatives and friends he'd seen on the road trip in Connecticut, he finally expressed his disgust over the season he was having. "I hit a homer in New Haven, and then could have had two more, but one outfielder caught it above the fence, and another made a great catch at the warning track. That's typical of this season. Instead of three hits, I had one. Then tonight I couldn't buy one."

"Be patient," Charley advised gently. "They will start to fall in if you keep hitting the ball hard."

"Be patient?" he retorted. "We're two months into the season!"

"Well," I pointed out, "you don't get twenty-two RBI's and five homers without doing something right! You've come a long way since the beginning of the season."

"The only time I was disappointed with your batting tonight was your last time up," Charley began. "With two strikes, you made no adjustments with your hands. Look at Walt McKeel — he's batting .330 because he chokes up and is so strong that he can still put them over the fence. You were swinging for a home run the entire last at-bat."

"No, I wasn't, Dad. Macha told me the same thing. I was supposed to just put it out there somewhere. He said I tried for a home run, but I didn't think I was swinging for a home run."

During Memorial Day weekend, Todd uncharacteristically played first base and was the only lefty batter in the starting lineup against their lefty pitcher. He went 3-for-3, with a double and two singles, before their right-handed reliever came in. His fourth time up, he probably said to himself, "What the hell! I'm 3-for-3 tonight, so I'm going for the right field fence." He flied out to center, instead. His swing had improved 100% since the previous evening, returning to the relaxed, smooth motion we recognized. It was definitely a mental game.

During the game, Todd's former roommate from Lynchburg days came and sat with us. John Graham, from Abington, Mass., had played in an independent California league after being released by the Sox in '95. His California coach had invited John and his brother to play a short season in the newly-formed independent "Big South" League, consisting of six teams. The Graham brothers were on their way to Mississippi to report when they dropped in on the Trenton game and spread out on two of Todd and Dana's couches for the night. We treated the four of them to an uproarious dinner.

The Sunday of Memorial Day weekend was another day game against the Sea Dogs. Brian Rose, a 20-year-old from Dartmouth, Mass., with a 5-1 record, pitched a 2-0 shutout. Trenton had swept the series. Incredibly, Randy Brown got his ninth homer at the 400' center field marker, while Adam Hyzdu also collected one. They were the Thunder's only two runs. Todd played third base and made some outstanding plays. In his first at-bat, he drilled a line drive into the hole between the shortstop and third baseman, which the third baseman caught in the webbing of his glove. The second time up, he hit a fly ball to center field. The third time, with a 3-2 count, one out, and the runner going from first base, he swung and missed. The runner was thrown out at second. It never got easier to watch the strikeouts.

The wives and fiancées of the players attempted to engineer Todd's social life. They called to include him and Dana, a bachelor with girlfriend Traci at home, in their evening activities. Several told us they had friends who would be "perfect" for Todd, but the friends were either in Colorado, some other faraway place, or had decided to marry guys who were "unworthy" of them. Todd noticed details of clothing and jewelry about women, just as he noticed architectural details on the exterior or interior of a building. He often avoided my questions about his social life by asking the same question in return. If he deemed my question was undeserving of his attention, he'd reply with, "Think about it!" Within a month, Todd found his companion for a lifetime. Trish, a Thunder intern getting her Master's in Sports Management at Florida State, would become his wife five years later. He didn't introduce us to her until August.

Sometimes, when Todd had had enough nagging, he'd thrust a quick, "Shut up, Mom!" toward me, or simply explode, which was Tim's pattern. Charley rarely exploded, but, instead, confronted me with silence. Fortunately, none of the three could match my menopausal mercurial moods. Sometimes I would wake up in the morning aiming to fight! I had no idea why and could only explain it with hormonal changes. Whatever Charley said was wrong and set me off, even if it was, "Did you sleep well?" He recognized when these moods appeared on the horizon and found numerous errands to do in the car. Charley and I had not had an easy winter adjusting to each other's constant presence in Florida. Since he had resigned from Fleet and had left the Ft. Lauderdale investment banking partnership, he'd had

continual meetings for his various boards of directors or for employment opportunities. Meanwhile, I'd devoted my time to moving out of our Rhode Island
house and Florida condo, in addition to moving my parents out of their Connecticut house. I played in golf and tennis leagues, had worked at my Rhode Island
design company refurbishing spaces from rooms up to entire buildings until I was
no longer a Rhode Island resident, and began transferring all of my baseball notes
into the computer. Certainly the freedom we enjoyed to travel, entertain guests in
Florida, or take four-mile walks each day outweighed all negatives. Nevertheless,
I found Charley peeking into the room where I sat over the computer, asking, "Are
you going to take a lunch break now?" I seldom ate lunch, and knew this was a
disguised request for a sandwich and company. Most difficult was his increasing
deafness in the left ear, something he denied vehemently. When he missed parts of
a conversation, discussions got diverted because he thought I'd asked something I
hadn't. Jim Hagan, president of the Providence Chamber of Commerce, used to
tell us a story about a man whose wife insisted he go to the doctor for a hearing
test. "Your hearing is perfect," the doctor pronounced after testing him. "Don't
you know that the majority of middle-aged men I test have perfect hearing, but
their wives insist the husbands can't hear a word they say?" There was certainly
more than a half-truth in that.

Back in our Massachusetts house for four and one-half months, we were able to
commute to New Britain, Conn., in June to watch Todd. His average stood at .277
before the game, with six homers and twenty-nine RBI's. General Manager Dan
Duquette and Chief Batting Instructor Steve Braun were among those from Boston seated in the stands behind home plate.

Todd struck out in the first at-bat we saw. When he came up the second time, he
went 0-and-2 and continued the agony by fouling off several balls. At least he was
choking up on the bat. By this point, watching the Boston management taking
notes on each batter, Charley and I could not contain our nervousness. Suddenly,
Todd smacked a home run over the right field fence. We led 3-0 in the fourth. I felt
like a wrung-out dishrag, but the tension headache I'd experienced for the first four
innings suddenly disappeared. Todd then hit a line drive double in the sixth that
rolled to the right field fence. He scored on a sacrifice fly to cut the lead that the
Twins had taken to 6-5. Having laid down a bunt (AT LAST!) in his previous at-
bat, Todd came up in the top of the tenth with the score tied 6-6. He ripped a
double to the 400' marker on the center field fence for his fifth at-bat, and scored
on a single by Adam Hyzdu. The game was three outs away from a Trenton win,
but, unfortunately, our closer, Reggie Harris, couldn't hold on. We lost 8-7 in the
bottom of the tenth inning. Todd played third base all weekend. His errors for the
season stood at five.The Twins' Rock Cats and the Sox Trenton Thunder were
among the three top home-run teams in the "AA" Eastern League. During the

Rock Cats -Thunder series, there were four combined homers in the first game, including Todd's, and six followed in the second game, including another by Todd. By the end of the weekend, Trenton was in first place in its division with 33-17. The new Rock Cats' stadium held its second largest crowd that Saturday night, with around 5,000 in attendance. They included four of Todd's Brown roommates, as well as Tim's friend Molly and her entourage. Todd's average stood at .291, with thirty-four RBI's and eight homers. He was playing for a manager who had great confidence in him; he'd worked with Steve Braun and made adjustments at bat; he'd added strength through weight-lifting. Most importantly, Trish was cheering for him back in Trenton.

Prior to the first game, Bob Schaefer, director of Field Operations for the minor leagues, had been talking to Todd and Randy Brown. When I asked what Schaefer had said, Todd replied, "Nothing." During the Saturday night game, Steve Braun recognized Charley and came over. "He's really worked hard on the off-speed pitches and has made a lot of adjustments. He's ready for the next step." Who knows what that meant!

We asked a pitcher's fiancée where Dan Collier and Don Sadler were. The wives, fiancées, and girlfriends were a pipeline to all the moves, up, down, and sideways. The Sox had repositioned Sadler in center field, but he had broken a finger. The Sox told Collier, batting .213, to report to a team in California. He was considering leaving baseball.We met Trenton Times reporter, Chris Edwards, in the Ramada Inn prior to game time that Sunday. "Did you know that Todd led the league in May with almost thirty RBI's?" he asked us. "If he keeps hitting this way, he might jump over a step before the season is over. He's still a real prospect." When we told Todd later that he'd led the league in RBI's during May, he responded, "That means nothing." He had learned that baseball wasn't a sprint, it was a marathon!

On June 6, 1996, the "AA" Eastern League named Todd "Player of the Month" for May. He got an inscribed cup to add to his collection in our Westport house. During that month, he'd batted .357 (30-for-84) for the Thunder, with five homers, eight doubles, and twenty-seven RBI's. When he was named "Player of the Month" for the entire Red Sox system, Sox announcers Jerry Remy and Bob Kurtz tossed his name around during a televised game in Fenway Park as being a "hot prospect being watched by the management."

I was ecstatic, but we didn't get Todd's reaction until we saw him back in Trenton on June 21, 1996. A sports page in The Trenton Times greeted us that featured Todd's photo as he was hitting a double in the previous night's doubleheader sweep against Bowie. The write-up said that he had gone 0-for-14 during the week, but had recouped during the doubleheader to smash three extra base hits. They were his nineteenth double, his second triple, and his thirteenth homer. His

RBI's had reached fifty in sixty-two games. He was touted in the paper as a possible All-Star selection. The All-Star game would take place at the Thunder field on July 8th. The team was 5-1/2 games in front of the second-place team in its division, with Macha a strong contender for All-Star managerial assignment.[27] Another article in The Times that day reported the diligence of Thunder players' workout routines. Todd was one of five players filing their workout sheets on a regular basis. The workout list was distributed by Boston Strength and Conditioning Coordinator B. J. Baker. The other four players were pitchers Mike Blais and Carl Pavano, infielder Randy Brown, and outfielder Trot Nixon.[28]

When we arrived at Waterfront Park that night and received the up-to-the-minute league stats, we realized that although his average had fallen to .283, Todd was among the league leaders in home runs, RBI's, doubles, slugging percentages, and extra base hits. We received further good news down on the field before the game. Quietly but with a huge grin, he told us after infield practice, "I've been voted to the All-Star team!" He'd been one of three from the Thunder voted to the team by league managers, scorers, and media. Accompanying him were Walt McKeel and Carl Pavano. The three "AA" Leagues across the country would compete, and the game would be broadcast nationally on ESPN2. Worldwide, it would be on Armed Forces radio. After that night's game, Todd received about $300 worth of Thunder clothing and a $100 check as gifts from Thunder GM Wayne Hodes, the same GM who had not treated the team to any celebration the previous season when they became Division Co-champions. We could never have imagined two months previous, while we were halfway around the world, that Todd would have accomplished such a complete resurgence by late June.

My whole attitude changed watching Todd perform. When he came to bat, I wanted men to be on base, because he seemed to concentrate more. I knew there would be more homers pulled over the right field fence. In the first six innings of the game, he went 1-for-4, including his fourteenth homer. In the last two innings, he added two singles. He was 3-for-6 on the night. His fourteenth homer broke a franchise record, as it was his twenty-second in two years as a Thunder player. He had outnumbered Tony Clark (1994) and Clyde "Chop" Pough (1995) in the record book.

The next morning we were again astounded to open The Times and see another large photo of Todd on the front page of the sports section, this time awaiting the throw at second base to tag out runner Juan Bautista. Todd had been selected "Player of the Game" the night before with four RBI's, although Woods and Holifield also had three hits that the evening, and Holifield made a fabulous diving catch in center field to rob Howie Clark of a hit with the bases loaded.

Todd displayed his first bit of "attitude" in the news report. Reporting that "Carey, for one, could use the exposure" (from media coverage for the All-Star game), John Nalbone reported Todd had stated "his game is good enough to be at the next level." Nalbone continued:

(He) has made it no secret that he'd welcome a trade from the Boston Red Sox organization, should they feel he's not in their plans. But Carey is also content doing well in Trenton with a chance to redeem himself with more at-bats after last year's disappointments (being sent down to Sarasota).

"I didn't think it was possible (to get selected after the terrible month of April at bat)," Carey....said.

"I learned that any time you have a setback in your career you have to overcome it."[29]

"Schaefer's here," Todd told us, "and I told him I definitely wanted to play Arizona winter ball. It's up to Kenney to place us, but he was very encouraging."

That day we picked Todd up at the Quaker Ridge Mall, where he and five other players were signing autographs with Manager Macha. We took Todd and Dana to eat at the Olive Garden Restaurant, where we met Nomar Garciaparra's ex-girlfriend, Jamie.

"How's Nomar's rehab going?" I asked. Nomar had torn a ligament in the back of his knee during the third game of the Pawtucket season.

"I really haven't seen him in a couple of months, but I guess he's gone to Florida to begin workouts," she reported.

"It's a shame he got hurt," Dana said. "He hit three home runs in the first three games of the season. I bet he'd be in Fenway if that hadn't happened, with all the injuries they've had up there."

An hour before game time, we were again at Waterfront Park when a horrendous storm hit. Lightning bolts struck outside the perimeter of the park, behind the light poles, and wind-driven sheets of rain made it impossible to see more than a few feet. The grounds crew had put the tarp over the infield just before the storm began, and even as lightning began to strike beyond the outfield fence, a few loyal workers tried to place heavy objects to hold the tarp in place. Just then the wind picked up, and the tarp's cylinder was lifted and blew back to the right field fence. The sit-down roller machine stayed in place on the edge of the tarp. Then the lights and scoreboard went out. Immediately, generators kicked in, as the sky turned purple. Our team took flight into the clubhouse, while the batboy stood in the dugout in six inches of water. The game was called off and would be played as part of a doubleheader the following day. Power was out for half of the city of Trenton, and some areas of Mercer County didn't get it restored for twenty-four hours. A tornado touched down in nearby Pennsylvania; one person died at Fort Dix. It was a flashback to the tornado in Lynchburg, Va., but at least there was no damage to

Waterfront Park. After one hundred sixty-some games without a rainout at Trenton's Waterfront Park, there had been two in one week.

A few thousand of us huddled there under the protection of the concourse and luxury suites' roof. Many of the team parents, spouses, and children were in town for the long home stand. Randy Brown's mom and grandma from Houston kept us amused during the delay with plans for Randy's upcoming wedding, and tales of his arrival on Cape Cod to play in that league during college. Randy had never left home before that summer, and got off the bus from Logan in the town square of Yarmouth, Mass., late at night. There was no one there to meet him, no one to take him to the home where he'd be living. He made his first call home from a public phone.

"What should I do?" he asked his mother.

"Just stay there a while longer, and then call a cab, if you have to."

Randy was delivered to a house "in some woods," according to the Houston boy. He made his second call home.

"Mom, I'm starving," he said.

"Well, walk down someplace to get something to eat."

"You don't understand. I'm out in the middle of the woods. I miss my car."

"Well, go down and ask the lady of the house for a sandwich."

"There is no lady here, Mom," Randy replied. "Only the man is here. The lady works up near Boston and only comes home on weekends."

"Well, go down and ask the man for a sandwich."

The following day, Randy's tribulations had not ended. He made another call home. "Guess what? My job out here fell through! What am I supposed to do all day? I have no money."

The one thing Randy wanted to hear from his parents was, "Come home." Instead of giving him that satisfaction, they suggested he talk to his coach. Randy stayed and got a taste of baseball life.

The atmospheric conditions at 1:35 p.m., on Sunday, June 30, 1996, were the opposite extreme from the night before at Waterfront Park. We sat in 90-degree burning sun for the first game of the doubleheader. Over 7,000 were in attendance. With the green plastic too hot to touch, let alone sit on, the liquids were flowing. Our All-Star pitcher, Carl Pavano, had eight runs posted against him in early innings by Canton/Akron. The opponents added two more by the fifth. In the bottom of the fifth, we began a comeback, which continued again in the bottom of the sixth. Down 10-1, we rallied to tie the game! Todd hit a double to the center field fence to collect his 55th and 56th RBI. He'd walked twice, including one intentional walk so they could pitch to Walt McKeel, whose average was around .330. We'd never seen anyone walk Todd intentionally.

As if the excitement weren't enough, in the bottom of the sixth, with score tied, we had the bases loaded and Trot Nixon, our ninth batter, up. His mother had her head down in her lap on top of folded arms each time he came to bat, as he'd been a first-round draft pick out of high school several years before, and his average stood in the .230's. Suddenly he smacked one over the fence at right center for a grand slam. He was named "Player of the Game."

Most of the fans left after the first game, since it had lasted almost four hours. Fran, from the Thunder staff, had her husband Anthony with her and they stayed to greet the players coming out of the locker room. Fran had curling popsicle-pink fingernails and lots of gold chains and bracelets. She was so tan she looked as if she lived on the equator, and she attended every home game. Fran knew every player's life history, and was on a first name basis with parents, wives, and girlfriends. She kept track of players' social activities, and had a warm hug for us the first time we met her. We'd never seen her husband before. He was as tan as Fran and no taller than his 5'4" wife, but hugely muscular. He'd won the "Mr. Trenton" contest, and like his wife, wore heavy gold chains over his tank top.

The Murphy clan (Todd's Brown teammate from Rhode Island and his siblings) arrived for the second game by pre-arrangement. Unfortunately, our team looked like Little Leaguers, dazed by the heat. Todd picked up his ninth and tenth errors at third base during the second game. He struck out and grounded out, going 1-for-4 in two games. Our inexperienced pitchers were pounded for ten runs early, and the game ended with an 18-1 revenge by the Ohio team. The opponents had scored twenty-nine runs in two games against us. Todd was so tired when we all went out afterward that he could barely eat. Nick Cafardo, writing in The Boston Globe on Sunday, June 30, 1996, published:

Red Sox General Manager Dan Duquette's only hope to build a championship team in Boston is if he somehow can match the number of players that emerged into stars or top prospects during the Lou Gorman regime...While those two (Rose and Pavano) and Jeff Suppan should give the Sox a formidable rotation at some point, they are sadly lacking in positional players. The best player for the system over the first half has been Todd Carey from Cumberland, RI. The Brown University alum was never considered more than a borderline prospect before this year. Now he has a .271 average with 14 homers and 56 RBI's in his first 70 games. He's still very streaky.[30]

By the beginning of July '96, Todd had played in fifty-six consecutive games, because five infielders were injured. On a major league roster, there would be utility infielders to rotate into the lineup or management would call someone up from the team below. He became fatigued and contracted a stomach virus; his batting suffered accordingly. He went 0-for-23 during a two-week period, until he hit a 3-run homer on July 3rd. When we arrived in New Britain, Conn., with my parents to watch him on July 4th, his stats read: .263 batting average, 15 homers, 59 RBI's. Manager Macha gave him the night off in a cold drizzle, because a lefty was pitching against the Thunder. After the game, Carl Pavano's (pitcher's) family had planned a cookout at 10 p.m., only minutes away. Todd told us Schaefer had contacted him to say Kenney would try to place him in winter ball in Puerto Rico. "It's up to Kenney," Todd was told, "but you're number one on our list." We'd heard that before! I kept a positive outlook, knowing this had been Todd's most productive, most fun, most publicized season.

Tim runs the marathon in Japan, 1995.

21

A Prospect at Last

Pawsox "AAA" Manager Bud Bailey contacted Todd. "Bailey said I would have been up there by now," Todd reported, "but they want me to stay in Trenton through the All-Star game. I'm glad, because I want to get my confidence back after the slump I've been in these two weeks."

"Are you hitting to all fields?' Charley asked him, like a broken record.

"No!" he replied curtly.

The Trenton team still led its division by five games. We planned to drive from Westport to New Britain for three successive nights, then proceed to Trenton to watch Todd play in the All-Star game there. A limo would pick up the three Thunder All-Stars and All-Star Manager Macha after the day game in New Britain and would drive them to Trenton for the All-Star banquet (July 7, 1996) the same night. Charley and I planned to attend only the luncheon prior to the All-Star game on the 8th.

Todd played the second game against the New Britain Rockcats at third base. We had an entourage of ten fans to watch the game. Todd got down in the count 1-2 or 0-2 almost every time at bat, but managed to pull out a base hit to the right side, as well as two walks. In a hit-and-run when he was on base, an outfielder bobbled a double, so Todd put on the jets for home plate. He slid under the catcher's tag to tie the score 2-2 behind Brian Rose's pitching. He made a great play in the field, with Bob Schaefer watching.In the bottom of the eighth, our infielders fell apart. Randy Brown, playing at second base, made his second error of the evening by throwing away a double-play ball that would have ended the inning. One run came home for the Rockcats. Then with two outs and men on second and third, Todd backhanded a ball hit up the third baseline and proceeded to throw it over our first baseman's head. Both runners scored. The game ended 5-2 against us, with a total of five errors made by our team. It was Todd's thirteenth.

Afterward, he was very cordial to all of us, then went out in New Britain with his friends who'd driven down from Fall River.

Over the course of the next two games, at least fifteen relatives and friends came to watch the teams split wins. Todd played first base, then third base. He told some of our friends that he no longer felt comfortable playing shortstop, since he hadn't played there much during the season. He went out afterward with his former Brown roommates who'd come to watch. That night, I dreamed that Todd was released.

We won the second game 13-7. Todd went 1-for-5, bringing his average down around .259. He ripped a double to the center field fence and walked once. He stroked the ball hard to the opposite field, as well as to the right side. Playing third, he made some heads-up plays, including catching a runner off base with too great a lead. Between opposing batters, he stood on the infield dirt practicing his swing with one hand.

Afterward, a limo waited for him, Walt McKeel, and Carl Pavano, the All-Star selections. The plan was to drive them directly to the banquet in Trenton. However, the game in New Britain didn't end until 4:30 in the afternoon (it had started at 1 p.m.), and it was a three-hour drive to Trenton. In addition, it was a Sunday, with beach traffic in every direction. As it turned out, the limo deposited them at the All-Star dinner just before it broke up. None other than Boston GM Dan Duquette introduced Todd as "Paul Carey" to the ballroom, as he made his appearance. Paul Carey had appeared on the Sox fields during spring training that year. Todd left his cold plate of chicken untouched, as he signed autographs and talked to Peter Gammons (ESPN announcer and Globe sportswriter). He and Carl Pavano spent the night in a prepaid room at the Princeton Hyatt site. When we checked into our room at the Novotel, we found a large All-Star sports bag awaiting us, loaded with goodies. The players received all of this, as well as jackets, T-shirts, and in Todd's case, $100 for hitting a ball into the Delaware River during the home run contest. Trish Kosloff, whom Todd was dating, was the intern from the Thunder office in charge of the entire week's All-Star activities, and had probably left us the extra goodies. But we weren't aware of Todd's liaison at the time.

The Trenton Times reported that attendance at Waterfront Park for the All-Star game set a stadium record of 8,369. And the crowd wouldn't soon forget the night. Covered live by ESPN2, with a fireworks display afterward whose finale brought tears and cheers to the fans, it was an evening of celebration. Smiles flowed everywhere, even when a thunderstorm started immediately following the fireworks. As sportswriter Chris Edwards remarked, "None of them (smiles) were forced."

Todd started at third base for the first five innings of the All-Star game, fielding four balls in the first two innings and throwing flawlessly to first. He scorched a fifth-inning RBI triple (after grounding out) past the right fielder, scoring Jackson-ville Tigers' left fielder Bubba Trammell with the American League's first run. Todd was then singled home to tie the score at 2-2. Our Thunder pitcher Carl Pavano started the game, and had given up one hit - a homer - to Orlando's Kevin Orie. The American League eventually lost 6-2 on three homers. Macha split the game in half among his positional players.

   The Trenton Times quoted Todd the following morning: "This is definitely a positive sign, especially in front of the home crowd. This is such a confidence builder." The crowd had come to its feet to cheer the triple.

   According to Edward's article, "Macha thought of removing Carey from the game so he could enjoy an ovation, but the modest Brown University product declined the offer."[31]

   The Trenton Times also reported that Ken Macha was one of four candidates for the managerial position with the Florida Marlins, after Rene Lachermann was fired.[32]

   "Wouldn't that be something if Macha ended up down in Florida and somehow Todd could go with him?" Charley mused to me.

   "They'll put a Hispanic in down there," the Thunder Pitching Coach Ralph Treuel speculated.

   We also noted in the paper that morning the reappearance of Trenton teammate Lou Merloni off the Disabled List. Lou had been injured on May 9th that year, after batting .232 in Trenton. Instead of returning to Trenton, the Sox had re-assigned him to Pawtucket. When we asked Todd about it, he responded, "Yeah, Macha's pretty upset about it, and so is the team. We need infielders, with all the injuries." But Bud Bailey was lacking infielders also. It was reported that Merloni would be Bailey's top utility guy in the infield and would play at third, shortstop, and second base. Garciaparra returned to shortstop from the Disabled List in Pawtucket the same week.

   On July 16, 1996, we traveled from our summer home in Westport, Mass., to Portland, Maine, to watch the series against the "AA" Marlins' Sea Dogs. We stayed in Gorham with my dear friend and former teaching colleague, Jackie Hill. The first night, in a light rain before a sellout crowd of 6,857 at newly-finished Haddock Field, the Thunder regained the league's best record with a 15-4 win. Todd made routine plays at third, as well as a spectacular one. He walked, hit a two-run homer (his sixteenth), and a double for his sixty-fifth RBI. We relaxed a little. Things were certainly a lot more fun when the team was winning (nine games in front of second-place Harrisburg), and when Todd was hitting well. His slumps seemed to last four weeks at a time!

   Todd had asked us to bring Tim's catching glove up to him, so he could use it in the bullpen. When we told Tim on the phone, he said, "He better not let anything happen to it! That's a good glove."

"Are you planning to make a comeback?" Charley asked him in Japan.

When Thunder catcher Walt McKeel tried out the glove and admired it, we joked that Todd might be after his job.

During the day, we either played golf or went to the beach in Pine Point, Maine. Todd slept, then worked out at the Portland YMCA before reporting to the field in the late afternoon.

In the first inning of the second game against the Sea Dogs, a thunder and lightning storm began for the sellout crowd of 6,861, followed by a spectacular double rainbow when the rain subsided. Before the delay, Todd had hit a single to right field to collect an RBI with our first run. Miraculously after the delay, his hitting continued with his seventeenth homer, his twenty-second double, and another single. He went 4-for-4 that night, almost all when he was ahead in the count, and with two outs. He had not taken strikes or fouled many off, and had raised his average from .253 to .266 in the course of two nights. The Thunder won 5-4, with a costly injury to the pitching arm of starter Brian Rose.

Todd and Manager Ken Macha were both quoted in The Portland Press Herald the following morning:

'Sometimes you start thinking about things too much when you're having a good year,' said Carey, who is among the league leaders in home runs (17) and runs-batted-in (68). 'You put too much pressure on yourself, trying to elevate every aspect of your game.'

'To me, his swing was still good,' said Trenton Manager Ken Macha, who gave Carey a few days off last week and told him to skip batting practice one day and just show up at game time. 'He was beating himself up mentally, getting himself out.' [33]

On July 17th, our last night in Portland, the Thunder got hammered. Each time a homer was hit by the Sea Dogs, a lighthouse with foghorn would rise from behind the center field fence, and rockets would erupt surrounding the lighthouse. Prior to the game, Navy Seals' demolition experts parachuted down onto the field, one atop the other's chute.

Afterward, the Thunder team ate dinner in the locker room before boarding their bus for the eight-hour ride back to Trenton. They would play a home game the next night, after arriving back around 6:30 a.m. Todd had a half-hour drive from the field, where the players had left their cars. He handed me a birthday remembrance before boarding the bus, saying, "I'm going to take two Benadryl so I can sleep." How the players could function with such fatigue was a mystery to me, especially when they faced fastballs traveling toward them at 90 mph! I knew that normally there would be extra players on the roster who could rotate in, but this year there were more injuries than normal in Trenton. Benadryl had always made Todd tired when he'd taken it for grass and pollen allergies.

We told him we'd see him in Norwich, Conn., in about three weeks, and he remarked, "Boy, I can't get rid of you guys!" Yet he'd made a point the night he got four hits in Portland to mention to the sports writer that we'd driven three hours to watch.

"Wait until you play in Pawtucket!" I responded. "Then you'll never get rid of us." Todd was still without a contract with an agent for the season.

We predicted that the Thunder and the Sea Dogs would meet for the championship of the "AA" Eastern League, since both were so far out ahead in their divisions. By that time, I hoped, the Trenton team would have perfected its bunting, its relay throws from the outfield, and its batting against pitchers throwing sliders. Although the Sea Dogs would make it all the way to the Eastern League finals, the Thunder would not.

The following Sunday, The Providence Journal stats revealed Todd had gotten another two hits the night the team had returned to Trenton. I congratulated him on the phone for having brought his average up to .271. He retorted, "Why do you look at that stuff, Mom? Do you realize that's the first thing you said to me?" He was not pleased with me, and he was entirely justified in his rebuke!

Thereafter, Todd's average took a nosedive. By August 4th, he was batting only .253, with 18 homers and 72 RBI's. He had struck out ninety-six times in 348 at-bats. Todd told us over the phone that his batting average "made him sick."

A bright note, though, was that a number of agents had been calling to represent him, indicating his name was being circulated. Nero had again done nothing, and we knew that Nero's nose would sniff out a fee as Todd approached "AAA."

Todd began a long home stand in Trenton by breaking the Thunder record for doubles, with thirty. On successive nights, both Hyzdu and Woods recorded their twenty-first homers, tying the Trenton record set by Tony Clark and "Pork Chop" Pough. We arrived in Trenton on Todd's birthday, August 14, 1996, but he wasn't in the lineup against the Binghamton Mets' lefty, Chris Roberts.

Prior to the game, Todd told us he was one of four Thunder players being sent to the Mesa team in the Arizona League that fall. This was a huge coup for him! The others included Walt McKeel (third appearance in the League), Don Sadler, and pitchers Mike Blais and Rick Betti. Ron Mahay, outfielder-turned-pitcher, was added to the list. Since management had mentioned the Puerto Rican (predominantly major leaguers) and Mexican leagues earlier to Todd as possibilities for him, the surprise must have registered on my face. Todd immediately asked me what was wrong with going to Arizona. I promptly quipped that I'd been hoping for a vacation out of the country during the fall or early winter months. "Well, you can go anyway," he replied.

After the game on his birthday, Charley and I were looking forward to sharing a meal with Todd, or at least having a drink with him to celebrate. However, Todd explained that 10 p.m. was too late to find anything open, so he and Trish, who was there to say goodbye to him, proceeded to share the birthday celebration together. Trish would return to Florida State to resume her Master's Program the following day. We had been displaced! Charley and I could tell that this was someone very important in Todd's life, especially when he asked us if we liked Trish. We had only gotten to know her briefly, but she was extremely easy to talk to, and we knew she and Todd would have a lot in common. Todd would never tell us his feelings for Trish, but we could tell he was a happier person. On our last night in Trenton, ace pitcher Brian Rose lasted only two and two-thirds innings, allowing seven runs on eight hits. The Thunder wore replica 1939 Trenton Senators' uniforms for "Nostalgia Night." The heavy wool didn't help Todd in the field - he looked sluggish and made an error at third, while a couple of other hard-hit balls glanced off his glove for singles. But at bat he collected two singles in three times up. The Thunder lost 14-8, as the Navigators got their revenge for the night before, with seventeen hits.

There was an article in the paper the next morning by Eastern League sportswriter Jed Weisberger, who selected Todd as All-Eastern League Honorable Mention at third base.[34] His average stood at .253 when we left to drive back to Westport the next day. Around that time, I began to collect lucky coins that I found along streets and sidewalks, hoping they would yield a few extra hits for our third baseman. Baseball players are very superstitious, so why couldn't their mothers be too?

We discussed Todd's inability to maintain a consistent batting average on the drive back to Westport. "Even if he ever got to the major leagues some day," Charley stated, "he'd be benched because he doesn't produce consistently. When he's hot, it lasts six weeks or so, and when he's cold, it lasts three to four weeks. He can't have such swings in his batting." As opposed to previous years when Todd came on strongly to finish the season, in '96 he slumped at the end, despite the Thunder's continued dominance of its division. Both Hyzdu and Woods finished the season with twenty-five homers, while Todd had twenty.

A slump can take the confidence out of a player. It is almost self-defeating, since the player comes to the plate remembering the failures of past at-bats. Only hard work can restore confidence and a few successes along the way on which to dwell. Then the slump usually turns around. Different distractions can prolong or shorten a slump, depending on the emotional make-up of the player. Todd's esteem had obviously been boosted by Trish's confidence in his ability, but she was absent from Trenton after the middle of August.

On September 1, 1996, Nomar Garciaparra debuted as a major leaguer. In a game against Oakland, he went 3-for-5, including a home run. Since his return in mid-July from the injury behind his left knee, Nomar had set the PawSox on fire. His additional twenty pounds created over fifty hits, including thirteen homers in 155 at-bats. The previous season in Trenton, he had hit seven homers by early September. He'd hired a personal trainer to work out every day during his rehabilitation.

The Thunder easily won its division of the Eastern "AA" League with a record of 86-56, and a 12-game lead over the Harrisburg Senators, who would be their opponents for Division Champion. The first game would be in Trenton.

The first playoff game on September 3, 1996, featured Thunder MVP Carl Pavano, the 20-year-old pitcher from Southington, Conn. The team had arrived back in Trenton by bus at 3 a.m. from Canton, Ohio, where they'd dropped three games out of four to end their regular season. The team was staying where we were staying in the Novotel in South Brunswick, N.J., since their apartment leases had all run out at the end of August. Their Harrisburg opponents were staying there, as well.

The first game of division playoffs was downright ugly for the Thunder. Pavano got pounded for nine hits, while Sadler made two errors, Holifield made one, and catcher Borrero made one. Two new pitchers and a catcher were called up from Sarasota. We had a total of six hits (including one by Todd), and lost 9-2. Todd began taking first strikes again, striking out twice before flying out to left field. When we bumped into Bob Schaefer in the parking lot of the Novotel, he reported he'd been in meetings until 4 a.m., moving players to fill roster playoff spots. The only one not pleased with the results was probably Amy McKeel. She and Walt had planned their wedding for late September, but Walt was in Fenway Park in the dugout on his wedding day. "He'll be able to buy her three weddings," Schaefer said to us.

Trenton players Don Sadler (shortstop) and Tyrone Woods (DH) had been conspicuously absent from the post-game champagne revelry on August 24th, after the team clinched first place in the division prior to playoffs. Woods had been vocal about being passed over for "AAA" at the end of the season, while buddy Reggie Harris (closing pitcher) went up to the majors. In the first two playoff games, Tyrone went 0-for-8 as fourth batter. Said Schaefer in The Trenton Times, "As soon as you realize there isn't anybody who's been in the game who hasn't been (bleeped) over, then you can deal with it. You've just got to keep on truckin."[35] Moral of the story: take what management deals you, and keep your mouth shut!

Don Sadler, having been Baseball America's "top Sox prospect" over the summer, freely admitted to reporters that with two errors and a total lack of concentration, he stunk up the Park in game #1 of the playoffs. Said one Boston official comparing him to Nomar Garciaparra, "Like Nomar, he had that approach and enthusiasm for the game. It's not that way anymore."

Incredibly, both Woods and Sadler arrived late to the on-field team meeting prior to the second game to further show their displeasure. One Boston official commented, "You've got all day to get here after a game like (Sadler's) and you stroll in here at 4:11. That's incredible."[36]

What Boston officials did emphasize, though, was that Sadler had just turned twenty-one, and had been thrown into a situation over his head, where for the most part, he'd responded well. Mrs. Pavano had provided Tyrone Woods with one of her special recipes, but neither Tyrone nor Don Sadler seemed to have a support system in evidence that season.

Before the second game, Todd took us to lunch at an outdoor restaurant in Forrestal Village, Princeton. He seemed relaxed and confident, showing us the literature he'd received from the Sox regarding his Mesa Saguaros team in the Arizona League.

Twenty-one-year-old Brian Rose from Dartmouth, Mass., (the town next to our summer home), took the mound for game two. "Brian Rose did it," Macha said in The Times the following day. "He handled the situation extremely well…He went out there and set them down."[37]

The Thunder fell behind 1-0 in the second inning on a lapse of attention by first baseman Kevin Coughlin. Arguing a close play at his bag, he failed to notice Harrisburg third baseman Jose Vidro sprinting home from third. Coughlin's throw to home was too late.

In the third, the Senators went ahead 2-0 on an RBI single, but in the fifth, our Joe Depastino, "A" catcher who'd been promoted from Sarasota, singled for his first "AA" hit and moved to second on Abad's single. Pitcher Mike Thurman made a throw into the visitor's bullpen on Allison's sacrifice bunt. Nixon added an RBI single to tie the game. The '93 first-round pick in the draft, Nixon had matured over the season, and in game one of these playoffs had driven in a key run with a double. He also made a spectacular catch against the center-field wall to rob MVP Vladimir Guerrero of a homer. Still, he threw his batting helmet all over the dugout as he strung swears together for all within hearing distance, whenever he was unable to get on base.

Todd worked the count to 3-2 his first two times at bat. The second time, Andy Abad was on third base. For the second time, Todd struck out and ended the inning.

Righty reliever Scott Gentile faced Todd with a 2-2 score in his third at-bat in the sixth inning. Again Todd went to a 3-2 count. With one out, Todd ripped a fast ball over the right field fence into the Delaware River. I jumped up, pointing to the river, commanding the ball, "Go! Go! Go!" Co-owner Sam Plumeri also jumped up from the sky box seat where he sat with Ed Kenney and Bob Schaefer, almost vaulting himself over the railing's edge. Schaefer and Sox Scouting Director Wayne Britton exchanged high-fives.

"The homer by Todd Carey lifted the whole team," Rose said in the media the following day. "We tied the score, Todd hit the homer right there, and the game is ours."

With two outs, Abad then followed Todd's example with a homer into the lights over right field. Without a double, he'd just missed hitting for the cycle. The series moved to Harrisburg's Riverside Stadium the following night, with the Senators' Eastern League MVP Vladimir Guerrero injured from an eighth inning run into an unpadded outfield gate in Trenton. Our lefty Brian Barkley (8-8) went against lefty Tommy Phelps (2-2).

Barkley got pounded for five runs on twelve hits in five and one-third innings. Trenton managed only one run in the first inning. In the sixth, Tyrone Woods slammed a two-out, two-run homer over the second tier of the center field wall for his second hit in three games. The score stood at 5-3. Senators' Manager Kelly sent his lefty pitcher back out in the ninth to face lefty batters Trot Nixon and Todd and right-handed batter Adam Hyzdu. Nixon flied out to center, and with two outs, Adam Hyzdu singled for his second hit in three games. Todd came to bat, having walked and hit hard line drives down the first baseline for outs, including a double play. With the count 3-2, he ripped the ball to the right field fence. Two busloads of Trenton fans, the Trenton co-owner, Charley, and I jumped in unison from our seats, believing the game had been tied. Instead, the Senators' right fielder Jesus Campos stood on the warning track and caught the ball as it died downward in the wind. The game was over, with the Thunder behind in the series two games to one.

The next day, Hurricane Fran veered northward along the Susquehana, after wrecking havoc in Wilmington, North Carolina, and its barrier beaches. Trot Nixon's family drove south from Harrisburg, hoping to find their primary residence, completed in 1994, still standing in Wilmington. They didn't hold out much hope for their beach place, and on a cellular phone the previous night at the ball game, learned of a tree that had fallen through the roof of their daughter's home. Harrisburg only got about an inch of rain. Nevertheless, by noon the players and fans were confined to quarters in the Hilton attached to Strawberry Square Mall.

The season ended unceremoniously for the Thunder on the night of September 7, 1996. There were only 2,302 fans at Riverside Stadium, on an island in the middle of the Susquehana River. Our knuckleballer Jared Fernandez gave up two runs and left the game with the score tied 2-2. Todd was unable to get a hit or an RBI with men in scoring position, including the bases loaded with no outs. In that situation, his shallow fly to center prevented Trot Nixon from reaching home plate. I was glad I wasn't sitting near Charley in the stands, so I couldn't see his clenched jaw. Todd had had two hits in four games, going 2-for-14 with two RBI's, four strikeouts, and four walks. In the end, mental errors caused our defeat. Nixon, playing center field, didn't hit his cut-off man. Macha brought Tweedlie, fresh up from Sarasota, to pitch with the bases loaded against us in the sixth. In the bullpen Doug Hecker remained, a veteran first-baseman-turned-pitcher. With two outs, the Senators' Stovall hit a triple to score three runs. Their three relievers shut us down. We'd had a total of six hits in the 5-3 defeat.

Outside the locker room after the game in Harrisburg, the loyal fans who'd driven from Trenton clapped and cried as each Thunder player emerged. The co-owner, Sam Plumeri, tried to put on a good face, although there would be much lost revenue by not having the team return to Trenton's Waterfront Park. As we said goodbye to team members and their families, <u>Trenton Times</u> sportswriter Chris Edwards approached Jared Fernandez to wish him luck, then rushed onward to file his story. He had written on Todd in his paper that morning, portraying Todd's up-and-down season and his commitment to school outreach programs in the Trenton area.

The team boarded the bus back to their hotel in Princeton, where they'd left their cars laden with apartment belongings. The following day they'd have post-season physicals and would clean out their lockers before dispersing. Harrisburg eventually beat the Portland Sea Dogs to become "AA" champions.

Todd and Nomar Garciaparra in Trenton, N.J.

22

Arizona League

We put Todd on the plane for the Arizona League on October 4, 1996. He had five Red Sox players joining him on the Mesa Saguaros (meaning "Cacti"), including Mike Blais, Rick Betti, and Ron Mahay (pitchers); Don Sadler (shortstop); and eventually, Walt McKeel (catcher). His former Trenton roommate who'd been traded to the Expos, Ryan McGuire, would also be on Todd's Mesa team. The team was managed by Pirates' "AAA" Manager Trent Jewett. Ryan McGuire and Mike Blais would share an apartment in Scottsdale with Todd.

The major league club lost their wild card bid in late September. We watched Todd's former teammates on TV, who were now on the expanded major league roster: Bill Selby, Nomar Garciaparra, Jeff Manto, Walt McKeel, Tony Rodrigues, and Trot Nixon. We counted seven infielders on the "AAA" or major league roster who could play third base. Arquimedez Pozo did a good job there at the end of the season, alternating between "AAA" and Fenway.

"That's one bad trait that I have of yours," Todd had told me before he left for Arizona. "I worry too much about things that are out of my control. Who gives a shit who's playing third base right now, or what's going to happen to him? All I have to do is concentrate on my own performance." Todd was repeating Charley's recorded message, and it seemed to have finally lodged in place, even when talking to dear, old Mom!By the beginning of October, Kevin Kennedy had been fired as Red Sox manager. Dan Duquette, GM, cited the team's unpreparedness coming out of spring training. Like Todd, the major leaguers had had an abysmal April. Duquette also cited Kennedy's inability to gain cohesiveness among the prima donnas before entering the wild card race. Yet, many of those same players had been hired by Duquette. Dan Duquette was not one to relinquish control, and hired Pitching Coach Joe Kerrigan before finding a new manager in Fenway, thereby undermining the authority of the manager, once chosen, to bring in his own staff.

Todd began his Arizona League stint with a homer, several doubles, and a triple in the first half-dozen games. His Mesa team, the defending champions, took the lead in their division early. Todd played every day, mostly at third, but sometimes replaced his apartment-mate, Ryan McGuire, at first base.

By the time we drove to Florida in the third week of October, the Boston papers announced that Bill Selby and Phil Clark would have contracts with Japanese teams. Jeff Manto, third baseman bouncing between "AAA" and the majors, had become a free agent. That was two less third basemen in Todd's path. Todd, meanwhile, had enjoyed a side trip to Sedona and the Grand Canyon with his apartment-mates.

Tim heard of Bill Selby's signing in Japan the day after it occurred. Although Bill would be at least five hours away from Tim, his team would go to play in Osaka, where Tim could watch him. Tim called us immediately for Bill's parents' number in Mississippi and had a lengthy conversation with Bill before he left, explaining the customs, the advantage of playing on the low-key Yokahama team, and the positive attitude Bill should display in order to gain from his experience. Bill would receive a speculated $500,000 for one year. Todd's reaction to the news: "What kind of security is that for his family? It's only a one-year contract." Since he was involved in a serious personal relationship, Todd's perspective on security (financial or otherwise) had altered.

Within two weeks of our arrival in Florida, Charley and I hopped a plane to Phoenix, using frequent flier miles for two free tickets. Todd had been playing for four and one-half weeks by the time we arrived.

He was living in Scottsdale in an apartment complex with a pool, golf course and line-skating/jogging trails, just east of the pedestrian mall containing the city hall, Center for the Arts, and library within the "Old Town" area. Their Mesa team was one game out of first place, and virtually the entire team was batting in the high .200's or better when we arrived. Todd was at .266.

He and Mike Blais had turned in their shared rental car after one month. He didn't plan to rent another until Trish arrived for Thanksgiving because Ryan had driven his car out from California and was taking them back and forth to work out and play ball.

No matter where these kids were playing, their lifestyle remained the same: two-bedroom apartment (this time with two baths), efficiency kitchen, someone sleeping on the pull-out sofa, dining table for four. The routine repeated itself daily: sleep, work out at the gym, errands or laundry, check-in at the field. Both Ryan and Mike were planning to get married within a year's time, so it became interesting when Trish and the fiancées visited, with only two bedrooms among them.

The 105-degree heat of early October in Phoenix lowered to 85 degrees, without a cloud in the sky during our four-day stay. Batting practice was occasionally abandoned before game time in this relaxed league. Six teams played at three different fields in the Phoenix/Tempe/Scottsdale area. Todd's Mesa team used the Phoenix Municipal Stadium, and only three times had they played in the evening, when the temperature dropped to 50 degrees. Almost every game was at 1:05 p.m. in the 85-degree heat. Mostly scouts attended, with around 500 fans on weekends.

Around mid-November, each major league team put together its forty-man roster in preparation for the choices it would make for the final roster during spring training. A player on the forty-man would receive an early reporting date in the spring, with additional meal money. Of course, any new player on the roster had to join the player's union and pay associated dues. This enrolled the player in a pension plan and assured a percentage of souvenir-shop sales the previous year from all stadiums (every major league player got the exact same amount on the same day). Todd reported that his new agent, Boston lawyer Ken Fishkin, had spoken to Kenney, and the Sox management was mulling over Todd's inclusion on the forty-man, thereby protecting him from other clubs. Todd, should he get on the roster in Fenway at some point, would need an individual meeting with player union reps, since he signed as a replacement player during the '95 season. Otherwise, the union would exclude him.

We counted among the rosters of the six teams in the league six names who had played major league ball that season. Todd had two singles in the first two games, collecting one RBI. He played third base in the first game, was DH in the second game. Charley's spin on his performance: "He was certainly more selective at bat, not going after curve balls out of the strike zone. That's how he got two base-on-balls today. And any time you get on base three times in one day, that's a good day."

In general, we were disappointed with the pitching performance of the three teams we saw the first two days, with the exception of Phoenix starter Chris Carpenter. The Phoenix team had excellent hitters, representing the Baltimore Orioles, Cincinnati Reds, Chicago Cubs, and Houston Astros. Perhaps the best overall player in the league, in Todd's opinion, was Phoenix third baseman Kevin Orie (Chicago Cubs), who was batting .392 and made some outstanding plays in the field. Todd's Mesa manager, Trent Jewett, had included four of his Pirates' positional players, as well as two pitchers, on the team. Expos' Ryan McGuire went 3-for-3 in the second game, with a single, double, and a triple. But as a first baseman, Ryan had had only nine RBI's and one homer in a month.

Todd talked of finances at dinner, and the results of his body fat test. His weight had increased to 201 pounds, with 15% body fat. That definitely didn't please him, since he wanted it at 10% or below. To Charley and me, he looked terrific. He and his roommates drank a protein supplement once a day that was the only proven nutrient to add muscle, not body fat.

He followed a pattern in the batter's box, taking the first strike, fouling one off or swinging at the second, getting down in the count with two strikes against him. When he became more aggressive, he pulled two hard shots to the first base side. His average reached .271.

Bob Schaefer, Director of Player Development, was there that week, along with Dan Duquette. Schaefer came over to us in the parking lot afterward, where we'd gathered with Todd and Mike Blais. "What did Schaefer have to report to you?" Charley asked Todd when we were alone.

"We talked a little about my hitting, and he asked me if I'd like to play in the Mexican League after I finish here. I guess Bo Dodson didn't show up."

"What did you say?"

"I didn't give him an answer yet. I'll have to find out their motivation for sending me down there. If they just need a body to fill Buddy Bailey's roster, I won't bother. I could use some rest. But if they plan to put me on the forty-man roster and play me every day down there, then I might go. If I'm already included on the forty-man, I'll pass. The Mexican League plays through Christmas until mid-January."

"Well, it's certainly important for you to be rested for spring training," Charley agreed. "Did Schaefer say anything about the selection for Kennedy's successor as major league manager?"

"No, but Schaefer was originally one of those being considered. Macha and Bailey are vying for that position now, and whichever of the two doesn't get it will go to Pawtucket as manager. Bailey won't be happy doing that again. They want someone with lots of major league experience to manage in Fenway, but I don't see what difference it makes, since he'll just be a pawn for Duquette."

Our last day in Scottsdale began auspiciously. The 40-degree temperatures during the night warmed to a sunny 75, and Charley and I spent the morning walking up the meandering roads into the Mummy Mountains. We had visited Phoenix at least twice before, once during Tim's Dartmouth College spring break tournament, in which the teams used the same Phoenix Municipal Stadium that was now Todd's home field. So there was no need to do more sightseeing around Camelback Mountain or up to the Grand Canyon five hours away.

Todd was not in the lineup that day. Instead, Yankee Matt Howard was taking a turn at third base, having played shortstop in previous games. With at least seventy-eight at-bats, Matt was one of the top ten hitters in the league (.322). Todd's roommate Ryan McGuire was close behind (.311), tied with Red Sox infielder Don Sadler. The Mesa team (Yankees, Red Sox, Pirates, Expos, and Cubs) was back in first place in its Southern Division.

Afterward, we met shortstop Kevin Polcovitch (Pittsburgh Pirates) and his wife, who would host Todd, Trish, and Mike Blais for Thanksgiving dinner. It would be the first turkey that Kevin's wife had attempted.

We drove Todd to Charley's Fall River friend's house for dinner. Todd informed us, "Schaefer asked me to play in the Mexican League when I finish here, because he wants me to see more off-speed pitches. So I asked him if the management intended to put me on the forty-man roster, because then I'd take advantage of the practice. He said they didn't intend to, but they think I'll play third base in Pawtucket ('AAA'). So if they're not going to include me on the forty-man, I'm not going down to Mexico just because they need a spot filled. I need a break, anyway. I've probably had almost eight hundred at-bats since the first week of April."

To protect Todd from being drafted to play on another major league team, under Rule 5 of the Minor League Draft provisions, the Sox would have had to put him on their major league forty-man roster. Entering his fifth full season in the minors, this step would be the final one in assuring him that the organization intended to use him in their major league infield at some point. It did not assure a spot on the final major league 25-man team at the end of spring training. By not including him on the '97 forty-man roster, management was leaving its options open to either put Todd back down on "AA," roster him at "AAA," or allow another team to draft him at the major league level (one level higher than the roster on which he was placed in his contract).

"Schaefer said he thought it might be an excellent opportunity for me, if some other team needs me immediately in the majors," Todd continued.

"That's true, Todd," I commented. "I know your future is uncertain at this moment, but it could be just what you need, especially if you have a strong finish in this Arizona League. Did he mention going to spring training early with the major leaguers?"

"No, but I'm going to call Ken (his agent) and have him do some pressuring."

"Well, I know you're probably disappointed about the 40-man roster, and the extra money would have been nice," Charley added, "but I really wouldn't read too much into their move. Schaefer might be privy to some inquiries about you from other teams. There are so many scouts at these games, and if they can make a good deal for themselves in a trade, they will."

I agreed. "Just remember, Todd, you are nothing but a piece of meat to them, to be traded to the highest bidder."

"Gee, thanks for the support, Mom. You always have such a negative attitude! You just can't handle disappointment," he told me, shaking his head in disbelief.

I felt really lousy after Todd reacted with such hurt. Mothers, after all, were supposed to be constantly supportive, and never display any disappointment or doubt about their offspring! After giving him a hug to say goodbye, telling him how much we loved him and how proud we were of the confidence he'd shown in this league, I watched him walk up the steps to his apartment in the dark, with his head hanging down near the flagstones. It was a sight I would long remember. I knew he was disappointed to find out he wouldn't be included on the forty-man major league roster for spring training in his fifth year, and should have watched my tongue. I felt tremendously guilty for contributing to his blues, and wrote a note of apology after we got home. He, too, must have felt some sense of regret for the sharp tongue, since he called us in Florida the day after we'd arrived, to make sure we'd gotten home safely.In the three weeks following our visit and Schaefer's announcement to Todd, his batting average plummeted to .216, the second-lowest on the team. If assigned to the "AAA" level in Pawtucket, there could be no such inconsistency at bat. Nevertheless, the Mesa team remained at the top of its division, and began playoffs on December 7, 1996. Ryan McGuire, Todd's Expo roommate and Mesa first baseman, had an MRI done on his ailing throwing arm after the team lost in the finals.

On December 4, '96, the Red Sox named Ken Macha Manager of the "AAA" Pawtucket Red Sox, with Rico Petrocelli Batting Instructor, and John Cumberland Pitching Coach. Many of Macha's former Trenton players would accompany him. The Sox named DeMarlo Hale as the new "AA" Trenton Manager.

Todd's contract arrived in mid-January, offering him $2,200/month, and assigning him to Pawtucket. He sent it to his agent without signing it, as he had expected to receive the same salary he had been paid by the Arizona League ($2,500/month). The Sox had disappointed him with their exclusion from the forty-man roster, their lower-than-anticipated salary, and exclusion from major league spring training. They threw him the bone of an invitation to mini-camp for selected minor leaguers within a week after the major leaguers reported. I did not have a good feeling about the upcoming season, knowing the Sox had dealt a severe blow to Todd's ego.

By invitation, Todd attended the Pawtucket team's press conference on January 31, 1997. Accompanying Manager Macha, in addition to Todd, were pitchers Brian Rose, Carl Pavano, and Mike Blais. Macha asserted that Walt McKeel, Don Sadler, Trot Nixon, and Adam Hyzdu would be playing in Pawtucket. When reporters asked about their local Rhode Island boy (Todd), Macha replied that Todd would be "in the mix of infielders at third base." This could have meant anything. Todd, in fact, felt that Macha honestly didn't know where Todd would end up. The Sox had signed another infielder, Mike Benjamin, age 31, the previous day, and had invited him to major league camp. If Benjamin ended up at "AAA," the infield would be two-deep at every position.

After the press conference, Ken Macha told Todd, "You take care of yourself." This non-committal comment greatly upset Todd. He'd expected to hear, "See you during spring training," or "See you back in Pawtucket after the spring."

23

Seizing
Opportunities

Todd reported to camp on February 26, 1997. He told us over the phone that he was in a mini-camp filled entirely with young kids. The remainder of the "young kids" would report at the opening of regular minor league spring training. Bob Schaefer stopped by the minor league complex and assured Todd that he'd spend a few days on the major league field, working out with the forty-man roster. Randy Brown and Don Sadler were working out there, as special invitees. Todd's spirits had risen, and Trish visited him after his first week. He said he was hitting well, but Bob Schaefer was trying to help him shorten his swing so he wouldn't strike out as much as the previous season.

True to his word, Schaefer called upon Todd to dress for his first major league exhibition game on March 6th. With major league infielders Cordero, Donnels, and Frye, as well as Nomar Garciaparra injured, Todd rode the bus to Winter Haven with the major leaguers to play against Cleveland. During batting practice in the cage, his uniform zipper broke. As the crowd of 7,000 began to filter in to watch, Todd had to walk the full length of the third base line back to the clubhouse when he was finished. "Your fly's open!" "Your fly's unzipped!' he heard over and over from those lining the baseline for autographs. What a debut!

It was, in fact, an excellent debut. Positioned at third base for the last inning, he came to bat and hit a double to drive in Boston's final run.

The following day, he started at third base in City of Palms Park in Ft. Myers against the Marlins in a split-squad major league game. He walked, singled to drive in one of Boston's two runs, and grounded out. NESN broadcast the game live back in New England, and we got several calls afterward. We'd decided not to go to Ft. Myers until the minor leaguers were all in camp. That way we'd know where to watch him. After one day back on the minor league fields, Todd played two more major league exhibition games. Schaefer had told Todd, "You are just as good as Donnels (third baseman backing up major leaguer Naehring)!" Jimy Williams, major league manager, had said to Todd after his first exhibition game, "Why aren't you on the forty-man? I knew you could hit!" Those comments had made all the difference in his confidence at the plate.

On March 8, 1997, among third, short, and second base, there were twelve infielders that would be assigned to either Fenway or Pawtucket. That meant four would be cut or moved downward. Naehring, Donnels, Arquimedez Pozo, and Todd were all working out at third base. Garciaparra, Valentin, and Randy Brown were at short; Frye, Cordero, Sadler, and Mike Benjamin were working out at second base. Incredibly, Rod Correia was signed on as another infielder. These numbers didn't take into account Tony Rodrigues or Lou Merloni, who were still not in camp. Lou, however, showed up early on his own to work out, and filled in for a few days in major league split-squad games. Lou had asserted to a <u>Boston Baseball</u> reporter that he'd rather play at "AA" in Trenton in '97 than in "AAA" Pawtucket, to get regular playing time.[38]

"Did anyone ask you about playing in replacement games in '95?" Charley asked Todd.

"It was never brought up."

After four games with the major league team, Todd was 4-for-6 at bat, with two doubles, a walk, and three RBI's.

On March 14, 1997, we arrived in Ft. Myers for our first weekend of spring training. It was pouring rain, but the minor leaguers had spent the morning in the batting cages. Todd's neck, shoulders, and torso appeared much larger than when I'd last seen him on January 2nd. He weighed 207 pounds, a gain of six pounds since early October. He still consumed his protein drink before breakfast and dinner.

There were two hundred players in camp, from the major league team through the lowest "A" Michigan team. Todd said that doing infield drills with his "AAA" teammates was like doing a line dance.

We were surprised to see Dan Collier when we arrived. He had been an outfielder released from Trenton in the summer of '96, who'd subsequently played in an independent league in California and been invited back to camp by the Sox. His son was now two and one-half years old. We began to see other familiar faces in restaurants around town: Marcy and Jared Fernandez; and Mike Greenwell, discussing a printout of his physical exam with a Japanese team representative. He'd had a contract with a Japanese team but had fled with an undisclosed injury.

Housed in the Sheraton where Charley and I stayed were the players on the forty-man roster, special invitees to major league camp, managers, and coaches. Todd's Trenton teammates Trot Nixon, Don Sadler, Adam Hyzdu, Walt McKeel, Randy Brown, and pitchers Brian Rose and Carl Pavano were there. Todd was again across the harbor at the Days Inn in North Ft. Myers with the minor leaguers. Dana LeVangie had accepted a job as major league bullpen catcher/coach, and lived in the Sheraton by himself. He would have another responsibility as part of his contract - catching during Mo Vaughn's batting practice.

Todd mentioned his agent, Ken Fishkin's, having taken all his clients on the Boston minor league teams to dinner, and the receipt of a new glove from Fishkin. With the selection of a low-profile agent without big names in baseball, there would be little likelihood that his minor-league clients could ride the stars' coattails into big promotional contracts. Todd had switched from agent Al Nero to Ken Fishkin purely on instinct. He respected Fishkin and felt a reciprocal congeniality with him and his family in Boston. Ken was not flashy and was personally involved with each of his clients.The Forrests, Paul and Edie from Cumberland, had stopped by to see Todd on the "AAA" field one day. "I hadn't been hitting after I got back to the minor league fields," he told us. "The day the Forrests came by was the day Yaz had been working with me, making an adjustment in my swing. I finally hit a line-drive triple to the fence, and Yaz pulled up in his golf cart with his cigarette dangling from his lips, screaming, 'I told you! I told you that would make the difference!' The Forrests couldn't believe it."

Trish was visiting on her last weekend of spring break during her Master's program at Florida State. At dinner with us, she ordered a salad with salmon chunks. Incredibly, Todd ordered salmon ravioli! Was this the same kid who had to have his hamburgers PLAIN growing up? Every time we went to a fast food restaurant, we would wait in line for his hamburger or hot dog WITHOUT pickles, WITHOUT ketchup, WITHOUT mustard, while ten people passed by us, got their food, and started eating. Likewise with chicken, meatloaf, prime rib—NO GRAVY - or pizza - JUST CHEESE - or fajitas or burritos - NO VEGGIES OR BEANS! Todd and Trish were clearly smitten with each other, and Todd smiled constantly, both on and off the field.

Trish told us that while she was working as an intern on the Trenton Thunder staff during the previous summer, she was warned not to fraternize with the ballplayers, who might prey on attractive, young females! She had begun doing promos in the Thunder dugout as director of the week-long '96 All Star festivities. "Trish the Dish" was quickly removed to the front office, viewed as too vulnerable.

During one major league exhibition game in which Todd played third base, Infield Instructor and Third Base Coach Wendell Kim told Todd he should continue doing whatever had gotten him to that point as a minor leaguer, not to change anything. "Too many guys get up here and try to impress, but you seem relaxed and focused," he told Todd. Wendell Kim was known for his full sprint to third base at the beginning of each inning, his positive outlook on life, and his strong desire to win. He had been the first Korean-American to wear a major league uniform, and had spent seven seasons as an infielder in the Giants system prior to 1980.

On Saturday, March 15, 1997, the sun shone brilliantly again, and we anticipated seeing an inter squad game on a minor league field. We met Josephine and Sam Plumeri at breakfast in our hotel, the delightful co-owners of the Trenton Thunder. They wished Todd well, although they said they would have liked to have him back in Trenton that season. We thanked them, but secretly wished we would never see another ball game in Trenton!

Todd caught the shuttle bus from the Days Inn to the practice field behind City of Palms Park at 7:45 a.m. every day. He'd left his car at our home in Westport, his first spring training without transportation, and had flown to Tallahassee to see Trish, then on to Ft. Myers. He got rides with Randy Brown or Gary Bennett, a newly-signed catcher who reminded all of us a little of Tim.

Speaking of Tim, after applying to graduate schools from his post in Japan, he'd received acceptance at University of California in San Diego, and was on the wait list for another. He immediately responded to California that he would matriculate, beginning September 15, 1997, for a "Master's in International Relations/ Pacific Studies." He was thrilled, and so were we! The owner of the school in Fukuchiyama City, where Tim and another American were teaching, had clearly been taking advantage of the two Americans. Tim and Alex had not been paid for outreach lessons to community centers and elementary schools three mornings per week, had not been offered the half-year salary increases for which they were eligible, and had not been offered vacations during all Japanese and American holidays, to which they were entitled. Needless to say, Tim was anxious to get home after two years.

When we arrived at the practice field with Trish at 10:30 a.m. on March 15, 1997, the parking lot was half full for the 1 p.m. major league game. Two full squads of "AAA" players contested against each other behind City of Palms Park. We would watch an intra-squad game, not an inter-squad game. Behind the major league field that morning were Scott Leius, a newly-signed Minnesota third baseman who'd played in the World Series, Tony Rodrigues at short, Lou Merloni at second, and Todd at first. First base was loaded with talent all the way up: Bo Dodson, Reggie Jefferson, and Mo Vaughn. The management's philosophy about keeping the players off balance regarding their daily status had trickled down to us parents, as well. There were clearly not enough positions for all the talented players on the field that day.

Behind the backstop was "AAA" Manager Ken Macha, and after the game, a close huddle developed among coaches, GM Dan Duquette, and outfielder Adam Hyzdu. Adam was being removed from the forty-man roster. "Dork" Duquette, as we called him, sported a new "beezer" haircut that stood up like porcupine quills. He wore his traditional inch-thick black elastic headband to hold his glasses around the back of his head, a patterned shirt, shorts, and white socks. If Duquette had been a supreme mastermind in Montreal, his business acumen was not in evidence that spring in Ft. Myers. It wasn't until after Valenin entered major league camp that he received the ultimatum to play second base, thereby substantially diminishing his value in a trade. He grudgingly took the field at second, never disparaging Garciaparra, who took his spot at short. Duquette apologized to Todd for having called him "Paul Carey" ever since the "AA" All-Star banquet the previous July.

"Don't worry," Bob Schaefer told the Dork. "You'll get to know his name soon enough."

The March <u>Boston Baseball</u> issue featured a two-page article on Todd entitled, "Now a Prospect, Carey Relishes Homecoming." Stressing that he wanted to focus on consistency throughout the '97 season, Todd summarized his problems thus far as having been "a lot of highs, but also a lot of lows, and it's hard for me to knock off the lows where I should." He stated that he had had 450 at-bats the previous year and his success had to do with developing physically and mentally, realizing what he could and couldn't do. "You can't go out there trying to impress too many people," he stated. "I can't worry about who they are signing up to the big-league level or even if they sign a couple of free agent guys down here..."[39]

When asked about an Ivy League fraternity among pro ballplayers, Todd mentioned Tim.

'He went to Dartmouth, and he used to play with Mark Johnson... and Bob Bennett.... They might have a little more of an uphill battle when it gets to the minor league system, because they're not used to playing every single day, or the amount of games, or they may not have had the coaching that the other kids have had.'[40]

Asked what problems would occur because he would be playing twenty minutes from home, Todd responded by saying that he was not going to let the pressure of playing before the home crowd get to him. "I think it's going to be a lot of fun," he stated. "I have a lot of friends and family in the area and they are going to come out to the games and offer their support."[41]

Unfortunately, I got in trouble again by voicing one of my fears when we were at dinner with Todd and Trish in Ft. Myers. Todd asked if we were planning to drive north from Florida at the end of May this year, as we usually did. Charley responded, "We haven't decided yet, but it stays cold up there, even in May."

I added, "We might go home in the middle of May if you're on the Pawtucket team. But if you're not playing much, we'll wait until Memorial Day weekend."

"W -H-A-T?" Todd almost jumped up on the table. "What did you say? Why would you even say that, Mom? You are always so negative, and I thought we'd discussed your lack of support in Arizona!"

"Todd, as far as I'm concerned, you should be on the major league roster right now. But none of us know if you'll play regularly. We don't have a clue what's on their minds!" I was sick of always having to defend my choice of words. The next day, after Trish had returned to Florida State, he was all smiles again.

In its first exhibition game, the Pawtucket squad lost to the "AAA" Texas Rangers 4-2. Todd played first base, while Scott Leius played third. Todd hit a ball high over the center field fence at the 400' mark, the second-longest homer we'd ever seen him hit (the longest was in Portland, Maine in July '96, which sailed over the trees beyond the right field wall). The next time up, he hit a single, then grounded out and struck out. His shortened swing was reminiscent of Minnesota's Paul Molitor. When Leius left the game, Todd moved over to play third base. Afterward, he said Dan Duquette, in attendance for Todd's home run shot, told Todd and Adam Hyzdu to begin running speed drills. "I had a really good time on the stop watch running the bases the first week we were here," he told us.

The '97 Red Sox minor league clubs would be in the same location as in '96, from top to bottom:

International League	**Pawtucket, RI**	**AAA**
Eastern League	**Trenton, NJ**	**AA**
Florida State League	**Sarasota, FL**	**A**
Midwest League	**Battle Creek, MI**	**A**
NY - Penn League	**Lowell, MA**	**Short A**
Gulf Coast League	**Ft. Myers, FL**	**Rookie**

We had had a really enjoyable weekend with Todd and Trish, and looked forward to five days hence, when we would all be together again. Todd had gone 3-for-6, including the home run, in the first two "AAA" exhibition games. Before we left to drive back to Delray, Manager Macha stopped to chit-chat.

Charley asked where he'd be living while he managed in Pawtucket. Macha responded that the organization provided a place close to the ball park. It would be a difficult summer for him to be away from his family, since his son, an excellent student, had turned sixteen and there were activities that the father wanted to be involved in, including baseball. "It will be a nice homecoming for Todd, though," Macha told us.

Although Ken Macha was an exception, we had remarked after brief conversations with Pitching Coach Treuel, Pitching Coach Jeff Gray, Manager Dick Berardino, and Coach "Gomer" Hodge that their assignments in the organization would bring them closer to family and business interests, as they had requested.

Perhaps the Red Sox were finally taking a humane interest in their staff!

"We don't envy your job, weeding out so many players," I said to Macha, fishing for some information about the final twenty-three on his roster.

"Well, in the long run you're doing them a favor, if they're 31 or 32 years old. It's time to get on with their lives. Of course, in the end, what happens is up to them, based on how they've performed."

We returned to Ft. Myers with my mother hospitalized in nearby Boynton Beach for blood clots in her left leg. She had had back pain for six weeks, and had lain prone during most of that time, while attempting chiropractic therapy, cortisone shots, muscle relaxers, and other pain killers. An MRI revealed a compression fracture in her lower left L4 vertebra, as well as herniated disks, for which she was to be evaluated for entry into a rehab hospital. Before that could be accomplished, however, the clots had formed. Unfortunately, she didn't inform anyone of her swollen leg except my father, whom she convinced that she had had an allergic reaction to one of her medications (in just one leg!).

After she'd been hospitalized for a week, with great trepidation I left her to travel back to spring training. In the back of my mind was the possibility that at any moment the clots could break up and travel fatally to the brain. However, I needed a diversion for the weekend! My sister did not get to Florida because all reasonable plane fares had been booked by spring breakers. Without a cellular phone, I was out of touch during the four-hour travel time to Port Charlotte, where Todd's "AAA" team was playing. I was as nervous as a prowl-cat. The weather was gorgeous in Port Charlotte, but there was no sign of Todd's team when we arrived. The game had been canceled in the late morning, during a downpour. We returned to Ft. Myers, where we checked into the Sheraton and then into my mother's condition. We continued calling twice a day, and her condition had improved significantly.

Todd's squad still consisted of players two-and three-deep at every position, without anyone's release. Some of those who'd been invited to major league camp had rejoined the "AAA" team, and infielders who had signed late were also on the "AAA" field. Todd played at shortstop during an intra squad game that replaced the scheduled game in Port Charlotte. He belted a triple to the fence with the wind blowing in.

Despite a migraine headache, I was able to catch up on some sleep, and each phone call to my mother assured me her condition was improving with the use of a blood thinner. Our second day in Ft. Myers featured a game against the "AAA" Pirates, under the guidance of Todd's Arizona manager, Trent Jewett. Todd again played shortstop, and then switched over to first base for the second half of the game. He went 1-for-3 with a single, but our squad lost 1-0 in the tenth inning. The major leaguers continued to lose their exhibition games. "It's always about pitching," Charley lamented.

After the game, Todd and Adam Hyzdu did speed drills with two strength/ conditioning coaches on a field by themselves. A twenty-foot rubber band was attached to the waists of the coach up front and the runner behind. We didn't want to be conspicuous and hang around to watch, so we never figured out the logic of the resistance training.

Bob Schaefer came over to Charley, who thanked Schaefer for his help in shortening Todd's swing. "He's too good a hitter not to be hitting consistently," Schaefer responded.

We learned that Ken Macha had taken three of his former Trenton players to dinner that week: Todd, Don Sadler, and Walt McKeel. Two others, Trot Nixon and Randy Brown, were still playing with the major leaguers during evening games. When I asked what Macha had talked about, Todd said it was mostly a social evening. I pressed him, and he said Macha had mentioned his hopes for the Pawtucket team. He wouldn't tell us, though, if Macha had any expectations of him, personally.

From those we met, both fans and sportswriters, we began to hear, "He may get a shot at Fenway by the end of this year if he keeps up the hitting." We began to believe it ourselves, while we answered, "We'll just be happy to see him playing in Pawtucket."

There were still many infielders bouncing between the major league team and "AAA." Although the Pawtucket team had two men for every infield position, still unresolved was the status of major leaguers Mike Benjamin, Chris Donnels, Randy Brown, Tony Rodrigues, John Valentin, and Bo Dodson. The players had nicknamed Lou Merloni "The Mayor" with good reason. Lou either knew everyone among those watching, or made it a point to know them. He had received the Fan Appreciation Award in Trenton in '95. At one of the games at our minor league complex during spring training, Lou had an entourage of aunts, uncles, and visitors from Italy and the U.S. in the aluminum bleachers. They sat apart from each other until the last couple of outs, as though they'd never met. One group was a low-key aunt, uncle, and their friends from the Boston area. We'd met them before in Port Charlotte. The other group appeared in silks, gold chains, and banded white straw hats to sit on the opposite end of the five tiers of bleachers that stretched twelve feet along the third base line. Within a few minutes of arrival, the bedecked Italian matriarch got Lou off the field to greet him in broken English. "Don't say anything bad about that kid!" she warned all of us jovially. Lou bantered with them not only from his position at shortstop, but also as he ran to and from left field, where he played during late innings.

Articles appeared in the press the third week of March about the unhealed wounds the '95 strike had left. The Providence Journal reported on the visit of

Donald Fehr, Players' Association Executive Director, to the Red Sox camp. A collective bargaining agreement, worked out in November '96, had been ratified the previous week. During the meeting with virtually the entire Sox roster, three replacement players were purposely excluded by the team, and relegated to the batting cage. Infielder Randy Brown, catcher Walt McKeel, and bullpen catcher Dana LeVangie had all participated as replacements. "This was a union meeting, and they're not members of the union," Fehr stated. "We still represent (their concerns), and at a later date, they can re-apply to the executive board (for entrance to the union). But they're not union members." Tim Wakefield would serve as '97 Sox player rep. Tim Naehring, '96 player rep, said he would "personally guarantee" that the replacement players, if called up to Boston, would not be ostracized.[42]

Such was not the case for Mets' pitcher Rick Reed, who got the job of number five starter while still at spring training in '97. Because he'd been a replacement player, his teammates did not congratulate him. Instead, they totally ignored him, except for pitcher Joe Crawford, also a replacement player. Reed had been a union member for seven seasons before pitching in replacement games for Cincinnati in '95. He had obviously needed the money, since the following January, '96, he'd supplied his needy parents in Huntington, West Virginia, with money for diabetic insulin and a replacement for their dilapidated car. The parents owned a car whose door was tied shut with rope.

The Yankees denied replacement players Matt Howard, Dale Polley, and Dave Pavlas even partial World Series shares for the Series games they had played. Eventually, Steinbrenner relented and granted them their money.

The major league team broke camp for exhibition games in Las Vegas. Randy Brown and Tony Rodrigues flew out with the team, although they were not on the forty-man roster. Randy's car was parked in the lot of the Ft. Myers Sheraton. He had asked Todd to drive it north for him, but the Sox had already secured Todd's plane ticket to Providence, and Todd was exhausted. Car carriers transported the major leaguers' cars. If Randy could find no one to drive his vehicle, he would have to pay the $650 himself, since he was not on the forty-man roster.

For the first spring training ever, Yaz became talkative to Todd. Having never said more than six or seven consecutive words to him that weren't swears, Yaz began to pat Todd on the back and would appear from the sidelines to give him support after each at-bat. Frequently, he and Steve Braun together watched Todd at the plate, and consulted with him immediately thereafter. "Prospects" were certainly treated differently!

Charley and I also noticed that coaching and managing staff were more solicitous toward us. Schaefer always gave us a wave and "Hello;" managers DeMarlo Hale, Ken Macha, and Dick Berardino would come up to talk, as did Hitting Coach

"Gomer" Hodge. Roving Batting Instructor Steve Braun had always stopped to talk, no matter what Todd's probability of success.

Three days before training ended, the twenty-three man "AAA" Pawtucket roster appeared to break down this way:

Five infielders chosen from:
Mike Benjamin
Randy Brown
Todd Carey
Scott Leius
Arquimedez Pozo
Don Sadler
Tony Rodrigues

Five outfielders:

Adam Hyzdu
Jose Malave
Trot Nixon
Jesus Tavares
Juan Williams

Two catchers:

Walt McKeel
Gary Bennett

Eleven pitchers.

Since the Pawtucket team traveled to many of their games by plane, as opposed to buses used at all lower levels, a mandatory dress code of pants and jackets was in effect. I had gone with Todd at Christmas to pick out two sports jackets as gifts, but in Ft. Myers he told us he needed some shoes that were not bankerish or L.L. Beanish, as well as a couple of shirts.

We decided to hit the Edison Mall in Ft. Myers with him after dinner, and get him the shirts. He would have to spring for the shoes himself. Thus began a two-hour ordeal during which he tried on shoes in five different stores. "I don't want loafers or tassels!" he declared after the first stop. It was harder to shop with him than with most of the women I knew, except for my sister.

"But, Todd, every tie-on shoe you tried makes you look like a priest!" I informed him. "At least get something with a little style in a color besides black!" The odyssey ended with a cordovan compromise, and two shirts from two separate department stores. Charley and I were exhausted when we'd finished, and went back to our room instead of to a movie.

The next day, Todd appeared exhausted in the 90-degree heat, as did many of the players. He was eighth batter because of his lack of offense that week. During the game, he struck out, grounded out, and popped up before getting a single to right field. In frustration, he had smashed his bat to the ground when he'd hit the pop up. All of the Boston management was in attendance in golf carts.

When we had dinner together for the last time, we asked if we should buy season tickets to the Pawtucket games. This would allow all of his friends and relatives to use the free-pass tickets. "I don't want to have to worry every night about a long list of names for the passes," he said. "I'm only going to put a few on it every night, besides you guys. Last year in Trenton, Shawn Senior got all upset before games because so many from New Jersey wanted to see him play. He always forgot somebody's name. That's not what we should be worrying about before game time."

"Just try to pay back all the people who have helped get you there," I suggested.

Charley's advice was the following: "We hope you have a really fun year! Let it all hang out, for better or for worse, because everybody there will be supporting you. It won't matter what happens. Right now I see you beating yourself up if you don't get a hit, and you know that's going to be counterproductive. Start the season in a positive frame of mind, and remember, a single or two a game is all you need, not home runs!"

I'd noticed on the Pawtucket bench that various players always grouped themselves together. The African-Americans and the Latinos sat together, often bantering in Spanish on and off the field, while the white players sat together near the coaching staff. Todd sat by himself that day on the end of the bench, in a funk over his hitting. The only ones who moved freely to talk up and down the bench were an occasional catcher or pitcher. The following day I noticed he slid into an opening on the bench with the black/Latino group. The jive stopped when Todd sat down.

The majority of the Pawtucket team was flying into Providence for a team workout before they opened their season in Charlotte, North Carolina. Todd planned to live in our house in Westport until he found an apartment. He was a good caretaker in our absence, and had the best "green thumb" of anyone caring for my house plants. A foot of snow fell in Providence before his flight left from Ft. Myers, so he enjoyed an extra day in the sun. Some of the coaches, managers, and players had begun their drive north, while others had left on planes immediately after the last spring training game and arrived before the snow did.

Todd's ability to play multiple positions in the infield was instrumental in keeping him on the Pawtucket roster. There were three infielders who ended up going directly from Las Vegas major league exhibition games back to the minors. Tony Rodrigues and Mike Benjamin went back to Pawtucket, while Randy Brown went down to Trenton.

None of their fates were as cruel as Mets' pitcher Joe Crawford's. Manager Bobby Valentine informed Crawford, who had spent his entire pitching career in the minor leagues, that he'd made the team on the last day of spring training, "unless we make some more moves." On the night before the team left for Las Vegas exhibition games, he and his wife went to invest in a suit for his plane trips. In Dillard's he met Steve Bieser, also in the same predicament. While Crawford and Bieser played exhibition games in Vegas, the Mets purchased pitcher Barry Manuel from Montreal. Crawford flew back to "AAA" in his new suit, while Bieser stayed.[43]

The Pawtucket team opened its season before a raucous crowd in Charlotte on the evening of April 3, after leaving Boston in two feet of snow. Because of delays, the team arrived in the Charlotte area at 12:30 a.m. The only one seemingly affected by the lack of sleep in the first game was starter Mark Mimbs, who got racked in the 11-8 loss with twelve hits, including four homers, one of which was a grand slam. Playing first base, Todd hit a three-run homer to left field, while Don Sadler, Juan Williams, and Archimedes Pozo also had home runs. Incredibly, in the third game in Charlotte, Todd hit another three-run homer over the left center fence.

On April 6, 1997, Todd's name was splashed in headlines in two separate articles in the sports section of The Providence Journal. One was a half-page feature on him by Bill Reynolds entitled, "Carey Fulfills His Dream at McCoy, 40 Miles Short of Another." Bill was the author of Success is a Choice (with Rick Patino) and Cousy: His Life, Career, and the Birth of Big-Time Basketball. Bill knew Charley's parents and was close to Christopher Herren, our nephew playing basketball at Fresno State. In his feature article, he traced Todd's background from Little League through "AAA" in Rhode Island. It was a "local player fulfills dream at Rhode Island landmark" nostalgia piece.[44]

After the team arrived in Richmond, Todd called us. He was, naturally, pleased with the way things were going, and enjoyed having the day off because of rain. He mentioned that at a luncheon with the Pawtucket Boosters Club and local Providence dignitaries, our friend, Jim Hagan, had been the guest speaker. He was president of the Providence Chamber of Commerce. "He had the guys on the team roaring because he told how I hated to stay in Westport growing up, and his daughter Kelley hated to stay in Little Compton. He said it was later you all discovered that we didn't want to miss the parties in Providence, and he told the team if they wanted some night life, they should follow me."

In the next two games Todd played in Richmond, with a night off in-between, he hit his third home run and added two more singles. Six games into the season, the PawSox were tied for first place in their division in the International League with a 4-2 record.

The team opened at home at 6 p.m. on April 11, 1997, in 30-degree weather. There was a full house, including thousands of school kids and some of Charley's family, as well as Cumberland and Brown University friends. Todd was not in the lineup against the Syracuse lefty. He went into the lineup as a pinch hitter, and struck out. The Sox lost 4-3, but retained their first place spot in the division, tied with Scranton/Wilkes Barre. It was certainly not the type of homecoming any of us had wished for him, after his strong play defensively and offensively in Charlotte and then Richmond.

After a hiatus of three games' playing time, Todd started at third base in Toledo for the ill Arquimedez Pozo. He had no hits, and had had only one, a single to the right side, during the Pawtucket home stand and prior eighteen at-bats.

Todd's pattern of the previous spring and the Arizona League seemed to be repeating itself. After an instant success in "AAA" during the first six games, he was slumping badly. Charley analyzed the reasons for his tremendous pendulum swings. "After he gets a few homers, he must subconsciously think that everything he hits has to be a home run. Then, when that doesn't happen and he goes 0-4 in a game, he loses confidence and can't seem to rebound. At this level, they won't keep him if he doesn't show consistency."

"You really should be discussing this with him," I told Charley. "It might help him focus on changing whatever is wrong. After all, he's the only one who can change what's happening."

"I've talked to him about his batting since he was nine years old," Charley responded. "He's smart enough to know what needs to be done."

"You assume that because you make one suggestion about his batting every month, you're having a discussion with him. Repetition never hurts if it's positive. A lot of the players' fathers talk with them constantly about their performances."

"Yeah, those players are either right out of high school, or they hate their fathers. I certainly don't want that to happen!"

Todd, the home-town boy, was certainly getting a lot of attention. Eight of Charley's relatives showed up for a day game on Sunday, April 27. Charley's father, sister, and Todd's American Legion coaches had attended the previous day, and Brown friends were there off and on. We found that Todd's aunt Gail had had the class she instructed write letters to him, but he had never received them at McCoy Field. A school principal in Cumberland had invited him to speak.

Against Ottawa on April 27, Todd homered, as he had the previous day. It was his fifth. The family in attendance was delighted. Todd's buddy, Ryan McGuire, had another big day for Ottawa. A 1993 third-round draft pick out of UCLA, he'd been traded from Trenton in '95 with a .333 average (seven homers, fifty-nine RBI's). He'd been glad at the time to get out from behind Mo Vaughn's shadow in the Sox system at first base. Thus far in '97, he had hit safely in fifteen out of seventeen games for a .366 average, one of the International League leaders.

We shared the Westport house with Todd during our stay that April, and because he left early for the field or gym each day, we had only three meals with him during the four days we were home. After the game on Sunday, April 27, the three of us went up to the Federal Hill section of Providence, where we believed some of the best Italian food in the country could be enjoyed. We chose Joe Marzilli's Old Canteen, where we'd taken the boys over the years to mark every special occasion in their young lives.

Charley and I had avoided any talk of baseball while we were with Todd, to prevent controversy and to provide positive support. We knew that Trish did the same. Over dinner at The Old Canteen, after his homer that afternoon, Charley offered a toast. Raising his wine glass, he said, "Here's to the beginning of a ten-game hitting streak!"

With that, Todd put his glass down and retorted, "Dad, is that what is always uppermost on your mind? After the pleasantries over the phone, the first thing you ask is, 'How are you hitting?' You already know how I'm hitting, since you get the box scores faxed down to you in Florida. I'm trying my best, and I don't need extra pressure from you!" Charley and I were flabbergasted, since we'd made a point of avoiding the subject of baseball the whole time we'd been visiting. "Well, Mom and I certainly don't intentionally try to put pressure on you, and if we ask questions about baseball, it's because we're over 1,000 miles away and extremely interested in our son's career." Charley took a gulp of wine and glared at Todd.

I added, "We don't deserve to be treated this way, Todd, and we're certainly not going to walk on eggshells to avoid setting you off! I hope you don't treat Trish this way, because she won't put up with it, either!"

I went on to point out that whether Todd played baseball or collected trash, we'd still be asking him questions about his activities. Furthermore, nothing could detract from our pride in him, no matter how he performed. "There are openings we give you over the phone, in case you want to talk to Dad about any problems you're having, including baseball," I said. "If you don't ask for his advice, we butt out immediately."

"You've never listened to my advice about baseball since you became a pro, anyway," Charley threw in.

"But I have always listened to your advice, whether you think so or not!" he retorted.

"Not true!" Charley countered.

"Yes, I have, Dad, but listening and executing are two different things, especially at this level. Right now I've got lots of professionals giving me advice, and I lie awake at night thinking about it. Why don't you just ask me if I'm having fun?"

"We can tell immediately from your tone of voice if you're having fun," I pointed out. Later, in private, I suggested to Todd that he make amends with Charley. "A major portion of your Dad's life has revolved around baseball, Todd, and it would be devastating if you shut him out. He only meant to wish you good luck by making the toast, so perhaps you should let remarks by parents, grandparents, or anyone else who means well just slide off your back a little more easily."

"Sure, just like you do, Mom!"

"Remember the adage, 'Do as I say, not as I do,' and learn from our mistakes." Despite a hug for each of us when we departed for Florida, Todd had not apologized for his outburst. He intended to look for house/apartment rentals the day before he left on a road trip to Syracuse and Ottawa. By the time we planned to return to Westport at the end of May, he would have settled elsewhere with Trish, her Master's Program complete.

"It's time he appreciated how much freedom he and Tim have had, and learn to hold his tongue!" was Charley's verdict when we were alone. "We exert no control over their lives, especially living so far away from both of them, and I'm not going to take any mouthing off from him because I'm interested in his career."

"I think he's still trying to please us," I pointed out. "When he's in a difficult slump, he's afraid of letting us down."

After an eight-day road trip at the beginning of May, '97, Todd's published average was .184. In seventy-six at-bats, he'd hit five homers, fourteen RBI's, walked nine times, and struck out sixteen. His only three errors occurred that week on the road, while he played second base.

The PawSox were only three games out of first place in their division and finished April with the second-highest number of victories in PawSox history. Still, three starting infielders, including Todd, and one outfielder were batting under .200 or a fraction above. Highly-touted Don Sadler and Trot Nixon were at .169 and .132 respectively after twenty-three games, while Pozo was at .207. The team ranked last in the International League in hitting (.231 accumulatively).

Manager Macha was quoted in The Providence Journal on May 4, 1997, as saying,

... 'I'm well aware of our hitting problems. Fortunately, our pitching has been extremely good or we would be in big trouble, but I don't anticipate any immediate changes. These kids will be here for a while.'

The article continued,

The word is that Boston will wait at least through May before making any roster changes. If these players are still having trouble making contact, the Boston brass will have to figure out what to do.[45]

In Trenton, Rod Correia was hitting .327, while Lou Merloni was at .330 and Andy Abad was at .319. Randy Brown had shown power hitting, with twenty-nine RBI's and five homers after twenty-three games. The conclusion for a neophyte like me was that the higher batting averages at "AA" indicated that pitching had lower velocity and less pinpointing over the strikezone than at "AAA." All of those players were anxious to get to Pawtucket in the infield.

In the May issue of Diehard ("The Magazine for Red Sox Fans"), Mike Scandura wrote a feature on Todd that, more than any other previous article, got to the heart of Todd's ball-playing abilities. Again, Ken Macha was quoted.

'This year, I want to start him out slow (Carey's frequently batted seventh) and make sure he has a little confidence going. The thing I'm pleased with is...the fact he's starting to feel it himself when he does things improperly at the plate.

'When he gets in trouble, it's because he's pulling off the ball a little bit. He opens his hip up a little too fast. He doesn't have a lot of lateral movement, he goes into rotation too quick. But he's starting to feel that and is trying to make adjustments.

'You've got to keep the peaks going and try to eliminate the valleys. He had a big peak last year, and he had a big valley.'

Getting lost in a big valley wasn't exactly Carey's most memorable experience.

'Any time you put up good power numbers, you start thinking power,' he said. 'When you pull the ball too much, you start pulling off the plate and you get away from what you used to do.

'I was trying to hit too many home runs and putting too much pressure on myself, instead of just hitting the ball to the other field. You look at Mo Vaughn, and he has a great blend of average plus power. That shows he's staying on the ball.'

'Sure, there's pressure. I think any time you get to a higher level, you've got to put up some numbers. But I don't think I've got as much pressure on me as the next guy because I have that degree. I can relax and try to have some fun here. I'm back home, so I want to enjoy the experience.'

So far, that hadn't happened. Macha summarized:

'Todd can play all of the infield positions. He's got some pop in his bat, and he's a left-handed hitter. If he can throw up some good numbers here, with the expansion draft coming up, at the least he might be a utility guy for somebody, if not for Boston.'[46]

On May 13th, the Pawtucket squad played the major league Red Sox in an exhibition game at McCoy. Todd got a double, going 1-for-4 at bat and playing first base. NESN televised the game throughout New England, and we got calls in Florida when it began and when it ended. "It was really fun," Todd told us. "That should boost his confidence," I remarked to Charley.

On May 14, 1997, The Providence Journal ran a column describing Todd's diligence to recover his swing. We knew he'd been working with Yaz in batting practice, and learned from the news account that Ken Macha had been watching tapes, and had spotted a loop in his swing. Todd took a look at himself, and began smoking line drives across the stadium during batting practice. In the game he played that night, he hit his sixth homer. "Maybe that's the start of something for him," said Macha, referring to Todd's 2-for-22 slump.

On May 17th, The Sun Sentinel in Florida ran an item under its "Extra Bases" (Boston Red Sox) column stating that Nomar Garciaparra was leading all American League shortstops in fielding percentages. In his first full season the previous year for the major leaguers, Nomar had handled 177 out of 179 balls cleanly. The only two errors he had were throwing errors. His teammates had nicknamed him, "Spiderman."

Charley and I began our trek north for the summer on May 17th. My mother was recovering at home, sleeping, eating, and entertaining in her new recliner, which allowed her compression fracture and hernial disks to heal. She continued to walk around 50 yards a day with a walker, after which her back usually ached. The blood clots were absorbed and the swelling in her left leg remained minimal, until she dangled her leg for any length of time. Eventually, she was able to walk back and forth against the resistance of the water in a pool.

When we arrived in Westport, Todd's average was a published .171 before the team went on the road for four games in Rochester and four more in Syracuse. Todd sat out two games and went 0-for-8 in the two games in which he played, the second as DH. We got a call from Sophie and Bob Havens in upper New York, who'd followed the team throughout their state and had taken pictures to send us. We'd first met the Havens when Todd played in Elmira. "Todd looked really down on himself," they reported to us. We could only guess how upset he had to be after working so hard. We hoped that management would give Todd a long leash before making any decision regarding his future. Certainly his leash would be shorter, though, than first-round picks like Sadler or Nixon, who had almost $1,000,000 invested in each of them and were in equally dismal slumps.

Before the road trip on May 17, 1997, The Providence Journal quoted Bob Schaefer as stating that no matter how tough it got for players like Don Sadler, Trot Nixon, and Todd Carey (who'd gotten off to slow starts), they would stay in Pawtucket.

'The first 100 at-bats don't mean a whole lot. I knew they would struggle but the only way they're going to get better is to play against better players and better pitchers. They're staying here.

'Those guys (hitting over .300 in Trenton) can play here (also) but, right now, we feel the guys at Pawtucket who are struggling now have a higher ceiling (better chance at the big leagues).'[47]

Whereas Don Sadler and Arquimedez Pozo began thirteen-game and ten-game hitting streaks respectively, Todd sat out three of the seven-game series in Rochester and Syracuse and didn't claim a hit until his thirteenth at-bat.

In addition, we learned upon our arrival in Massachusetts that Charley's mother would enter Charlton Hospital in Fall River, Mass., the following day for a procedure to locate blockages that prevented circulation from entering her left foot. The foot was swollen and purple, and sported ulceration as a result of diabetes. We hoped for the best scenario, whereby surgery could treat the blockage, when discovered, with bypasses. Because Mary had had three previous strokes, she was on Coumadin treatments daily.

Todd had decided to talk with the team psychologist, on call for all the Boston teams. Trot Nixon had been consulting with him, and by early June, Trot's hitting had turned around. Ken Macha had informed local reporters that he'd asked Trot to set a goal of reaching a .200 batting average by June, and a .250 average by July. Todd was still struggling to reach .200 by June 4th, so we were pleased with his decision to see the psychologist. In '97, the slump lasted two months.

The team bussed from Syracuse after the last game there, and arrived in Pawtucket at 5 a.m. on May 23rd. That afternoon, Todd's girlfriend Trish arrived by train for the summer. The same night, Brown University graduation weekend began. Todd got two hits playing second base in a losing effort against Norfolk, before he and Trish headed to the campus. There they joined the 10,000 alums that return to the upper and lower greens every year for Brown class reunions.

Todd had looked like a different ballplayer against Norfolk - confident and aggressive. He was definitely on a high, even when he didn't take the field the following afternoon. In attendance at the sunny stadium were Todd's first Brown University coach, Dave Stenhouse, and his family. Mike Stenhouse, Dave's son, was a broadcaster for NESN. In addition, four Brown friends, including Todd's roommates from N.Y.C. and Washington, D.C. were at the game, as well as Westport friends of ours.

Tim had called us twice from Japan to check on Todd's status. "You see, if he went to left field with outside pitches, then they'd eventually stop throwing over the left side of the plate and lay one in there that he could pull to the right side," Charley explained. "But he doesn't even let me finish telling him, and cuts me off.

Maybe he would listen to you, Tim. No matter what, though, we're really proud of what he's already accomplished."

"I agree, Dad. All these films and the crap about loops in his swing are just that - crap. He's got to get his confidence and he can hit anyone. Once he lets the bat flow wherever the pitch takes him, he'll be confident again. Tell him to call me."

Todd did, indeed, talk to Tim at length, and to Charley during the succeeding road trip. Charley uplifted his spirits by advising him to begin the season over again, without any regard for stats. "They'll only remember if you changed things for the second part of the season," he told Todd.

Former Brown Coach Stenhouse had been very encouraging. He told us, "Don't worry about him. Rico Petrocelli (Pawtucket Batting Instructor) found something, and he'll work with him.

"He's going to make it. (To Trish) You'd better get ready!! What a thrill this is for me! I've only had three that I coached get this far, and it's gut-wrenching. You must be thrilled, too."

*Charley and Pam Carey, center, enjoy a game
at McCoy Stadium, Pawtucket, R.I..*

24

Obsession

By the end of May, in three home games out of four, Todd hadn't played in the field. In two out of three, he hadn't played at all. His average was into the .190's. Todd had gone to the field every day confident of playing first, second, or third base. He had rotated through all of those positions, with only a high throw from third to mar all of the outstanding back-handed stops and throws from his knees.

Together, Charley, Trish, and I proceeded to rehearse every scenario: Todd wasn't playing because management was showcasing players that might be involved in a trade; Todd might be sent down to "AA"; or the worst, Todd might be released. Then we went through all the recent conversations Todd had had with Macha and we had had with Bob Schaefer, all of which indicated the opposite. In retrospect, Ken Macha wrestled daily with the lineup, to try to rotate all of his many infielders. In all honesty, the management had shown great patience and generosity toward Todd.

Todd and Trish had scrubbed and washed and scrubbed again their summer cottage. Trish was allergic to dog and cat hairs and the previous tenants had owned three dogs and two cats. During the morning of a game in which he got two hits against Rochester, Todd weeded around the front of the house and planted flowers. "It was the best therapy in the world," Trish told us. On the team's day off, he and Trish did a walking tour of Boston.

Todd had prepared Charley and me for his co-habitation prior to Trish's arrival. He'd simply stated that Trish would be joining him, wherever he rented for the summer. We had not questioned his decision, knowing how serious their relationship was and how long it took Todd to decide anything important. Besides, we had nothing to say about it and loved Trish! We wondered how Trish's parents were accepting the news in New Jersey. As it turned out, they had actually helped locate the cottage through a New Jersey friend, whose son subleased the cottage to

Todd. Before Trish's arrival, Tim asked us by phone, "Did he drop the bomb on you yet?"

"What bomb?" I asked.

"The bomb!" The silence of the brotherhood was still intact, and Tim was not about to let the cat out of the bag if Todd hadn't mentioned to us that he intended to live with Trish that summer.

"If you mean that he is going to live with Trish," I answered, "he told us they were going to find a rental together for the summer."

"What did you say?" Tim asked.

"We said we were happy for him and wished him luck finding a place."We listened to the PawSox games on the radio. Whereas Charley hung on every word, I usually had a stomachache if I listened. Even if we went to a movie, Charley had the car radio tuned in to the station so that the moment he turned on the ignition, he could catch up with the live action.

At home games, our freebie seats were always amid the wives, girlfriends, and children of the players, as well as the other parents. My favorite playmates were the Latino players' children, especially Jose Malave's and Tony Rodriguez's daughters, as well as the Hyzdu children, Zack and Alexa. The Latinos' wives chattered continuously in Spanish, and almost none of them spoke any English. The Rodriguez children were bilingual, but none of the others had taken advantage of the opportunity to learn English while living in the States six months per year. I bought pre-school books in English that taught numbers and colors, so that I could read to them while we watched the games. I guess the old teacher in me surfaced again, or maybe I was practicing for grandchildren!

The team left the morning of May 30th at 5 a.m. by bus for Scranton, Pennsylvania. As DH and ninth batter against a lefty pitcher in Scranton, Todd struck out twice and popped up once, twice leaving a runner in scoring position, before hitting a double against the wall at left center. According to Trish, Todd was aware of an article by Bob Dick in The Providence Journal that morning (June 1,'97) that prospects Nixon, Carey, McKeel, and possibly Sadler were "overmatched" at "AAA".[48] Todd had responded that reporters had to create news to sell papers. Rose worked seven and one-third innings and gained the 4-2 win, his eighth.

Todd went 2-for-11 on the road through five games. "Jesus, what's the matter with him?" Tim asked when he called from Japan. "Maybe he needs a wakeup call like they gave him when they sent him from Trenton down to Sarasota."

"He certainly has all the tools to make it to the majors," Charley responded, "but he is a head case. I really think right now, though, that it would be counterproductive to send him down. He's hitting the ball hard to all fields, but they're just not dropping in. If they sent him down now, it might finish him. They'll start to fall in."

Meanwhile, Andy Abad played first base when Todd didn't, and played in the outfield as well. In his first 105 "AAA" at-bats, Andy had 6 homers, 21 RBI's, and a .317 average by mid-July. He had easily adjusted to the pitching at the "AAA" level.

Unexpectedly, Todd played first base in the last game in Rochester against lefty pitcher Rick Krivda. Todd usually sat on the bench when a lefty pitched. Krivda threw ten innings and gave up just four hits, one run, and struck out nine. Three of the strikeouts were Todd's, who batted eighth and also grounded out down the first base line. Our pitcher, Mark Mimbs, surrendered four hits and struck out eleven in seven and one-third innings. Jose Malave hit his tenth homer for our only run. Malave had hit safely in fourteen out of fifteen games.

With the score tied, 1-1, Todd made "the defensive play of the game," according to the radio announcer. He scrambled between first and second base to retrieve a ball that caromed off our pitcher, Mahones, and threw the batter out. The game continued, and in the twelfth inning, the PawSox mounted a mild threat when Gary Bennett (our catcher) singled, and Todd followed with a single up the middle off right-handed pitcher Chris Bennett. The runners were left stranded.

In the bottom of the thirteenth inning, Danny Clyburn hit a one-out triple off our pitcher, Carlos Valdez, into the right field corner to score Tim Laker from first base. The relay throw from second baseman Tony Rodriguez eluded our catcher.

Jesus Tavarez and Jose Malave had each had two hits in the game, and Todd was one of three others to get one hit. He'd had three in sixteen at-bats on the road trip. The team bussed back to Pawtucket after the game, and arrived at 6 a.m. Todd had called Trish at 3 a.m. when the team stopped at a rest stop, so that she would be there to meet the bus when it arrived. The day he arrived home, his Trenton and Arizona roommate, Ryan McGuire, was elevated from the Ottawa Lynx to the major league Expos.

When asked about Sadler's 3-for-47 slump at the beginning of June, Macha said Sadler, Nixon (now hitting everything hard to the opposite field as a lefty batter), and McKeel (.231) would stay in Pawtucket for the season. As for the rest, including Todd, Correia, Rodrigues, Pozo, and Abad - "Make a spot for yourself in the lineup," was Macha's advice. "I've encouraged everyone. I've had them fill out forms about how they can improve themselves... I hope they are (keeping their notebooks on opposing pitchers), but I can't make them. They have to show me what they can do."[49]

Todd had spent two days prior to the June 8th game at Mo Vaughn's house in Massachusetts, where there was a batting cage within the house. Mike Easier had flown in from Texas to conduct sessions with Mo and John Valentin. Todd had been one of several minor leaguers invited by Easier the first day, but had been alone to work with Easier the second day. He sported new blisters taped by the trainer but didn't play that night.

In the following three games against Ottawa, he moved around the infield, playing short, then second for the injured Sadler. It was the first time all year that he'd played shortstop, and the game was televised live on NESN. Todd had played twenty-seven games at first base and eight games at third base before playing short. Waiting with the ball to tag a runner out at second base, his arm came down over the runner's leg as it slid into the bag. The Ottawa runner was called safe. Todd got heated about the call, but Macha restrained him before he was ejected. The instant replays showed the play again and again, supporting the call. At bat, Todd hit a pop foul that was caught, struck out, walked, and then hit a single over the first baseman's head, as the bat flew toward the Lynx player stationed there. Andy Abad saved the game with a two-run bases-loaded single in the bottom of the ninth for a 9-8 win.

Catcher Walt McKeel was struggling in a .231 slump, despite a big RBI double in the first game of the Lynx series. His wife, Amy, had been working full-time in Providence. Pregnant and very ill, she decided to go home to Carolina to stay with her folks for a while to be near her doctor. Walt was always one of the first players to rush out of the clubhouse, after Amy had left.

"It's no longer a question of 'if,'" Charley said to me after Todd's average had sunk to .185. "It's a question of 'where' and 'when' they lose patience with him. He's refused to adjust at the plate by not hitting outside pitches and by standing and taking curve balls. They set him up with curve balls, and he gets down in the count so they can blow a fast ball past him. He's not a Wade Boggs who can get hits with two strikes on him."

There were others struggling at the plate. Nixon, Sadler, Correia, Bennett, and Todd were all around or under .200. Walt McKeel was around .230. The group of wives, girlfriends, and relatives were totally supportive of each other in the stands, as well as in the room adjoining the clubhouse in Pawtucket, where immediate family could get warm, set up the kids' toys, or use the private bathroom. Unfortunately, that room was off-limits to parents, so Charley and I went to an enclosed hallway with seating to warm up during the early months. While the games were being played, the girlfriends and wives held each other's children, entertained them, and fed them treats. Parents like me were able to take a turn with the kids when the others needed a break. That's when I brought out the pre-school books in English for the Latino sons and daughters.

The Pawtucket team became more cohesive as June came to a close, even as more players were added from Trenton and from Fenway. Todd and Trish had had a get-together at their cottage, attended by a few players and girlfriends, as well as by one of the team trainers. Mike Blais' fiancée, Janna Venice, had invited six couples from the team to her parents' house for a clambake, and Todd and Trish planned to invite most of the team for a Fourth of July cookout at their cottage. After the last game of the home-stand, we took Trish and Todd out to dinner in Providence, to celebrate Father's Day, June 12, 1997. It was just too much distance to drive back to Westport for a home-cooked meal. Todd began to brighten up, and on our way out of the restaurant, he and Charley had a tête-à-tête in the men's room. Charley told Todd not to give up, and without getting technical about his swing, advised him to do something drastic to change his batting - e.g., open his stance, move his hands, etc. I kissed both of them, telling Todd, "Keep your chin up and your shoulders back. We love you." Something got through to him, because he collected five hits in three games in Toledo - two to left field, two to center field, and a bunt he beat out. Pawtucket bombarded the Toledo Mud Hens and retained first place in its division.

The Columbus series was another story. The team lost three straight in Columbus, and Todd went 0-for-6, playing first base and DH'ing. He sat one game out. After the fourth game, his average stood at .194. In that game, he hadn't gotten any hits, but had driven in the third run by flying out to the right center field fence with the bases loaded. Both teams led their divisions.

On June 24,1997, two days before our thirty-second anniversary, Lou Merloni was called up from Trenton to play the infield in Pawtucket. Lou had batted .310 in Trenton, and had been named to the "AA" All-Star team that same day. Manager Macha, Batting Instructor Rico Petrocelli, and Pitching Coach John Cumberland had a meeting with Todd at that time, with the result that Todd would see a lot less playing time. His average stood at .192, and as Macha pointed out, he had the potential to be a major league player but hadn't proved it yet, because of his inconsistency. In addition to Todd, Rod Correia and Tony Rodrigues would get less playing time in the Pawtucket infield. Both were twenty-nine years or older, with few years left to progress. Todd would celebrate his 26th birthday in two months.

June 24th was the first home game in a three game series against Rochester, who stood one-half game behind Pawtucket in the same division. Lou Merloni was, indeed, in the field at shortstop, and the Merloni entourage was in the stands from Framingham. Todd was the DH. He told Trish later that he hadn't even seen the pitches his first two times at bat that night, because so much was going on in his head after the meeting he had had that day. He struck out twice and grounded out. It wasn't until his fourth at-bat that he collected a double off the left center fence. Trish had tears in her eyes with that hit, knowing Duquette and Kenney were in attendance from Boston. I could hardly breathe each time Todd came to bat, and my stomach was in an uproar between the tension and the antibiotic I was taking for a respiratory infection. The PawSox got the win and Pavano pitched superbly, becoming a "AAA" All-Star, along with Brian Rose and Arquimedez Pozo.

We were grateful that Trish was able to boost Todd's spirits. Otherwise, he'd have internalized everything. Instead, he talked out the scenarios, and refocused. She reminded him every day that he would be a major league player and pointed out to him that he'd be the same person, with or without baseball, and the same people would love him. The other options in his life, grad school or a career, were surfacing in Todd's conversations, although he didn't want to dwell on anything but the job at hand. He was working double time to practice his batting. "He regards this season as being over right now, and he sounds totally defeated," Trish told us. "Macha hasn't spoken to him since that meeting, and Todd is convinced Macha has lost all confidence in him."

"As long as he's in the lineup, Macha hasn't lost confidence," I said. "But he should regard every game as the beginning of a new season for himself. Someone has to restore his confidence - he needs Steve Braun, or maybe Easier could fly in from Texas to work with him. We would be happy to pay for it. But in the end, he's got to make the mental change himself - no one else can do it for him."

"He has two choices: he can either suck it up, work harder, and get some confidence; or he can march into Macha's office, and tell him it's over," Charley added to Trish.

Over the phone, Tim reviewed the techniques he was neglecting, as Todd tried to stay awake during the late-night call from Japan.

"Whatever he's going through, don't let him take it out on you," I advised Trish. "I know it's easiest to lash out at the people around you, but he's got to realize that his biggest supporters will be there no matter what happens."

"Don't worry, I won't let him, Mrs. Carey. The only time he talked after the game with the three strikeouts was when we listened to a message on the answering machine that told me I hadn't gotten the job at Towson State. Then the attention shifted from him to me."

At that time, the media were focusing their attention on Wil Cordero, the Red Sox left fielder whose wife had been found by the rescue squad at 1 a.m., beaten over the head in the couple's apartment. Cordero admitted having hit her, but Ana refused to press charges. Records surfaced of previous beatings to Cordero's first wife while she was pregnant, for which she still carried scars. At that time, Cordero was playing for the Montreal Expos, and Duquette was the GM there. Duquette claimed that what had happened in Montreal was between Cordero and the counselor he'd been seeing. Meanwhile, Cordero had played immediately after the latest incident, on the road.

On the road in Scranton, the PawSox lost the first two games. Merloni was 3-for-19, with two homers, since coming up to "AAA." Todd didn't play until the second game, when he pinch hit for Sadler and struck out looking. He'd worked with Steve Braun that afternoon, and the radio announcer mentioned how Braun had repositioned Todd's hands.

"It has nothing to do with his hands," Charley commented after the strikeout. "It's all a matter of confidence." With the bases loaded and no outs in the bottom of the ninth, Todd hit into a double play. The only person more miserable than Charley, Trish, and myself was probably Todd. Charley's mother and mine were praying, while Lou Merloni's mother lit altar candles for Lou.

In the third game in Scranton/Wilkes Barre, playing first base, Todd collected a single, and hit a sacrifice fly to drive in a run. Most importantly, he hit the ball deep to the outfield every time except when he got his single through the right side of the infield. He had used the entire field, and hadn't struck out. That night, Walt McKeel and Arquimedez Pozo were sent up to Fenway. The third base position opened up in Pawtucket for one infielder.

Talking to Tim in Japan, Charley said, "There are two characteristics of Todd's that bother me about this season. One is that for someone who has had tremendous success in all aspects of his life, his confidence waxes and wanes. I can't figure out why this occurs, but the pendulum swings seem to have begun in college. I remember Coach Castelli telling me during the tournament in Hawaii, that Todd had come to him and said he had no confidence then. Even Castelli was astounded, and couldn't figure it out.

"The other thing that bothers me is that he hasn't shown an ability to adjust in situations that don't work. No matter what he says, he's still trying to pull the ball for home runs. In any job in life, it takes some intellectual sophistication to rethink a situation and find new solutions."

The long home-stand over the July 4, '97 holiday began with three games lost to Richmond. Walt McKeel and Arquimedez Pozo were playing up in Boston, and instead of Todd, Lou Merloni took over at third base. He was batting .368. Todd played the second game at first base, and as the team pounded nineteen hits in the 11-8 loss, Todd went without a hit in his first four at-bats, striking out twice. Charley and I became increasingly agitated in the stands, watching his average sink back into the .180's. We had Trish's parents with us, visiting from New Jersey, so we had to hold ourselves together. They, too, felt the stress; but Martha Correia, infielder Rod Correia's wife, kept chattering to me through the final innings. "You should be a sports psychologist," I told her. In his fifth at-bat, Todd hit a sharp grounder through the right side for his first hit of the day. I decided that in future games I would go for food or make a pit stop when Todd batted. A couple of beers also helped.

The next day, The Providence Journal carried Todd's picture in Bob Dick's column with the caption, "On downward spiral." The column carried a paragraph entitled, "Carey on thin ice" that read:

Even though he was in last night's starting PawSox lineup, Cumberland native Todd Carey has played himself into a backup role, according to Manager Ken Macha. Carey entered last night's game with a .189 average and 35 RBI's and eight home runs. According to Macha, Carey has had over 200 at-bats and has failed to have an impact. Macha also has been unsatisfied with Carey's defense and base running.[50]

Todd had heard none of this to his face. Instead, he'd read it in the paper while leading Trish's parents on a tour of Brown University. Macha had not said one word to Todd since the meeting they'd had together with Rico Petrocelli and John Cumberland on June 24th, two weeks prior. When Todd came to bat, if there were no signals or instructions to be given, Macha often turned his back, walking along the third baseline toward the bullpen, or simply spread his feet apart and, with his hands on his knees, stared at the grass underneath him.

Todd continued to be in Macha's shithouse, and, instead of taking the field, was the DH in the last Richmond win. Since I'd begun the habit of going to the ladies' room or to the snack bar during his at-bats, I learned to judge whether he'd reached base from the roar of the crowd, the silence of the crowd, or the PA systems' music to ignite a rally. His hits began spraying sharply to different fields, and he didn't strike out in two games. As DH in the first game against Norfolk on Independence Day, he had a breakthrough, collecting three hits, three RBI's, and a walk. Before the evening game, he'd invited a majority of the team for a barbeque at their cottage, for which I volunteered to do much of the cooking.

"You know, they almost cancelled the whole thing because you took over!" Tim told me on the phone later.

"No way! Really?" I asked, astounded. "I always have so much food ready for the Fourth of July cookouts that I pulled a lot of stuff from the freezer and brought it over. They still had to cook the hamburgers and hot dogs and set everything up." Trish had, indeed, appeared annoyed that I'd usurped her function that afternoon in the yard. I learned to imitate her parents by showing up at precisely the appointed time for future events.

Bob Dick, The Providence Journal reporter who'd written the unfavorable article about Todd the day before, walked right past him in the locker room to interview Lou Merloni. What other 25-year old, paid $2,500/month would have his job performance evaluated daily in the city paper?

We met Ben Mondor, owner of the PawSox, before the third Norfolk game. "He'll turn around," he said about Todd.

"Yes, if we can live through it," I responded.

With that, he gently pulled me by the arm, closer to him. "I've told them (management), 'You have to be patient! It's their first year in 'AAA.' Mo Vaughn couldn't hit the side of a barn here, and do you know what John Valentin batted here? He batted .214!'"

Besides Todd's Cumberland Coach Bruce Villeneuve offering encouragement, even reporter Bob Dick had a turnabout and gave Todd a headline in The Providence Journal sports section on Monday, July 7:

Hard Work Finally Paying Dividends for Carey

His double in the first inning of yesterday's game gave him (Todd) a modest five-game hitting streak and hiked his average to a season-high .206. During the home stand, the left-handed hitting infielder has gone 7-for-15. Carey has struggled since the start of the season, hitting .194 in April, .176 in May, and .197 in June. 'I feel a lot better up at the plate and I hope the hard work is paying off,' said the Cumberland native and Brown University graduate. 'It's a confidence thing. Getting some hits with men on base helps. I'm holding my hands higher, getting a more level swing and waiting on the ball a little longer.' Carey was on base three times yesterday with a double and two walks.[51]

While all these encouraging things were happening, Todd and Macha still weren't getting along. Asking each team member in the locker room if he were interested in being put on the list for fall/winter ball, Macha skipped right over Todd. Todd spoke up and said he wanted to go, and needed to go. "You don't have the numbers," Macha responded.

"That's bullshit," Todd retorted. "Neither does Nixon (batting .209) or Sadler (batting .223)!" Fortunately, Todd's agent, Ken Fishkin, was very friendly with Ed Kenney, who found spots for the players on teams in Arizona, Mexico, Venezuela, Puerto Rico, and Australia.

Todd wasn't the only one upset with Macha. Carl Pavano had been diagnosed by Pappas with a bone spur in the elbow of his pitching arm, but Macha pushed him back in the starting rotation, rather than taking him out, while the media reported "elbow stiffness." He had experienced stiffness the previous season in Trenton.

The last game before the All-Star break was the third win in five games against the Western Division leaders, the Norfolk Tides. Todd played third base and collected two doubles, raising his average to .213. He was also patient at the plate, walking once. Even the Merlonis began rooting for him. Andy Abad hit his sixth homer after reaching Pawtucket, and Adam Hydzu hit a two-run homer, his seventeenth. But it was Don Sadler, benched for two games during the series for lazy base running, who cleared the bases on a drive to deep right and snapped the 4-4 tie. Ron Mahay, promoted from Trenton to Fenway and back to Pawtucket to pitch in relief, got the win. Ron was an outfielder reincarnated as a pitcher.

After the game, a surprise fan waited for Todd outside the clubhouse entrance of the stadium. Mrs. Diane Hardy, Todd's first grade teacher at Community School in Cumberland, approached him for autographs with her family. Mrs. Hardy had dug out Todd's first grade class picture. After his initial surprise, he was able to identify half a dozen classmates without looking at their names. Trish was highly amused at the photo of the cute little urchin! Todd later spoke before the entire student body at his alma mater and gave a mini-clinic, after which he signed baseballs for everyone.

Tim called us during the All-Star break, while Todd and Trish visited Cape Cod. He had spoken to Todd and learned of Todd's turnabout at bat. "Before his five-game hitting streak began," Tim told us, "I told him that everyone was sick of babying him and that he needed a swift kick in the butt to get his act together, or he'd soon be out of a job. He was trying to pull the ball every time he came up to get a home run. Mom was crying, and Trish was sympathizing, but those were crutches for him to use to feel sorry for himself."

"Macha did the same thing in <u>The Providence Journal</u>," Charley told Tim. "He came down hard on him."

"That must have been what he needed," Tim answered. "As much as Trish is trying to help, he's going to have to make it or break it on his own."

Todd's hitting streak extended to nine games during a road trip against Norfolk and Charlotte, while the PawSox fell four and one-half games behind Rochester. Todd batted .500 going into the eighth game of the streak. Our summer revolved around home games in the stadium, or away games on the radio. During this road trip, I refused to listen to the radio, and made plans to go out with friends while Charley sat tuned in to every word. Or I simply found another room in the house where I could pursue an activity behind a closed door.

Todd didn't play in just two games of the road trip, although in one of those he pinch-hit and drove in the eighth, winning run during a 7-7 tie against Norfolk. He had four RBI's on the trip, and upped the number of doubles he had hit to thirteen. He remained at first base in every game except one in Charlotte, when he didn't play because a lefty pitched.

On July 15, his average after the road trip stood at .215. People began to ask us, "What's he thinking of doing when this is over?"

The president of Butler Hospital, a private psychiatric hospital in Providence where Charley remained chairperson of the board, asked me, "How did Todd handle the frustration this spring?"

I responded by answering, "We heard him on a pre-game radio interview during the last road trip, and the announcer asked him essentially the same thing. Todd said it had been extremely frustrating to play in front of his hometown crowd and 'not put on a good show.' He had greatly increased his batting practice, as a result.

He put a positive spin on it by saying that, with all those supporting him in Rhode Island and Massachusetts, he had a lot of people to talk to when he needed help! He can be witty when he wants to be! His confidence level sounded high. He was asked where he liked to bat in the lineup and he said, 'Anywhere there are men on base ahead of me, so I can drive them in, usually fifth or sixth.'"

Ken Fishkin, Todd's agent, and his family were in attendance for Todd's ninth home run in a Pawtucket game against Syracuse around the end of July. When Charley asked Ken whether Todd would be placed into winter ball, Ken responded, "Right now he doesn't have the numbers (stats)."

To me Charley said, "We're not going to let Fishkin off the hook that easily. He's spouting the party line from management and wants Todd to feel indebted to him when he does find a spot for him. Then Todd will rehire him for next year. I let him know we fully expect Todd to play this fall, since he's begun to hit consistently."

We sat with Brian Butterfield, the newly-appointed third base coach for the '98 expansion Arizona Diamondbacks. Charley had played ball for Colby College against Brian's father, who was then head coach at the University of Maine (John Winkin's predecessor). Coach Butterfield subsequently left the University of Maine for the New York Yankees. Brian knew all about Todd, having watched him in the Arizona League, and felt his best position in the field was at third base. Also in attendance were the Bryant University and Providence College baseball coaches. Todd found out about Master's Programs in Business at Bryant, as well as about graduate assistantships there for coaching the baseball team. He planned to help the Brown coach with his team that fall of '97.

During the Toledo series, Bob Schaefer, minor league Director for Player Development, approached Charley after one of the games. He had had a conversation with Todd, and reported to Charley that Todd was in a good groove at bat, and as a result, the Sox were trying to place him in winter ball. Todd elaborated by saying that there were a couple of slots on a Mexican team that four of the Sox players would share, each playing half a season. "I'd want the first half of the fall season," he said, "because I'd just as soon be home for Christmas and get rested for spring training. Anyway, Tyrone Woods just came back from the Mexican League and told me some horror stories about living down there. I'd rather not stay four months anyway." Trish pointed out to Todd that playing the second half in the Mexican League would be meaningless, since the expansion draft, as well as the forty-man roster, would be determined by November 1st. She had her Master's in Sports Management and was able to explain to me all the nuances of pro ball.

The baseball season had wrecked havoc with Charley's and my sleep, as well as with our sex life. Aside from the schedule of getting to Pawtucket for home games at 7 p.m., we were beginning to feel sleep-deprived because of the coffee or Coke at the games or worry after the games. By the time we arrived back in Westport from McCoy Stadium, it was usually 11:30 p.m. We didn't know how regular attendees like the Merlonis, Roses, or Pavanos could function, holding full-time jobs and traveling in excess of an hour to Pawtucket. Mrs. Rose worked the third shift at a factory from midnight until eight in the morning, after watching the games Brian pitched. All of us knew we had to be there for the short life-span of our sons in pro ball. However, I spent a week in Florida checking up on my parents during both June and July, and mostly slept.

Trish had started working full-time for the Ivy League Group in Princeton, New Jersey, as an assistant compliance director. On July 28, driving home on Route 1 in Princeton's bumper-to-bumper traffic, she was hit from behind in a multi-car accident, with muscular injuries to her back, neck, and side. The aerobic classes she taught and her workouts were sidelined indefinitely. In his first game in Scranton following the accident, Todd struck out three times and popped up. "When he gets on the ball field, he's got to block everything else from his mind," Tim advised us. "Just like when he and I used to step on the ice for a hockey game." Todd was 1-for-13 in his last four games.

Snatches from the lives of minor leaguers and their families... Robinson Checo had been purchased from a team in Japan for $2.5 million to pitch for Pawtucket. However, when the PawSox crossed the Canadian border to play in Ottawa, Checo couldn't find his passport, and was left stranded with the border authorities. Jared Fernandez and his wife Marcy, re-assigned from Pawtucket back down to "AA" Trenton when Checo was purchased, still had no place to live. Jared flew to Ottawa, pitched as the starter in place of Checo for the Pawtucket team, then flew back to Trenton.

Periodically, team members, such as infielder Tony Rodrigues, went on the Disabled List, even though they were perfectly healthy. Tony's empty slot was filled by Tyrone Woods, when he was recalled from Mexico to become the Pawtucket DH. Joe Hudson's wife and son reappeared in Pawtucket when Kerry Lacy and his family were sent back up to Boston. Most of the players who bounced between Pawtucket and Fenway had their residences midway between the two. After the first week of August, when the team left on a road trip, many of the families returned to their permanent addresses, where the children would enter school. The "AAA" regular season ran through Labor Day, after which playoffs began.

The Scranton bus followed the Pawtucket bus back to Rhode Island for an eight-day home stand after the series in Scranton. We didn't see or hear from Todd much, except at games, or when Trish took a train up for the weekend. He was involved in clinics on the field, public relations functions, errands, or he slept. The PawSox were still 6 and 1/2 games out of first place.

"I heard Ken Macha interviewed on the radio," a friend of Charley's family told us. "He said that Todd had worked very hard, his average was going up, and he would play in the final game against Charlotte." At least fifteen people had come to see him for the third game in which he didn't play, and his Cumberland High Coach Bruce Villeneuve and family took Todd to dinner afterward. On August 7, 1997, Todd hit two homers over the right field fence, then walked in the 7-2 win. Ironically, his best-hit ball was probably his last, when he drilled one that looked like it would clear the left center fence for his third homer of the day. But with the wind blowing in, left fielder Clifford Floyd jumped against the fence and caught the ball as it dropped inside the park. On his way down, the outfielder landed on his ankle, but held on to the ball.

Todd's homers were featured on the local sports clips on TV that night, and several people called us. The most rewarding publicity, though, was the quote by Ken Macha in The Providence Journal the following morning:

'I spoke to Todd about a few things this week. He batted .300 in July and now his swing is a lot flatter and (he) has made some improvements. You have to take your hat off to him, he carried the team today,' Macha said. 'We had him in the office earlier (July) and told him his playing time would be limited because of non-production but he has gone to work on his problems.'[52]

Bob Dick's column that day also underscored Todd's efforts, and quoted Todd:

'I've tried to flatten my swing out and am trying to put the ball in play more often and not strike out so much...Today, with runners on, I just wanted to put the ball in play and I stayed flat through the ball and it happened to go out of the park. I think my swing is a lot shorter and quicker.'

Todd's last homer had been on July 18th, and although his average hovered just under .230, his RBI's had risen to 55, the fourth highest on the team.

'I don't think I have really contributed that much. My RBI's are fine, but I feel they should be better. I had some chances early in the year to drive some runs in, but didn't do it. Some baseball people say it's better to have a good second half than a first half.'[53]

That last statement was something Charley had taught his younger son!The PawSox remained in second place in their division on August 8, 1997. The team had a decent chance as of that date to tie or better its all-time single season total wins. The 1978 PawSox under Joe Morgan held the record of 81-59. The '97 team had had 86 roster moves at that point in the season, using 44 different players (25 pitchers). Thirteen PawSox players had been promoted from Pawtucket to Boston that season.

Todd played in three games in Norfolk at first base, shortstop, and then third.

The PawSox swept the three-game series behind Checo, Pavano, and Rose (his fifteenth win). But it had been a costly series in Norfolk. Adam Hyzdu was injured in the first game, when he jammed his ankle. Arquimedez Pozo was hit by a pitch in the face, and in throwing his bat in disgust, he hit Lou Merloni in the temple in the dugout. Todd replaced Pozo at third base.

I had stomach pains AGAIN and couldn't sleep after listening to the game in Norfolk in which Todd went 1-for-5. I repeated my request to Charley to take the radio to another room so that I was unable to hear the action. Charley had no tolerance for my emotionalism.

By mid-August when Todd turned 26, the PawSox drew within four games of Rochester, their division leaders. These same teams would eventually play against each other in the first round of playoffs, beginning September 3rd. In a regular season series against Rochester, Todd replaced Lou Merloni at second base. Lou had torn the anterior cruciate ligament in his left knee in the first inning on a hard but clean slide by P.J. Forbes. In the third inning, Forbes went out of the base path, intending to wipe out Todd at second base on a forceout. Fortunately, Todd escaped the attempt. Things got tense in the fifth inning after our starter, Derek Lowe, drilled Forbes on the upper left arm. Rochester pitcher Steve Schrenk then plunked our first baseman, Bo Dodson, who calmly trotted to first base. Todd hit his twelfth homer to add to DH Tyrone Woods' two that game (six in one week), and Trot Nixon's two. Todd also singled in a run, for his 56th RBI. His average remained at .220, his errors at twelve.

We noticed that Tony Rodrigues, who was spending his second season in Pawtucket and had played in Fenway Park for a brief stint in '96, took the field even more rarely than Todd. Our speculation was that he was probably much older than the declared age on his visa from Puerto Rico. However, he signed his first contract in the minor leagues the same year as Todd, and would have one year left before free-agency. Most importantly, he had been a replacement player with Todd. Tony's agent was Ken Fishkin, Todd's agent, as well as Walt McKeel's. None of the three players had had good seasons, but Charley, Trish and I hoped Todd would switch to a more aggressive agent, nevertheless.

The last road trip to Ottawa and Syracuse in late August was disastrous for Todd. Arquimedez Pozo had left the team to attend an operation on his newborn, so Todd filled in at third base. While Trot Nixon hit his twentieth homer, Adam Hyzdu hit his twenty-second, and Chris Allison (elevated from Trenton to replace the injured Lou Merloni in the infield) hit consistently, Todd only managed two hits in over twenty at-bats on the road. His average slid to .212, as he tried hard to obtain a roster spot in the Mexican winter league. Trot Nixon was assured of returning to Mexico, and the rest of the Mexican slots would be announced by Ed Kenney over Labor Day weekend. Charley felt that as a parent, he should advise

Todd to get on with his life. Todd had been handed the most golden of opportunities - a starting position every day at "AAA" under a manager who was confident of his abilities and a Player Development Director who believed in him. The expansion draft was just months away. For whatever reason, he hadn't been able to capitalize on the opportunity, and major leaguers had to have the total package - talent, an even temperament, mental toughness, dedication to hard work, and a total belief in themselves. Until that season, I had always believed Todd had the package to make it all the way.

The team returned by bus from Syracuse at 5 a.m. to begin its last home stand that same night, August 28th, against Columbus. Pawtucket would definitely be in the playoffs, and eventually ended up in second place. They would begin divisional playoffs on their home field. By the end of the regular season, the '97 team would tie the most-win record of any PawSox team in history, with 81 wins and 59 losses.

Todd entered his sublet house in East Providence after traveling all night from Syracuse. He was aware that the renters had returned, together with their three dogs and a cat. He crashed there until noon, then started the moving process down to Westport. Tim, who'd returned the previous week from Japan, helped him in the pouring rain. We also had my parents and my sister in the Westport house, visiting during Labor Day week so they could enjoy the company of both boys. Tim would remain with us until he left for graduate school at the University of California in San Diego on September 12th. Trish also joined us for Labor Day weekend.

Steve Braun, roving batting instructor, was in town for the team's last home stand. Between ten to fifteen of our friends and relatives attended each of the last five games. Playing for Pozo at third base in the first game, Todd collected two hits and a walk. Pozo was benched inexplicably for the first home game after he returned from his baby's operation. Todd joked that Arquimedez had taken his third "vacation" of the season, resting before being placed on the expanded roster in Boston. Rumor had it that Arquimedez had gone back to the Dominican Republic immediately after the second baby's birth, distraught that he'd had another girl. His wife and newborn had remained in Pawtucket Memorial Hospital in Rhode Island.

After the first win against Columbus during the final home stand, our friend, John Cipollini, demonstrated to Todd outside the clubhouse how Todd had been moving his feet, preventing consistent hitting. After working all day with Steve Braun, Todd was not happy to be further critiqued, even though John was extremely complimentary.

In Boston, Nomar Garciaparra had had a thirty-game hitting streak and would be named "Rookie of the Year" in the American League. Sadler would not replace him at the major league level in the near future. Donnie had written off his Pawtucket season, giving up with a .212 average. With the exception of injured Lou Merloni (Venezuela), and Trot Nixon (Mexico), as well as the Latino players, few of the other players had received word about winter ball by the end of the season. Neither Trish nor the two of us asked Todd any questions about it. Everyone we knew, especially close friends, questioned us about his plans for the future and what had gone wrong with his season. Catcher Gary Bennett and his girlfriend, Ruby, had an agreement not to talk baseball after he left the field. "He was making himself so miserable, why make two of us miserable?" she told us.

The last regular season game on Labor Day featured a cookout, along with an open bar, for players' families under the corporate tent along the left field line. There was an hour's rain delay during a torrential downpour, while we ate and drank. Todd was not in the lineup, because Lou Merloni's injury had healed.

Three of Tim's Dartmouth friends joined us for the cookout. After eight and one-half innings, rain again descended, and the game was called in a 4-0 loss to Scranton. Most of the team enjoyed steaks under the tent after the game, while four of its members went to another tent to sign autographs for "Fan Appreciation Day." We would surely miss the most accommodating, congenial staff under Ben Mondor's ownership that we had ever encountered at any ball park. We gave them gifts of appreciation for their genuine helpfulness over the summer. The park would expand after the season to increase the capacity from 7,500 to 10,000 fans, and new parking and corporate entertaining facilities would be added. The raised seating that had necessitated autograph-seeking fans to lower souvenirs and pens in buckets to the players would drop almost down to the backstop area, and home plate would move forward to the pitcher's mound.

The following players received the team awards at the end of the '97 season:

Rookie of the Year - Carl Pavano
MVP - Brian Rose (received a 27" TV)
Defensive Player of the Year - Trot Nixon
Slugger of the Year - Arquimedez Pozo
10th Player Award - Adam Hyzdu (received a 27" TV)

The International League awarded "Rookie of the Year"
and "Most Valuable Pitcher" to Brian Rose.

25

On to the
Next Season

It was not until several weeks after the playoffs that I forced myself to recon-
struct the end of the '97 season. It was a dismal blur in my mind, literally (pouring
rain) and figuratively, although our Brian Rose delivered his most masterful performance of the season in game one, pitching eight shutout innings and gaining ten
strikeouts. Unfortunately, pitcher Doug Johns did also, during eight innings for
Rochester. Pawtucket reliever Toby Borland was tagged for a pair of doubles in the
ninth, giving up the only run of the game. Pawtucket had failed to score in twenty-
two innings. Todd sat on the bench against lefty Johns during game one.

The second game of that round of the Governor's Cup proved even more exciting than the first, and more frustrating for Todd, who again sat on the bench while
right-hander Yan pitched against us. Prior to the game, we saw Macha and Todd in
an intense private discussion in the dugout. Todd had not started in three straight
games.

Our pitcher, Carl Pavano, was trying for his fifth win over Rochester, but was
not as sharp as he'd been in recent outings. However, in the second inning, after an
error on Abad's grounder to Rochester third baseman P.J. Forbes, Merloni singled
Abad to second base, then Sadler singled Abad home for our first run in 23-2/3
innings.

Forbes came back to single-handedly tie the game at 1-1 with a homer in the
third. But the PawSox went ahead 3-1 in the bottom of the third when Abad hit a
ball over the wall in right with Pozo on base.

In the fifth, Pavano ran into trouble as Danny Clyburn hit a soft, bases-loaded
single that dropped before Trot Nixon could grab it in center field. That tied the
game at 3-3.

In the eighth, reliever Kerry Lacy replaced Pavano. Lacy pitched two innings of
hitless relief and escaped a Rochester Red Wing threat in the top of the ninth,
when he walked two.

Rochester starter Esteban Yan had retired thirteen in a row prior to the bottom of the ninth. With the score tied 3-3, he fanned Merloni, but the splitter in the dirt got away from catcher Ryan Luzinski. Merloni headed down the line to first, complete with a brace on his rehabilitated left knee. Luzinski, who'd just entered the game, pounced on the ball, but threw wildly down the right field line, well beyond Merloni, who chugged to second. Twenty feet from that bag, Merloni took his last look down the line, and raced for third. Manager Macha held his hands up all the way, but our Lou didn't even look up.

With Merloni ensconced on third base, it was up to PawSox catcher Jason Varitek to deliver the runner home. On a 1-and-2 pitch, he sacrificed to the outfield. The PawSox had tied the series at one apiece. Rose and Pavano, contrary to rumors, would not pitch for Boston during the remainder of the big league season. The PawSox would then have to clinch the first round in Rochester at Frontier Field, where the Red Wings had posted the best home record in the league at 49-22.

Game three was unlike the first two. Our starter, Robinson Checo, was tapped for six runs in five-plus innings, giving up eight hits before being relieved by Carlos Valdez, then Pete Walker (who gave up another run) in the 7-1 loss. Checo had won his last four regular season starts, and was called up to Boston immediately after the playoffs. Newcomers Keith Johns and Julio Pequero, who'd both been with the Red Wings less than a week, combined to drive in five runs in their Frontier Field debuts.

Todd started that game at second base, replacing Lou Merloni. He hit a double and a single in four at-bats. He and Arquimedez Pozo (also two hits) had two-thirds of the team's total hits that night. Our only run came in the third inning, when catcher Gary Bennett was brought home by Adam Hyzdu. The PawSox still had to win two more in Rochester.

But it didn't happen. Although Pawtucket dominated Rochester during the '97 regular season (12-5), Rochester eliminated the PawSox in the fourth game of the first round, as they had the previous year. The Red Wings would go on to play the Columbus Clippers for the Governor's Cup.For the fourth game out of five, Todd was not in the starting lineup. We listened to the radio as he pinch-hit in the sixth, replacing Abad at first base after Abad dislocated a finger diving for a ball. Abad rotated between the outfield and the infield. Todd failed to get a hit in two at-bats. The Paw Sox had batted just .235 and scored only five runs in the first three games of the Division playoffs.

After the fourth game, Robinson Checo, Arquimedez Pozo, Curtis Pride, and Jason Varitek joined Boston for the remainder of the big league season. Lou Merloni, Trot Nixon, and Kerry Lacy were asked to leave numbers where they could be reached in case of an emergency call-up.

Todd had no final meeting with Macha after the season ended, and returned to an empty clubhouse to pick up his belongings the next day. As numerous team members made plans for winter ball, Todd's agent, Ken Fishkin, informed Todd that he was still in contact with Ed Kenney about Todd's placement in the Mexican League.

The season had ended on September 6, 1997. While Todd played golf, jogged, and spent time in both Westport and Princeton (visiting Trish), he still had not heard about winter ball by September 19th. His agent asked him to stay by the phone September 22nd through 24th, since negotiations were proceeding between Kenney and the Mexicans to send Todd as a replacement for a player who had declined. The sight was pathetic, seeing Todd sitting on the sofa reading day after day, awaiting the call. He'd complete his daily jog, do his errands or mine, then come home for the rest of the day. He even drove me to the beauty parlor, while he had his hair cut next-door. "He looks lost," a friend of ours said who had run into him at the grocery store.

Wednesday, September 24th, came and went, and still he had no word. On the 26th, Friday, he called Schaefer in Boston. "He washed his hands of winter ball, and told me it was Kenney's job to place us, which I knew," Todd told us.

"What else did he say?"

"Basically, he said he saw a lot of good things in my play this year, but I had to cut way down on the strikeouts. I'll be back in Pawtucket again, fighting for a starting position next season."

Around dinner time that day, Fishkin called. "The Sox are having trouble finding a spot for everyone, and the first baseman you were going to replace decided to go to Mexico after all," Fishkin reported.

Over dinner, Charley and I asked if he were disappointed. "Sure, of course! But this will give me time to get some perspective, forget baseball for a while, and then refocus on what I need to improve before spring training. Schaefer said he wasn't sure yet who'd be on the forty-man roster to go to camp early. I only know that I want to get out of here, where everyone knows every detail about my season, and asks all kinds of questions."

That was certainly the truth! The constant questions from family, friends, and coaches had not helped Todd's performance, nor had Charley's and my presence at the games. "Well, there was one positive feature of the summer," I ventured.

"What was that?" Todd asked.

"You refocused at the end of June and even told the media about some of the things you changed. Those adjustments resulted in less strikeouts and a .300 batting average during July. Dad and I were really proud of you for working so hard."

"What are your plans now?" Charley asked.

"I'll leave and go down to Princeton with Trish and find a job just to pay the rent."

"Well, this could be a blessing in disguise," Charley said. "Up until now, you've told us that you wanted to focus completely on baseball. But without a decision from Kenney about winter ball, I think you should consider dual career paths at this point."

"What does that mean, Dad?"

"It simply means that you shouldn't put all your eggs in one basket. Take the preparatory course for the Graduate Management Admissions Test while you have time off. The test results are valid for five years, so if you ever decide to leave baseball, you could apply immediately to grad schools."

"I plan to take the course and the test, but at my own pace and on my own schedule. I know you both think I should leave baseball, but whether you like it or not, I'm going to stick with it. You think you've been supportive because you attended all the home games this summer, but I know how upset you got in the stands, and I know, Mom, that you were crying on the phone to Tim in Japan when I had a real bad stretch. If you can't take it, stay home!"

I was taken aback, and it was a few seconds before I could control my voice to speak. "Todd, the hardest thing in the world is seeing a child of mine trying to fulfill a lifelong dream, and watching him struggle, without being able to help. Someday you may experience the same thing. Trish found it difficult to watch at times, too."

"Yeah, but she never took baseball out of the ball park."

"Well, I admire her for that! But I find it difficult to accept that you honestly believe we have not supported you 100% while you've been playing pro ball. We were the ones who believed in you when you didn't believe in yourself. We know you have more tools to make it to the majors than some of the guys who have made it already. But *you* have to believe that, and *you* have to want it too."

"I do right now."

Todd packed that night, and left the next day to join Trish in their search for a four-month rental apartment. He began work at Princeton University in the book store, and planned to conduct baseball clinics with Coach Gallagher, the Trenton batting coach. He kept in shape by working out with the Princeton team and signed up for the preparatory course for his GMAT's. The moral of the story for Charley and me: "Get a life!!" The following March, we did not plan to visit spring training as frequently, and would spend fewer summer evenings in '98 at McCoy Stadium in Pawtucket. Instead, we resolved to plan some trips and wean ourselves off baseball. Todd's comments had hit a nerve, and it was time to admit that our addiction to our son's career was not beneficial for any of us. I resolved to begin to let go of my role as nurturing parent and step back into the role of bystander until called upon. Trish would help him in my place.

Tim had set up his graduate apartment in a refurbished residential housing complex at the University of California in San Diego (La Jolla). He was one of 90 first-year students in a two-year Master's program in Asian Studies/International Relations, and despite the demands of the program in Japanese, Statistics, National Security Policy, Managerial Economics, and optional Chinese, he loved it. Many of his fellow students were foreign nationals working for their consulates. Those governments sent the employees through the program, and all were fluent in English.

Prior to the expansion draft in early November, Todd asked Trish to collect any articles she found on the Internet regarding the possibilities for trades or draft picks that involved Boston. He wanted to be prepared for any eventuality. Boston paid $75,000,000 for Montreal pitcher Pedro Martinez, with several of our minor leaguers involved in the trade, including Pawtucket starting pitcher Carl Pavano. Undoubtedly Carl would become a major leaguer immediately for Montreal. His parents, Carl and Ann Pavano, and other relatives from Connecticut would miss seeing him play on a regular basis. For every game Carl had pitched in Pawtucket, Ann had occupied a seat on a vertical aisle directly behind home plate. His dad tracked his pitches on paper. Seats in our "family pass" section were not able to be reserved, but Ann had claimed her stake on that seat. One day, the office staff gave Charley a ticket placing him in that seat, but Ann politely asked him to find another when she arrived.

Excluded from winter ball and the forty-man roster, Todd decided to take advantage of the invitation from Bob Schaefer for minor leaguers to use the training facilities in Ft. Myers at their own expense. He would travel to Florida prior to the opening of minor league camp in mid-March. For the sixth straight season, Todd would not join the major leaguers who were housed at the Sheraton Harbor Place. Many of his Pawtucket teammates on the forty-man roster would also live there, including Arquimedez Pozo, Jason Varitek, Lou Merloni, Don Sadler, Trot Nixon, Mike Coleman. In addition, the above-named would be participating in major league exhibition games in the City of Palms Park beginning in mid-February. Todd did not get invited to participate as he had been the previous year, despite being in camp three weeks early. "Well, if you're sick of it," Schaefer told Todd, "have a good year!"

Todd made plans to fly to Ft. Myers in mid-February with pitcher Mike Blais. Three minor leaguers would share an apartment when they arrived, thus avoiding the Days Inn accommodations. He completed the GMAT preparatory course, and scored high enough on that exam for entrance requirements at Bryant University in Smithfield, R.I. A friend of his was the head baseball coach there, Jon Sjogren, and mentioned that a graduate assistantship might be available if Todd were to become their assistant baseball coach. Time would tell, but before departing for Ft. Myers, Todd obtained an application for a Bryant University M.B.A.

He brought the rough draft to show us when he visited over two weekends in February. Meanwhile, Trish purchased her ticket for a week's visit during spring training.

At first, I had a hard time dealing with the fact that among those still playing for the Red Sox who had started with Todd, almost all had either been promoted to the big leagues or had been included on the 40-man roster. There was no denying that the Sox management had treated Todd fairly, but the talent that lay within him had only one year left to emerge before free agency. After the '98 season, he could be signed by anyone if he were to have a successful year. Others with less talent were playing in the big leagues, but they exuded confidence and made things happen. The bonus factor that management had paid was also a key, Todd's bonus being negligible compared to those in the first few rounds of the draft. Big bucks meant big playing time.

By the end of the third week of January,'98, contracts had been mailed out of the Boston office. On January 20, the media reported that the Sox were close to a long-term contract extension, under arbitration, with infielder John Valentin. Valentin's agent, Dick Moss, was doing all the talking, and announced that there were relatively minor things to clear up. In the end, Valentin succeeded in obtaining $25 million over four years. Infielder Julio Cesar Guerrero agreed to terms with Boston management; infielder Mike Gallego was invited to major league camp; infielder Mike Benjamin signed a $242,500 one-year contract. Some of these infielders would, of course, end up in "AAA."

In late January, '98, Charley and I visited Tim at University of California, San Diego (La Jolla). We arrived just five days after the Denver Broncos left the practice fields on that campus to become Super Bowl World Champions. The San Diego area is a tourist's Mecca. We had planned our visit to coincide with the Fresno State basketball game against San Diego State. Our nephew, Christopher Herren, was a junior guard for Fresno under Coach Jerry Tarkanian. He had just returned to the team a month before, after undergoing drug and alcohol abuse rehab. Perhaps the greatest basketball player for Durfee High (Charley's alma mater) in Fall River, Mass., Christopher had scored 2,000 points there before being named to the '94 McDonald's All-American Team. He did not disappoint us.

Christopher scored twenty-six points in the win for Fresno State, and played even better in a nationally-televised game from Hawaii immediately following. "He's the best college guard I've seen all year," the announcer commented. Tormenting opposing fans with finger-pointing, quick smiles under burning eyes, as well as self-congratulatory bellows and hugs into the TV cameras, Chris fed off the frenzy. Most importantly to us, he looked healthier and happier. As he climbed into the bleachers after the San Diego State game to give me a bear hug, I whispered in his ear, "We're so proud of what you've done, Chrissy! You look wonderful!" Although Charley and I had been unable to see Christopher play for several years, the cousins had stayed in touch and we all gathered together at Christmas. "It's so good to see family out here!" he exclaimed. The day we arrived back in Florida, February 9, 1998, Sports Illustrated was on the news stands, containing Gerry Callahan's article on Christopher. It concluded:

The NBA remains Herren's goal, but he says he has learned not to concern himself with next year or even next week. His demons are always around the next corner, waiting to renew acquaintances. For every positive influence on Herren, there are a dozen dubious characters buzzing around, looking, as he says, to kick it with him...[54]

By the third week of May, advance word from NBA scouts indicated Chris would not be chosen in the first round of the '98 draft. He decided to return for his senior year at Fresno State, where he received almost 24-hour support from the graduate students in sports management and the counseling groups on campus. Over time, Christopher reached the NBA, but his career there was short-lived. His demons returned, and he departed for China, Italy, Turkey, and Iran to play ball.

Todd's contract for 1998 arrived for $2,700/month. It went unsigned until the end of spring training, while Todd's agent negotiated for $2,900/month.

Todd and Mike Blais, his apartment-mate, worked out every morning from 9 a.m. until noon in the City of Palms Park, while the major leaguers and invitees switched over to the five fields at the minor league complex. Todd awaited the opening of minor league camp on March 13th, a week later than in previous years. We attributed the late opening to a lack of funds after the Sox signed pitcher Martinez for the immense sum of $75 million over six years. The early weeks of March rolled by and Todd was not invited to participate in exhibition games with the major leaguers, as he had the previous season. There was an old adage in baseball: "You're only as good as your last at-bat."

There is March Madness in basketball and March Madness in spring baseball camps, as every year, rumors abound. Hundreds of players report and perform for three weeks, before making the rosters or getting cut. Some faces are "missing in action," while new faces appear. Todd's '97 traveling roommate, catcher Gary Bennett, had been traded to Philadelphia. Infielder Tony Rodrigues did not receive a new contract. Japanese teams bought outfielder Jose Malave and pitcher Rafael Orellano. Outfielder Adam Hyzdu signed a deal with the Diamondbacks expansion team, near his Arizona home. Those of us who had sat in the family seats at McCoy Stadium would surely miss the Hyzdu children. They were among my favorites. I twisted Alexa's hair into pigtails while she and her brother recited a history for the pages they crayoned during the game.

The Sox had acquired, among others, "AAA" first baseman Nick Delvecchio, a former rival of Tim and Todd's at Harvard. Nick entertained Todd with tales about his Harvard friend, Matt Damon (co-writer of the movie script "Good Will Hunting" and rising movie star). Ken Macha returned as the Pawtucket "AAA" manager for his second season.

On February 24, 1998, four days before the first Sox major league spring training game, second baseman Jeff Frye suffered a season-ending ACL (ligament) injury to his left knee during a seemingly harmless rundown. "I heard something pop," said Darren Bragg, the runner on the play. "It definitely didn't sound good. It definitely didn't look good." Frye, at age 31, was coming off his best season as part of an infield of outstanding hitters in '97 - Mo Vaughn (.315 with 35 homers), Nomar Garciaparra (.306 and 30 homers), and John Valentin (.306 with 18 homers).

The Sox mulled their alternatives to replace Frye: unsigned ex-Braves' second baseman Marke Lemke; former Dodger's shortstop Greg Gagne, who wanted to play close to his Massachusetts home; veterans Mike Benjamin or Mike Gallego, already in camp; or Triple A players Lou Merloni or Donnie Sadler.

Lou Merloni and Nomar Garaciaparra had become bosom buddies. We began reading in the south Florida papers about Lou's gold Italian baby bull's horn that he wore as a good luck charm around his neck. He had received it from his Great Uncle Dom Merloni, who'd inherited it. In the spring opener behind pitcher Martinez's victory over the Twins, Don Sadler got first crack at second base and Merloni went in to replace Garciaparra at short. Over the course of the next few weeks of major league camp, no less than fourteen infielders took their places on the diamond, Todd not among them.

Todd and Mike Blais traveled to our condo in Delray Beach the last two days of February for a change of scenery. They spent one day at the new Roger Dean Stadium in Jupiter, where the Expos and Cardinals both trained. They watched Ryan McGuire, Todd's former buddy, play in the major league Expo exhibition game, then accompanied Ryan and his wife out to dinner. Todd had attended the McGuires' wedding in Michigan the previous fall.

We called Tim in California while Todd visited us. When Tim heard that Todd had not participated in major league games, he advised Todd, "Find out what the hell's going on!"

Todd returned for a second weekend in Delray Beach to pick up various graduate school applications that had arrived at our address. He asked us to look over his rough draft for the Bryant University application in Rhode Island. Upon his return to Ft. Myers, Todd had a quick conversation with Bob Schaefer. Back in early February, Todd had mentioned to Schaefer his disgust at being excluded from the forty-man roster. Schaefer had advised, "Well, if you're sick of it, have a good season!" This time, Schaefer's terse response was, "The spots are all full right now, but I'll keep you in mind." True to his word, within two days Schaefer called Todd to accompany the major leaguers on a two-day road trip up the west coast of Florida. Todd dressed for both games, but never took the field. "He thought it was a big waste of time," Trish informed us. "He could have been back in Ft. Myers working out."

Before the middle of March, 24-year-old Nomar Garciaparra became American League Rookie of the Year for '97. He led all AL rookies in thirteen categories, and the entire American League with 209 hits and 11 triples. With a .306 batting average, 30 homers, 98 RBI's, 122 runs, and 22 steals, he was quoted as saying:

'I wasn't happy because the team didn't go anywhere. We have to concentrate on pulling together. We have to concern ourselves with team chemistry, picking each other up and winning. The individual honors take care of themselves if the ring is there.' [55]

On March 11, '98, Nomar and the Red Sox came to terms for a landmark $23.25 million over five years. The salary could escalate to $44.25 million if the team exercised two option years. Nomar's salary the previous season had been $150,000. He got a $2 million signing bonus, plus $600,000 in '98; $900,000 in '99; $3.3 million in 2000; $6.85 million in 2001; and $8.6 million in 2002. We were genuinely happy for him, as he was a selfless player and an unbelievable talent. In addition, he kept in touch with us every Christmas!

The very next day, first baseman Mo Vaughn claimed in the press that the Sox were conducting a smear campaign to gain leverage in contract negotiations after his three-year, $18.6 million contract had expired. He was referring to an acquittal in a two-day trial in Massachusetts for his arrest on drunken driving charges on January 9, 1998. Despite police testimony during the trial, Mo had been found innocent because of dense fog the night of the accident. "They almost wish that I had been found guilty (of drunken driving) so they could have sat back and had control" said Vaughn, who refused to undergo the alcohol evaluation that management was requesting. "They took care of who they wanted to take care of," he said. "If I had a general manager who liked me, my deal would have been done, too."[56] Mo had an Opening Day deadline and wanted a five-year deal for an estimated $50 million. The Sox had offered three years. The Boston media had continually documented Mo's philanthropy among inner city residents, and he was invaluable as a public relations tool for the Sox. By the end of exhibition games, he had homered ten times, leading all major leaguers that spring.

On March 21, 1998, Charley and I arrived at spring training in Ft. Myers and proceeded to the minor league fields to watch the "AAA" game against the Pirates. Trish, her dad, and Mike Blais' wife met us there. Trish and Janna were spending a week's vacation in Todd and Mike's apartment.

I knew I had to keep the faith that Todd and Trish had, and once I reached the furthest three fields, the familiar sounds of the crack of the bat and minor league coaches yelling for runners to round the bases drew me in. The parking lot was packed, since three games were in progress against the Pirates' "A," "AA," and "AAA" teams. Randy Brown, traded from the Sox to the Yankees to the Pirates the previous season, was not in sight.

There were so many minor leaguers in camp again that instead of being resentful of those who'd proceeded up the ladder to City of Palms Park, I became grateful to see Todd out on the field. Despite a bad head cold, he fielded flawlessly at short for the first half of the game and collected a line-drive single to center field that drove in two runs. After a certain pitch count, the teams would switch from the field to the plate, whether there were three outs or not. After Todd rotated out of the game we saw, Coach Santana brought him and Bo Dodson to a separate field, where Todd fielded another fifty balls at third base and short. "Looks like they'll try to use him as a backup utility man," Charley surmised. On the "AAA" bench sat twenty-five pitchers waiting to see some action.

We were greatly encouraged to see that the Sox were still working so intensely with Todd. There were two "AAA" players on the bench for every infield position. Pozo was at third base, having cleared waivers over the weekend. Gallego, Merloni, and Sadler were still in contention to play second base with the major leaguers.

Roving Batting Instructor Steve Braun chatted with Charley, as did Manager Macha and Player Development Director Bob Schaefer. After inquiring about Tim, Steve Braun commented, "Todd should have a good season this year. He always does better the second year he's on a team." That was music to our ears, reassuring us that he wouldn't be released in the spring and would be back in Pawtucket.

"There's one thing we can be infinitely grateful for," Charley said later to me. "The Red Sox have been extremely loyal to Todd, and have hung in there with him through the bad times."

Ken Fishkin, Todd's agent, had visited prior to our arrival. Although Todd wanted more money per month before signing his current contract, even with a contract the management could release minor leaguers at any time, since they had no union representation. For the present, Fishkin was concentrating on laying some groundwork with other teams. That way, once Todd became a free agent, Fishkin could manipulate the teams' interest on Todd's behalf.

Mike Blais' wife, Janna, reported on the bus trip that Mike, a backup reliever, had taken several days before with the major leaguers. There had been a torrential downpour, and upon arrival at the Cincinnati spring stadium, the bus driver learned that the game had been canceled. He was given instruction to proceed to the clubhouse. Assuming the practice fields were connected to the major league field, as in City of Palms Park, the driver proceeded across the outfield as a shortcut to the clubhouse. One outfield led to another outfield, then another outfield, before the bus encountered a brick wall. There the bus became mired in the mud. The Sox major leaguers spilled out to walk all the way back to the clubhouse, just as Reds' owner, Marge Schatt, appeared screaming at the top of her lungs. Two hours later, a tow extracted the bus and pulled it back out the way it had come, defacing the three fields all over again.

Charley met Trenton's Hitting Coach Gallagher, whom Todd had worked with in January at Gallagher's private batting cages. "He told me," Charley reported, "that of all the players he has ever coached, Todd knows most instinctively what he's done that's technically wrong or right. He said he works hard and has all the tools, but lacks confidence. I blame myself for always telling the boys to be humble and not to ever brag about their accomplishments. I wish now that I'd given them some attitude."

Wow! What unconscious values parents exhibit when raising their kids! Do we teach them "attitude" by boasting about all their accomplishments in front of them and encouraging them to do the same? Or do we teach them humility by supporting their efforts and congratulating them privately? Obviously it is a thin line and Charley and I had believed that humility was never a fault; that accomplishments spoke for themselves. The successes that our sons achieved had allowed them the confidence to proceed to each new level, both in athletics and academics. As they rose to the highest levels in pro sports, successes were harder to come by. Therefore, their confidence waxed and waned more frequently. Interestingly, their confidence levels never diminished while they attended graduate school.

What upset Charley the most that day was seeing Todd take a called third strike over the outside corner at-bat. When Todd called our hotel, Charley recounted to him all of Gallagher's compliments. Then he said, "Gallagher said you still lack confidence, and that is exactly what I saw in your hitting today, particularly when you took that third strike. When you did that, it's because for a fraction of a second, you didn't believe you could punch it into left field."

Todd's Dad was giving detailed baseball advice, but he needed to take a breath to gather his composure. I knew he was going back to the basics he had taught Todd, but also knew that Todd would take the advice from his batting instructor a little more easily. Impatiently, Charley emphasized the urgency of the changes that had to occur. "At least take a cut at it! You would have reduced your strikeouts by maybe fifty last season if you'd just had the confidence to hit to left field. And frankly, time is running out."

"But you don't know how hard it is to go through a season like last year and to have to pull yourself up again, Dad!"

"Maybe I don't know from a baseball standpoint, but I know that in anything you do, you have to totally believe in yourself. How would I have survived being fired from Fleet if I didn't have total confidence in myself? Stop second-guessing yourself. You're too good a player to have such self-doubt. There are nothing but young kids around you, and experience alone should get you a starting position before them!"

With my parents in tow, we journeyed back across Alligator Alley on March 28th for our last visit to spring training in '98. We never knew when the saga would end, and as addicted as we were, we couldn't stay away. The day we arrived was the last major league game before the players traveled to Atlanta for a pre-season exhibition.

We set up our paraphernalia at the minor league fields - lawn chairs for my mother's ailing back and my dad's knees, cooler with drinks and sandwiches, suntan lotion, camera, hats - and waited for the Pawtucket team to dribble out for infield practice after filing through the chow line. The weather was 85 degrees and gorgeous, the type of Florida day that northerners dream about. Around Easter, the mass exodus from the state always began, and those of us who stayed behind waved them joyous farewells.

We settled in, commenting to some of the players we knew about the contrast in temperatures from 50 degrees the previous weekend. Manager Macha stopped to say, "If you're waiting to see Todd, you'll have a long wait! He's playing in the big league game against the Twins over at their complex (also in Ft. Myers)." We scurried as fast as we could with an eighty-six and eighty-two-year-old across town. Fortunately, Todd had left us tickets at the press booth.

He did not start, but in the bottom of the fourth inning, went in to give Nomar Garciaparra a rest at shortstop. What a thrill to see him in a major league uniform! Behind screwballer Wakefield, the Sox ran up six runs off Twins' starter Hawkins. Todd hit his first pitch - outside over the left corner - in a line drive to the left field fence, caught by the outfielder there above his head. It was exactly what Charley had suggested he should do. The second time up, he drove a ball to right center for an RBI single. Lastly, he grounded to second base off Rick Aguilera, the closer. Todd moved to third base for the last three innings in the 10-5 win. What a day! We took him to dinner, and despite his bloodshot eyes, red neck, and heat exhaustion, celebrated the day with two rounds of beers over Italian dinners. It was easy to forget the tremendous physical demands on these ball players, participating in daily hitting and fielding drills, games in the heat (or cold), often lengthy travel, and the demands of relearning positions in the field.

The next day, many of the special invitees to major league camp were back on the minor league fields. The major leaguers had boarded a plane at 6:30 a.m. that morning for Atlanta. Back on the minor league fields were Lou Merloni, Trot Nixon, Mike Coleman, Ron Mahay. In the game against the "AAA" Twins, Todd started the game at second and reached base on an error. Pozo shared the position with Todd, playing the second half and collecting a double. There were seven infielders vying for four starting positions before camp broke up on April 6th. That didn't include Don Sadler, who was in Atlanta playing with the major league Sox. The "AAA" roster would again reduce to 23, and with 25 pitchers on the Pawtucket bench, the most nervous group on the fields the last weekend in March was, understandably, the pitchers.

Our last day at spring training, '98, we watched Brian Rose pitch for Pawtucket at the Twins' minor league complex. Todd had played with the Sox major leaguers two days prior at the Twins' stadium. Brian Rose had not traveled to Oakland with our major leaguers because he would be pitching his first start at Fenway in the home opener, quite a thrill for the young Dartmouth, Mass. native. Our summer home was in Westport, the very next town to Brian's. He was pitching the "AAA" game for us that day.

Merloni was again at shortstop; Liniak was again at third; Pozo was at second; Andy Abad was at first. Halfway through the game, newly-acquired (WITH ONE WEEK OF SPRING TRAINING LEFT!) shortstop Keith Johns went in for Merloni. Johns came from the "AAA" Rochester Orioles, in exchange for our first baseman, Bo Dodson. Todd was the DH as ninth batter, but at least he had a place in the lineup. Nick Delvecchio, his Harvard buddy, was no longer on the roster. Rumors floated that deals were being negotiated to send Pozo and outfielder Hurst (6'7" tall) to Japan. They still would have to make room for Sadler when he came down from the major league team.

Todd looked aggressive and confident in most of his at-bats. He hit his first two outside pitches to be caught at the left field fence, then collected an RBI single with a ball hit so hard that when it bounced six feet in front of the second baseman, it caromed up ten feet above his head. The last time he struck out.

"You're hitting the ball well," Charley told him when he said goodbye to all of us. "Keep it up! I'll see you in Pawtucket in a month when I go up for the hospital board meetings."

"And I'll see you in two months," I said as I gave him a hug and kiss. "We love you! Please give us a call before you leave Florida." I was staying in Florida until we drove north in late May.

We talked to Lou Merloni at length, and congratulated him on the fine spring he'd had with the major leaguers. He complained about not getting many at-bats the last couple of weeks with the "big team." He had a really bad head cold, complete with sore throat, cough, the whole works. "We needed Bo (Dodson) on this team for his cool head and experience," Lou said. "Our outfielders, excluding Nixon, are off the wall. And that Liniak kid had one-and-a-half months of 'AA' ball last season. He came to this team mouthing off about what a superstar he is." Lou was not alone in his sentiments about the missing Bo Dodson and his family. Hunter and baby Tanner would join the album of PawSox alums who were held close to the hearts of those still playing and those who had sat in the stands. Hunter knew the name of every species of dinosaur and what they ate, and always carried a knapsack full of toy soldiers to the games.

Charley talked to "AA" Batting Coach Gallagher before we left, who had complimented Todd the previous week. "Looks like he's coming on!" he said.

By March 29, 1998, the major league Sox had the best record of the spring, with 19 wins and 8 losses. But every baseball fan knew that spring games meant nothing, and a long season lay ahead. Doris Kearns Goodwin brilliantly described the Red Sox in her book Wait Till Next Year as "perpetual bridesmaids, exciters of hope and destroyers of dreams."[57]

On April 6, 1998, Todd flew to Providence. The following day, twenty-four players assembled at McCoy Stadium for workouts. One would either have to go on the Disabled List (even though he wasn't injured) or leave the roster, in order to reduce the number to the maximum of twenty-three.

Todd at McCoy Stadium, Pawtucket, R.I., with grandparents Evelyn and Walter Plumb.

26

A New Uniform

The Biltmore Hotel in downtown Providence was the site of the '98 PawSox press banquet. A restored landmark, the hotel was a far cry from the King's Inn Restaurant in Lincoln, R.I., where it had been held the previous year. At the press conference, Todd renewed acquaintances with some of our old friends: Jim Hagan, president of the Providence Chamber of Commerce; Dean Holt, President of Fleet Bank of Rhode Island; Bill Murray and Bill Darcey, fathers of Todd and Tim's Cumberland friends.

Todd played in only one game during the three opening losses, April 10 -12. All other infielders played in at least two games. Liniak played every game at third base and Merloni played every game, rotating between second base and short. Keith Johns, the shortstop acquired during spring training from the Orioles' Rochester "AAA" team, played opening night and one following game, while Merloni and Pozo shared second base.

Before the team left on April 13th for a road trip, Macha informed Todd that because Donnie Sadler was returning to the Paw Sox from the big league team, Todd would be put on the Disabled List. He apologized for having to do so, but said the roster had to reduce down to twenty-three. Todd immediately tried to get Bob Schaefer on the phone to find out if Schaefer could trade Todd from the organization. In this case, he had hit the ball well during spring training, but was, nevertheless, the first positional player to go on the DL. I surmised that Todd was low man on the totem pole in Pawtucket and was happy that he had taken some action instead of waiting for Boston to make another move. Schaefer's response was no response: he told Todd he had too many players and no answers for him - everyone would rotate on the DL, except the "Golden Boys" favored by GM Duquette.

Todd took the news of being on the DL calmly, trying to hide his disappointment over the phone when he told us. My heart was breaking for him, but I had to maintain a "stiff upper lip." Trish urged him to call his agent. Even at the "AAA" level, especially with his '97 stats, he had no leverage. He and Trish joked about what week would be convenient for each player on the roster to have to sit out, and what their medical excuses would be. "Maybe I have PMS," Todd joked.

"You've already used that excuse to me before," she quipped back.

Dreams die hard, particularly if they have been the object of hours, months, and years of fielding thousands and thousands of ground balls, or of hitting a baseball with bleeding hands, or of sacrificing any other activity that might interfere with that dream. In his essay for graduate school expressing his Statement of Purpose, Todd described his newfound objectives of obtaining an MBA, applying it in the world of finance (having already spent six months as a financial analyst intern for Citizens Bank in Providence), and eventually becoming the president of a major league baseball organization, thus combining his expertise in two worlds. He was subconsciously trading one dream for another. Yet he held onto the graduate school application for at least a month before submitting it. The deadline for matricula-tion in the fall semester was July 1st. "I really think that he's planning to work out again during the off season, hoping he's going back to baseball," Trish told us confidentially. "But he told me privately that the last time he truly enjoyed himself on the field was during the 'AA' All-Star game in Trenton."

Charley and I had other concerns on our minds. My mother began therapy for her herniated disks, which she had re-injured during a fall in the bathroom three weeks prior. During therapy, she could hardly walk and needed round-the-clock painkillers. As it turned out, an MRI revealed four herniated disks and two com-pression fractures. Charley's mother in Massachusetts was coping with her con-stant health problems after three strokes. A health aide and a nurse visited daily. What she couldn't cope with was Charley's father's increasing irascibility, a symp-tom of what she called a "cloud on the brain" in his MRI. At home, she found a new focus by tuning into the PawSox games on the radio every evening. At 7:45 a.m. every morning, we would receive a phone call in Florida giving us the result of the previous night's game, along with an update on Todd's play. This was fol-lowed around 9 a.m. by a fax from Butler Hospital, where Charley was chairman of the board of trustees. The fax relayed that morning's Providence Journal article on the game and the box score and division standings.

The major leaguers returned from their opening road trip with a record around .500, then went on to win nine games in a row during their opening home stand at Fenway. Nomar Garciaparra hit safely in over thirteen games, and on April 14, 1998, collected five RBI's in one game. Mo Vaughn, on one occasion at Fenway, hit a grand slam to win the game. The fans would not tolerate any talk of Mo's leaving Boston.

On April 23, playing first base, Todd hit a single at McCoy Stadium in the ninth inning against Rochester for his first hit of the season. He also walked and made a spectacular defensive play, which Charley was able to witness while he was home for board meetings. With runners at second and third and one out in the fourth inning for Rochester, Todd made a leaping grab toward the first baseline to rob Howie Clark of a hit. In addition, he stole a base during the 7-6 loss. At the end of the night, he was batting .187, with no RBI's.

In addition to loss of players due to injuries, the PawSox lost Lou Merloni to the major league team on May 8th. The day before, All-Star shortstop Nomar Garciaparra went down with a minor shoulder separation in Kansas City. Lou joined the team there. After the PawSox home stand, Lou led the International League with a .386 batting average. His slugging percentage of .716 was good for fourth overall, and his eight home runs were only two off the league lead. He had had twenty-two RBI's by May 8th. In his first game at Fenway Park, filling in for the injured Valentin at third base, Lou had a perfect night at bat; he hit a homer his first time up, and collected a double and a walk. We could imagine the busloads of Merlonis from Framingham, Mass., who had filled Fenway on that Friday night for Lou's home debut.

Of course, with two infielders out of the PawSox lineup, Todd played at short or first base regularly, even after infielder Bill Ashley came off the Disabled List. By May 10, Todd had hit three homers, was batting ninth, and his average stood at .200. The PawSox had slipped to third in their division, with a record of 14-14. By May 20, they would be second from the bottom, with a record of 16-21, although Todd's average rose to around .220. More and more young pitchers (average age 22 years) were promoted from Trenton: Peter Munro, Brian Barkley, Juan Pena, Jim Farrell.

One of the bright spots on the roster was Trot Nixon. Although his average was .259 by May 7th, he had begun the season batting .302 during the month of April, with six RBI's. During the previous season of '97, Trot had struggled with a .123 average during the month of April. In addition, Walt McKeel, catcher, had shed at least twenty-five pounds because of the strain on his back, and was batting .305; Arquimedez Pozo, DH, was batting .297.

Playing in Buffalo, Todd went to dinner after the game with Tim's ex-Lynchburg roommate, Bill Selby. The "AAA" Cleveland team had purchased Bill when he returned from playing in Japan. Bill had always had trouble fielding ground balls when he'd played the infield, and still lacked a position on the diamond. He remained a DH. Against Indianapolis, Todd reacquainted himself with hard-hitting first baseman Mark Johnson. Mark was the Senior Captain of the Dartmouth team when Tim was a sophomore, and had been part of a trade from Pittsburgh's major league team to Cincinnati's "AAA" team.

On May 21, 1998, the major league Sox invited Trot Nixon to take batting practice in Fenway, since center-fielder Buford was complaining of an injury. That night, Trot was sent back to Pawtucket to play. He cleaned his apartment in anticipation of his wife's arrival for the long Memorial Day weekend. The next day, he was recalled to Boston when Buford was put on the DL. Such is the life of a minor leaguer, up and down like a yoyo.

As we prepared for our drive north for the summer, Todd's average rose to .230, and we began to hope that he might have a future left in baseball. I even went so far as to begin collecting pennies again on sidewalks and streets for good luck. Of course, they had to be face up to count, as Trish had taught me.

Pawtucket had promoted Lou Merloni, Trot Nixon and Keith Johns to Fenway Park. Don Sadler went back to Florida to rehabilitate his hand, and both Mike Coleman and Walt McKeel were on the DL. At least Todd would get a lot of playing time. Charley had a balanced view of events: Todd is playing right where he should be.

We stopped at Sea Island, Georgia, for the first two nights on our drive north to Massachusetts and managed to forget baseball, pampering recent aggravations of plantar fasceitis (torn ligament under Charley's foot), and a calcium deposit on my shoulder that burgeoned forth like an ugly little fungoid from demanding exercise routines in Florida. In order to "Get a life!" we were returning to the Cloister Hotel, where we had spent our honeymoon almost thirty-three years before. This time we stayed in one of the beautiful new buildings on the beach, complete with spa, beach club, Jacuzzi, two pools, cabanas, and restaurants. The original golf course and tennis courts remained, but a new convention center and post office building had been added. The monks' cloister, where we dined at night, retained its genteel southern formality. A second dining room the size of the first had been opened, along with a disco/ballroom for after-hours dancing or lessons - a concession to the times.

We found our group photo labeled "1965" among the honeymooners' albums resting behind glass inside the hotel lobby's secretary. "We certainly looked beefy!" was Charley's comment. The exorbitant cost of a beachfront room in 1998 included three four-course meals per day (two of which were buffets). Naturally, we took full advantage! I doubted that the differential in our girths between 1965 and 1998 would be consequential after we left, even without the birth control pills which I'd used as an excuse for my added weight in the '60s.

Our next stop driving north was Norfolk, Virginia, where Todd's Pawtucket team was playing. With lefty Pulsipher pitching for the Mets' Norfolk Tides, both Todd and Andy Abad (lefty batters) were out of the lineup. I never understood why the manager took Todd out against lefty pitchers. Contrary to established baseball lore, Todd seemed to see the ball out of the pitcher's hand just as easily if he were a lefty. When Pulsipher was relieved by a righthander in the seventh, Todd and Andy still didn't go in to play shortstop, first base, or the outfield (where youngsters from Trenton were planted as if a meteor spray had deposited new stars).

However, with one out in the ninth and our catcher B. J. Waszgis on second base, Todd and Andy were summoned to don batting helmets. On the second ball pitched to him, Todd hit a two-run homer over the right field fence. Andy then grounded out, and two batters later, the game was over in a 5-3 loss.

Wearing a new Brown baseball shirt after the game, Todd appeared relaxed and happy. He had asked Ben Mondor, owner of the Pawtucket team, to supply a recommendation for graduate school at Bryant University. He had also asked the President of Citizens Bank of New Hampshire, who had hired him in Rhode Island as an intern. With a day off for the team following the game, Todd, Andy Abad, and the Pawtucket trainer planned to go on a deep-sea fishing expedition out of Norfolk. Andy was a Florida resident, and he and his dad made frequent trips on their boat to the Bahamas.

Charley and I stopped next in Baltimore - a totally revitalized city we had somehow missed in our previous travels. The seaport area had been historically renovated so that literally millions of people roamed the streets day and night. It reminded us a lot of Boston's historic Faneuil Hall Marketplace. One had the sense of a pulsating, thriving harbor with its new Science Museum, Convention Center, Aquarium, and World Trade Center set against historical Little Italy and Fort McHenry. The city struck me as being one of sharp angles everywhere - in its new structures and its sculptures - as if pushing toward the millennium, saying, "Look at me!"

The setting of Camden Yards against the old Baltimore and Ohio brick warehouse (the longest continuous building east of the Mississippi) blended history seamlessly with modern convenience. On a 75-minute tour we roamed the state-of-the-art press boxes; the $11 million electronic room that controlled the music, scoreboards, and TV spots; the club level, where companies leased box seats and lounges, complete with a travel agent. We walked on the lower level to the dugouts beneath miles of pipes that carried, among other things, beer to all the concessions. We were told of the research demanded to bring the history of previous downtown ball parks (Wrigley Field, Fenway, Memorial Stadium) into the design of Camden Yards. The only places we could not venture were the locker rooms or the turf of the field. Upon returning to our hotel room, we had a message light blinking. Todd's voice said, "Call me in Norfolk. I have some interesting news," and he left the Doubletree Hotel number where the PawSox were staying. We knew he'd been out deep-sea fishing all day, and surmised there had been a trade.

We were right! "I got traded to the Norfolk Mets today!" he told us. "Schaefer called and told me. He said he thought it would be a great opportunity for me, because their 'AAA' team is light on infielders, and their major league second baseman and first baseman have been around for a while. I had to get right to the field and change because the 'AAA' team was playing their major league team tonight. I played third base."

"What great news! Wonderful!" Charley and I both shouted at once into the hotel phone. "You'll certainly get a lot of playing time," Charley continued in his best fatherly voice. "Just don't try too hard to impress them. They already know what you can do. Have you seen Ken Macha?"

"No, not yet. I have to switch hotels because the next two nights I still have to play against Pawtucket, and it's pretty awkward."

"I bet your Pawtucket teammates are really ragging on you!" I commented, grabbing the phone for a minute.

"Yeah, they are. Now I might need you to get into my apartment in Pawtucket for my clothes, so you can ship them down here. And you'll have to store my furniture and return the pieces I borrowed from the Laffeys. Also, would you mind checking on my Jimmy to make sure it is still locked up inside the Stadium? I'll leave it there until I figure out how to get it down here." At least I was good for something, even if it wasn't baseball advice!

"Of course not. You make a list of what you want us to do, and over the next couple of weeks we'll get it done. You might want to rent a car in the meantime."

"Maybe. But I really don't want to pay another month's rent on the apartment in Pawtucket." Todd still watched his pennies!

"Okay. We'll get in this week. Just make arrangements with the landlord, since we have no keys. Have you called Tim?"

"Not yet. Just Trish. I'm excited, and so is she."

I had gotten my wish not to spend the summer of '98 at McCoy Stadium again! Todd had been traded for "AAA" Mets' outfielder Dwight Maness, who was immediately activated for play on the Red Sox "AA" Trenton team. Over the next days, we stayed in touch with Trish and dropped in at her family's home in New Jersey on the ride north. "I told him he's like an adopted child," she reported. "They want him, they chose him, and he doesn't have to prove anything to them. It's a great opportunity! When my job with the Ivy League ends at the beginning of July, I can spend some time in Norfolk while I'm interviewing for a new position. I'm familiar with Virginia Beach."

Trish called Tim while we called the grandparents. We were thankful Todd wasn't heading to some west coast team. If he some day made the majors, we could easily get to Shea Stadium. With spring training for the Mets in Port St. Lucie on the east coast of Florida (about ninety minutes from our condo), I wondered if I would have less of a life next spring than I'd had while traveling to

Ft. Myers to watch the Red Sox. The choice would be mine.

The next two weeks were a blur, trying to open the Westport house for the season, get Todd's belongings distributed, visit Charley's mother (re-hospitalized), attend a Colby reunion in Maine, and a wedding back in Florida.

The first nights in Westport we were able to listen on the PawSox radio network to their games against the Tides, still in Norfolk. Todd debuted in a regular season game as a Tide on May 30, 1998, with two hits against Pawtucket. He started at third base.

Trish's father, Ira, was a more devoted fan that we could ever be! He supplied us with faxes every morning in Westport. He would look up the articles from the Norfolk paper on the Internet, then fax them the next morning. We still had no Internet capability on our old computer (purchased in '89 while Todd was at Brown). Any information Charley and I needed we usually retrieved from libraries or book stores. Ira supplied us with over thirty pages from Sporting News, CBS Sportsline, CNN, and Norfolk Tides' websites, describing every Mets player that had been on their spring roster, top prospects, and major trades the Mets had made. We didn't request any of this information, but nevertheless, devoured it!

Todd left Pawtucket with a .205 batting average in twenty-eight games. He'd had four homers, ten RBI's, two errors, thirteen strikeouts, a slugging percentage of almost .400, and an on-base percentage of .247.

Bob Dick reported the trade in the Providence Journal. The PawSox were his regular beat, but Dick had not always been kind to the players:

It came as no surprise that the Red Sox finally jettisoned utility infielder Todd Carey and sent him to Norfolk Thursday for outfielder Dwight Maness, who was sent to Trenton. The real surprise is that it took this long to do so. Carey struggled almost from the first day he arrived at the Triple-A level last year. In 113 games, the left-handed hitter batted .216 with 12 homers and 58 RBI's. This year the Cumberland native was off to a slow start, batting .205 with four homers and 10 RBI's in 28 games. 'He couldn't correct his swing. It was too big and he struck out a lot and hit fly balls,' PawSox Manager Ken Macha said of Carey.[58]

Within a few days of our arrival in Westport, we called the Pawtucket stadium to arrange to pick up Todd's car. The players all left their cars locked under the stadium when they went on a road trip, and the team was still away. Ben Mondor, the Pawtucket owner, invited us into his office, along with President Mike Tamburro.

"We want to thank you for everything you did for Todd and for us while we were here," I began. "You made our stay extremely comfortable."

"Well, we want to thank Todd for all his P.R. work in the schools and at clinics, and especially for getting us the team batboys from Cumberland," Mondor responded. "We hope he's pleased with the trade, because it's a real opportunity for him."

"We're all excited about it, and especially the way he's started out! He's played third base every night since it happened, and has had five hits in thirteen at-bats," Charley responded, taking a seat across from Mondor's desk.

"That's great! We've been keeping track of him. The Mets called here every night for a week asking to acquire him before it took place," Mondor responded. "You know, we've never seen a local kid do well here," he told us. "There's too much pressure on him. Look at Ken Ryan."

"Well, we're certainly indebted to Bob Schaefer," I told the two men, "and to you." We believed Schaefer had had Todd's best interests at heart, and Todd thanked him in writing at the end of July, when management demoted Schaefer within the Boston organization.

We stacked all Todd's belongings into our car and into his Jimmy, and our friends, the Laffeys, met us at his Pawtucket apartment to pick up their pieces of furniture. Their son, Derek, had lived in our Cumberland house with Tim and Todd at various times while we were in Westport or Florida. Derek had moved to Mexico as a technical engineer for Teknor-Apex. In addition, Todd had worked for the Laffeys during high school at their deli.

Posted on the refrigerator of Todd's apartment we found the 1998 PawSox team rules:

Fines

Curfew - Three hours after game or 1 a.m., whichever is later $250

Insubordination - Fighting, etc. $200

Tobacco Rule - No chewing! Pay my fine also.

Lateness -
    Stretching $ 25
    Infield Practice $ 25

Lateness - Bus $ 25

Plus you pay for your transportation to the next city!

Dress Code - Flights: Coat, dress shirt, slacks. No tennis shoes - $ 25

On road: No shorts

Batting Practice & Infield: Numbered practice tops

General: Neat facial hair: No beards or goatees

In general, we are professionals. We expect conduct to be according. Play hard, have fun, and advance your career. Other unprofessional behavior to be fined at discretion of the manager!

On Todd's answering machine was a message from Batting Coach Gallagher in Trenton. It had been recorded before the trade, but Charley passed it on to Todd anyway:

1. At bat, think middle but react inside. (If a pitch is outside or up the middle, hit up the middle or to left.) If a pitch happens to be inside, react to it as opposed to looking for a ball over the plate.
2. Be good with the eyes - go up the middle. (Keep your head on the ball. Use the middle of the field as opposed to trying to pull it.)
3. Whenever you go backward, use the middle of the field. (Whenever you feel you are leaning back on your heels, hit ball up the middle.)
4. Concentrate and lock in. (Compose yourself, don't get distracted by the pitcher or anyone else.)
5. Get in a position (with PawSox) to get called up. (Play well so that if there's a vacancy in Fenway, you'll be called up.)

By June 3, 1998, the Norfolk Tides were 27-24, having won seven of their previous eight games. Todd was second or third in the batting order. Like a phoenix risen from the ashes, he was transformed. On June 2nd he had a three-hit night, bringing his average with the Tides to .444. His combined average (PawSox and Tides together) was almost .250. Confidence was everything, in this game or any other. The Norfolk General Manager treated the team to steak dinners at the restaurant he owned in Norfolk, *Grate Steak.* There, the players chose their own cuts of beef from the meat locker, then cooked on a grill in front of them.

Our transformation was almost as complete. Charley had bought Mets' hats and Todd bought all the men in the family Tides' shirts. After the PawSox games ended each night, Charley would tune into their radio network for the International League scores. However, he couldn't force himself to disconnect from the TV when Red Sox games were on.

After we attended Charley's Colby reunion in early June, classmates of his who'd attended the reunion and lived in Rochester went to Todd's games against their hometown Red Wings there. Todd went 2-for-8 with a homer in the first two games, then had a 3-hit night, including a bunt single, behind the Tides' pitcher, Mark Mimbs.

The last day in Rochester, by prior arrangement, Todd met with all of the fourth and fifth graders in the gym of the elementary school where Charley's Colby classmate, Sue Pineo, was employed. She faxed us afterwards to say that there had been about 125 children sitting together on the floor at Todd's feet as he spoke about the importance of cooperating with classmates, communicating with one another, and the discipline required in school and in sports. After he answered lots of questions, he had the children come up and showed them good fielding form, batting stances and swings, and pitching grips. Last but not least, he pitched soft indoor baseball and everyone got a chance with a soft bat before he signed about 100 autographs.

The following morning the team tried to fly back to Norfolk, but instead sat on the runway in Rochester due to horrific weather in Philadelphia, where they were connecting. After waiting out the storm inside the Rochester airport, they eventually arrived in Norfolk at 4 p.m. for the 7 p.m. game. Todd picked up a rental car at the airport so he wouldn't have to walk from his hotel to the park or get rides from his teammates. He intended to move into an apartment at the beginning of July, when Trish joined him. Her contract with the Ivy League Group in Princeton expired on July 1st, and she began interviewing for a permanent position on an athletic staff at colleges and universities on the east coast.

The following week was disastrous for Todd in the field. In twenty-eight games with Pawtucket, he'd had only two errors. In one game on June 16, 1998, he committed two errors, which festered and eroded his confidence until he had a total of eight by week's end! "There's a huge dip in front of my playing area," he told Charley. "Everyone who's come in here to play third has had a problem."

My reaction was from a mother's perspective: "Can't the grounds crew fix it for their own team's sake?" Todd's defense had always been the strength of his game.

The Tides came into Pawtucket for the last time in '98 over Fathers' Day weekend, the third week of June. "He was really nervous about it," Trish told us, "and said he hoped he never had to play in Pawtucket again." As it turned out, Todd performed flawlessly at third base and collected three hits during the series. The two teams split at two apiece. It was a chance for everyone local to say goodbye to him, from friends to former coaches to relatives to neighbors. So many people attended the series with us that on just one night Todd had to leave twenty names on the pass-list for tickets.

He stayed with us in Westport during the four games, jogging along the beach, eating at some favorite spots, and packing all of his belongings into his car. He had lived out of one duffel bag since he was traded on the road trip May 28th. The PawSox bus driver from Cumberland volunteered to help Todd in any way he could, so Todd paid him to drive his car to Trish's house in New Jersey. She would then bring it to Norfolk when she joined him the 1st of July.

On June 22nd, Bob Dick of the Providence Journal followed up his previous article at the time of Todd's trade:

The only problem Todd Carey says he's had since being traded by the Red Sox organization to the Norfolk Tides last month is his defense. Carey has been asked by Tides manager Rick Dempsey to play a lot of third base. 'And I have booted a number of balls (10 errors, total season) because I haven't really played there in the past year and a half.' Otherwise, Carey, in the middle of a homecoming series against his former Pawtucket teammates, has been doing just fine with his bat, he says, because he's getting a chance to play every day. 'I've been in there pretty much hitting in the two slot every game and I know if I go 0-for-4, I won't sit for a while,' the Cumberland native and Brown University grad said...At the time he was dealt away, Carey was struggling with a .205 average in 28 games for the PawSox. But, in his first 21 games for the Tides, Carey has done much better and was hitting .299 with 3 home runs and 11 RBI's...'I'm not bitter at Boston for the trade. They did a lot for me in six seasons, especially Bob Schaefer (Boston's Director of Player Development) who believed in me when, at times, I didn't believe in myself,' Carey said. In 113 games last year for Pawtucket, Carey batted only .216 with 12 homers and 58 RBI's.[59]

Around the third week of June, Tim's old Lynchburg roommate, Bill Selby, went from the "AAA" Buffalo affiliate of Cleveland to their "AA" Aeros. Bill had played 40 games with the Boston Red Sox before the Yokohama Bay Stars in the Japanese League bought him. "It was a great experience for me and my family and it was what the Lord wanted us to do. I'm grateful for the opportunity," Bill was quoted as saying. In Buffalo, he'd hit .266 as a utility player.

All-Star ballots were due around this time for the "AAA" game, to be broadcast on July 8th from Norfolk (ESPN2). Without pitcher Mark Mimbs, sold from Norfolk to a Japanese team, the Norfolk team could not find a representative for the All-Stars. Steve Decker, batting .364 for the Tides, had joined the team around the same time as Todd, and therefore wasn't a serious candidate. Ruben Sierra had joined the team the third week of June and therefore was also ineligible.Every team in the league gets at least one at-large representative to the All-Star game, if no team member is voted in by the media. Thus, Benny Agbayani became the Tides' representative. Benny had planned to get married to his sweetheart from Hawaii over the break, so he declined the invitation. He'd promised Neila that they'd be married as soon as he made it to the major leagues, and Benny had gotten that call for a brief stay at the end of the first week in June. Tides' President Ken Young stepped in and offered to cover the cost of the wedding if Benny participated in the All-Star game. Only one catch: the wedding would have to take place at home plate. So, on July 8, 1998, before a national television audience, the ceremony was performed, complete with Hawaiian shirts, leis of real flowers, and a receiving line of bat-toting ball players.

Ken Macha of Pawtucket was chosen as a coach of the International League All-Stars, while Dave Miley of Indianapolis managed. Pawtucket's representative, Trot Nixon, hit a triple to lead the International League to an 8-4 win over the Pacific Coast League. Joel Bennett, Rochester's 10-0 starter, got the win. Joel was the pitcher who had requested Tim as his catcher every time Bennett pitched for the Lynchburg Red Sox team.

Meanwhile, back in Boston, Nomar Garciaparra continued hitting in a 24-game streak, and Sox management awaited word on their number one draft pick in June, Adam Everett. Adam was another shortstop and had been offered over $1 million, but had not yet signed on the dotted line. Mo Vaughn rested his pulled hamstring instead of participating in the All-Star game, then rejected the Sox four-year, $36 million offer.

"The management is trying to make Mo look bad," Tim surmised from California, where he was working for SONY during the summer. "They've fed the press a lot of negative releases since the drunken driving incident, and now they want him to look greedy. There's bad blood between Mo and Duquette, but in reality, Nomar got offered incentives for more of a total package than Mo, and Mo's value to inner-city Boston is invaluable."

"Yeah, he was just in Providence running a kids' clinic," Charley agreed.

In the Mets' organization, players moved up and down more frequently than in the Red Sox. The major league Mets were in a race for the wild card, like the Sox. Jeff Tam went up as a right-handed reliever from Norfolk to Shea on June 27th, after refining his split-fingered fast ball over the winter and going 2-2 with five saves in '98. Todd Hundley and Matt Franco rehabbed in Norfolk before being recalled. Catcher Todd Pratt also went up, down, and up again, while catcher Rick Wilkins joined the Tides June 4, after being designated for assignment. Reuben Sierra quit the Norfolk team while we visited around July 17, 1998, then rejoined by the end of the month. Of Baseball America's top ten minor league Mets' prospects named in January, '98, only one was an active starter on the Norfolk roster by the end of July: right-handed starter Octavio Dotel.[60]

On July 27, 1998, Todd's ally in the Red Sox system, Player Development Director Bob Schaefer, was reported to have been removed from his post. Speculation was that Buddy Bailey would move into Schaefer's post, and Kent Qualls into Ed Kenney, Jr.'s, post as Director of Minor League Operations. Kenney was rumored to have resigned and Steve August, Director of Major League Administration, likewise.

'He (Duquette) didn't say why (the change was made),' Schaefer said from his home yesterday. 'He just said he had someone else he wanted for the job.'

Steven Krasner, Providence Journal writer, expressed his opinion:

The overriding feeling in the organization, though, seems to be one of fear, in which employees are concerned that if they offer a differing opinion to Duquette's, they'll be gone. If Schaefer, who received credit for helping to turn around Boston's farm system, could get summarily shunted to a lower level job, then they could, too.

If Kenney, a third generation Red Sox baseball man, could get yanked from his job, then whose job is safe?[61]

Charley, center, with Todd and Tim, Great Lakes League, 1991

27

Up and Down Again

My birthday was coming up, and Todd and Trish wanted to give me their present in person. Charley and I decided to drive to Norfolk for an eight-game Tides' home stand around July 19, 1998. The drive down turned into one of the longest twelve-hour rides we could ever remember. There was the perennial construction through parts of Rhode Island and especially Connecticut, with increased congestion from traffic around the beach towns. We hit New York at rush hour, then New Jersey was a caravan of vacationers the entire length of the Turnpike. The Garden State Parkway was even worse. Virginia around D.C. was stop-and-go, with better than an hour's delay on Route 95. The Route 64 Bypass around Richmond to Hampton reduced to two lanes eastbound, due to construction.

We arrived at Harbor Park on a muggy, hot night and enjoyed a couple of beers overlooking the Elizabeth River. Todd was playing third base and was batting eighth with a combined average of .254 for the season. The Tides were coming off a five-game losing streak.

Todd looked healthy and relaxed as he took his place in the batter's box, and seemed as confident as we'd ever seen him at the plate and in the field. Trish's presence always worked wonders for him! Our long hours driving down seemed a distant memory. Todd banged a single into the opposite field, walked his next time up, and then was intentionally walked. "It's great to see how selective he has become at the plate," Charley remarked. The Tides pulled out a win over Syracuse with a two-run homer by Benny Agbayani in the eighth. The Tides remained alone in second place in the International League Southern Division.

Newlywed Agbayani had been optioned back to "AAA" from the Mets the day before. There was so much movement up and down off the Tides' roster that second baseman Ralph Milliard was the only starter who'd been on the roster at the end of spring training. Syracuse's Pat Kelly left the stadium in the second inning, fueling rumors that Boston had made a deal for him. That would not bode well for the second basemen in the top two tiers of the Boston organization, six in all: Frye (injured), Lemke (injured), Sadler, Merloni (injured), Pozo (leading the I.L. with a .348 average), Benjamin. As it turned out, St. Louis had outbid all the others for Kelly.

The following day it poured, so we visited Todd and Trish at their apartment in the Virginia Beach area of Runaway Bay. "We feel really safe here, and everyone gets along well," Trish said. "The guys all ride with each other and the women do things together when they're not working." We had met several of the wives at the game the night before, and eventually, some of their children. Steve Decker, first baseman/catcher, had moved into the second bedroom at Todd and Trish's apartment, while his wife and two children remained in Oregon. Although every other room in the apartment was completely furnished, the only furniture in his room was an air mattress. Tinfoil covered the windows to prevent him from waking up at 6 a.m. Steve had played in the majors for five years and was the proud owner of a Lexus! He thought it was a waste of money to furnish a rented bedroom.

During our shopping expedition that day, we read in the local paper that another player was expected on the Tides' roster, down from the major league team. "Todd automatically goes into the mentality he had in Pawtucket, worrying that he'll be dropped to make way for the new arrival," Trish confided in me. "I told him he'd better start believing that he's proved himself here, and that he'd be one of the last to be dropped. He's hoping that even though he'll become a free agent, the Mets will put him on the expanded forty-man roster and send him to winter ball for a couple of months."

Back at their apartment, Trish learned that she had a job offer awaiting her on the Athletic Department staff at Hofstra University, the first of several offers over the summer. "I need a good springboard," she said, "to lead eventually to an Assistant Athletic Directorship. But I have to be somewhere on the east coast." At the beginning of August she received an offer too good to pass up at Brown University, while Todd gained acceptance for his MBA at Bryant University in Rhode Island.

We walked the Virginia Beach cement boardwalk, then watched a miserable Tides' loss (7-3) to Louisville. Todd struck out twice with men on base, something we thought he'd reduced considerably by being more selective. He also grounded out twice to the first baseman. "They're jamming him and he's not getting his bat around fast enough," Charley said, exactly what Coach Gallagher had talked about in his phone message back in June. I hated baseball again!

The following morning in the paper, Manager Rick Dempsey was quoted:

'We were only five in back of Pawtucket last week, now we're eight' (Dempsey said). 'This is what happened to teams that aren't clicking, teams that lack chemistry. We need somebody to start hitting homers. We need to get guys in from third. I feel like this clubhouse hasn't had a leader in it since Todd Pratt was called up midseason last year. I know it's a rarity to find a guy like that, but we need to find one.' [62]

The next game was a win over Louisville, but Todd did not play. Apartment-mate Steve Decker played first base. Since Steve had had surgery on both knees, he rarely caught behind the plate. He iced both the knees at the apartment immediately after every game.

The highlight of the evening with Trish and her parents (visiting for the weekend) was watching the kids in attendance under the age of ten run the base paths after the game. One boy in a wheelchair captured our hearts as he struggled to keep up with those around him. His arms were shaking from the strain of spinning the wheels of the chair as fast as he could, but as he crossed home plate, his father grabbed him in a bear hug and the remaining crowd stood up and cheered.

The next night, after a wonderful birthday celebration that Todd and Trish orchestrated for me, Todd again did not take the field. In the stands, we tried to make sense of it, but our years of experience taught us that there was never any logic to what happened on the diamond. The over-thirty group was again out there in the 5-3 loss to Louisville. Todd pinch-hit for Sauerbeck, the pitcher, in the seventh inning and hit a sharp grounder near the second base bag, then went in to play third base. He made a great backhanded stop behind the bag to throw the batter out.

"Dempsey told me we needed to win and some guys were hot with the bats right now. But that doesn't explain why he didn't put Haney in the outfield. Then I could have played third. And he left our pitcher (Sauerbeck) in one too many innings going into the seventh with a 3-3 tie. So naturally they hit a two-run homer off him."

"Just keep your confidence level up. You hit the ball really well tonight and I want you to get in the same mental frame of mind that you had when you came here," were Charley's words of advice as we said goodbye. "Don't go into a tailspin at the end of the season. We hope you'll play tomorrow, even if a lefty pitches."

"I hit well in three games against lefties, but Dempsey said I might not play if one pitches tomorrow."

Charley said to me later, "I'm glad we're going home, since I couldn't stand to watch another game with him bouncing balls off the dugout steps while the others are playing." Todd did, indeed, play against the Louisville lefty, going 0-for-3 with a walk.

Tim had left on July 19, 1998, for nine days in Japan. He had been invited to participate in a third-degree black-belt exam in one particular form of karate, the first American to be included. He worked out with the instructor between five to eight hours a day prior to the test and passed easily.

Before we drove thirteen straight hours from Norfolk to Massachusetts, we had listened to a discussion between Todd and Trish regarding different types of agents for professional athletes. When she had been a graduate assistant at Florida State during her Master's program in Sports Management, she had dealt with many agents interested in Florida State athletes. She explained that some of the bigger agencies can perform numerous functions if the athlete needs it: negotiating, overseeing financial affairs, promoting and marketing.

"I don't trust anyone to do all that for me," Todd said. "I know that a big enough star wouldn't have to be promoted. And certainly I don't need financial advice." While Todd remained silent, the rest of us agreed that although Ken Fishkin hadn't yet received a dime as Todd's agent, Todd needed a change.

"I have an idea," Charley broached to Todd, Trish, and her parents. "Since I'm retired and had twenty-three years experience in the world of finance, and since you had two years experience dealing with agents, Trish, why don't we team up and become Todd's agent? We could certainly do as much as Fishkin has. The only thing we'd have to farm out is the marketing and promotion when he makes it big."

"Sounds good to me!" Trish heartily agreed.

Todd called his agent, Ken Fishkin, and dictated the name of teams he wanted Fishkin to contact for future contracts in the upcoming season. He also asked Ken to call Jim Duquette, Mets' Minor League Director in New York to get some details regarding the possibility of playing winter ball. By the end of July, he had received the course offerings for the '98 fall semester in the MBA program at Bryant University, Smithfield, Rhode Island. The College required a tuition deposit by the end of August to register. On August 6, 1998, Trish accepted a job offer on the Athletic Department staff at Brown University.

Trish would become Assistant Director in charge of compliance for the athletes (grade point averages, drug testing, community service, etc.). On Todd's birthday, August 14, 1998, she moved into our house in Westport with us so she could commute to work. The Tides' last game would be in Richmond on September 8th. After that, Todd planned to join her in an apartment search in Providence. He would miss the first week of classes for his MBA.

Charley and I left to attend the wedding of a Colby friend's daughter in Vermont over the weekend of August 14-16. That Sunday morning, we departed the Londonderry (Vt.) Inn at 7 a.m. to drive 3-1/2 hours to Boston to catch a plane to make our last trip to Norfolk. We wanted to celebrate Todd's twenty-seventh birthday with him. The timing of our trip was unfortunate, since our nephew

Chris Herren was married during the week we were away. Chris had an important upcoming year in '99. He would not only become a parent, but would become a point guard at Fresno State instead of a shooting guard, in order to better hone his skills for the NBA draft.

My parents' health had improved. They flew up from Florida to join us at Ronald Reagan Airport in D.C., where Charley and I deplaned from Boston. We rented a car to drive another 3-1/2 hours to Norfolk in pouring rain. After a two-hour rain delay, the game against Columbus began at 8 p.m. By the time it was over, we were all exhausted.

Todd had not stepped onto the field in two nights, not even to pinch hit. Although he seemed frustrated with all of us in attendance, he put on a good front when he came out of the locker room. He gave my parents and Charley a hug and kiss, but neglected me during the chaotic interchange. I displayed my own sign of affection by planting a big kiss on him. Moms are taken for granted sometimes, even if we do make eight-hour trips to say, "Happy Birthday!"Since Mike Kinkade had been acquired by the Mets from "AAA" Milwaukee on July 31st, he was batting around .300 combined for the season. He had taken over at third base in Norfolk. Todd was used primarily as a pinch hitter, which meant that when there were two National League "AAA" teams (the Mets being one) playing each other, the pitchers batted, there were no DH's, and Todd saw no action. When a pitching change occurred, a pinch hitter batted. If one team was from the National League and the other wasn't, they used the D.H. rule, since American League pitchers had had no previous experience batting. So when Todd went in to pinch hit, it signaled there would be a pitching change. When he had finished batting for the pitcher, he retired from the rest of the game, as the new pitcher took the field. He was one of several positional players sitting on the bench when we arrived, but the only positional player who sat out as many as seven straight games without being in the starting lineup. At least in Pawtucket, all the infielders rotated onto the field to start. By the second night we were there, Robert Eenhoorn, the shortstop who also sat out with Todd, retired from baseball and went back to Holland to coach a team and manage a stadium.

The Mets' major league team was still in a run for the wild card spot in the playoffs. As a result, many of their players were on the Tides' roster, to keep them active until the teams expanded to forty in September. Benny Agbayani had returned to Norfolk from the major league team for the seventh or eighth time that season. The Tides were in second place in their division, ten games out. Todd Haney (in his early 30's) had replaced Eenhoorn at shortstop, while Todd's roommate, Steve Decker (age 32), rotated at first base with Pratt and Agbayani. Kinkade played every day at third base.

During the second game we saw against Indianapolis, Todd got in once to pinch hit for pitcher Wilson. He grounded out to the first base side, scoring a runner from third. When third baseman Kinkade was ejected from the game for arguing with the home plate umpire after his strikeout, Manager Dempsey had to put outfielder Rick Parker in to play third, since Todd had already pinch hit and been removed from the game. The Tides lost badly in the first two games we saw.

Their Harbor Park was a double-decker stadium that held 12,000. It reminded us of newly-constructed Waterfront Park in Trenton, but in Trenton the luxury boxes sat on the top level. In Norfolk, there was a covered grandstand above the boxes, along the first and third base lines. In left field beyond the fence there was a hillside for picnic groups. At the far end of the first base line, by the foul pole, an air-conditioned restaurant was perched behind a wall of glass where one could watch the game without the 95-degree temperatures and 90% humidity we experienced the first three nights there.

The Norfolk attendance was around 5,000 on each of the four nights we attended in August. The fans consisted mostly of families, and they were definitely there to be entertained. There were exceptions like ex-Orioles manager Davy Johnson, who sat in the seat directly behind us and was scouting for a Japanese team. Some of the biggest ovations during the game occurred when there were contests on the field between randomly selected fans at the end of the innings, or during the Rip Tide mascot's antics. We were always amazed at the efforts of the fans as they dived under seats or did somersaults in efforts to retrieve foul balls. If a fan caught a ball directly on the fly during the game, everyone within view gave him a standing ovation. In Pawtucket, the fans seemed more knowledgeable and much more engrossed in the game. The atmosphere there was tenser, especially for us parents.

My parents treated Todd's apartment-mate, Steve Decker, Todd, and us to lunch the afternoon of the third game we saw. Steve, originally from Illinois, held a $1,000/month mortgage on a home in Oregon where his wife remained during the season with their two daughters. Steve's hayseed freckles, strawberry blond crewcut, and "Big Sky" lingo belied his veteran savvy as a major leaguer. He was one of three Tides' players featured in the local paper in Norfolk the next morning with the headline, "This is no Way to get Rich." Steve, it explained, "signed a 'split' contract with Pittsburgh in the off-season that would have paid him $300,000 if he made the major league Pirates, and $60,000 at 'AAA.' When the Pirates released him, he signed with the Mets for comparable numbers."[63]

Another player featured in the article was shortstop Todd Haney. "The Tides have four six-year minor league free agents. They're players who signed with the Mets who had at least six years of professional experience, but were not on anyone's forty-man roster. They generally make from $25,000 to $40,000."[64]

Our Todd received his free-agency notice that day from the Mets, effective Oct.

15, 1998. His agent, Ken Fishkin, had contacted several other teams on Todd's behalf in preparation for his free agency. There is no mandated minimum salary at the minor league "AAA" level. The Mets paid a minimum of $2,100/month for six months to their "AAA" players, establishing their own budget and salary scales. Factors affecting salaries were free agency, inclusion on the forty-man-roster, and experience.

My Dad and Mom, ages eighty-six and eighty-two, were real troopers. They marched behind Charley and me to walk the one-third mile to the ball park from the Norfolk hotel every evening. Dad was hunched over with his bad knees (from a polio attack when my sister and I were youngsters) wrapped in foot-long elastic bandages, within which magnets were attached. The bandages emerged beneath the hem of his Bermuda shorts. He trailed at the end of the caravan, and we stopped often to check on him. My mom's four herniated disks and two compression fractures had had a remarkable recovery by means of pool therapy - daily walking against the resistance of the water in the clubhouse pool in Florida. She was able to keep up with us on our treks, but the glaucoma that had been in remission had reasserted itself with increased pressure on the cornea. Therefore, she couldn't distinguish depths of objects, and shadows presented perilous obstacles she never saw. Without our help, she would have stepped right off curbs or fallen upon steps that lay in front of her. Once she walked right into the side view mirror on a van.

The schedule was the killer for them. Todd's games began at 7:15 p.m., and often ended after 10 p.m. We all slept late each morning, and after meeting for breakfast, we would split up so Charley and I could power walk for an hour. Mom and Dad would just be finishing their last cup of coffee when we returned. Then they would set off for an abbreviated stroll. Afternoons we took water cruises of the Norfolk harbor, shopped, or went to the pool, and Todd sometimes met us for a late lunch between 1:30 or 2:00 p.m. He had to report to the field shortly after 3 p.m. for batting and infield practice, and a cold-cut buffet. On our final day in Norfolk (August 20th), the team had its last day off before Labor Day. Therefore, Todd could escort us for a bayside lunch and tour around Virginia Beach, occupying most of the afternoon. My parents relived their honeymoon there on what had been a deserted beach fifty-seven years before. At that time, World War II had begun and a German sub had sunk one of our ships offshore. The beach's golden sand was turned into a slimy carpet of black tar, forcing my parents to retreat to Skyline Drive, Virginia, for the rest of their honeymoon.

By 4 p.m., Mom and Dad had to lie down. At 6:30 we met again, allowing 45-minutes for our walk one-third mile to the ball park. After the games, we sometimes accompanied Todd to the mall behind our Sheraton for a light dinner wherever a kitchen remained open. By then, of course, we had snacked on the poison-

ous meats, French fries, fried dough, charcoaled pretzels, frozen yogurt, or peanuts at the ball park.

Following a visit to my sister's new home in Annandale, Virginia, Charley and I
flew back to Boston from D.C.'s Reagan Airport on August 21, 1998. Todd was
batting almost .280 for the Tides when we left, with a combined average of .257 for
the season. He had not been in the starting lineup in the last two games we saw. In
one game he went in at shortstop in the sixth inning and in the last game he was the
DH.

President Clinton announced an all-out war against terrorist Osama bin-Laden,
and the day before we flew north, our missiles had struck terrorist training camps
in Afghanistan and a chemical plant (supposedly producing chemical warfare) in
the Sudan. We couldn't wait to get out of the D.C. airport!

On August 31, 1998, Charley, Trish, and I watched a televised Red Sox game in
Westport, during which Lou Merloni broadcast the "color segment" of the game in
place of the ailing Jerry Remy. Lou gave insights into the strengths and weaknesses up and down the Sox lineup. He had just learned from a CT-scan performed
by Dr. Bertram Zarins that he was suffering from a stress fracture (crack) of the
left tibia, injured in late June. Team physician Arthur Pappas had diagnosed
Merloni's condition as a bone bruise.

On the last day of August, Norfolk Tides' pitcher Brian Maxcy was mugged in
Durham, North Carolina, after a Norfolk victory there that evening. He was
walking between the Bulls' Athletic Park and the hotel where the Tides were
staying when he was hit in the head with a steel beam ripped off a light pole. Brian
did not relinquish his wallet or his watch, but instead blocked a third swing, at
which time the assailant threw down his weapon and fled. Maxcy was stitched up
and released, while police arrested the assailant within 30 minutes of the attack.
Maxcy had pitched briefly in the major leagues in 1995 and 1996 and was assigned
to Norfolk when signed by the Mets in '98. Two days after the attack, Maxcy still
had not heard from either the Norfolk management or the Mets' management
regarding his recovery.

On September 3rd, Tides' third baseman Mike Kinkade was called up to the
expanded roster at Shea Stadium. As a result, Todd played regularly in the infield
for the last week of the season at "AAA." On September 1st, he went 3-for-5 with
a home run (9), double, and a single. His combined average was .256 for the season,
.275 since the trade. After the Tides' season ended, Todd Haney, batting .325 at
the top of the International League, was also called up to the Mets. He'd been
demonstrative in his disappointment at not being called up sooner, slamming his
batting helmet to the ground after each at-bat.

The Norfolk Tides had no hope of a playoff spot. Eventually, the boys' old
friends Bill Selby and Jeff Manto (Cleveland's Buffalo affiliate) battled against old

friend Mike Blais (Astros' New Orleans affiliate) in the "AAA" World Series in Las Vegas. The Astros won the title.

Todd In Norfolk Tides uniform, 1998.

28

Another World

The day after the Tides' season ended on September 8th, Todd came home to Westport to belatedly begin his graduate program at Bryant University. Trish was still living with us and had asked me to accompany her in the selection of an apartment for them in Providence. Tim flew home from California for a visit before his classes began in the final year of his MA program.

Shortly thereafter, Tim left for another survival course in the wilderness of New Jersey and Charley and I left for an eagerly-awaited three weeks in Prague, Budapest, Sicily, and Dorset, England. When we turned on the CCN broadcast in London to learn that Mark McGuire had broken Maris' record, we saw Boston MVP Nomar Garciaparra being hugged by his buddy, Lou Merloni. The Red Sox had just clinched a wild-card playoff spot, to be paired against the Cleveland Indians. On October 3rd, the Sox playoff dreams ended in Cleveland. Alone, Nomar stood on the field after the last home game in Fenway and clapped for the fans that had been so supportive all season. The Yankees took over and became American League Champions, then World Series Champions, sweeping the San Diego Padres in four straight games. The Yanks were dubbed the "greatest baseball team" ever assembled, with an accumulated record of 125 victories and 50 losses.

Todd had had no word from the Mets about playing winter ball, and was not free to talk to other teams until the Mets decided on October 15 whether to retain him or let him go.

On the last day of the regular season, September 27, '98, Mark McGuire slammed his seventieth homer. Unfortunately, McGuire hit the home run off Todd's former teammate in Pawtucket, Carl Pavano. Carl had been traded from Fenway Park in the deal for Pedro Martinez of Montreal and would go down in history as the starter called in to relieve, who gave up the record-breaking homer in St. Louis. A medical researcher in the stands, Phil Ozersky, caught the ball and was later the beneficiary of $2.7 million, paid by a comic book publisher for the ball. Yet it was Pavano who was hounded for autographs. Maintaining his composure and his quiet sense of humor, Carl joked in The New York Times, "I wish I could have gotten to the stands a little faster...If I could've gotten to that ball, it would have been a nice check."[65]

Sitting in the back seat of Anthony's car (a taxi we'd hired) as we left Palermo for the eastern Sicilian city of Taormina, I felt ignored while Charley chatted continually in Italian with Tony in the front seat. Although I was more fluent and often suggested the correct phrasing, my voice was not acknowledged until Charley had repeated the phrase to Tony. This reminded me of the place mothers had in the world of baseball – nowhere! I asked Charley if he wouldn't mind coming back as a Sicilian in his next life. Always the pragmatist, he answered, "With a 20% unemployment rate, I'd be lucky to be driving a cab!" I knew I relied on Charley's realistic approach to life, and so did Todd and Tim.

On October 14, 1998, Todd officially became a free agent. His team, the New York Mets, told his agent that they would be happy to have Todd back at "AAA" in Norfolk, but he would again be playing behind Mike Kinkade (third base) and Ralph Milliard (second base). They did not envision Todd as a shortstop. Fishkin personally talked to half the major league teams by week's end. Todd's objective was to get signed by a team with a small market and less expensive budget, without any mega-star contracts!

Immediately after the Yankees captured the World Series Championship on October 21st, 31-year-old Mo Vaughn declared his free agency in Boston - a severe blow for Boston fans and race relations in that city. No other active Boston athlete had done as much for charity within the city, including the establishment of his own "Mo Vaughn Youth Development Program" for after-school tutoring and life skills. After Vaughn turned down Duquette's final Boston offer, including a "character clause," he got a tattoo on his left forearm that read, "Still I Rise."

On October 24th, the Mets made catcher Mike Piazza baseball's richest player ever, with a seven-year contract for $91 million. Although his $13 million average yearly salary wouldn't compare to Michael Jordan's $33 million (Chicago Bulls), Piazza topped Pedro Martinez's annual $12.5 million (Boston Red Sox), Greg Maddux's $11.5 million (Atlanta Braves), Barry Bonds' $11.45 million (S.F. Giants), as well as Albert Belle's (Chicago White Sox) and Gary Sheffields's (L.A. Dodgers) $11 million, Eric Lindros' $8.5 million (Philadelphia Flyers), and Steve Young's $8.2 million (S.F. 49'ers). Mo Vaughn signed an $80 million contract in November, '98, to play first base and bat third for the California Angels. It was obvious to us that these baseball teams could afford their superstars only because they were paying their minor leaguers a mere $2100/month at the highest level. And the minor leaguers only got paid for the months they were on a roster! Off-season jobs for the minor leaguers had to pay well, unless the players were guaranteed spots in fall/winter ball.

We were happy to learn that Ken Macha had reached the major league level, this time as bench coach in Oakland. Boston had countered with its own offer, too late. The Norfolk Tides' manager, Rick Dempsey, became the third base coach with the major league L.A.Dodgers.

By the end of the second week of November, Todd and Trish had attended Dana LeVanie's wedding. Dana was the bullpen catcher in Fenway and had been Todd's roommate in Lynchburg. They had also heard from Steve Decker. Steve reported from the state of Oregon that he had signed with Anaheim immediately after the season had ended, but told Todd that it was more typical for free agents to get their deals solidified during the month of December.

The first week of December, '98, the Boston media announced that Terry Murray, CEO of Fleet Financial Group and Charley's former immediate boss, was interested in buying the Red Sox! We were glad Todd was out of that organization, so that there would be no possibility of our encountering Fleet management again. By then, Vaughn had signed with Anaheim; Randy Johnson had signed with Arizona; and Albert Belle had signed with the Orioles. All three salaries surpassed Piazza's annual salary. Then on December 12, the L.A. Dodgers gave Kevin Brown, pitcher, a seven-year $105-million contract, making Brown the game's highest paid player at $15 million per season. Todd's agent pushed hard in talking with the Dodgers, as Todd would be a cheap contract after the expense of signing Brown. In addition, Rick Dempsey, Todd's manager in Norfolk, would be an invaluable liaison in Los Angeles at the major league level. Other teams that seemed interested in Todd were the Oakland A's and the Pittsburgh Pirates.

Christmas '98 came and went in Massachusetts for the Carey family, with Tim visiting from his Master's Program in California, and my parents flying in from Florida, though delayed until 2:30 a.m. on the Philadelphia runway because of a blizzard. They were forced to spend the remainder of the night sitting in the Philadelphia Airport at ages 87 and 83! Todd and Trish stayed with us briefly while traveling back and forth to Providence.

Todd had himself begun calling directly to management within the Dodgers. With Christmas and New Year's immediately following management meetings, agent Ken Fishkin was unable to reach those making contract decisions. So Todd called the GM directly, and was told the Minor League Director was in the Dominican Republic (probably watching major leaguers in the winter league). Fishkin didn't pursue the man down there, and waited to be contacted, while Todd became more and more stressed. Todd called Dempsey, his former Norfolk Manager now in the Dodgers' system, who spoke on Todd's behalf. Nevertheless, it was January 14, '99, before the Dodgers firmed up a $7,500/month contract offer, and that didn't include an invitation to major league spring training in Vero Beach, Florida, nor inclusion on the 40-man major league roster. In contrast, Mo Vaughn would receive $82,000/game! Meanwhile, the Pirates had been trying to reach Fishkin regarding a contract for Todd, but Fishkin was unavailable! We were all supremely disappointed in the agent's performance. On January 13, the Pirates offered a contract without an invitation to major league spring training, but with a salary of $8,000/month. All things being equal, the Dodgers seemed to offer a better opportunity for an infielder, since the Pirates had signed so many. Todd's letter of intent was signed on January 14, 1999, but his actual contract with L.A. was signed in Fishkin's office in Boston on January 28, 1999.

The January 2-26, 1999, issue of USA Today Baseball Weekly featured six articles on the L.A.Dodgers, stressing Davey Johnson's leadership in establishing a new identity for his team. Although taking heat for the sport's spiraling salary scale after signing the first $100 million man (Kevin Brown), the Dodgers' GM Kevin Malone wasn't contrite: "To me, it's just sour grapes. Everyone is jealous of the Dodgers."

The new major league Dodgers "want to establish the attitude that we are no longer going to be the laid back, unaggressive team, as the Dodgers have been classified the last few years." said Malone.[66]

The '98 season had brought unprecedented change in an organization known as one of baseball's most stable. The club had been sold to Fox's Rupert Murdock, and a seven-player trade involved third baseman Todd Zeile and catcher Mike Piazza. GM Fred Claire and Manager Bill Russell were fired; the minor league system and scouting departments were restructured and shored up.

"Put all your hopes and aspirations for Todd's baseball career in your back pocket," Charley advised me. "Right now he's just living out the dream." I bit my lip!

On Thursday, February 18, 1999, major league pitchers and catchers reported to spring training camps in Florida. The remaining major leaguers reported three days later. As it turned out, four third basemen, four second basemen, and three short-stops were included on the L.A. forty-man roster. Todd was not.

It would be two weeks later, March 8th, before all minor leaguers not on the forty-man roster were expected in camp. Any earlier would result in expenses being paid by the ball player, with nowhere to stay. Todd was frustrated and anxious to report to Dodger camp in Vero Beach to prove himself. After he and Trish visited Tim in San Diego, Tim reported he had never seen Todd in such great shape, totally focused on one goal: achieving the major league roster this season. Todd anticipated a lot of up and down movement within the Dodger organization, and he seemed mentally ready to make a good first impression. There were 167 minor leaguers who reported to Dodgertown on March 8, 1999.

Meanwhile, the Dodgers signed Pete Rose, Jr., to the forty-man roster as a third baseman, thereby becoming a rival with Todd for the third baseman's job. The media made much of Pete Rose, Sr.'s, attending his son's training camp. Pete, Jr.'s, 1997 season two years prior had produced a batting average over .300 with almost 100 RBI's, and he was reported to have bulked up to 230 pounds in the years following, but had been released from Cincinnati in '98. Both father and son were quoted as saying they fully expected Pete, Jr., to make the major league roster in the '99 season. He had been able to participate in only one major league game while a member of the Cincinnati organization, and father Pete said he had been "used." Aren't all ball players used? In the first week of minor league inter squad games, Pete Jr. played the outfield while Todd played third base.

29

Last Stop: Dodgertown

The Vero Beach, Florida, spring training facility for the Dodgers was an institution in itself, a "baseball utopia" in its 52nd season in 1999. Founded in 1947 by Branch Rickey and Walter O'Malley, Dodgertown was first used for spring training the following year, and the team had not missed a season since.

...Military barracks — razed to make way for golf courses and tennis courts — once housed 750 players, along with managers, coaches, writers, and the O'Malley family....Stars and scrubs, legends, and no-names, coaches and players...'There was no real heat in those barracks,' (Vin) Scully (Dodgers' announcer in his 50th season in '99) says....'There was an actual chow line, and there might be a Class B player with his tray and right behind him would be Walter and Kay O'Malley.'[67]

The story is told that Mr. O'Malley would ride around in a golf cart and would stop to pick up a Class D pitcher who might have a number in the 400's on his back. Then another player would join the group on the cart and they'd go play eighteen holes. Whatever trees Mr. O'Malley's ball hid behind would be tied with a ribbon and those trees would disappear the next day![68]

With nowhere to go at night, the front entry of the barracks became the place to congregate for Pepper Martin, Roy Campanella, or Frankie Frisch. There, baseball stories would get swapped or infielder Chuck Connors (later star of "The Rifleman") would arm wrestle Branch Rickey, Jr. Walter Alston patrolled curfew, pounding on the door of Sandy Koufax and Larry Sherry's room until his World Series ring broke, when Koufax and Sherry were late rumbling in.

In a section known as "the string area" (which we did not see), Branch Rickey positioned strike zones made of string in front of home plate. This turned hopeful pitchers like Sandy Koufax into great ones by making them hit the corners.

Todd's 1999 Dodgertown was like a summer camp among the Australian and assorted pine trees. The unmarried players lived three to a spacious room in one-story brown stucco "dorms" which resembled long wings of a motel surrounded by bright impatiens. An office with "Dodgers" on its bright blue awning guarded the entrance to the circle of dorms from the main road. The dorms fanned out around three paved roads that formed a large elliptical circle, with a sentry posted at the south end to keep everyone, including parents, out. Two minor league fields were on the east side behind the dorms and another guard sat on the dirt road leading to the fields from the dorms. A large swimming pool and volleyball court were available to the players on the south end. Access to the minor league fields for spectators was behind a restaurant coming off Route 60 from the Interstate.

West of the dorm complex was the locker room facility, indoor batting cages, players' dining hall, and conference rooms (which also doubled as movie theaters). Todd raved about the quality of the three meals a day he received - no metal military cafeteria trays these days! Further west were additional minor league fields for the "AAA" players, the major league Holman Stadium, and the golf course.

Holman Stadium was an historical site, not only because it was the first stadium built specifically for spring training, but also because it was sunk down into the ground with trees and hillsides behind it, and no dugouts. Fans sat directly behind the open players' benches. Todd's neck was severely burned after he appeared in a major league exhibition game there. It was in this Stadium during Todd's "A" Ft. Lauderdale season that Charley and I had been chosen King and Queen for the game.

The players felt in Dodgertown either like grade-school campers within a campus, or like kings, grateful for the enclosed surroundings and activities. Players like Todd without a car, or those from foreign countries, were mostly grateful.

He arose every morning around 7 a.m. and by 10 a.m. filed out of the locker room for instruction, drills, or an away exhibition game. Kevin Brown walked among the players on the Dodgertown grounds along the same paths that Don Drysdale, Roy Campanella, and Jackie Robinson had walked. O'Malley's son had sold out to Rupert Murdock's Fox Group, which was complaining about property taxes on the 470-acre site 3,000 miles away from the Dodger's home base. And so the Ft. McDowell Indian community in Arizona had offered to put up a 12,000-capacity stadium in a $20-million complex for Dodgers' spring camp. Only trouble: there was a gambling casino on the property that took in $200 million a year and major league baseball did not want to be associated with gambling.

Two days after Todd had reported, he called to say he'd gone into the major league exhibition game to replace Eric Karros at first base. Because Karros decided to linger in the game, Todd didn't get in until the last inning, and never got an at-bat. But he was encouraged that the organization knew who he was after only two days. He had walked to the game with Mike Piazza, an opponent for the Mets.

"He's the biggest catcher I've ever seen!" Todd reported.

We drove up to see him several days later. His feet were sore because of blisters from his new cleats and he tiptoed gingerly. Of course, he was exhausted from the long days of instruction, drills, and batting practice, but he was on a high. There were movies every night for the players, and Todd had had a couple of conversations with Rick Dempsey, one during a movie in the conference room/theater. Dempsey had been Todd's Norfolk Mets' manager the previous summer and was the major league third base coach for L.A. in the spring of '99. Dempsey filled Todd in on the poor treatment he'd received from the Mets at the time of his dismissal.

"I don't like their training schedule down here," Todd told us. "We meet as a group - all the minor leaguers - for instruction, and stand and watch. Then we have to walk over to our field, behind the dorms. Then if there's indoor batting practice we have to walk all the way back to the indoor cages behind the major league field. I only had seven live pitches thrown for my batting practice before the guy said his arm hurt and I should go inside to the cages. We've been here almost a week and I've hardly seen any live pitching!"

Inter squad games started eight days into minor league camp, with Todd starting at third base for the first five innings of the "AAA" game before rotating out. "I felt really comfortable fielding, but I walked and grounded out at bat. I'll get my eye back soon." When "Grapefruit League" games started among the "AAA" teams, Todd was the starter at third base and by the third week of March, was usually rewarded with a hit per game, sometimes off the outfield fence, and sometimes off opposing major league pitchers who were rehabbing or sent down.

By March 24,1999, only a handful of players had been released, while eight infielders remained on the major league roster. There would be movement down onto "AAA" still, since minor league camp didn't break up until the day after Easter, April 5, 1999.

During our first visit to Dodgertown, Charley and I sat on bleachers watching Tommy Lasorda work on a minor league field with five unidentified players during batting practice. Not once during the 30 minutes we watched did Lasorda have anything negative to say to any of them. Instead, he yelled, "That's your zone!" or, "That's the way I want you to swing! You own that pitch and you know where it's going to go!"

On March 26, 1999, I picked Charley up at the West Palm Beach Airport upon his return from several days of meetings in Providence, and we proceeded directly to Vero Beach to see Todd and to join Trish and her dad, Ira, for the weekend.

Saturday, the 27th of March, the "AAA" team was playing at the shared St. Louis Cardinals' and Montreal Expos' facility in Jupiter. So we drove an hour south from Vero Beach along the highway to Jupiter, with Ira and Trish following us.

Although the facility was only two years old, it was a disaster for fans of minor leaguers, like us. The access road to Roger Dean Stadium led off Donald Ross Road from Route 95, amid miles of soon-to-be-developed sand dunes. Pipes lay over the dunes which would connect to a satellite campus for Florida Atlantic University and to a gigantic mall. Further down the access road near the Stadium, colonial-looking townhouses had been recently constructed.

Unfortunately, there were no road signs anywhere along the access road for parking for the minor league fields. We pulled up to the grass lots next to Roger Dean Stadium and asked directions. "Five dollars, please! You'll have to park here and walk clear around the stadium. There's no parking on that side." So Trish's father pulled his car in behind us and we both paid the fee. As it turned out, the major league Cardinals, with Mark McGwire in the lineup, were starting a game at the same time that their "AAA" team was playing against our "AAA" Dodgers. So we began out trek with coolers, newspapers, and lawn chairs clear around to the other side of the major league stadium. It literally took 30 minutes. We battled the throngs entering from the stadium side until we got to a paved pathway that led to the back of the minor league fields. The pathway ran out behind the first outfield fence, so we circled two outfields in the grass before coming to the "AAA" field.

Todd was DH'ing. "He's worried about making this roster," Trish confided in me. Like many others, he was an outsider trying to become part of the inner circle.

Otherwise, he seemed relaxed and extremely happy to be with Trish. He had two at-bats that day, grounding out to second by topping the ball, and hitting a hard shot up the middle. Unfortunately, the hit-and-run play was on, so what would ordinarily have been a single was handled by the shortstop, who was moving toward second when the runner left first. At least Todd had done his job by safely advancing the runner. In the last half of the game, another infielder replaced Todd.

The next morning Todd and Trish met us at 7:30 a.m. for breakfast before he reported to the field and she departed for Providence. After breakfast, as Charley and I walked two miles of entirely unpaved roads around a subdivision off 88th Avenue, I thought of all the roads we'd walked on baseball trips, and wondered if these would be our last.

The "AAA" Dodgers would play the "AA" Dodgers in an inter squad game in Dodgertown in the late morning. Todd did not take the field, but those who did talked with Tommy Lasorta and joked with "AAA" Manager Mike Scioscia. Those not in the game were sent for indoor batting practice, while a major league Dodger game proceeded on the other side of the complex. Todd reappeared halfway through the game, but was the second-to-last among the sixteen position players to be called into the "AAA" game. Every left-handed batter the lefty "AA" pitcher faced struck out.

We tried to avoid the reality of numbers and playing time in our conversation with him over dinner, but it was obviously uppermost in our thoughts with only a week of camp left. We made plans to watch his team play in Jupiter two days hence. "Don't be surprised if we get a call this week to come pick him up," Charley warned me privately.

"Well, if it's to end now, at least he's got a lot to look forward to. He can jump right into a summer semester for his MBA, and he will still get engaged no matter what!" I tried to be optimistic. Todd had asked us before we'd deposited him at Dodgertown whether we'd like to have Trish as part of our family, and of course we were ecstatic! It was three months shy of their three-year anniversary when he questioned us. No one could accuse Todd of rushing into anything! It had taken him six months to decide on a new car.

The day after we all returned to our respective homes, Trish called to say that Todd had reported several more cuts from the "AAA" Albuquerque roster that morning, including Pete Rose, Jr. "He told me tonight, more would be notified by phone if they're cut," she said, "and he told me to stay by the phone. I'm afraid to answer it!"

So were we. In fact, I took the receiver off the hook for an hour, to allow us to get some paperwork done. The final game of the NCAA basketball championship between Connecticut and Duke on TV diverted our attention. Nevertheless, each hour dragged by endlessly until around 11 p.m. when we knew Todd would no longer call us and we could safely assume he'd be making the trip the next day to play the "AAA" Dodger game in Jupiter.

"My stomach has hurt since I left Florida," Trish said. "I just wish we could fast-forward to the day after Easter when they break camp, so we'd know one way or the other. Todd wants another team to pick him up if he's cut, but rosters for all the teams will be set this week. Of course, Fishkin has no plans to place him anywhere else, in case he's cut. He claims it's unethical to talk to any other team while Todd's still under contract. We all know those contracts are meaningless, because management can dump the players any time, even with contracts." None of us could figure Ken Fishkin out. He and his family appeared to genuinely like Todd. Yet he had not gone out of his way to lay the groundwork to relocate him, either because he didn't believe in Todd's ability or because he was uninterested.

I thought about the people directly affected every spring by the ruthless employment tactics carried out by professional baseball's minor league systems: not only the players and their immediate families (there were many sons and daughters two and under on this team), but also girlfriends/fiancées and their families, grandparents, aunts and uncles, former coaches, and whole communities who had supported the players' rise through the levels of minor league ball.

We were on the road again the next day, back to Roger Dean Stadium in Jupiter.

And once again, Mark McGwire would be drawing huge crowds to the field at the same time as the "AAA" game on the back field. At that time, Todd's playing time was immaterial, as long as he was still on the roster.

We arrived in Jupiter one and one-half hours prior to game time, so that we could park in the minuscule area allocated for St. Louis minor league parking along the street, instead of in the major league lot for $5/car. We set up our lawn chairs and picnic lunch under a couple of palm trees behind the bleachers to watch Todd's Dodger team take infield practice. Todd spotted us and came over when they concluded. We munched on sandwiches and asked if he were playing that day. As it turned out, he had started at shortstop the day before and would be out of the lineup while we were there. Charley and I were on a visiting schedule for the off-days he wasn't playing. "Do you want to write the lineup?" he asked me. Of course, I did!

None of the Dodger players wore names on their backs. Todd went in for Wes Chamberlain as DH in the top of the eighth inning and struck out on three pitches. When he met us after the game, he asked us to bring all his belongings from our residence to the game the following day. I would be driving my parents up to Vero Beach to see him for the last time before the players broke camp. "There are twenty-nine still on the roster, and it has to get down to twenty-three. If anything happens, I'm going right to the plane to fly to Providence. I can contact Ken (Fishkin) from there."

"You've got to think positively!" I warned.

"This is one hell of a way to live!" I concluded later to Charley. "Every day for a week we've all been afraid of a phone call, and Todd isn't concentrating on the job he has to do."

"I'm trying to be positive," Trish told us over the phone, "but I'm really glad I've been busy at work and I'm not there!"

Tim explained, "When Todd and I were in camp the last week, we knew you were there to support us. But it was an extremely difficult position to be in, just in case anything happens. I think if Todd made the cuts so far, he'll be okay, but if that's not the case, it's embarrassing, especially with you there. He'll internalize everything. If he does make the 'AAA' roster, his talent had better start to kick in!"

With Charley conducting a condo association meeting, I drove my parents to Vero Beach to see the "AAA" Dodgers play the "AAA" Mets, Todd's Norfolk team of the previous summer. Norfolk third baseman Mike Kinkade (who'd re-placed Todd the previous August) was up with the major leaguers, but infielder Todd Haney, age 33, was in the lineup. He and his wife, Kira, were expecting a baby. Kira told me, "After the fantastic season my Todd had last year, the Mets told him he'd be the utility player on the major league team this year. Then they signed three other utility infielders."

Our Todd did not take the field. In the previous six days, he had been in the starting lineup only twice. Still, he put on a good face for my parents after the game ended, and we had a lot of laughs over dinner. We never mentioned baseball. Despite remaining in an extremely stressful profession, Todd had become a much more caring, thoughtful person. We had observed the change during the several years he'd been dating Trish, and we attributed it directly to her influence. Todd began to send cards <u>before</u> the actual anniversary, birth date, Mother's, or Father's Day. He began calling regularly as well, even with nothing specific to tell us. We became the beneficiaries of hugs when we arrived to see him, as well as when we departed.

My dad commented during dinner on the beautiful Dodgertown facilities. Todd responded that although there were amenities like a golf course, swimming pool, volleyball court, and movies, the playing fields were much too crowded together, and there was too much distance between fields and locker room/batting cages. And still there were too many players. With four days left in camp, the "AAA" team had sixteen positional players on the bench. There would be only twelve going to Albuquerque.

We lived by the phone the next forty-eight hours, carrying it with us when we went anywhere. Still no word as the team traveled to play the "AAA" Marlins in Melbourne. We recalled that the Red Sox had released Tim on almost the last day of camp.

The week dragged on endlessly until Friday at 5 p.m., when we received a call from the manager of an Elmira, N.Y., team in the Northern Independent League. He asked for Todd. When told that Todd was still at camp in Dodgertown, he expressed surprise, saying, "I read over the press wires that he was released two days ago!" Todd had been fired in the media, but not face to face.

Surmising that the end had occurred or was near, we called Trish. "What the hell is this about a press release?" Charley asked her.

"I got the same call last night," she said, "so I spoke to Todd this afternoon. The situation has become very complicated, and the Dodgers are using some disgusting tactics. They obviously sent out a press release two days ago saying he and Jason Thompson (first baseman) were released. But then Livingstone and some other major leaguer refused to accept assignment to the minor league Albuquerque team, so suddenly the 'AAA' team was short two players. At that point they couldn't withdraw the press statement."

"How did Todd take that?" I asked, concerned about my younger son.

"Todd didn't find out about it until Jason Thompson was moping around, and Todd asked him what was wrong. Jason told him that he'd heard his name and Todd's had been sent over the wires about being released. So Todd marched into the Player Development Office and demanded to know what was going on."

"I can only imagine the story they dreamed up," I interjected. I was doubled over like a pretzel in my chair, listening to this, with my hand over my eyes.

"The Dodger minor league administrator said there had been no press statement and that Todd was bound for Albuquerque on Monday unless the major leaguer Livingstone decided to go instead. Todd said every other position player on the 'AAA' team had been on the forty-man roster. And Fishkin refuses to approach other teams because Todd's still under contract to the Dodgers. Todd demanded that he call them, anyway. I think Todd's at the point where his pride will tell them to stick it if Livingstone decides to go to Albuquerque, and he won't put himself through this degradation any more. He should just go back to Bryant and finish his MBA. He's got so many options after that!" Trish was as frustrated as we were and had decided she didn't want the uncertainty of baseball life indefinitely.

"Not only does he have another life," I ventured, "but he will know he saw one dream through to the end. He accomplished what only a select few among hundreds of thousands have done!"

"Well, I'm going to hang out in the apartment this weekend, just in case," Trish concluded.

The next morning we got a call from Todd, but we missed it and played phone tag. At 6 p.m., Trish reached us. "Have you heard?" she asked.

"No, we've been leaving each other messages," I said.

"He was released at 4 p.m. today. There were several major leaguers that accepted assignment to Albuquerque, so Jason Thompson, Todd, and a couple of pitchers got their final notices. Let him tell you about it."

My first reaction was not disappointment for a dream that had died. I had anticipated this moment for weeks. I was a parent, and my concern was for Trish and Todd. "Are you okay?" I asked her.

"Yeah, I'm okay. I know he's very upset at the way it was handled, but he's going to first contact Fishkin and then come home. If nothing works out with another team, he can enroll in the May semester at Bryant."

I could see Charley grimacing as he slumped in his chair. Always the pragmatist, he responded, "We'll pick him up in Vero Beach as soon as we hear that the Dodgers have supplied him with a ticket to Providence. Right now, with Easter and spring breaks, Florida is packed with people, and flights will be pretty booked."

Todd filled us in immediately thereafter. "I had asked the Minor League Coordinator Schofield for today off, because with everything going on, I wanted to talk to Ken (Fishkin) today. There was a message light on my phone late this afternoon, and when I went back in, they said they were letting me go anyway, because several major leaguers decided to go to Albuquerque." Like a kid he asked, "Can you come pick me up tomorrow?"

Charley was the first to answer. "Of course we can. We're so sorry to hear the news, Todd! But you have given it your all, and sometimes life hands us unexpected turns that force us in a new direction. Like when I lost my job, or when Timmy was released." A family dream was over, killed, ended! But a parent has to rally for the sake of the child. I didn't care if Charley was speaking platitudes at that moment. At least he was saying something, until I could speak without my voice cracking. "You don't have to hang your head to anyone!" he concluded.

"Todd," I added, "I want you to remember something that Kate Sidwell told us when Dad lost his job at Fleet. Kate told us that when Steve (her husband and Defensive Coordinator of the New Orleans Saints) had been fired from his first pro football team, someone told her, 'You may not believe it at this moment, but you will survive! And you will be much stronger for the experience.' You have a bright future ahead of you, loaded with options."

"Yeah, but that doesn't make it any easier!" We knew he felt angry and humiliated and only wanted to get on the plane to see Trish. She would help him more than we ever could.

"Of course not! Give it time. Trish and your family will always be there for you."

We drove up the next morning to Dodgertown to pick him up. He was waiting in the bright sunshine at the curb in front of the housing office. All his belongings, including his gloves and bats, were jumbled in duffel bags piled on the curb. The most pathetic sight for a mother is to read failure in the sloping shoulders and downcast eyes of her child. His baseball cap was pulled down low over his eyes and his head never looked up. Without speaking, Charley and I jumped out and gave him a hug. Then he opened the back door, threw his gear on the floor, and climbed in. Todd kept his eyes closed all the way back to Delray to avoid conversation.

"I'm so proud of him!" Trish told us disjointedly on the phone after we'd arrived at our condo. "But he doesn't think I've told him that often enough since this happened, or it's just not sinking in right now. And he's not willing to give up the dream yet, until he talks to Fishkin. I don't want to have to go through this again, and I hope he goes back to school."

Within days Todd had received offers for assistant coaching positions in Rhode Island, including high school, college, and American Legion, all of which would conflict with his schedule of graduate classes. He chose to work in the Bryant University Career Services Office during the first summer semester, and received an assistantship in the fall of '99 for his full tuition. His contacts in the world of finance gave him entry to an internship with Lehman Brothers in New York City during the second summer of his graduate program.

And so, two months shy of seven years later, the saga ended. Ironically, Todd had been released from pro ball almost the same day as his brother, two days before the end of spring training. Neither had defied the odds to become the one player in one hundred who goes on to play at least one inning as a major leaguer. Neither, in a mother's humble opinion, had "swilled" or "chugged" during his career in minor league ball - derogatory terms for being really sucky performers. But then, didn't every mother think that even <u>her</u> baby beetle could turn into a gazelle, as the old Moorish proverb stated? After it was over, there followed many moments when I had a sinking feeling in the pit of my stomach, knowing there would be no more spring training camps to see a son of ours on that sparkling green background. I found myself unable to watch many of their former teammates, whose families had followed the same arduous road toward the major leagues with us, but who, instead, had seen their sons achieve their dreams. I could not shake my bitterness at the injustices that minor leaguers received across the board. But I had so many years of proud memories, happy friendships, and a wonderful new daughter-in-law we could attribute only to baseball! As Richard Bode eloquently stated in <u>First You Have to Row a Little Boat</u>, "How I get there is more important than whether I arrive, although I will arrive...."

A lot had changed, and a lot remained the same. Todd's structured lifestyle, discipline, and drive had shifted toward a new goal, providing enduring interests beyond it. In a follow-up article on him eleven months after he left baseball, <u>Providence Journal</u> reporter Steve Krasner shadowed him during a day in graduate school.

'I miss it (baseball),' admitted Carey.... 'I'm going to school full-time, and they're (the players getting ready for the pro season) working out....It's an adjustment, but I've had other things I've wanted to do. And I'm looking forward to other challenges in my life. [69]

The value any person may have in our lives, or any object, or any experience, is in the lessons we are taught which will remain a part of us. Life draws meaning from its journey, not its destinations. In <u>Under the Tuscan Sun</u>, Virginia Mayes draws upon writer Tim Parks' explanations of the ubiquitous statues of the Virgin throughout Italy as a reminder that all will go on as before, that we need not " 'imagine that what was happening to you here and now was unique and desperately important.'"[70] I knew that I would miss them all: the battlefields, the combatants, the pilgrimages, the excruciating moments, and the moments of glory. My acceptance of the abrupt ending of a family's dream came slowly. I gathered together the journals I had kept over the years, and with the writing of this manuscript, the catharsis began.

Tim in 2009 is working for the U.S. Government. He is married with one daughter. Todd in 2009 is a Vice President of J.P. Morgan in Boston, working as a private banker. He is married with two daughters.

Todd and Trish, Dodgertown, 1999

Footnotes

1 Pat Jordan, A False Spring (New York, 1975), p. 19-20.

2 Peter Golenbock, Fenway: An Unexpurgated History of the Boston Red Sox (New York, 1992), p. 436.

3 Bill Reynolds, Fall River Dreams (New York, 1994), p. 333.

4 Jim Lee, "Todd Carey Marking His Mark on Brown Baseball," The Providence Journal, (May 7, 1992), Sec. D, 1.

5 Bruce Chadwick, Baseball's Hometown Teams (New York, 1994), p. 31, 57, 63, 87, 84, 104, 117, 125-126, 133, 136, 143-144.

6 Wayne Price, "Dunn Deal for Baseball," Star Gazette, (September 1, 1992), Sec. A, 1.

7 Conversation among Clyde Smoll, Pam Carey, and Charley Carey at Dunn Field, Elmira, N.Y., August 1, 1992.

8 Jim Bouton, Ball Four Plus Ball Five (New York, 1985), p. 280.

9 Jordan, p. 86.

10 Rich Pedroli, "Local Ballplayers Getting Set to Pack Their Bags," Woonsocket (R.I.) Call, (February 17, 1993), Sports, 11.

11 Bouton, p. 128-129, 213.

12 Ibid., p. 76.

13 Richard Ford, "Stop Blaming Baseball," The New York Times Magazine Section, (April 4, 1993), 40.

14 Ibid., p. 42.

15 Donald Hall, Fathers Playing Catch with Sons (San Francisco, 1985), p. 40.

16 "Lynchburg Red Sox," Lynchburg News and Advance, (June 3, 1993), Sec. D, 5.

17 Hall, p. 128.

18 Gary Crockett, "Carey's Talents Go Beyond the Lines," Lynchburg Times, (June 29, 1993), Sec. B, 10, 1.

19 Scott Cole, "The Road to the Top Gets Bumpy for Carey," Woonsocket Call, (August 18, 1994), Sports, 15.

20 Scott Cole, "Tim Carey Tries Life in the 'Real World,'" Woonsocket Call, (August 18, 1994), Sports, 15.

21 "Red Sox," The Providence Journal, (September 16, 1994), Sec. B, 7.

22 "Minor-Leaguers Might Have Leverage for Once," The Palm Beach Post, (February 27, 1995), Sec. C, 1.

23 Judith Blahnik and Phillip S. Schulz, Mud Hens and Mavericks (New York, 1995), p. 1.

24 Kim Haban, "Sucker-punch Sparks Thunder Rumble," The Trentonian, (August 1, 1995), 3.

25 "Red Sox Recap," Ft. Myers News Press, (March 30, 1996), Sec. B, 5.

26 David Lamb, "A Season in the Minors," National Geographic, (April, 1991), 68-69.

27 Chris Edwards, "Carey's Bat Keys Sweep," The Trenton Times, (June 21, 1996), Sec. C, 1.

28 Chris Edwards, "Manto to Rehab with Thunder," The Trenton Times, (June 21, 1996), Sec. C, 3.

29 John Nalbone, "Pavano Rewarded with 'All-Star' Quality," The Trenton Times, (June 22, 1996), Sec. B, 3.

30 Nick Cafardo, "Success in the Stars?," Boston Sunday Globe, (June 30, 1996), 52.

31 Chris Edwards, "Attendance Marks Are Smashed at Waterfront," The Trenton Times, (July 9, 1996), Sec. C, 3.

32 Chris Edwards, "Carey Makes an All-Star Splash," The Trenton Times, (July 9, 1996), Sec. C, 3.

33 Glenn Jordan, "Dogs Lose Lead, Game to Thunder," Portland Press Herald, (July 17, 1996), Sec. D, 1.

34 Jed Weisberger, "This EL Team Proves '96 No Down Season," The Trenton Times, (August 18, 1996), Sec. C, 3.

35 Chris Edwards, "Woods Wants a Promotion," The Trenton Times, (September 5, 1996), Sec. B, 5.

36 John Nalbone, "Sadler's '96 Effort Leaves Some Things Wanting," The Trenton Times, (September 5, 1996), Sec. B, 5.

37 Chris Edwards, "Thunder Rally to Tie EL Series," The Trenton Times, (September 5, 1996), Sec. B, 5.

38 Larry O'Rourke, "Less Thunder, More Lightning," Boston Baseball, (March, 1997), 30.

39 Michael Rutstein, "Now a Prospect, Carey Relishes Homecoming," Boston Baseball, (March, 1997), 23.

40 Ibid.

41 Ibid., p. 22.

42 Sean McAdam, "Sox Find a Few Strike Wounds Still Unhealed," The Providence Journal, (March 19, 1997), Sec. D, 1, 8.

43 Buster Olney, "The Unkindest Cut of All," The New York Times, (April 1, 1997), Sec. C, 22.

44 Bill Reynolds, "Carey Fulfills His Dream at McCoy, 40 Miles Short of Another," The Providence Journal, (April 6, 1997), Sec. C, 1.

45 Bob Dick, "Macha Gives Weak Hitters Another Month to Improve," The Providence Journal, (May 4, 1997), Sec. C, 5.

46 Mike Scandura, "Todd Carey Enjoys His Homecoming," Diehard, (May, 1997), 21.

47 Bob Dick, "With the Paw Sox," The Providence Journal, (May 17, 1997), Sec. D, 5.

48 Bob Dick, "Some Top Prospects Slow to Shine," The Providence Journal, (June 1, 1997), Sec. D, 5.

49 Bob Dick, "Young but Tough, Team Has Solid Hold on 2nd Place," The Providence Journal, (June 8, 1997), Sec. C, 5.

50 Bob Dick, "Paw Sox Journal," The Providence Journal, (July 3, 1997), Sec. D, 5.

51 Bob Dick, "Hard Work Finally Paying Dividends for Carey," The Providence Journal, (July 7, 1997), Sec. D, 3.

52 Bob Dick, "Lowe's Pitching, Carey's Hitting Power Paw Sox Win," The Providence Journal, (August 8, 1997), Sec. D, 6.

53 Bob Dick, "Correction Equals Production," The Providence Journal, (August 8, 1997), Sec. D, 3.

54 Gerry Callahan, "Bulldog Determination," Sports Illustrated, (February 9, 1998), 46.

55 Craig Barnes, "Garciaparra Not Satisfied as Top Rookie," Sun Sentinel (Fla.), (March 9, 1998), Sec. C, 7.

56 "Vaughn Angry about Boston's 'Smear Campaign,'" Sun Sentinel (Fla.), (March 12, 1998), Sec. C, 14.

57 Doris Kearns Goodwin, Wait Till Next Year: A Memoir (New York, 1997), p. 254.

58 Bob Dick, "Carey Never Hit Stride," The Providence Journal, (May 31, 1998), Sec. D, 6.

59 Bob Dick, "Carey Hitting His Stride Since Joining the Tides," The Providence Journal, (June 21, 1998), Sec. D, 2.

60 "News from the Field," The Virginian Pilot, (July 24, 1998), Sec. C, 8.

61 Sean McAdam, "Schaefer Removed from Post as Head of Farm System," The Providence Journal, (July 27, 1998), Sec. D, 6.

62 Rich Radford, "Barker's Slam Is Another Blow to Tides' Fading Playoff Hopes," The Virginian Pilot, (July 18, 1998), Sec. C, 3.

63 Robin Brinkley, "This Is No Way to Get Rich," The Virginian Pilot, (August 19, 1998), Sec. C, 1.

64 Ibid., p. 7.

65 Murray Chass, "One Pitch Put Him in the Record Books," The New York Times, (February 23, 1999), Sec. D, 3.

66 Jorge Valencia, "Dodgers Armed with New Attitude," Baseball Weekly, (January 20-26, 1999), 5-6.

67 Jayson Stark, "Such a Terrible Shame for the Grand Old Game," (Philadelphia) Inquirer Daily News, (March 7, 1999), Sec. D, 16.

68 Ibid.

69 Steven Krasner, "Todd Carey Moves on to His Next Challenge," The Providence Journal, (February 3, 2000), Sec. C, 1.

70 Frances Mayes, Under the Tuscan Sun: At Home in Italy (San Francisco, 1996), p. 269.